Foreword

"IT IS REMARKABLE TO THINK ABOUT WHAT HAS BEEN ACHIEVED IN AVIATION SINCE THE WRIGHT BROTHERS' EXPLOITS OF 1903. EVERYONE INVOLVED IN THE AEROSPACE BUSINESS CAN CELEBRATE WITH PRIDE IN 2003 A CENTURY OF SUCCESS, TECHNICAL INNOVATION, COURAGE AND SHEER INFLUENCE ON THE WAY WE ALL LIVE. HOWEVER, IMPORTANT AS IT IS TO CELEBRATE THE FEATS OF THE PAST AND HONOUR THOSE WHO GAVE EVERYTHING TO THE ENDEAVOUR – EVEN SOMETIMES THEIR LIVES – IT IS IMPORTANT THAT WE USE THE OCCASION TO INSPIRE A NEW GENERATION TO TAKE UP THE CHALLENGES OF THE SECOND CENTURY OF FLIGHT. THAT IS WHY BAE SYSTEMS WAS THE FIRST FOUNDATION SPONSOR OF THE '100 YEARS OF FLIGHT' BEING CO-ORDINATED BY THE ROYAL AERONAUTICAL SOCIETY. THE FUTURE IN THIS BUSINESS WILL BE AS EXTRAORDINARY AS THE PAST. IT WILL NEED EXTRAORDINARY PEOPLE."

SIR RICHARD EVANS CBE
CEO BAE SYSTEMS

BAE SYSTEMS

CENTURY OF FLIGHT

Editor: Mark Nicholls

Design: Lee Howson, Austin Smith,
Mike Carr, Martin Froggatt, Andy O'Neil,
Patrick Juggins

Chief Designer: Steve Donovan

Staff Photographers: Duncan Cubitt,
Steve Fletcher

Production Editor: Sue Blunt

Sub Editor: Sue Naden

Production Manager: David Sopher

Commercial Director: Ann Saundry

Marketing Manager: Sari Bouvet

Circulation Manager: Kieron Jefferies

Advertising Sales: Emma White, Al
Evans, Ian Swain

Advertising Production: Cheryl Bayley

Director of Aviation: Ken Delve

Publisher and Chief Executive:
Richard Cox

Printed in England by: St Ives
(Plymouth) Ltd

Colour and Origination by: Final
Repro of Sawtry

Distributed by: Seymour Distribution
Ltd, London. **Tel:** 020 7396 8000, **Fax:**
020 7396 8002

Published by Key Publishing Ltd
PO Box 100, Stamford, Lincs, PE9 1XQ
Tel: +44 (0)1780 755131 Fax +44
(0)1780 757261
e-mail: edspecials@keymags.co.uk
Website: www.keypublishing.com

CONTENTS

Editor's comment
The first century of powered flight encompasses a massive amount of achievement consequently this special magazine is designed to provide an overview of man's accomplishments during the past 100 years. Every effort has been made to guarantee the accuracy of specific dates throughout this publication. However, in some cases a definitive cannot be established and so the most widely accepted date has been used.

Paving the way

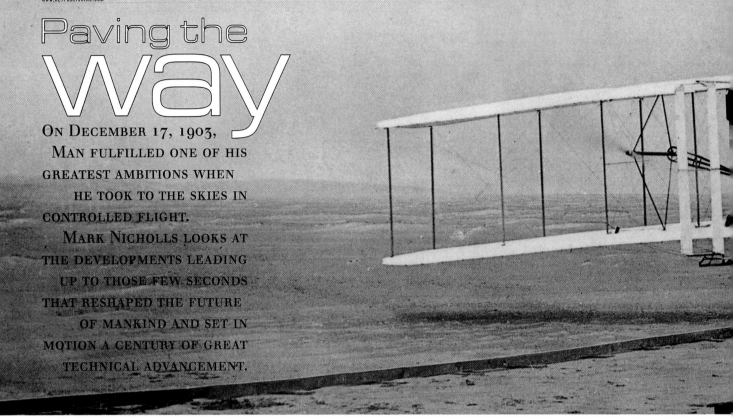

On December 17, 1903, man fulfilled one of his greatest ambitions when he took to the skies in controlled flight. Mark Nicholls looks at the developments leading up to those few seconds that reshaped the future of mankind and set in motion a century of great technical advancement.

Although great credit is due to Orville and Wilbur Wright, due recognition must also go to the aviation pioneers who preceded them. Chanute, Lilienthal, Langley, Maxim and Pilcher had all made their own experiments before the Wright brothers' flight, but had met with less success. Indeed, experiments with gliders had been going on for almost 100 years, but many of the early proponents of flight had merely tried to copy the actions of birds or had no basic grasp of aerodynamics and consequently had met with failure.

The Wrights employed a much more measured approach and clearly had a better understanding of the basic physics and requirements needed to get a heavier-than-air machine off the ground - and to be able to control it once it was airborne. Their approach was a cautious one and they set themselves goals on their way to building the Wright Flyer. They required a suitable airframe structure, an engine of sufficient power, a wing able to produce enough lift to get the whole aircraft airborne and - most importantly, in their view - a practical flight control system. Work carried out by others into the structure best suited to building an aeroplane was a great help, as were the developments made in the field of the internal combustion engine. But it was a near-infatuation with control that gave them the edge because, probably more than any of their predecessors, they grasped the realities of controlling an aeroplane in three dimensions. Others imagined that an aircraft would turn flat, making use of a rudder only. The Wrights made the correct assumption that if the aircraft rolled around its longitudinal axis (banking) it would accomplish the turn

much easier. Initially, the means of achieving this was by 'wing warping', though it was not long before the aileron was invented to better accomplish this movement.

To evaluate their work the brothers built a number of experimental full-size kites and later, gliders. Gradually they incorporated their new ideas, some more successful than others, and it was this measured but practical approach that in the end guaranteed them success. They built their first man-carrying glider in late 1900. This was a biplane design with no tail but a rudimentary elevator mounted in front of the wings. The pilot had to lie flat on the lower wing, using hip controls linked to cables to warp the wings and enable the glider to turn.

The lack of available data meant the brothers made some fundamental mistakes, but it was a case of learning from them. There was so much to learn too - how an aircraft's centre of gravity affects its flight characteristics and what aerodynamic and control layout would best provide stability in flight. It is interesting to note that the Wrights' preference for a forward 'canard' elevator is, in fact, an inherently unstable design and one they should, perhaps, have avoided. Today, with the aid of fly-by-wire control systems, aircraft are deliberately made unstable - often with canard foreplanes - because such an aircraft is very manoeuvrable. However, on-board computers keep the unstable aircraft in the air - and in 1903 none of this was available.

The Wright brothers began their early gliding trials at Kill Devil Hills, Kitty Hawk, North Carolina, in September 1900. A series of test flights over the next couple of years revealed

flaws in their designs, but at the same time proved that in many areas they were on the right track. Stability and control were still proving difficult and they proceeded to work out their own theories concerning aerofoil shapes and performance. In 1902 they built a new glider, still with the canard elevator in front of the wing but with a vertical tail to improve longitudinal stability. This glider had a completely new wing design with a much higher aspect ratio, though a droop (anhedral) was also built into each wing tip to make the aircraft less susceptible to gusty conditions. This design caused more control problems and the glider crashed - though not before a great deal more had been learnt. The brothers persisted with their calculations, even making use of a small wind tunnel they had built themselves. The solution proved to be a simple one - to make the vertical tail movable so that it acted as a rudder, linked to the wing

WRIGHT FLYER DATA	
Wing span	40ft 4in (12.28m)
Length	21ft 1in (6.4m)
Wing area	510 sq ft (47.4 m2)
Max weight	605lb (274.6kg)

warping hip controls. The result was that with both surfaces linked, the turn was much more smooth and controlled. The suitably-modified glider made 375 flights in just six days, vindicating the Wrights' hard work.

Efforts were now directed at constructing a powered version of the glider and consequently an engine needed to be sourced. This was easier said than done as the internal combustion engine industry was still in its infancy. Once again, the brothers had to go it alone, building their own engine with the help of mechanic Charles Taylor. Two propellers were to be used, both mounted behind the wings and counter-rotating so as to cancel out each other's torque and chain driven by the engine. Again, a great deal of

The Wright brothers. It was their ambitious but measured approached to building a successful powered aeroplane that paved the way for 100 years of some of the greatest technical achievements man has accomplished. (KEY collection)

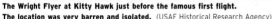

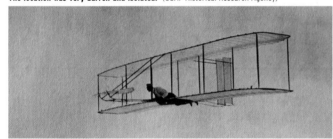

**The Wright Flyer at Kitty Hawk just before the famous first flight.
The location was very barren and isolated.** (USAF Historical Research Agency)

research was necessary to produce an efficient propeller since none had been made before and it was a matter of good aerodynamics to produce a good propeller – it has nothing in common with a ship's propeller, as many believed! At last, all their efforts reached fruition with the construction of the powered 1903 aeroplane, the Wright Flyer. Basically it was very similar to the 1902 glider, though with the addition of engine and propellers, plus a few other detailed changes. A good deal of fine-tuning to the propulsion system was needed as a result of breakages and other technical problems, but these were gradually overcome. The aeroplane still had a level of inbuilt instability, though at the time the brothers did not realise it and pressed ahead with plans for a first flight on December 14, 1903. Wilbur Wright made this attempt using a 60ft (18.3m) launch track to assist take-off and got airborne, but then overcompensated with the front elevator and the aircraft settled to the ground a little, damaging part of the elevator assembly. Two days of repairs were necessary before the aeroplane was ready again. At 10.35am on December 17, 1903, Orville Wright took the aircraft into the air for what was to be the first

controlled powered flight – it lasted just 12 seconds and covered 120ft (36.5m). Wilbur also flew the machine, and then at noon Orville made a 59-second flight covering 852ft (259.7m). The aircraft rolled over on landing, was extensively damaged and never flew again. But history had been made – Man could fly a machine in a controlled manner. John Daniels captured the event in aviation's

most famous photograph, and despite shunning publicity the Wright brothers had earned themselves a place in the history books. Today we take flying for granted, but it is worth remembering that although that first flight covered less than the length of a Boeing 747, without it and the Wright brothers' perseverance and ingenuity Man might not be soaring where he is today.

**The Wright 1902 glider had a twin vertical
tail to assist in longitudinal stability.**
(USAF Historical Research Agency)

One of the early Wright gliders, without a vertical tail, is steadied during a brief flight.
(USAF Historical Research Agency)

1903-19

1903-19

1. First Flight
On December 17, 1903, Orville Wright achieves the world's first controlled powered flight at Kill Devil Hills, Kitty Hawk, North Carolina in Wright Flyer. (KEY collection)

2. Briton flies
Alliot Verdon Roe becomes the first Briton to fly in a British aircraft when he completes a 100ft (30m) flight at Lea Marshes in Essex on July 23, 1909. (KEY collection)

3. Channel flown
On July 25, 1909, Frenchman Louis Blériot becomes the first man to fly across the English Channel when he lands on British soil after a $36\frac{1}{2}$-minute flight.

4. Early Avro
The Avro Triplane appears in 1910, the first in a very famous line of aircraft from the Avro company. This replica example is operated by the Shuttleworth Collection at Old Warden in the UK. (KEY - Robert Rudhall)

SIGNIFICANT DATES

October 7, 1903: American Samuel Langley's Aeroplane, powered by a 59hp engine, attempts a flight from a modified house boat but crashes into the river. Another attempt on December 8 also fails.

September 20, 1904: Wilbur Wright completes the first-ever circular flight by an aircraft.

January 17, 1905: The Zeppelin LZ 2 airship is launched.

November 12, 1906: Alberto Santos-Dumont completes Europe's first recognised sustained powered flight when he travels 722ft (220m) in a 14-bis biplane.

November 13, 1907: The first free flight by a helicopter is completed by Paul Cornu at Lisieux, France, though it lasts only 20 seconds and reaches an altitude of 1ft (30cm).

November 30, 1907: America's first aircraft company is formed by Glenn Curtiss. The company is to become synonymous in both military and commercial aviation.

February 10, 1908: The first military contract for aircraft – the Wright Model A biplane – is signed by the US Army.

May 14, 1908: Wilbur Wright takes the world's first passenger, Charles Furnas, aloft on a 29-second flight.

September 17, 1908: The first death in a powered aircraft. Lt Thomas Selfridge is killed when the Wright Army Flyer, flown by Orville Wright, crashes during a test flight. Orville Wright is severely injured.

February 1909: Shellbeach on the Isle of Sheppey is the UK's first recognised aerodrome.

June 12, 1909: Two passengers are carried by an aircraft for the first time, in a Blériot XII.

November 4, 1909: British aristocrat Claude Moore-Brabazon shows that pigs can fly when he takes a small pig for a 4-mile (6.4km) flight at Shellbeach, Isle of Sheppey.

December 1909: The first aircraft designed by Geoffrey de Havilland makes its first flight.

September 8, 1910: The first known mid-air collision occurs in Austria.

November 7, 1910: The first-ever cargo flight takes place when a Wright Model B biplane carries silk between Dayton and Columbus in Ohio.

Dec 17, 1903: Wright Flyer Sept 30, 1907: Voisin-Farman 1 1919: Curtiss No.1 Jan 23, 1909: Blériot Type XI Aug 18, 1911: RAF Fe.2 1912: RAF BE.2 Jan 1915: Airco DH.1 Dec 12, 1915: Junkers J1 1916: Albatros D.III

1903-19

5. Zeppelin

Count Ferdinand von Zeppelin establishes the world's first commercial airline company – Die Deutsche Luftschiffahrt Aktiengesellschaft (Delag). It operates six airships flying passengers within Germany from 1910 until 1913. (KEY collection)

6. Bristol Boxkite

The Bristol Boxkite makes its first flight on July 31, 1910, and is typical of the early biplanes, featuring an open frame with fabric-covered wings and tail. (Cliff Knox)

7. Avro 504

The Avro 504 makes its first flight on September 18, 1913 and is destined for widespread use, particularly as a trainer. (Gordon Swanborough collection)

8. Revolutionary Scout

The Bristol Scout biplane makes its appearance in 1914 and brings with it a number of innovations, soon to be found on many World War One combat aircraft. (Gordon Swanborough collection)

9. Famous Fokker

The Fokker M.5K makes its first flight in April 1914 and becomes the prototype for the famous Eindecker, represented here by this example from Personal Plane Services. (Cliff Knox)

10. Sunk by Torpedo

On August 12, 1915, Short 184 seaplanes successfully torpedo a Turkish supply ship, the first ship to be sunk in this way. (Gordon Swanborough collection)

November 14, 1910: The first flight from a ship is accomplished by Eugene Ely, who flies a Curtiss Hudson Flier from the bows of the USS *Birmingham*.

September 17, 1911: Calbraith P Rodgers sets off on the first coast-to-coast flight across the USA in a Burgess-Wright aircraft, completing his journey on November 5.

September 23, 1911: The first airmail flight takes place in the USA using a Blériot monoplane.

October 22, 1911: The first use of an aircraft under wartime conditions takes place when the Italian Air Flotilla uses a Blériot monoplane to carry out reconnaissance of Turkish troops.

September 1912: The Australian Army Aviation Corps is established.

May 13, 1913: The world's first four-engine aircraft, the *Le Grand*, makes its first flight in the hands of Igor Sikorsky.

November 1913: The first aerial combat takes place over Mexico when Dean Lamb (flying for the Army of Venustiano Carranza) exchanges handgun fire with another aircraft flown by Phillip Rader (flying for General Huerta).

December 28, 1913: The first flight in excess of 20,000ft (6,096m) is achieved by Georges Legagneux in a Nieuport Type IIN who reaches 20,079ft (6,120m) over St Raphaël, France.

July 27, 1914: A Short seaplane flown by the company's test pilot Gordon Bell is the first to drop a standard naval torpedo.

March 3, 1915: The National Advisory Committee for Aeronautics (NACA), the forerunner of today's NASA, is established in the USA. It is tasked with various evaluation and experimental research projects and is responsible for some momentous achievements.

April 1915: Anthony Fokker perfects a method of synchronising a machine gun and an aircraft propeller, allowing the gun to fire cleanly through the propeller arc.

November 6, 1915: A Curtiss AB-2 flying boat becomes the first aircraft to be catapult-launched from a moving ship.

12

11

13

14

11. Giant seaplane
The Zeppelin-Lindau Dornier Rs III makes its maiden flight on November 4, 1917. The aircraft features extensive use of steel and aluminium and has a long endurance, making it ideal for long-range operations. (KEY collection)

12. Atlantic non-stop
On June 14-15, 1919, Capt John Alcock and Lt Arthur Brown make the first non-stop crossing of the Atlantic. Their Vickers Vimy is seen departing from St Johns, Newfoundland. The flight to Clifden, Ireland, takes 16 hours and 27 minutes. (Gordon Swanborough collection)

13. Breguet beauty
The Breguet 14 is one of the most famous French aircraft: by December 1918 some 5,300 had been built. This example can be seen at La Ferté Alais in France. (KEY - Duncan Cubitt)

14. First Boeing
The first Boeing commercial aircraft to be solely designed and built by the company, the B-1 flying boat, makes its maiden flight on December 27, 1919. (Boeing)

SIGNIFICANT DATES

July 15, 1916: William Boeing forms the Pacific Aero Products Company (which became the Boeing Company on April 26, 1917) in Seattle.

October 5, 1916: The UK's first airline, Aircraft Transport and Travel Ltd, is established.

May 20, 1917: The German submarine U-36 becomes the first submarine to be sunk by an aircraft, following an attack by a RNAS flying boat.

August 2, 1917: RNAS pilot Sqn Cdr E H Dunning makes the first successful landing on a moving ship when he sets his Sopwith

Pup down on HMS *Furious*.

April 1, 1918: The Royal Air Force is established in the UK.

May 15, 1918: The US Army and the US Post Office commence the first regular airmail services between Washington DC and New York via Philadelphia.

May 15, 1918: Using a Liberty 12 turbocharged engine, a Packard-Le Pére LUSAC-11 fighter, flown by Capt Rudolph Schroeder, sets a new altitude record of 33,113ft (10,093m) over Dayton, Ohio.

February 5, 1919: The world's first regular passenger airline service commences between Berlin and Weimar, operated by Deutsche Luft-Reederei (DLR).

May 24, 1919: Avro Civil Aviation Service commences the first domestic flights in the UK by an airline, linking Blackpool, Manchester and Southport.

August 25, 1919: Aircraft Transport and Travel Ltd begins the world's first scheduled international airline service with flights between Hounslow, UK, and Paris Le Bourget, France.

October 7, 1919: Dutch airline Koninklijke Luchtvaart Maatschappij voor Nederland en Kolonien (Royal Dutch Airlines) is formed. Better known as KLM, it is today the world's oldest airline, having never changed its name.

December 10, 1919: The first flight from the UK to Australia is completed when Ross and Keith Smith land their Vickers Vimy at Darwin.

December 12, 1919: The first trans-Australia flight is completed by a B.E.2 flown by Capt H Wrigley and Lt A Murphy. Their intrepid flight takes 46 hours.

Sept 1917: Handley Page O/400 **Nov 30, 1917:** Vickers Vimy **Jan 1918:** Fokker D.VII **May 1918:** Handley Page V/1500 **Oct 4, 1918:** Curtiss NC-1 **Jan 1919:** Farman Goliath **June 25, 1919:** Junkers F 13 **Oct 1919:** Fokker F.II

"Knights of the Air"
Normandy - July 25th, 1944. Operation COBRA

Non-fiction:
The Battle for Europe 1943

Unless you were actually there, you've never seen WWII like this. Extreme low flying action, realistic land targets and genuine war missions. You're going to use planes like the P-47 "Thunderbolt", the Fw 190 and the Hawker Tempest V to stop the enemy's advance.

It's you and your squadron versus the entire enemy's arsenal: their guns, hardware and planes. So choose between 34 authentic planes from the United States Army Air Force, Royal Air Force or the German Luftwaffe. The skill and perseverance you and your squadron bring to each battle will determine whether your campaign in Microsoft® Combat Flight Simulator 3 mirrors historical events or diverges from history and evolves along lines you create.

Tactical Air War Simulation has never been this real.

www.combatflightsim3.co.uk

Microsoft
game studios™

Microsoft®
Combat Flight Simulator 3
Battle For Europe

KEN DELVE EXAMINES
THE FIRST MILITARY
USE OF THE AEROPLANE
AND THE MANNER IN
WHICH IT REVOLUT-
IONISED WARFARE.

First World War
Birth of Air
Power

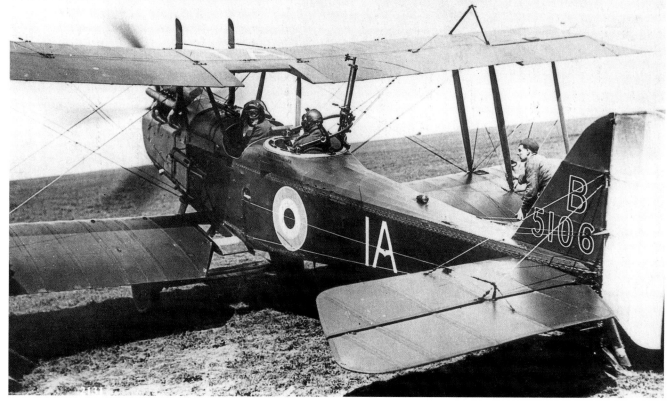

The outbreak of World War One in August 1914 ushered in a conflict that changed the face of the military art. New weapons were brought into use which rendered 19th Century strategies and methods of warfare obsolete. On land, the most significant changes involved the greater destructive potential of the machine-gun and the tank, but more significant for the future trend of warfare was the appearance of the aeroplane. Air Power had arrived. Although the aeroplane had been put to limited military use before 1914, in the war fought in North Africa between Italy and Turkey, it was the Great War of 1914-1918 which saw its rapid development as a key weapon of warfare. Initial development was slow, but by 1916 the aeroplane had come of age and was employed in a number of roles. By the time of the Armistice in November 1918, the major powers all had large air forces and their aircraft bore little resemblance to those which had been available at the start of the war. Throughout history, armed conflict has provided an impetus for technological development.

Army 'Eyes'

At the outbreak of the war the notional air capability of the participants was less than impressive. Most of the major European powers fielded something in the order of 300 aircraft, by no means all of these being 'operational' types. For example, the British Royal Flying Corps (RFC), which had been established in 1912, had only four operational squadrons capable of being deployed to France. Most army generals of the time considered the aircraft to be little more than an extension of the light cavalry which for decades had provided the army with its 'eyes' – the ability to 'see over the hill' and so determine the enemy's position, strength and intentions. This reconnaissance role was vital and remained so throughout the war. Such a sortie by an RFC aircraft prevented the British Expeditionary Force from making a strategic error during the initial German advance and the retreat from Mons enabled the Allied front line to stabilise. The German Air Service was equally active in seeking aerial reconnaissance and it was inevitable that opposing aircraft would come into contact.

Inadequacies

At this early stage of the war there was no concept of a fighter aircraft whose role was to seek out and destroy the enemy, and other than ad hoc weapons such as pistols and rifles there was little with which to attack enemy forces. The RFC scored an early success, however, when three BE2s of No.2 Squadron chased a German Taube, forcing it to land in a field. Lt Harvey-Kelly landed nearby and he and his observer, Lt Mansfield, chased the enemy pilot into a wood. They were unable to catch him, although they managed to burn his aircraft before climbing back into their own machine and returning to base. The greatest danger to pilots apart from the unreliability of their machines, was from ground fire, as soldiers on both sides tended to fire at anything that flew near them. In addition to the reconnaissance task, aircraft were used as observation platforms in conjunction with artillery, spotting fall of shot, though until the advent of air-to-ground communications any aiming corrections had to be

By the latter years of World War One aircraft were being used in large numbers by both sides for reconnaissance, bombing and air-to-air combat. Most aircraft were either two-seat, such as this RE8, with a pilot and observer, or single-seat.

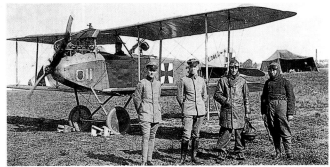

Above **The Bleriot XI monoplane equipped a number of Allied squadrons in the early years of the war.**

Above Right **The German Air Service achieved dominance of the air in 1916, allowing its reconnaissance aircraft, such as this Albatros CVI, relative freedom of manoeuvre.**

Below **'Stick and fabric' is a frequently-used description of early aircraft, a view supported by this pusher (engine at the back) Maurice Farman .**

Centre **Large bombers, such as these Staaken R.VIs, were used for strategic bombing, a role which became a cornerstone of air doctrine in the post-war period.** (All photos Ken Delve Collection)

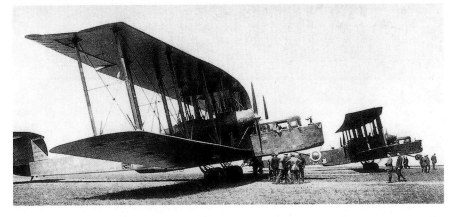

Strategic Bombing

Although aeroplanes were restricted to reconnaissance and artillery spotting for the first few months of the war, the Germans used another aerial weapon to open up a new type of warfare - strategic bombing. At the start of hostilities, the German High Command had six airships for reconnaissance and bombing (although it has become common practice to refer to all German airships as 'Zeppelins' this is not strictly accurate, as airship were also made by other manufacturers). The first bombing sorties took place in August and although not a great success, they revealed the potential of such operations and the difficulties faced by the defenders, the airships outperforming the aeroplanes. A small number of bombing sorties was also flown by aircraft, though as with much that happened in these early months of the war, success was often due to individual initiative rather than to military strategy. One such example was Hermann Dessler's 'attack' on Paris in a Taube on August 29, 1914, when he circled the Eiffel Tower and dropped a number of small bombs, killing one civilian. The British Royal Naval Air Service (RNAS) adopted a more aggressive approach, and the squadron based at Ostend undertook a number of attacks on German airship sheds with some success, Lt Marix destroying Z9 in its shed at Dusseldorf in October 1914. An increasing number of bombing raids was flown by all sides during 1915, although this was still small-scale action using relatively ineffective bombs. The first air VC (Victoria Cross) was won on such a mission, Lt Rhodes-Moorhouse of No.2 Squadron receiving this highest gallantry award following an attack on the rail yards at Courtrai. By the summer of 1915, the French GHQ (General Headquarters) was calling for a bomber force of 1,000 aircraft with which to win the war by attacking military-industrial targets and lines of communication. The Imperial Russian Air Service, meanwhile, was developing large bomber aircraft for long-range missions.

However, it was the activities of German Zeppelins over the UK, and especially London, which established strategic bombing. The first such attack on England took place on

passed by flying over the battery and dropping message bags. The RFC developed a number of techniques, among them coloured lights, to improve this artillery co-ordination. Trials of Wireless Telegraphy (W/T) systems in the latter part of the year showed the most promise, although it was some time before this type of equipment came into widespread use. September 15 also saw the first use of aerial photography, Lt Pretyman of No.3 Squadron exposing five

photographic plates. This photographic role, which enabled the land commander to study a picture of the enemy positions, became a vital requirement for military planners. A great deal of effort was expended on such sorties - and on protecting them from enemy interference - while at the same time trying to prevent the enemy from obtaining similar intelligence of one's own position. These latter considerations led to the development of fighter aircraft.

● **Line up of Sopwith Dolphins of No.1 (Canadian) Squadron. By the middle years of the war, new types were entering service at regular intervals and aircraft were being built in their thousands.**

January 19, 1915, when two airships bombed targets in East Anglia, though it was not until London was attacked on May 31 that public outcry at this 'outrage' led to a call for increased air defences of both guns and aircraft. Further raids during 1916 led to the responsibility for Home Defence being transferred from the Admiralty to the RFC, and a new defensive system of guns and aircraft was positioned around London. By the end of 1916 this had proved effective and a number of Zeppelins had been shot down, leading the German Airship Service to scale down its operations over England. However, the impact which this small-scale and generally ineffective bombing had on politicians was enormous. Combined with an increase in bombing attacks by aircraft against targets behind the front lines, it led to a general belief amongst politicians and the military that this aspect of air power could be decisive – a belief that led to the doctrine of the bomber as a 'war-winning' weapon. The need to prevent such bombing provided another impetus to the development of fighter aircraft.

Fighters – and Aces

The need for an aircraft designed for aerial combat had been evident since the latter part of 1914, and by spring 1915 dedicated fighter types such as the Vickers FB.5 entered service with the RFC. The problem of mounting and aiming the machine-gun was solved either by using a pusher type of aircraft, with the engine at the back so there was a clear field of fire ahead of the aircraft, or by mounting the guns on the upper wing in such a way that they fired over the propeller arc of a tractor-type aircraft (i.e. engine in the front). A better solution was to mount a gun on the front of the fuselage so that it fired through the propeller. French pilot Roland Garros adopted the simple principle of putting metal plates on the back of the wooden propeller blades so that those bullets from his machine-gun that did not go between the blades would bounce off the metal plates. He scored a number of successes using this system, though a truly practical solution only came with the development by Fokker, and subsequently others, of an interrupter gear which stopped the gun firing when a propeller blade was in the way.

Once this development was incorporated onto more manoeuvrable aircraft, such as the Fokker Eindecker, true

fighters entered the fray. Max Immelmann scored his first success with the Eindecker and its synchronised guns on August 1, 1915. He was accompanied by Oswald Boelcke, who enthused: "With the single-seater, my ideal is achieved – now I can be pilot, observer and fighter all at the same time". These two men were amongst the first of a new breed of aviators and became household names as fighter aces. The Germans gained control of the air with superior aircraft and tactics, leading the RFC headquarters to state: "Until the RFC is in possession of a machine as good as or better than the German Fokker it seems that a change of tactics becomes necessary ... a machine proceeding on reconnaissance must be escorted by at least three other fighting machines". The so-called 'Fokker Scourge' remained in evidence for much of 1916, the use of elite fighter squadrons contributing to the effectiveness of German fighters. The French attempted to counter this by putting together an elite squadron in the Verdun sector. This proved effective and aces such as Jean Navarre were soon popular heroes in France. In typical flamboyant fighter pilot style, Navarre's Nieuport was painted red so that friend and foe alike could see who he was. Though Navarre's name is not well known, the name of another pilot of a red fighter is still synonymous with the idea of the fighter ace - Baron Manfred von Richthofen in his red Fokker Triplane. The British had their aces, too, despite some initial reluctance on the part of their military leaders to promote such a concept. However, if only for reasons of morale the exploits of aces such as Ball, McCudden and Mannock soon became popular and provided a useful focus for national sentiment.

Mass Air Battles

Whereas in the early months of the war aircraft were a rare sight, towards the end of 1916 each of the major combatants had air strengths measured in thousands of aircraft. This was a significant achievement, both in terms of aircraft production (the five main combatants – Britain, France, Germany, Italy, Russia – had built over 22,000 aircraft in 1916) and training to provide aircrew and support personnel. The balance of power over the Western Front remained with the Germans at the end of 1916 as their fighter aircraft and tactics were still superior, but the Allies were introducing new aeroplanes, such as the Nieuport,

Spad, Bristol F2.B and SE.5 that in early 1917 would redress the balance. A last surprise awaited the Allied flyers.

By the time the British offensive – that became the Battle of Arras – began in May, the Germans had prepared an elite grouping of squadrons under von Richthofen for the first 'Circus' operation (known later as Richthofen's Flying Circus). Initial Allied losses were high, at least four to one in air combat.

However, of more importance to the evolution of air power was the first large-scale tactical use of aircraft in direct support of ground forces, the Close Air Support (CAS) role whereby aircraft bombed and strafed targets in and around the front lines. The Germans adopted a similar concept with their Sturmflieger (storm flyers) units.

By this time, air power had also gone to sea – the ultimate development of which was the aircraft carrier, a ship designed for the operation of a number of aircraft rather than the earlier concept which had seen single aircraft being launched from a platform aboard a battleship. The Royal Navy adapted the light cruiser HMS *Furious* to feature a flight deck and hangar for the operation of ten aircraft, and although this vessel did not enter service until March 1918, a new element of air power was firmly established.

As far as the war was concerned, the major development of 1917 was the entry into the conflict of the United States of America in April, although it would be many months before the Americans arrived in the combat theatre.

Turning Tide

As far as the air war was concerned, the tide had turned by mid-1917 with Richthofen commenting: "you would not believe how morale is among fighter pilots at the front because of their sorry machines ... we must unconditionally support and use every firm that produces a type somewhat better than this damn Albatros." Furthermore, the German High Command believed that an additional 40 fighter squadrons would be needed by early 1918 to counter the American presence. Large numbers of aircraft supported every major offensive as the land commanders continued to launch massive, murderous (on both sides) and futile attempts to break the stalemate of trench warfare.

Strategic bombing was, on the other hand, showing

The BE2c was one of the most widely-used Allied types. This particular example belongs to 39 Squadron and the pilot is Lt William Leefe Robinson, the picture being taken shortly after he shot down a Zeppelin over London – a feat for which he was awarded the Victoria Cross.

Attacking troops on the ground became a regular task for specialist squadrons. This Brandenburg C1 has an array of weapons with which to attack ground targets.

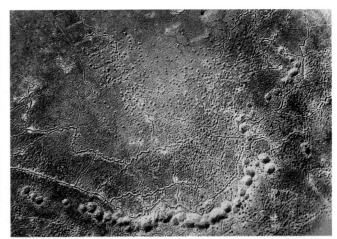

One of the main roles for aircraft was reconnaissance, and from 1916 onwards this included photographic reconnaissance, pictures such as this one proving very useful to military planners. The zig-zag of trench lines is distinctive, as are the impact craters from shells and mines.

Attaching bombs to the underside of the wings. Most bombs were of small calibre but the ability of aircraft to fly over the front lines and attack distant targets was one of the main advantages of air power.

Twin Lewis Gun mounting in the back seat of this Bristol F2b Fighter, an aircraft which served with distinction in the latter part of World War One and on into the 1920s.

promise. German attacks on England had started to use long-range aircraft rather than airships and whilst the physical damage inflicted by these attacks was small, the effect on morale (on the politicians and public of both sides) was significant. The ability to fly over the entangled masses of men involved in the ground war and strike deep into enemy territory was a new aspect of warfare, one that could be used to destroy targets of military importance, as well as weaken the spirit of the enemy's home population. With increasing numbers of

aircraft, new purpose-built bombers types, such as the DH.9 for short-range work and the Handley Page bombers for longer ranges and dominance of the air, the Allies were planning a major extension of strategic bombing.

It was indeed to be a decisive year. The Germans realised that they had one last chance for a war-winning offensive before the arrival of the Americans. All the basic air power roles, as outlined above, had been established by mid-1917 and between then and the end of the war in November 1918, all that changed was

the scale of operations, the types of aircraft and weapons, and to some extent the tactical employment of aircraft.

The formation of the Royal Air Force as an independent arm of the British military took place in April 1918, around the same time that the Germans launched their spring offensive. Allied aircraft were vital in helping to stem the massive German push that for the first time in years broke the routine of trench warfare. It was during one of the great air battles, on April 21, that von Richthofen was shot down and killed. The German offensive took place and in August the Allies launched their own. This was given direct support by large numbers of aircraft, whilst the new strategic bombing arm, the Independent Force, attacked targets behind the front lines. Larger bombers entered service, the HP 0/400 began operations in August, and work was progressing on a 'super heavy bomber' that would be able to bomb Berlin, the V/1500 otherwise known as the 'Bloody Paralyser'. However, the war ended before it could enter service but its development – and the doctrine under which it was to be employed – showed the direction in which air power was heading.

With the Armistice of November 1918 this 'war to end all wars' came to an end – millions of lives had been lost, empires had collapsed and Europe would never be the same again. For the military a new weapon of war had arisen and had shown its potential. From a flimsy contraption of little apparent value, the aeroplane had developed into an effective weapon.

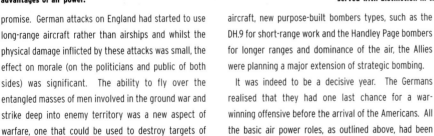

The Nieuport series of fighters was amongst the best of the war: this Nieuport 23 with its cartoon horse served with the French squadron Escadrille N561.

destruction from the air

KEN DELVE PROVIDES AN OVERVIEW OF AIR-TO-GROUND WEAPONS DEVELOPMENT.

Air-to-ground weapons are intended to destroy ground targets – sounds obvious, but those targets vary from troops and vehicles to bridges and airfields, as well as reinforced structures such as bunkers and moving targets at sea. With such variety comes the problem of what type of weapon to employ and how to deliver it.

In the Vietnam War the Americans dropped thousands of bombs on jungle areas in an attempt to kill isolated groups of Vietcong – an operation that has been likened to "using a sledgehammer to crack a walnut". Weapon to target matching, ie using the correct type and number of weapons to destroy a specific target, sounds easy but numerous variables make up the equation and all too often, one of those variables might be missing or in error.

In recent years, buzz words such as 'surgical precision' have been used to describe the accuracy with which aerial weapons can be delivered, often followed by media reports that a bomb has gone astray causing 'collateral damage' (killing civilians) or resulting in 'friendly fire' (killing one's own troops). Here we will look at the development of air-to-ground weapons, and whilst overall progress will be revealed as one of increased destructive capability for each aircraft/weapon employed, there are basic considerations that remain unchanged. An accurate bomb will only destroy the target if it hits it (ie aiming, delivery and weapon effect) and it will only hit the right target if it

knows where the target is (target intelligence and planning). In both of these broad areas, there remains plenty of scope for error in this so-called precision age. Those who task an attack on a particular target may have got it wrong, those who deliver the weapon may have misidentified the target, the weapon may malfunction, and

so on. This is the real world and not the sanitised environment that some politicians choose to promote.

Attack from the Air

As mentioned in the article on World War One (page 12) the initial military employment of aircraft was for

The destructive power of modern air-launched weapons is quite incredible – and often spectacular. (KEY collection)

Loading GP and anti-personnel bombs on to a Hawker Hind; most of the bombs in RAF service in the early 1930s (as here) were of World War One vintage. (Ken Delve Collection)

Above: **A 4,000lb 'cookie' blast bomb waits to be loaded into a Lancaster of RAF Bomber Command. The use of a mixed load of blast weapons and incendiaries proved effective against built-up areas.** (Ken Delve Collection)
Right: **The unguided rocket was used extensively during World War Two. Among the most effective was its employment by RAF Typhoons in the anti-armour role after the D-Day landings.** (KEY collection)

British cities from 1915 onwards. The weight of bombs dropped never amounted to much, but the ability of the Germans to bomb London, even though casualties and damage were insignificant, had a major effect on civilian morale and political opinion.

The earliest bombs used by aircraft were adaptations of artillery shells but it was not long before purpose-designed bombs were introduced that were easier to carry, with improved ballistics (the way the bomb falls) and more explosive power. With the creation in 1918 of the RAF's Independent Force, tasked with attacking targets in Germany, the first major strategic bombing force had been created and new large bombers, capable of carrying more and heavier bombs over greater distances, entered service.

For attacks on troops in the trenches, or more ideally when they were on the march behind the lines, aircraft used small anti-personnel bombs, hand grenades and machine-guns. This type of air attack could prove very effective especially

reconnaissance rather than for direct offensive activity, for example, directing the massed firepower of the artillery and making sure that it was falling in the right place. Weapons began to appear on aircraft for self-defence against other aircraft and aerial combat, and the development of the fighter aircraft, duly followed. However, even before World War One, Italian aviators had dropped weapons, 'hand bombs' thrown over the side of the aircraft, and fired guns at targets on the ground – with little hope of either hitting anything or doing much damage.

The European air arms that took to the skies in August 1914 had no policy for the employment of aircraft against ground targets and with little carrying capacity and no special air-to-ground bombs, it seemed as if aircraft would play little direct part in the land battle. By 1916 this situation had begun to change and by the end of the war, the bomber had become an important tactical and strategic weapon, and one that would dominate post-war military doctrine.

World War One is remembered as a struggle in which millions of soldiers faced each other across barren

stretches of 'no man's land' and where an offensive by one side would result in thousands of casualties. Artillery fired millions of high-explosive shells, whilst machine-guns wreaked havoc amongst advancing lines of infantry. When compared to firepower and destruction on this scale, the part played by aircraft might seem small but it was the nature of air bombardment rather than its scale that was to prove important.

The uniqueness of the aeroplane was its ability to fly over the front line trenches and attack targets in the rear areas or even in the enemy's homeland. One of the first examples of strategic bombing was the German airship offensive on

against ill-disciplined soldiers – as was the case in the Battle of Nablus when British aircraft attacked the retreating Turkish army and played a significant part in the success of General Allenby's attack on Damascus.

World War Two

The 'war to end all wars' had a profound effect on politicians in the 1920s and early 1930s but there was little attention paid to military development. For example, it was not until 1935 that the RAF undertook a detailed survey into the types of bomb it had and service requirements for the future. Interestingly, it concluded that little needed to

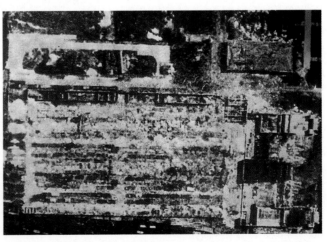

The before and after effects of a World War Two Allied bombing raid. As can be seen in the post strike image, the factory is heavily damaged, but the machinery within could be substantially intact. (Ken Delve collection)

change, except that 20lb anti-personnel bombs and 30-50lb General Purpose (GP) bombs should be developed. This reliance on GP bombs, the standard one being the 250lb GP bomb was to prove a gross error. When war broke out in 1939 the RAF had to rely on such weapons (the largest of which was 1,900lb) for the first two years. The array of weapons also included Armour Piercing (AP) and Semi Armour Piercing (SAP) types but all suffered from the same lack of

Above: **Royal Navy Swordfish aircraft achieved a number of notable successes with the torpedo during World War Two. The torpedo was one of the most effective anti-shipping weapons of the period.** (KEY - Duncan Cubitt)

effectiveness, as in general terms their charge ratio was too small; i.e. too much metal and too little explosive.

The RAF was not alone – all the major air forces suffered a similar lack of effective weapons; even the Luftwaffe, with its experiences of the Spanish Civil War, was little better placed and in terms of strategic bomber air doctrine was behind the RAF. With the exception of guided weapons, the RAF led the way in the development of air-to-ground weapons and their delivery, it is worth therefore focusing on these developments.

In the article on World War Two (pages 40-46) mention is made of the bombing offensive against German industry, which commenced in May 1940; and it was this offensive that had the greatest influence on bomb development.

The basic aim was to destroy industrial complexes and the machinery they contained, although such targets were the aiming points of any attack, the inevitable result of inaccurate delivery of the bombs was destruction over a wide area. Whilst the industrial complex remained the aiming point, an 'area bombing' strategy stated that de-housing (and killing) workers would also hinder German war production.

This led to the adoption of weapons and tactics that would cause maximum destruction to buildings. The British experience of the German blitz on London and other cities in 1940 showed the blast effect of bombs and the nature of the destruction caused by various types of weapon against various types of target. It was apparent that a mix of blast bombs and incendiary bombs was most effective.

Incendiary weapons had been part of the aircraft's armoury for many years, and in the late 1930s the RAF produced a number of new variants, the most effective of which was the 4lb incendiary. For maximum effect, the buildings in a target area had to be knocked down, thus giving the incendiaries access to flammable material,

including ruptured gas pipes. Traditional bombs were not particularly good at this as they did not produce enough blast effect. The Luftwaffe used a high-capacity (i.e. high proportion of explosive to casing) 'parachute mine' for attacks on UK cities, and the RAF developed the 4,000lb HC blockbuster bomb, usually referred to as a 'cookie' (first used against Emden on March 31, 1941).

The combination of such blockbuster weapons and incendiaries was devastating and was responsible for laying waste to large parts of many German cities. Blast effect on

heavy industrial machinery was invariably less than the planners had predicted, and whilst a factory might appear badly damaged – burnt-out buildings on aerial photographs – in many instances the actual machinery survived. An 8,000lb HC bomb was introduced in early 1942, but the 4,000lb weapon remained the most popular, along with a new 1,000lb MC bomb.

Improvements in the type of explosive – Amatol, Torpex and Cyclonite to name but a few – made each individual bomb more effective. However, what really increased destructive power was a change of tactic that enabled a more accurate and more concentrated pattern of bombing. This was primarily due to the use of special Pathfinder units to mark the target with incendiaries or with Target Indicators, the latter providing colour patterns on which the main force of bombers would drop their bombs.

From the middle years of the war specialised air-to-ground weapons were introduced, albeit invariably employed in small numbers and against specific types of target. One of the best-known is the 'bouncing bomb' (although it was technically a mine) used by the RAF to attack German dams in May 1943 under Operation Chastise. The weapon devised by Barnes Wallis required pinpoint delivery for it to impact

the back wall of the dam, sink down the wall and then explode, with the water pressure behind causing the dam wall to crack and fail. A specialist squadron was formed, 617 Squadron under the inspired leadership of Wg Cdr Guy Gibson, and Lancasters were converted to carry and deliver the weapon. The attack on the night of May 16/17, 1943, suffered heavy losses but the Mohne and Eder dams were destroyed.

Debate has raged post-war over the raid's effectiveness in slowing German war production, but this aside, the impact

● **The aftermath of the world's first nuclear attack at Hiroshima, Japan. The devastating effect of nuclear weapons was in the long run to guarantee peace between East and West during the Cold War.** (Ken Delve collection)

● **Developed during the Vietnam conflict, the laser-guided bomb was to makes its mark during the 1991 Gulf War. Here an Iraqi hardened aircraft shelter proved less than hard to destroy with the aid of a Paveway LGB.** (Ken Delve collection)

● **Throughout the Cold War and in conflicts like Korea, Vietnam, the Gulf War, Kosovo and even Afghanistan – the free-fall iron bomb has remained one of the most employed weapons.** (KEY collection)

on the enemy's morale was enormous. Barnes Wallis developed a number of other specialist bombs, most significantly the Tallboy (12,000lb MC) and Grand Slam (22,000lb MC), both of which were used by a small number of Lancaster squadrons and with a specific weapons effect in mind. An RAF study stated that: "the 12,000lb MC bomb was not designed for attack on very hard targets but for the production of large craters and maximum earth shock by deep penetration into the ground with a large charge. It is noteworthy that all the serious damage to the large V-weapon sites was caused by near misses in which the structure was undermined by the crater."

Before leaving World War Two, it is worth noting that we have so far only covered a selection of the air-to-ground weapons developed since 1939. It is appropriate to highlight two used against naval targets (mines and torpedoes) and one multi-use weapon, the rocket projectile (RP). In the early years of the war, the main weapon for use against shipping was the standard GP or AP/SAP bomb, and whilst there were some successes with this type of weapon, especially in the Pacific, these were largely due to tactics, luck and the nature of the target (e.g. non-armoured flight decks on Japanese carriers). When bombs managed to hit ships they caused damage, often fatal damage, but in proportion to the effort expended, this was not the most effective use of air power. As the 'Airpower at Sea' article (pages 140-143) makes clear, the Pacific campaign is to some degree at variance with this general statement. The loss of the British capital warships *Prince of Wales* and *Repulse* to Japanese air attack whilst manoeuvring at sea, the devastating attack on the docked ships at Pearl Harbor and the decisive Battle of Midway, all revealed the capability of aircraft against shipping. However, in the bigger picture, the attacks on merchant shipping were more significant as they affected more than one land campaign.

Mines were a standard part of the anti-shipping inventory but the large-scale use of air-dropped mines was a particular feature of RAF operations, with Bomber Command alone dropping an average of 1,000 mines a month from 1942 onwards. Larger aircraft, such as the Halifax and Lancaster, could carry six mines, referred to as 'vegetables', on these 'gardening' sorties. Whilst the exact number of ships lost to mines is impossible to calculate, it is generally accepted that this air campaign played a major part in the overall anti-shipping and anti-submarine war.

Bombs and guns were also used extensively against shipping and cannot be ignored, but it is the torpedo that had the potential to prove particularly lethal. This type of weapon had been used in World War One, albeit on a limited scale and with limited success, but it really came of age in World War Two and was employed by all the major air arms. The torpedo was not an easy weapon to use as it required the launch aircraft to fly toward the target, often a heavily defended warship, on a steady course at low level. Amongst a number of other parameters, it required accurate delivery in terms of height and speed at release. Its major advantage was that a single hit below the waterline of the target could prove fatal. The tell-tale plume of water rising up from the target showed the aircrew that their 'tinfish'

had struck home. One campaign in which anti-shipping operations by aircraft played a major part was the Western Desert, when Allied aircraft operating from Malta and Egypt succeeded in reducing Rommel's shipborne supplies, especially of vital fuel oil, to a trickle.

The rocket projectile was also used against ships to good effect - RAF Beaufighters and Mosquitoes, especially those of the Coastal Command Strike Wings, caused great loss to enemy shipping in the latter years of the war. The standard RAF weapon was the 60lb RP and this also proved to be a devastating weapon against land targets. Indeed it was this role that saw its major employment, with aircraft like the Typhoon specialising in using RPs (and cannon) against vehicles, tanks, and fixed targets such as radar sites.

Fleeting mention has been made of aircraft guns and whilst we have not focused on this subject, guns of various calibre have always been an important part of an aircraft's air-to-ground weaponry, at times comprising the main weapon. The 20mm cannon fitted to the Hurricane, for example, were lethal in the hands of Desert Air Force pilots strafing targets in the Western Desert. Special guns, such as large-calibre anti-tank weapons, appeared on a number of aircraft - the Luftwaffe for example, employing this type of weapon against massed formations of Russian tanks on the Eastern Front.

Cold War

Dropping the atom bombs on Japan in August 1945 raised the importance of air power as a strategic weapon from dominant to decisive. With a single aircraft able to destroy an entire city, air war changed almost overnight and from a defensive point of view it was even more imperative to prevent enemy bombers penetrating your airspace. This destructive capability increased with the introduction of the hydrogen bomb and the spread of atomic capability to other countries, the 'nuclear club' soon included Britain, France and Russia.

Delivery by aircraft remained the main technique into the late 1950s when the development of surface-to-surface missiles (SSMs) reduced dependence on aircraft, and eventually replaced them as the main delivery system. In terms of air delivery, the nuclear weapon evolved quickly making it more destructive, more accurate and giving it longer range. The latter aspect, known as stand-off - ie no need for the bomber to actually fly over the target - was one of the main features of air weapon development in the latter half of the 20th Century.

● **Anti-shipping missiles have replaced the torpedo in modern warfare, with the helicopter often providing the desired launch platform.** (KEY collection)

● **An RAF Tornado GR.1 operates its JP233 weapon during a test mission. Designed to destroy Warsaw Pact runways during the Cold War, it was only used in anger during the 1991 Gulf War and has since been withdrawn from use.** (KEY collection)

The basic set of weapons in use at the end of World War Two remained in current for the next 50 years, for example, a standard weapon for aircraft such as the Vulcan and Tornado was still the 1,000lb bomb. This is also true of a number of other basic weapon types, such as the cannon and the unguided rocket (RP). In many respects all that had changed from 1945 was the way in which the weapon was delivered, and a study of the major conflicts (Korea 1950, Suez 1956, Vietnam 1960s) shows the same basic types in use. It is in the area of precision-guidance that the real changes have taken place over the last 25 years, with the Vietnam War providing one major impetus for change. Amongst the many developments that took place during this conflict, the most significant saw improvements to aiming systems. The Paveway series of LGBs entered service in the mid-1960s and the latest variants, such as Paveway III, are operational today.

The basic principle is to attach guidance and control units to existing 'dumb' bombs, with laser being the preferred guidance sensor. In essence the bomb(s) are dropped by the launch aircraft such that they fall within a cone of reflected laser energy produced by a laser fired at the target by an aircraft or by a ground operator. The bombs then guide to the laser point with a high degree of accuracy.

Heavily defended targets are best attacked from a distance to reduce the threat to the attacking aircraft. The best way to achieve stand-off is to power the bomb – at which point it becomes a missile.

Air-to-surface missiles (ASMs) only became a standard part of the aerial arsenal in the 1970s and then in combination with sensors that enabled the missile to be guided to the target area. Early types of missile, of late 1960s vintage, included the AS30 which was visually guided by the operator in the aircraft tracking flares on the missile and sending radio guidance signals to correct its flight path. Later and more effective ASMs used sensors on the missile to feed information to the launch aircraft, TV-guided missiles proving particularly accurate. One drawback with all such weapons was their cost, although the trade-off of guaranteed destruction for fewer resources (fewer aircraft) was used to counter the argument.

Of the TV-guided missiles one of the most effective is the AGM-65 Maverick, first introduced in the 1960s but with continuous development that has kept the basic weapon in service; for example, over 800 AGM-65s, in TV and Infra-Red guidance modes, were fired during the 1999 Kosovo conflict.

To summarise the last 20 years: excluding nuclear weapons, the RAF's array of air-to-ground weapons in 1984 comprised:
1 Conventional iron bombs – 540lb and 1,000lb – in free-fall, retard of laser-guided modes.
2 Cluster bombs – a CBU (cluster bomber unit) with 147 bomblets.
3 Unguided rockets – 68mm rockets in a pod.
4 Area denial weapon – the specialist JP233 system.
5 Ant-radiation missiles (ARM) – for use against enemy ground radar.

The same range of basic weapon types was used by most air forces, although specialist weapons, such as the ARM and JP233 varied and were not universally employed. The anti-radiation missile was developed in response to the growing threat from radar-guided surface-to-air missiles and guns, and was designed to home in on the transmissions from such

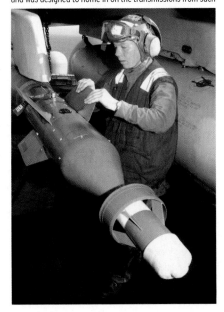

radars, flying down the beam and destroying the radar. This type of air-to-surface missile has increased in importance since its introduction in the 1970s and now forms a key part of most major air forces – the USAF having become particularly adept at what it calls the 'Wild Weasel' role. In the 1991 Gulf War, the principal weapon of this type was the HARM, and hundreds were fired as part of the offensive against Iraqi air defences in order to secure air superiority. Cluster bombs were developed as part of NATO's armoury against the

Warsaw Pact superiority in land forces and especially armour and other fighting vehicles. The bomb opens and distributes its bomblets over an area the size of a football pitch, although the general footprint can be adjusted.

Another important aspect of securing air superiority is preventing the enemy from using his aircraft, and one of the most effective ways of achieving this is to destroy them on the ground or at least to prevent them from flying. The RAF's JP233 airfield denial weapon was designed to destroy airfield surfaces, runways and taxiways, and slow down any repair attempts. A combination of penetration munitions and 'area denial' mines to prevent repair teams patching up the airfield surface, gave the weapon its overall effectiveness. Although developed for the Cold War task of attacking Warsaw Pact airfields, a number were dropped during the Gulf War.

Torpedoes are still carried by aircraft (and helicopters) but the main use is now against submarines rather than surface ships – the primary weapon against these is the anti-ship missile. The Argentinean Air Force scored a number of successes in the 1982 Falklands Conflict using Exocet missiles. This weapon, along with the likes of Sea Eagle, Harpoon, Penguin and SLAM-ER, remains an effective part of the airborne arsenal.

More range, more accuracy

In the decade since the Gulf War the major development in air-to-ground weapons has centred on delivery accuracy, making the surgical strike even more surgical (though still with the capacity for error) and stand-off capability. It has not always been a question of developing new bombs, but rather enhancing the sensors that are used to direct the bomb to the target. Inertial Navigation, Laser, GPS (Global Positioning System) and a variety of other sensor options are often integrated into the weapon's guidance system and accuracy is now measured in feet in almost any weather condition, day or night.

As with all of aviation, the world of modern weapons is laden with acronyms – JDAM, LGB, PGM, JSOW, WCMD, JASSM, SCALP to name but a few – each of which refers to type of weapon or its delivery. The USAF is very much a leader in the field of aerial weapon development and typical of the new breed is the AGM-154 JSOW (Joint Stand-Off Weapon) which is now carried by a variety of aircraft, such as the F-16 and the B-2. The launch range depends on the height of the aircraft and the weapon type – 12nm being typical for a low-level launch, 40nm for a high-level launch and 120nm+ for a powered launch. The JSOW is essentially a weapon carrier and it can be fitted with a variety of munitions depending on the target type. Basic guidance is GPS/Inertial Navigation but an Imaging Infra Red (IIR) sensor can be used for terminal guidance. These types of weapon are modular in construction, allowing a 'mix and match' of guidance and munitions as well as making future development easier.

Today more emphasis is being placed on material destruction than killing people – the US employed smart weapons during the Kosovo campaign to neutralise Serbian electrical power output. Air-launched weapons have come a long way since the days of dropping a small bomb over the side.

Some of the latest air-launched weapons, including the new Storm Shadow stand-off weapon, on display beside a French Air Force Mirage 2000D. The Storm Shadow, and the Apache behind it, will offer NATO forces and other operators a new level of stand-off accuracy. (KEY - Malcolm English)

An armourer prepares a GBU-12 laser-guided bomb aboard the USS Abraham Lincoln. (US Navy)

21

1920-29

1

2

3

1. First troop transport

The world's first dedicated troop transport, the Vickers Vernon, is introduced to the RAF on August 1, 1921. It is the first in a series of similar aircraft designes from the Vickers factory.
(Gordon Swanborough collection)

2. Successful Siskin

On May 7, 1923, the Armstrong Whitworth Siskin III makes its first flight. This successful all-metal RAF biplane fighter of the 1920s also attracts considerable export orders. (Gordon Swanborough collection)

3. Airliner evolves

The Fokker F.VIIa flies for the first time on March 12, 1925. It was derived from the earlier F.VII (seen here at the Aviodome Museum in Amsterdam, The Netherlands), though retained the single engine. The subsequent F.VIIa-3m made use of three Wright J-4 Whirlwind engines and was a huge success. (KEY - Steve Fletcher)

4. Boeing mail plane

The Boeing Model 40 makes its first flight on July 7, 1925, and after an initial lack of orders goes on to serve the San Francisco-Chicago airmail route operated by Boeing Air Transport. This was fulfilled by the Model 40A, fitted with a Pratt & Whitney Wasp radial engine. (Boeing)

SIGNIFICANT DATES

FEBRUARY 1, 1920: The South African Air Force is born.

FEBRUARY 5, 1920: The officer cadet training school at Cranwell is opened by the RAF – 82 years later it is still fulfilling its role.

MARCH 29, 1920: Situated just south of London, Croydon airport begins operations as the city's main airport.

APRIL 17, 1920: The Venezuelan Military Air Service is established.

JUNE 4, 1920: The US Army Air Service (USAAS) is formed following the passing of the Army Reorganisation Bill. On July 2, 1926, it becomes the US Army Air Corps.

SEPTEMBER 28, 1920: The Dayton-Wright RB Racer competes in the Gordon Bennett Aviation Cup Race. It is the first aircraft to be fitted with retractable landing gear.

NOVEMBER 16, 1920: Two ex-Australian Flying Corps pilots establish the Queensland and Northern Territories Aerial Service, or QANTAS, using just three biplanes.

DECEMBER 14, 1920: First fatal accident for a British airline when a Handley Page O/400 crashes just after taking off from Cricklewood.

JANUARY 15, 1921: Etienne Oehmichen flies a twin-rotor helicopter equipped with a large balloon for stability and lift.

FEBRUARY 22, 1921: Transcontinental American airmail services commence between San Francisco and Mineola, New York, using de Havilland DH.4Ms on the 14-stage route.

MARCH 4, 1921: The Caproni Ca 60, a giant eight-engine, nine-wing flying-boat designed

to carry 100 passengers crashes just after becoming airborne on its first and only flight.

MARCH 31, 1921: The Australian Air Force is formed from the Air Corps. On August 13 it adds 'Royal' to its title.

JUNE 8, 1921: A USD-9A (American-built DH.9A) flies with a pressurised compartment in place of the original open cockpits.

JUNE 15, 1921: Bessie Coleman is the first African-American woman to receive a Fédération Aéronautic Internationale (FAI) pilot's licence.

AUGUST 3, 1921: Aerial crop spraying takes place for the first time at Troy, Ohio.

OCTOBER 15, 1921: Spanish airline Compania Española de Trafico Aero commences operations. Today it is better known as Iberia.

DECEMBER 5, 1921: The first scheduled airline service in Australia is inaugurated by West Australian Airways.

JANUARY 11, 1922: First helicopter to hover for over a minute – built by Spaniard Marquis Pateras de Pescara – occurs in a hangar at Issy-les-Moulineaux, Paris, France.

FEBRUARY 9, 1922: The Royal Air Force Reserve is formed.

MARCH 20, 1922: The US Navy commissions its first aircraft carrier, the USS *Langley*, a converted collier.

APRIL 1922: The Colombian Army Air Arm is established.

APRIL 7, 1922: The first mid-air crash involving two airliners kills seven near Thieuloy-Saint-Antoine, France, when a

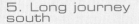

1920-29

5. Long journey south

On November 16, 1925, Alan Cobham sets off from Croydon on a civil air route survey flight to South Africa, eventually arriving at Cape Town on February 17, 1926.
(Gordon Swanborough collection)

6. Three-engine Ford

Powered by three Wright Whirlwind engines, the Ford 4-AT Trimotor makes its maiden flight on June 11, 1926. With more than a passing resemblance to the Junkers G 23, the American airliner is set to enjoy great success with US airlines. (KEY collection)

7. Atlantic Solo

On May 20-21, 1927, the first solo non-stop flight across the Atlantic is accomplished by Charles A Lindbergh in a Ryan NYP called *The Spirit of St Louis*. The aircraft is now on display in the National Air and Space Museum, Washington DC. (NASM)

8. Giant Dornier

The huge Dornier Do X flying-boat, powered by 12 Bristol Jupiter 525hp engines, makes its first flight on July 25, 1929. On October 21 it carries 150 passengers, ten crew and nine stowaways on its maiden passenger flight. (KEY collection)

Daimler Airways DH.18 collides head-on with a Grands Express Aériens Farman Goliath. This results in different routes for London-Paris and Paris-London flights.

OCTOBER 23, 1922: The American Propeller Company displays the first reversible-pitch propeller.

DECEMBER 1922: The Irish Air Corps is formed.

JANUARY 9, 1923: The first successful flight of a rotary wing aircraft takes place at Cuatro Vientos military airfield, Madrid, Spain. The aircraft is the Autogiro C.4, designed by Juan de la Cierva.

MAY 2-3, 1923: Lts Oakley Kelly and John Macready perform the first non-stop transcontinental flight from New York to San Diego in 26 hours, 50 minutes in a Fokker T-2.

MAY 23, 1923: A new airline, the Société Anonyme Belge d'Exploitation de la Navigation Aérienne (SABENA), is established as Belgium's national carrier.

JUNE 14, 1923: The New Zealand Permanent Air Force is established.

AUGUST 28, 1923: A flight endurance record of 37 hours 15 minutes is established by a USAAS DH.4B after being refuelled 15 times in the air using a 50ft hose from another DH.4B.

APRIL 1, 1924: The Royal Canadian Air Force is formed.

APRIL 28, 1924: Imperial Airways commences operations with a 13-aircraft fleet. The state-owned company is established by combining the assets of private companies Daimler Airway, Handley Page Transport, Instone Airline and British Marine Air Navigation.

SEPTEMBER 28, 1924: Two out of four USAAS Douglas World Cruisers (DWCs) arrive back at Seattle following a 175-day 26,345 mile (42,397km) round-the-world flight, the first such circumnavigation.

MARCH 1925: A number of German airlines begin to offer in-flight movies in the shape of short single-reel silent films projected onto a small screen at the front of the cabin.

MAY 1, 1925: The Japanese Army Air Corps is established.

MAY 15, 1925: A new three-engine airliner, the Junkers G 23, enters service with Swedish Air Lines, beginning a trend for tri-motor designs.

JANUARY 6, 1926: German national airline Deutscher Luft Hansa is formed by the amalgamation of Deutscher Aero Lloyd and Junkers Luftverkehr.

FEBRUARY 6, 1926: The Pratt & Whitney Aircraft Company produces its first engine, a nine-cylinder radial air-cooled engine, developing some 400hp at 1,800rpm.

MARCH 16, 1926: The first successful launch of a liquid-fuelled rocket takes place at Auburn, Massachusetts. Dr Robert H Goddard's rocket reaches just 184ft (56m) but its descendants go on to reach for the stars.

MAY 9, 1926: First flight over the North Pole is achieved by Lt Cdr Richard E Byrd and Floyd Bennett in a Fokker F.VIIA-3m.

JULY 1, 1926: The Kungliga Svenska Flygvapnet (Swedish Air Force) is established.

DECEMBER 1926: The Lockheed Aircraft Company is founded by Allan Lougheed – he chooses to call it 'Lockheed' because it is easier to pronounce than his own name.

SELECTED FIRST FLIGHTS

July 19, 1920: Vickers R.80 airship	**August 23, 1923:** Polikarpov II-400	**1926:** Letov S 118	**January 7, 1928:** Polikarpov U-2/Po-2
November 24, 1920: Dornier Cs II Delphin	**September 9, 1923:** Curtiss R2C-1	**March 16, 1926:** Armstrong Whitworth Argosy	**February 15, 1928:** Short Calcutta
December 12, 1920: Blériot-Spad S.33	**October 2, 1923:** de Havilland DH.53	**March 19, 1926:** Fairey IIIF	**June 1928:** Hawker Hart
April 19, 1921: Short N.3 Cromarty	**1924:** Nieuport-Delage Ni-D 42	**April 1926:** Blackburn Ripon	**June 25,1928:** Boeing F4B/P-12
May 1921: Boeing GA-1	**1924:** Douglas O-2	**May 7, 1926:** Blériot 127	**April 1928:** Vickers Vildebeest
August 1921: Caudron C.59	**May 1924:** Fokker C.V	**June 11, 1926:** Ford 4-AT Trimotor	**August 1928:** Boeing Model 80
March 26, 1922: de Havilland DH.34	**May 26, 1924:** Tupolev ANT-2	**August 17, 1926:** Short Singapore	**November 1928:** Hawker Tomtit
May 1922: Breguet 19	**June 23, 1924:** Focke-Wulf A 16	**September 1926:** Avro Avian	**November 14, 1928:** Fairey Long-Range
August 22, 1922: Vickers Victoria	**1925:** Potez 25	**September 30, 1926:** de Havilland DH.66	Monoplane
October 9, 1922: Dornier Komet II	**January 3, 1925:** Fairey Fox	**September 30, 1926:** Dornier Do R Super-Wal	**1929:** Avro Tutor
November 6, 1922: Dornier Do J Wal	**February, 1925:** Gloster Gamecock	**October 27, 1926:** Blériot 165	**February 1929:** Morane-Saulnier MS.230
November 18, 1922: Dewoitine D 1	**February 22, 1925:** de Havilland DH.60	**November 3, 1926:** Boeing F2B-1	**March 1929:** Great Lakes 2-T-1
November 24, 1922: Vickers Virginia	**March 10, 1925:** Supermarine Southampton	**March 1927:** Westland Wapiti	**July 25, 1929:** Dornier Do X
November 28, 1922: Fairey Flycatcher	**March 12, 1925:** Fokker F.VIIA	**March 2, 1927:** Boeing F3B-1	**September 11, 1929:** Fokker F-32
January 1923: Curtiss PW-8	**May 10, 1925:** Armstrong Whitworth Atlas	**May 17, 1927:** Bristol Bulldog	**September 11, 1929:** Tupolev ANT-7/R-6
January 9, 1923: Cierva C.4	**July 6, 1925:** Douglas DAM-1	**July 4, 1927:** Lockheed Vega	**October 25, 1929:** Fairey Fox
May 7, 1923: Armstrong Whitworth Siskin III	**July 7, 1925:** Boeing Model 40	**1928:** Dewoitine D.27	**November 1929:** Lockheed 8 Sirius
June 2, 1923: Boeing Model 15 (PW-9)	**July 29, 1925:** Blériot 155	**1928:** Farman F.190	**November 6, 1929:** Junkers G 38
July 30, 1923: de Havilland DH.50	**November 24, 1925:** Tupolev TB-1	**1928:** Polikarpov R-5	**December 9, 1929:** de Havilland DH.80

1920-29

1. British Bulldog

The Bristol Bulldog single-seat fighter makes its first flight on May 17, 1927. The aircraft is designed to meet Air Ministry Specification F.9/26 for a new day/night radial-engine powered fighter.

Powered by a Bristol Jupiter engine it is widely used by the RAF and is also exported to Australia, Denmark, Estonia, Finland, Latvia, Sweden and Siam. (KEY collection)

2. Airborne luxury

On March 16, 1926, the Armstrong Whitworth Argosy makes its maiden flight and although only seven are built they leave a lasting impression on commercial aviation. Star feature aboard the aircraft was the first class silver service, complete with steward. This level of comfort is of course available only to the very rich because at the moment air travel is only open to the privileged few. The Argosy suffers three major incidents, including one in-flight fire that causes the aircraft to crash and results in 15 fatalities. The type is eventually withdrawn from use by the end of 1936. (Gordon Swanborough collection)

SIGNIFICANT DATES

March 14, 1927: Pan American Airways is formed and is set to become one of the most influential airlines over the next 50 years.

May 25, 1927: Lt James H Doolittle completes an 'outside loop', the first time this manoeuvre has been accomplished

June 29, 1927: The first flight between the USA and Hawaii is completed in an Atlantic Fokker monoplane by Lt Albert Hegenberger and Lt L Maitland in 25 hours and 50 minutes.

July 4, 1927: Lockheed's new streamlined Vega four-passenger aircraft makes its maiden flight, powered by a single 220hp Wright Whirlwind engine.

September 8, 1927: The Cessna Aircraft Company is formed and is destined to become one of the worlds leading manufacturers, particularly of light aircraft.

October 14-15, 1927: Flying a Bréguet 19, Frenchman Dieudonné Costes and his navigator, Joseph Le Brix, complete the first non-stop crossing of the South Atlantic.

February 22, 1928: Australian aviator Bert Hinkler completes an 11,000 mile (17,702km) solo flight from London to Darwin, Australia, in an Avro Avian. He departs London on February 7 and routes via Rome, Malta, Libya, India, Burma and Singapore.

May 15, 1928: The Australian Flying doctor service is introduced with help from the Australian Inland Mission and Qantas.

June 9, 1928: A Fokker F.VIIb-3m, flown by Australians Charles Kingsford Smith and Charles Ulm, and Americans Harry Loon and James Warner, completes the first crossing of the Pacific from the USA to Australia with stops in Hawaii and Fiji.

June 11, 1928: The world's first rocket-powered flight takes place when the seaplane Ente flies for three-quarters of a mile in the hands of pilot Friedrich Stamer.

June 18, 1928: Amelia Earhart becomes the first woman to fly across the Atlantic as part of a three-person crew in a Fokker F.VIIb-3m.

October 15, 1928: The huge Graf Zeppelin airship completes an east-west crossing of the Atlantic when it arrives at Lakehurst, New York. The airship had left Friedrichshafen, Germany, on October 11.

January 1, 1929: Poland nationalises its airlines, thus forming one operator - Polskie Linje Lotnicze (Polish Air Lines or LOT).

August 1929: Several small solid-propellant rockets are fitted to a Junkers 33 seaplane which then performs the first rocket-assisted take-off.

August 8-29, 1929: The German airship Graf Zeppelin is the first of its type to circumnavigate the world in a journey lasting 21 days, 5 hours and 31 minutes - covering a distance of 21,873 miles (35,200km).

September 1, 1929: In the USA the Aeronautics Branch of the US Department of commerce decrees that all licensed aircraft in the USA must carry the designation 'N' followed by identifying numbers and letters.

September 24, 1929: James H Doolittle, flying a modified Consolidated NY-2, is the first pilot to fly solely by use of instruments and radio aids from take-off to landing without any visual reference.

December 1929: The Hellenic Combat Air Force is established, forerunner of the modern day Greek Air Force.

SOLO DESCENT:
As the sun sets over the Rocky Mountains
and you prepare to descend onto an isolated
lake – this is one moment when our Interactive
ATC won't be necessary.

That's how real it gets in Microsoft® Flight Simulator 2002 Professional Edition

If you're serious about flying, Flight Simulator 2002 Professional Edition will take you to new heights of realism. Pilot over stunningly detailed terrain, realistic cities and dramatic landscapes that are rendered in unprecedented depth. Experience spectacular visual and lighting effects including contrails off your wing tips and smoke from your tyres at touchdown. Climb into the cockpit of any one of a wide variety of aircraft including a Boeing 747-400, interact with ATC to ask for clearance during take-off or landing and get to grips with landing a Cessna 208 Caravan floatplane onto rivers and lakes.

Flight Simulator 2002 Professional Edition adds a whole new dimension to your flying experience.

Microsoft®

www.flightsim2002.co.uk

PISTON

POWER

The piston engine made possible that memorable Wright brothers' first flight. Bill Gunston OBE FRAeS charts the development of the piston engine through the past 100 years.

At the end of World War Two, the invention of the turbojet was thought by some to herald the death-knell of aircraft piston engines. This proved to be true for large or fast aircraft, but today the production and variety of smaller piston engines has never been greater.

Basic principles

Piston engines are also known as reciprocating engines, because they generate their power by the reciprocating motion of pistons moving to and fro inside cylinders. Each movement is called a stroke. Such engines come in various families, operating in different ways – in aviation, about 98% operate on the Otto, or four-stroke, cycle.

The size of such engines is measured by their capacity, or swept volume. This is the area of each piston multiplied by the stroke (the distance the piston travels along the cylinder) multiplied by the number of cylinders. Thus, the famous Merlin engine of World War Two had 12 cylinders with

Above: **The mighty Wright Cyclone radial was one of the leading engines of World War Two. Fitted to the Boeing B-17 Flying Fortress, as illustrated here, it played a vital part in securing the Allied victory.** (KEY - Duncan Cubitt)

1903: First piston-engined flight **1908:** Gnome Rotary engine **1915:** Rolls-Royce Eagle **1918:** Bristol Jupiter **1919:** Armstrong Siddeley Jaguar **1924:** Wright Whirlwind **1925:**

a bore of 5.4 inches and a stroke of 6 inches, giving a capacity of about 1,649 cubic inches, or just under 27 litres. This can be compared with typical car engines which have about 2 litres!

The four-stroke cycle is how almost all aero engines (and car engines) work. A major difference is that, while most car engines are cooled by water flowing round the cylinders, the majority of aero engines are air cooled, with closely-spaced fins dissipating the heat from the cylinders. Another obvious difference is that, while car engines drive via a gearbox or automatic transmission, aero engines drive the propeller directly, though many drive via a speed-reducing gear so that the crankshaft can turn at high speed for maximum power while the propeller turns more slowly for maximum efficiency.

A few aero engines are two-strokes, similar to those found

Above: **A Rolls-Royce apprentice works on a Bristol Pegasus radial engine from one of the Royal Navy Historic Flights Swordfish aircraft. The Pegasus was developed between the wars but as can be seen, its design certainly made maintenance access easy.** (Rolls-Royce)

in many motorcycles. Near the bottom of the power stroke, the inlet valve or port opens and pre-pressurised mixture rushes in, while the exhaust escapes through a port on the other side of the cylinder. This seems an excellent idea, because the engine gets one power stroke on each revolution of the crankshaft instead of on every two revolutions as with a four stroke. But it is not very efficient, because on each stroke some exhaust gas is left in the cylinder and some fresh unburnt mixture can escape with the exhaust.

The third fundamental type of piston aero engine is the diesel. This resembles both the others except that no spark plug is needed and the down-going piston sucks in pure air. This air is compressed so tightly by the up-going piston that, near the top of the compression stroke, when a tiny spray of fuel is squirted in it burns instantly. Because of the extreme compression, diesels are thermodynamically more efficient than spark-ignition engines, and another good feature is that instead of highly volatile petrol (gasoline) they can use

fuel oil, which some people consider safer. The main drawback is that they have to be massively constructed, which is bad news for aircraft designers. ▶

Top: **The Sopwith Camel was one of a number of aircraft powered by the Gnome rotary engine. The propeller and engine both rotated around a fixed crankshaft, though the principle was very inefficient.** (Gordon Swanborough collection)

The de Havilland DH.60G Gipsy Moth is a fine example of how a non-inverted inline engine hampered forward visibility of the pilot.

27

Even today the Merlin is still being refined, though for racing purposes rather than combat. The annual Reno air races witness a huge gathering of exotic warbird racers, including this P-51 Mustang powered by a highly-tuned Merlin engine, probably producing almost double its original power output. (KEY - Duncan Cubitt)

At the upper end of the radial power curve was the Bristol Centaurus, a two-row 18-cylinder radial, sleeve valve engine developing 2,500hp. This engine is most famous for its use in the Hawker Sea Fury but four pairs of them also powered the Bristol Brabazon airliner in 1949. (KEY collection)

Lack of an engine prevented any would-be aviator from achieving success until the Wright brothers began flying on December 17, 1903. They used a primitive home-made Otto-cycle engine, with motorcycle chains driving two slower-turning pusher propellers. By 1907 improved Otto engines were made, with a row of four or even six water-cooled cylinders. Such engines powered almost every German warplane in World War One, but in 1905 two Frenchmen, Laurent and Louis Seguin, began designing an engine that was literally revolutionary. They called it the Gnome rotary.

Early engines

The cylinders of the Gnome were arranged like spokes of a wheel. Even stranger, the crankshaft was fixed to the aircraft and the propeller was fixed to the engine. Thus, when the engine started, it spun round, driving the propeller with it. Fuel mixture was sucked in via the hollow crankshaft and escaped from the crankcase via one-way flap-valves in the crowns of the pistons. The operating cycle was extremely inefficient, and the engine burned almost one-third as much castor-oil lubricant as it did of fuel. Not least, the powerful gyroscopic effect of the spinning engine often made aircraft tricky to fly. For example, the Sopwith Camel, the most successful British

fighter of World War One (usually powered by a version of the Gnome with ordinary inlet and exhaust valves called the Clerget) tried to climb when turning left but tried to dive when turning right.

The main idea of rotary engines was that spinning the cylinders round kept them cool. However, the fundamental limitations of the rotaries meant that at the end of World War One they faded from the scene. In their place came water-cooled inline engines, powerful eight- and 12-cylinder

Above: **Arguably the most famous piston engine ever built, the Rolls-Royce Merlin helped to win the Battle of Britain. As well as being fitted to the Spitfire and Hurricane, it also powered bombers, such as the Avro Lancaster, and was to see constant development throughout the war, resulting in 168,040 engines being built.** (KEY collection)

fighters. A new species, the static radial. At a glance, the radial looked like a rotary, with cylinders arranged like wheel spokes, but such engines are more conventional in that the engine is fixed to the aircraft and the propeller is driven by the crankshaft.

Vee engines (with two banks, or rows, of cylinders forming a V when seen end-on) and a new species, the static radial. At a glance, the radial looked like a rotary, with cylinders arranged like wheel spokes, but such engines are more conventional in that the engine is fixed to the aircraft and the propeller is driven by the crankshaft.

In 1917 a Bristol engineer, Roy Fedden, assisted by L F G 'Bunny' Butler, designed an impressive 400hp nine-cylinder radial which they named the Jupiter. With this they formed an Engine Department at the Bristol Aeroplane Company. For six years nobody wanted to buy an expensive new engine, because thousands of wartime powerplants could be had for almost nothing. Then in 1923 the RAF bought 81 Jupiters, and Fedden's team escaped being shut down. By the mid-1930s more than 7,100 Jupiters had powered 262 types of aircraft, and an improved version, the Pegasus, was in production. Though it was the same size (1,753 cubic inches, or 28.7 litres) as the Jupiter, the Pegasus eventually gave over 1,000hp, and by 1942 17,000 had been made.

More power

By 1930 Fedden could see that eventually even more power would be needed, so that capacity would have to be increased. Bigger cylinders were not a good idea, because it would take too long for the combustion to spread from the spark plug throughout the available volume above the piston. More cylinders could not be packed into one radial row because where they were fixed to the crankcase they were already touching each other. The obvious answer was to use two rows of cylinders, but when Fedden tried to do this he found it impossible to design the valve gear, needed to drive the four valves (two inlet, two exhaust) at the head of each cylinder. He wanted four valves to get better 'breathing', with an easy flow path for the incoming mixture and outgoing exhaust.

In the end, he decided to replace the poppet type of valve with the sleeve valve, in which the piston oscillates inside a sleeve, a steel tube fitting precisely inside the cylinder. Each sleeve is driven by a small crank geared to the crankshaft so

Above: **The Continental R-670, as fitted to the Boeing Stearman trainer, will have been a familiar engine to thousands of wartime American pilots. The simplicity of the seven-cylinder radial design is readily apparent here.** (KEY - Duncan Cubitt)

The water-cooled option

Meanwhile, other companies were busy with water-cooled Vee engines. In France Hispano-Suiza V-12 engines powered thousands of fighters and bombers, and much greater numbers (to be precise, over 129,000) were improved by Vladimir Klimov in the USSR and used for the famous Yak fighters and SB and Pe-2 fast bombers. In Germany both Daimler-Benz and Junkers decided to put the two banks of six cylinders under the crankcase in the inverted-V, or ^, arrangement. They considered this gave a fighter pilot a better view ahead (and they were right) but, amazingly, the German DB601 of 34 litres, the DB603 of 44.5 litres and the Junkers Jumo 211 and 213 of 35 litres were repeatedly out-powered by the Rolls-Royce Merlin of only 27 litres.

The monstrous Napier Sabre engine as fitted to an RAF Typhoon. Featuring four horizontal banks of six cylinders, the Sabre ultimately developed 3,000hp, making it one of the most powerful British piston engines ever built. (RAF Museum)

The Grumman F8F Bearcat was powered by the 18-cylinder Pratt & Whitney R-2800-34W Double Wasp. Coupling this huge 2,100hp engine to a small airframe produced outstanding performance, hence its popularity among the modern-day warbird racing fraternity. (KEY - Duncan Cubitt)

that specially shaped ports (apertures) in the sleeve are alternately brought in line with inlet or exhaust ports in the cylinder. It took ten years and millions of pounds, but Fedden won in the end. Starting with the 900hp Perseus, he went on to produce the 1,200hp Taurus and 1,400-2,000hp 38-litre Hercules, both with 14 cylinders, and the 2,500-3,000hp Centaurus with 18 bigger cylinders.

His success inspired Frank Halford to design for the Napier company a complex liquid-cooled engine called the Sabre. It had four horizontal banks each of six small cylinders, and by running at the exceptional speed of 4,200 rpm (revolutions per minute) it generated 2,400hp for the RAF's Typhoon and Tempest fighters and later reached 3,000hp.

American radials

In 1925, a group of engineers in the USA broke away from the Wright company and set up as Pratt & Whitney Aircraft. Led by Frederick B Rentschler, their chief engineer was George Mead and chief designer Andy Willgoos. They created a neat nine-cylinder radial named the Wasp, and though it had only two valves per cylinder, and a capacity of only 1,344 cu in (22 litres), it gave 400hp, and soon was giving 600hp, the same as the big Jupiter. The Wasp and an enlarged version named the Hornet soon rivalled the Jupiter as the world's No 1 best-selling engine, and they had a big advantage. With only two

valves per cylinder, it was easy to double up and add a second row of cylinders.

Thus, by 1935 the Pratt & Whitney Twin Wasp was on test. Whereas the Wasp was known as the R-1340, from its capacity, the Twin Wasp had slightly smaller cylinders but it had 14 of them, in two rows of seven, so it was designated as the R-1830. It soon gave 900hp, and in World War Two it was made in astronomic numbers,

mostly rated at 1,200hp. For example, two were needed for each of the 10,000 DC-3/C-47/Dakota/Skytrain transports and four were required for each of the 19,000 B-24 Liberators. Meanwhile, by 1938 the mighty R-2800 Double Wasp was being tested. This had 18 cylinders, each much larger than those of the R-1830, and vast numbers were made at powers over 2,000hp, for such aircraft as the F4U Corsair, F6F Hellcat and B-26 Marauder. In World War Two Pratt & Whitney horsepower totalled 603,814,723 from 363,619 engines. No rival even came close.

Rolls-Royce had produced some of the most powerful engines of World War One, but then wanted to concentrate on making cars. Marshal of the Royal Air Force Hugh Trenchard got them to make a neat V-12 of 1,296 cubic inches which became famous as the Kestrel. By the late 1930s, a total of 4,750 had been made, rated at 480 to 745hp. In parallel, the famous Derby firm had produced the bigger 2,239 cubic inch Buzzard, rated at up to 825hp, and then derived from this a special engine for Schneider Trophy seaplane races. Named simply the R, this racing engine was by 1931 developed to give an amazing 2,783hp at 3,400 rpm.

A key factor in this fantastic power was use of special fuels. Such fuels were useless for worldwide air force use, but by adding special materials such as TEL (tetra-ethyl lead) ordinary petrols were produced with an octane number of first 87 and then 100. Octane rating is a measure of resistance to detonation, a dangerous condition in which the mixture effectively explodes. With high-octane petrols the power of engines can be dramatically increased, and one way of doing this is by supercharging.

Merlin power

Ordinary engines are naturally aspirated; like humans, they just suck in air. When fitted with a supercharger the air is forcibly pumped in under pressure, and the power developed is directly proportional to the mass of air ▄▄▶

Top: **Today the Rolls-Royce Heritage Museum in Derby rewards the visitor with a wonderful celebration of the company's heritage, which includes this section Griffon engine.** (KEY - Duncan Cubitt)

Above: **The Daimler Benz DB603 is typical of the 'inverted V' designs by the German company. Fuel injection gave its products an edge in some combat situations but the smaller capacity Rolls-Royce Merlin regularly out-performed these bigger capacity engines.** (KEY collection)

Merlin **1935**: Daimler Benz DB 600 **1936**: Jumo 211 **1937**: Napier Sabre **1937**: Wright R-3350 **1938**: Bristol Centaurus **1938**: Lycoming O-145

Today literally thousands of light aircraft are still powered by piston engines driving a propeller. Among the most prolific of the engine manufacturers is Textron Lycoming – its 'flat four' engine can probably be found at most general aviation airfields in the Western world, its heritage can be traced back to 1938. (KEY collection)

The largest piston-engined bomber ever to enter service in significant numbers was the huge Convair B-36 Peacemaker. The aircraft featured six 28-cylinder Pratt & Whitney R-4360 Wasp Majors as well as four turbojets. (KEY collection)

taken in on each induction stroke. Supercharging is especially important for high-flying aircraft. A naturally-aspirated engine rated at 500hp at sea level will give only 250hp at 20,000ft 6,096m), because at that altitude the atmospheric pressure has fallen by half. If the crankshaft is geared up to drive a rapidly-spinning centrifugal blower (a supercharger), almost all the lost power can be restored. As atmospheric drag has for the same reason fallen by almost half, a supercharged aircraft can fly much faster at high altitude than at sea level.

By 1934 Rolls-Royce was testing an engine a little bigger than the Kestrel, with 1,649 cubic inches, or about 27 litres. Named Merlin (the bird, not the wizard), it began life powering the Hurricane, Spitfire, Whitley, Halifax and many other aircraft at powers around 1,000hp. During World War Two this modest V-12 engine was transformed. In 1940 newly hired aerodynamicist Stanley Hooker (who knew nothing about engines and had never even seen one) redesigned the Merlin supercharger to increase power to over 1,400hp. He then designed a two-stage supercharger, the air passing through two spinning compressors one after the other. At a stroke this doubled the power of the Merlin at high altitude. By the end of World War Two, production of the Merlin totalled 32,377 at Derby, 26,065 at Crewe, 23,647 at Glasgow and 30,428 by Ford Motor Co near Manchester. Packard, the US car firm in Detroit, added 55,523 Merlins, known as V-1650s for P-40s, P-51 Mustangs, Mosquitos and Lancasters. Later versions gave up to more than 2,200hp, an incredible figure for a small engine running on mass-produced 115/145-grade petrol. Rolls-Royce also produced a 36-litre (R size) engine name Griffon, which at up to 2,500hp powered later Spitfires, Fireflies and the Shackleton.

American power

In 1930 work began in Indianapolis on the Allison V-1710. It was designed for airships, but found its niche as an engine for US fighters in World War Two. Most went into the twin-engined Lockheed P-38 Lightning and various types of Curtiss P-40 Tomahawk/Kittyhawk, but another application was the superb NAA P-51 Mustang. Earlier types of Allison lost power at high altitude, so the Mustang was dramatically improved by being fitted with two-stage versions of Packard Merlin. However, American use of the Merlin stopped in 1945,

and later aircraft such as the F-82 Twin Mustang were fitted with 2,200hp Allisons.

Wright, meanwhile, had produced over 200,000 nine-cylinder R-1820 Cyclones (1,200 hp) and 14-cylinder R-2600 Cyclones (1,600-1,700hp), and went on to make the R-3350 18-cylinder Duplex Cyclone of 2,200hp for the Boeing B-29 Superfortress. Like the R-2800 Double Wasp of the P-47 Thunderbolt and the V-1710 of the P-38, the B-29 engine was fitted with a turbosupercharger to maintain power to high altitude. Instead of being geared from the crankshaft, a turbocharger is connected to a small turbine driven by the white-hot exhaust gas. This harnesses power that would otherwise go out of the exhaust pipe.

Wright chief engineer Bill Lundqvist hit on the idea of making a turbo drive the crankshaft, and by 1949 the Wright Turbo-Compound was on test. It was an R-3350 with three exhaust turbos, which raised power from the basic 2,700hp to 3,400hp. It was an efficient but complex engine, used in the DC-7, L-1049 Super Constellation, P2V (P-2) Neptune and P5M Marlin. A rival was the 3,000-3,700hp Pratt & Whitney R-4360 Wasp Major, which had 28 cylinders in four rows. It powered the C-97/Stratocruiser, B-50 and the enormous B-36 Peacemaker. Even more powerful was the USSR's Dobrynin VD-4K, engine of the Tu-85, which gave 4,300hp at almost 33,000ft (10,058m) and was the most powerful piston engine ever to fly. This was impressive, but Tupolev replaced the Tu-85 with the Tu-95, featuring turboprops of almost 15,000hp! However, the most powerful, largest and heaviest piston engine ever built, though never flown, was the Lycoming XR-7755 of 1944 which produced 5,000hp from nine banks of four cylinders.

Smaller pistons

By 1955 the only piston engines under development were for lightplanes. Though there were still large numbers of such classic engines as the de Havilland Gipsy in use, and one should not forget the deliberately simple Shvetsov M-11 five-cylinder radial, of which some 130,000 were made, almost the whole world market was being met by the American Continental and Lycoming products. These have four or six (rarely, two or eight) air-cooled cylinders arranged horizontally in left and right banks driving a central crankshaft. Today these still dominate the world market, and Textron-Lycoming deliveries easily exceed 250,000, but competition is growing.

In Austria the Rotax company has shown that if you want to make a neat lightplane you can do it with an engine that is smaller, lighter and in most ways more efficient than the traditional US products. Originally designed for snowmobiles, the Rotax engines completely dominate the world market in powers up to 150hp, despite competition from over a dozen other makes. Many new engines are exciting. In France SMA has succeeded in getting US certification for the SR305 diesel, a 230hp engine able to run on ordinary jet fuels whilst cutting consumption (and costs) by a claimed 40%. And in Canada, Orenda has shown that its 600hp liquid-cooled turbocharged V-8 can most effectively replace turboprops!

The piston engine was literally the driving factor at the start of this century of powered flight – as can be seen, 100 years on it still has a lot of potential.

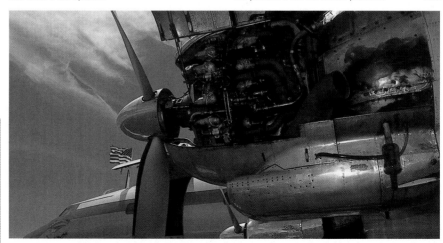

● Above: The massive and complicated Wright Turbo-Compound radial powered the Lockheed Super Constellation, illustrated here on a military C-121C variant. (KEY - Steve Fletcher)

1939: Pratt & Whitney Double Wasp **1940:** BMW 801 **1941:** Rolls-Royce Griffon **1942:** Pratt & Whitney Wasp Major **1951:** Dobrynin VD-4K **1997:** Orenda OE600

1930-39

1930-39

1. Outdated Heyford

The Handley Page Heyford bomber makes its first flight on June 12, 1930. The RAF receives 124 examples, but its design is already outdated, with open crew stations, biplane configuration and a very poor performance. (Gordon Swanborough collection)

2. Zeppelin to South America

The Graf Zeppelin airship (LZ 127) performs its first crossing of the south Atlantic, setting off from Friedrichshafen. (KEY collection)

3. Long-range airliner

Designed to meet an Imperial Airways' requirement for an aircraft to fly its long-distance routes to the far reaches of the British Empire, the Handley Page HP.42 first flies on November 14, 1930, though some sources claim it flew as early as June 30. Despite being extremely slow, the aircraft proved to have an excellent safety record.
(Gordon Swanborough collection)

4. Auntie Ju

In April 1931, the all-metal Junkers Ju 52/3m makes its maiden flight and becomes one of the most famous transport aircraft in history. It is a three-engine development of the original Ju 52, which first flew on October 13, 1930. Initially intended as an airliner, it gains fame when used as a transport by the Luftwaffe, mostly for troops. Almost 500 examples are built.
(KEY - Duncan Cubitt)

SIGNIFICANT DATES

JANUARY 16, 1930: Flying Officer Frank Whittle files a patent for his turbojet engine. At the time his work goes unappreciated.

JANUARY 25, 1930: American Airways is created through the merger of 12 independent airlines. It is subsequently renamed American Airlines on May 13, 1934.

MARCH 21, 1930: The Fuerza Aérea Chilena is created by combining the air arms of the Chilean Army and Navy.

MAY 15, 1930: Female passenger attendants are introduced by American carrier United Air Lines, all are qualified nurses.

MAY 24, 1930: British pilot Amy Johnson arrives at Fanny Bay aerodrome in Australia after a 19-day flight from the UK. She is the first woman pilot to complete the epic journey and uses a de Havilland Gipsy Moth.

JULY 16, 1930: Transcontinental and Western Airlines (TWA) is created with the merger of Transcontinental Air Transport and Western Air Express.

SEPTEMBER 1930: The Taylor Cub makes its first flight. Later taken on board by Piper, the Cub and its derivative - the Super Cub - are set to become two of the most famous light aircraft ever built.

SEPTEMBER 3, 1930: The first non-stop east-west crossing of the Atlantic is accomplished by two Frenchmen, Dieudonné Costes and Maurice Bellonte flying a Breguet 19 from Paris to New York in 37 hours 18 minutes.

DECEMBER 22, 1930: The Tupolev ANT-6 four-engine bomber makes its first flight. Designated TB-3 in service, it is the world's largest aircraft.

JANUARY 7, 1931: The first solo flight from Australia to New Zealand is completed in 12 hours and 15 minutes by Guy Menzies.

MARCH 26, 1931: Schweizerische Luftverkehr (Swiss Airways - later Swissair) is formed from the merger of two Swiss carriers, Balair and Ad Astra.

MAY 27, 1931: The first full-size wind tunnel, with working cross-section of 60ft (18.2m), begins operations at NACA's Langley Field Laboratory, Virginia.

JULY 1, 1931: United Air Lines is established, though as a holding company for four existing airlines: Boeing Air Transport, National Air Transport, Pacific Air Transport and Varney Air Lines.

JULY 1, 1931: Intrepid aviator Wiley Post and navigator Harold Gatty complete a flight around the Northern Hemisphere in their Lockheed Vega. The journey takes 8 days, 15 hours and 51 minutes.

SEPTEMBER 18, 1931: Hostilities begin in the

Apr 29, 1930: Polikarpov I-5 **Sept 1930:** Taylor Cub **Dec 22, 1930:** Tupolev ANT-6 **Apr 1931:** Junkers Ju 52/3m **Aug 14, 1931:** Tupolev ANT-14 **Sept 1931:** Heinkel He 59 **June 18, 1932:** Dewoitine D 500 **Feb 3, 1933:** Boeing 247

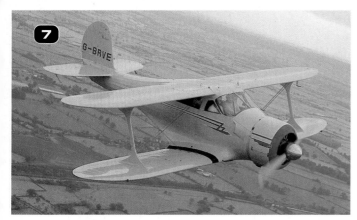

its first flight on November 4, 1932. As well as its unusual back-staggered wing layout, it also features a retractable undercarriage and fully-enclosed cabin. (KEY collection)

I-16 puts up courageous resistance. (KEY - Steve Fletcher)

1930-39

5. Magic Moth
One of the classic aircraft of all time, the de Havilland DH.82 Tiger Moth makes its first flight on October 26, 1931. Designed as a training aircraft for the RAF, it also enjoys massive export success and is sold on the civilian market. Over 8,000 are eventually built and a number of these remain airworthy today. (Gordon Swanborough collection)

6. Boeing Peashooter
Boeing P-26 Peashooter makes its first flight on March 20, 1932, and is the first all-metal fighter- it goes on to serve in the pursuit role for the USAAC. (Boeing)

7. Staggerwing
The beautiful Beech 17 Staggerwing makes

8. Revolutionary Rata
The small but fast Polikarpov I-16 Rata makes its first flight on December 31, 1933, and is the first low-wing monoplane with a retractable undercarriage to enter service. Although outclassed by Luftwaffe opposition when Germany attacks Russia in 1941, the

9. Flying Pencil
The slim Dornier Do 17 - nicknamed 'the flying pencil' - is designed to be a six-passenger mail plane and flies for the first time during 1934. It is not taken up by the airlines but instead finds favour with the Luftwaffe and spawns a line of bomber variants. (KEY collection)

Far East as Japan attacks China. The conflict is set to last for many years and witnesses an increasing use of air power.

OCTOBER 5, 1931: Clyde Pangborn and Hugh Herndon complete the first non-stop flight from Japan to the USA in a time of 41 hours and 13 minutes flying a Bellanca Skyrocket.

DECEMBER 29, 1931: Grumman flies the prototype FF-1, the first naval fighter to incorporate a retractable undercarriage.

MARCH 25, 1932: The Soviet Union forms a national airline officially called Grazhdanskii Vozdushnyi Flot (Civil Air Fleet) but referred to as Aeroflot. Initially it is responsible surveying, aerial

photography and crop-dusting, in fact just about civilian aviation application, as well as carrying passengers.

APRIL 1, 1932: The Beech Aircraft Corporation is formed by Walter Beech and his wife Olive Ann. It is set to become one of America's most successful aviation manufacturers of the next 70 years.

APRIL 27, 1932: Imperial Airways commences passenger services between London and Cape Town, South Africa.

MAY 9, 1932: A USAAC pilot, Captain A Hegenberger, becomes the fist solo pilot to perform an entirely blind landing using only cockpit instruments in a modified

Consolidated NY-2. A pair of Kreusi radio compass transmitters help him to locate the runway.

MAY 21, 1932: American aviatrix Amelia Earhart becomes the first woman to fly solo non-stop across the Atlantic when she lands near Londonderry, Northern Ireland, after departing from Harbour Grace, Newfoundland. Her flight lasted 14 hours and 54 minutes.

DECEMBER 1, 1932: The Heinkel He 70, designed by the Günter brothers, makes its first flight. Built to a very streamlined specification, the aircraft was very fast for its time and set new standards in European aircraft technology.

FEBRUARY 8, 1933: Boeing ups the stakes in the airline field when it performs the first flight of its new Model 247 twin-engine all-metal monoplane airliner.

APRIL 1, 1933: France gets its own air force when l'Armée de l'Air (Air Army or French Air Force) comes into being.

APRIL 1, 1933: The Indian Air Force is established.

APRIL 21, 1933: The giant US Navy airship USS *Macon* makes its first flight. It can carry five fighter aircraft inside a bay, which are then lowered by trapeze for launch and recovery during flight.

1934: Savoia-Marchetti SM.79 **Feb 23, 1934:** Lockheed 10 **Apr 17, 1934:** DH DH.89 **Sept 12, 1934:** Gloster Gladiator **Sept 12, 1934:** Hawker Hind **Jan 7, 1935:** Avro Anson **Sept 17, 1935:** Junkers Ju 87 **Mar 10, 1936:** Fairey Battle

1930-39

1. Electric Lockheed

February 23, 1934, witnesses the first flight of the Lockheed 10, an all-metal cantilever low-wing monoplane able to carry up to ten passengers. The aircraft is very successful and enjoys healthy sales. (KEY collection)

2. Stringbag

The legendary Fairey Swordfish makes its maiden flight on April 17, 1934. Nicknamed 'the stringbag' due to its outdated biplane configuration and construction, it nevertheless proves to be a vital asset to the Fleet Air Arm and scores some memorable victories during World War Two. (British Aerospace)

3. Bomber in disguise

On February 24, 1935, the first Heinkel He 111 flies - although designed as an airliner, it finds more work as a Luftwaffe bomber. Over 7,300 are built but many suffer at the hands of the RAF during the 1940 Battle of Britain and so are confined to night operations or use against less heavily-defended targets. (KEY collection)

4. Tubby Grumman

A development of the earlier F2F, the Grumman F3F makes its first flight on March 20, 1935. It serves aboard the US Navy carriers until the late 1930s. (KEY - Stephen Bridgewater)

5. Famed flying-boat

Arguably the most famous flying-boat to fly, the Consolidated PBY Catalina is in fact an amphibian which goes on to provide outstanding service during World War Two. It makes it maiden flight on March 28, 1935. (KEY collection)

6. Definitive Trainer

The North American NA-16, soon to be called the Texan or Harvard, makes its first flight in April 1935. Over 17,000 are eventually built, and as well as serving with the wartime allies, the type sees considerable use around the world. Many are still airworthy in private hands today. (KEY - Duncan Cubitt)

7. B-18 Bolo

A new bomber for the USAAC, the Douglas B-18 Bolo, makes its maiden flight in April 1935.

SIGNIFICANT DATES

August 1933: Hamilton Standard introduces the world's first variable-pitch propeller on a Curtiss Condor.

October 31, 1933: France gets its own national airline with the inauguration of Air France by French Air Minister Pierre Cot.

November 4, 1933: Brazilian carrier Viacao Aerea São Paulo (VASP) is created.

February 1, 1934: South African Airways is established, assuming the assets of South Africa's Union Airways in the process.

April 11, 1934: A new altitude record is set at 47,352ft (14,433m) by Cdr R Donati flying a Caproni 113 over Rome.

April 17, 1934: What is without doubt a truly beautiful design, the de Havilland DH.89 Dragon Rapide, makes its maiden flight.

May 11, 1934: The Douglas DC-2 enters service with TWA and embarks on the Los Angeles-New York route.

May 19, 1934: The enormous Tupolev ANT-20 *Maxim Gorkii* becomes the world's largest aircraft to fly. It can carry up to 50 passengers and even has space for a kitchen, photo lab, radio studio and cinema. It crashed on May 18, 1935, after colliding with a fighter killing 56 people.

May 29, 1934: The 1934 Collier Trophy is awarded to the Hamilton Standard Propeller Company for its development of the variable-pitch propeller.

October 23, 1934: Italian pilot Francesco Agello pushes the world speed record up to 440.68mph (709.2km/h) in the Macchi MC.72 racing seaplane. The aircraft is powered by a pair of Fiat engines positioned one behind the other to produce 3,100hp.

October 24, 1934: Charles Scott and Tom Campbell-Black land in Melbourne, Australia, to win the MacPherson Robertson England-Australia air race in their de Havilland DH.88 Comet *Grosvenor House*.

March 9, 1935: It is announced that Germany has indeed formed a new air force - the Luftwaffe - in blatant contravention of the Treaty of Versailles.

April 15, 1935: The first aircraft equipped with hydraulically-operated folding wings, the Douglas XTBD-1 torpedo-bomber, makes its maiden flight.

July 24, 1935: British scientists successfully track a Hawker Hart for 34 miles (54.7km) using radio direction finding (Radar) equipment. Radar is set to become vital in the defence of the UK during the 1940 Battle of Britain and remains an every day tool in the realms of commercial and military flying.

September 17, 1935: The Junkers Ju 87 Stuka dive bomber makes its first flight. Designed for

Mar 17, 1936: AW Whitley May 12, 1936: Messerschmitt Bf 110 June 10, 1936: Westland Lysander June 21, 1936: Handley Page Hampden June 25, 1936: Bristol Blenheim Oct 15, 1936: Nakajima Ki-27 Dec 21, 1936: Junkers Ju 88

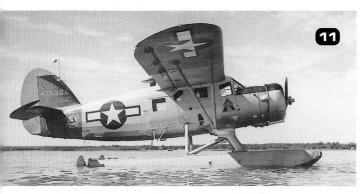

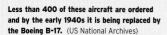

Less than 400 of these aircraft are ordered and by the early 1940s it is being replaced by the Boeing B-17. (US National Archives)

8. Luftwaffe Ace
The Messerschmitt Bf 109 first flies on May 28, 1935, and is set to revolutionise the German Luftwaffe. The fast and manoeuvrable monoplane is synonymous with the Battle of Britain, yet it serves throughout World War Two on all fronts. With around 35,000 built, it remains the second most prolific aircraft in history. (Cliff Knox)

9. Flying Fortress
Without question, the most famous American bomber ever built, the Boeing B-17 Flying Fortress prototype, the Model 299, makes its first flight on July 28, 1935. Later models, heavily armed with machine-guns, formed a large part of the Eighth Air Force armada that targeted Nazi Germany by day. (US National Archives)

10. Unsung Hero
The Hawker Hurricane, designed by Sidney Camm, makes its maiden flight on November 6, 1935. It is destined to live in the shadow of the Supermarine Spitfire, despite being responsible for the lion's share of enemy kills during the Battle of Britain in 1940. (Gordon Swanborough collection)

11. Ultimate utility
November 14, 1935, witnesses one of the all-time great utility aircraft making its first flight, the Noorduyn Norseman. Designed specifically for the harsh climate of northern Canada, the Norseman can be fitted with wheels, floats or skis and can carry up to eight passengers. (KEY collection)

12. Dakota legend
On December 17, 1935, what is to become the most famous piston engine airliner in history makes its maiden flight. The Douglas DC-3 Dakota proves immensely popular with the airlines and the military during World War Two. Sixty-seven years on and some are still in commercial service. (KEY - Duncan Cubitt)

precision ground attack, the Stuka drives fear into the population of many Europeans during the first years of World War Two.

October 3, 1935: Italian aircraft attack targets in Abyssinia, but the action against a country with practically no air force brings international condemnation.

December 1, 1935: The world's first airways traffic control centre opens at Newark, New Jersey. Initially it is manned by staff from the larger American airlines.

March 2, 1936: Frank Whittle founds Power Jets with an initial investment of £10,000 to begin development work on the turbojet engine.

March 4, 1936: The world's largest rigid airship, the Zeppelin Company's LZ 129 *Hindenburg*, makes its maiden flight.

May 12, 1936: The first Messerschmitt Bf 110 twin-engine fighter makes its first flight. It has more range than the Bf 109 but is not as agile and becomes easy prey for Allied fighters during World War Two.

June 10, 1936: The prototype Westland Lysander makes its first flight at Yeovil. The aircraft has amazing short field performance and is able to take off in just 490ft (149.3m). It is destined to be a very useful means of inserting agents behind enemy lines during World War Two.

June 25, 1936: The Bristol Blenheim Mk.1, developed from the Bristol 142 *Britain First*, makes its first flight. The all-metal monoplane bomber is even faster than the RAF fighters of the time

June 26, 1936: Focke-Wulf flies its Fa 61 helicopter for the first time. The unusual machine has two large rotors mounted on outrigger struts, as well as a normal propeller to cool the radial engine and provide some forward thrust. In the hands of German test pilot Hanna Reitsch it sets a helicopter distance record of 67.7miles (108.97km) on October 25, 1937.

July/August 1936: The situation in Spain deteriorates into civil war with Germany

backing General Franco and sending aircraft of the Condor Legion in October to support the nationalists. However, Soviet-supplied Polikarpov fighters inflict heavy losses on the Condor Legion.

September 28, 1936: Squadron Leader S R Swain sets a new world altitude record of 49,944ft (15,222m) in a Bristol 138A.

October 27, 1936: Pan Am commences regular flights between the USA and the Philippines using Martin M-130 flying-boats.

January 15, 1937: The Beechcraft 18 makes its first flight at Wichita, Kansas. The all-metal monoplane proves very popular with both commercial and military operators.

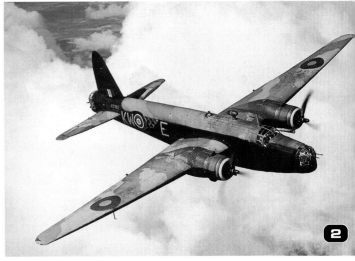

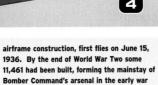

1930-39

1. Beauty in the air
One of the most beautiful aircraft designs ever built, the Supermarine Spitfire, takes to the air for the first time on March 5, 1936. After its valiant service during World War Two the Spitfire continued to fly with air arms for a number of years, and today around 50 remain airworthy. (KEY - Steve Fletcher)

2. Geodetic bomber
The Vickers Wellington, masterpiece of designer Barnes Wallace and featuring geodetic airframe construction, first flies on June 15, 1936. By the end of World War Two some 11,461 had been built, forming the mainstay of Bomber Command's arsenal in the early war years. (Gordon Swanborough collection)

3. Queen of the skies
The Short Empire Flying-Boat makes its maiden flight in July 1936 and goes on to serve Imperial Airways' routes to the Middle East, Asia and South Africa. (KEY collection)

4. Popular Goose
The Grumman G-21 Goose takes to the air for the first time on May 29, 1937. It proves to be a very popular amphibian and is used by the military and commercial operators. (KEY - Steve Fletcher)

5. Dornier Do 24
Another flying-boat from the Dornier stable, the Do 24 was originally designed to meet a Dutch Navy requirement and the prototype makes its first flight on July 3, 1937. Used by the German military throughout World War Two, deliveries to the French Navy continue after the war, with Spanish examples flying well into the 1970s. (KEY collection)

6. Undaunted Dauntless
The Douglas SBD Dauntless dive-bomber becomes one of the most influential US Navy aircraft of World War Two. The prototype completes its first flight on April 22, 1938, and Fleet examples go on to wreak havoc with the Imperial Japanese Navy, notably at the 1942 Battle of Midway. (KEY - Duncan Cubitt)

SIGNIFICANT DATES

APRIL 2, 1937: Swedish aircraft manufacturer SAAB (Svenska Aeroplan Aktiebolaget) is formed.

APRIL 9, 1937: The prototype Mitsubishi Type 97 makes a record-breaking flight from Japan to England in just 2 days, 3 hours and 17 minutes.

MAY 6, 1937: One of the most infamous aviation accidents happens at Lakehurst, New Jersey, when the *Hindenburg* airship explodes and crashes while attempting to land. Sixty-one people survive but 36 are killed. The event sounds the death knell for the hydrogen-filled airship.

JUNE 30, 1937: The world altitude record goes up once more as Flt Lt M J Adam reaches 53,937ft (16,440m) in a Bristol 138.

JULY 1, 1937: Continental Airlines is born out of the former Varney Air Transport.

JULY 2, 1937: Aviatrix Amelia Earhart and her navigator Fred Noonan disappear over the western Pacific while attempting a round-the-world flight in a Lockheed Electra.

JULY 27, 1937: A new four-engine transport aircraft, the Focke-Wulf Fw 200 Condor makes its maiden flight. Although intended as a long-range airliner, it eventually sees considerable use as a maritime patrol aircraft with the Luftwaffe.

JULY 30, 1937: The Royal Navy assumes control of the Fleet Air Arm, which up until now has been controlled by the RAF.

AUGUST 23, 1937: The first ever completely automatic landing takes place at Dayton, Ohio, using a modified USAAC transport aircraft. With the aid of radio instruments and gyroscopes, the aircraft is guided to the ground along with assistance from radio equipment at the airfield.

OCTOBER 1, 1937: The wearing of seat belts is made compulsory aboard all British commercial airliners.

OCTOBER 16, 1937: The Short S.25, the prototype of the Sunderland flying-boat, makes a successful first flight. Throughout World War Two, the Sunderland earns a reputation as a long-range patrol aircraft and is feared by U-boat crews.

JANUARY 20, 1938: A successful air-to-air refuelling is made between an Armstrong Whitworth AW.23 and a Short C-class Empire flying-boat. The system has been pioneered by Alan Cobham and his company Flight Refuelling - a name set to become synonymous with mid-air refuelling in the coming years.

JUNE 7, 1938: The prototype Douglas DC-4 makes its maiden flight. The four-engine aircraft is fitted with a nose wheel and is larger than the DC-3.

JULY 14, 1938: American tycoon Howard Hughes smashes the record for flying around the Northern Hemisphere when he completes the feat in 3 days, 19 hours and 8 minutes flying a Lockheed 14-N Super Electra.

Dec 24, 1937: Macchi MC.200 **Jan 1938:** Aichi D3A Val **Apr 6, 1938:** Bell P-39 **May 23, 1938:** Fiat CR.42 **July 1938:** Focke-Wulf Fw 189 **Oct 11, 1938:** Westland Whirlwind **Oct 14, 1938:** Curtiss P-40 **1939:** Henschel Hs 129 **Jan 1939:** NA B-25 **Jan**

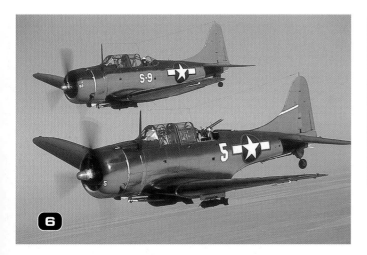

7

10

8

11

9

7. Zeke!

The Mitsubishi A6M Zero, or Zeke, is the most famous Japanese fighter of World War Two. First flight is on April 1, 1939, with the type proving to be quite a handful for Allied and USA Navy pilots during the early days of the conflict. (Frank B Mormillo)

8. Stirling performer

Powered by four Bristol Hercules engines, the Short Stirling bomber makes its first flight on May 14, 1939. It is the RAF's first four-engine monoplane bomber and bravely performs this role until September 1944 when it is replaced as a frontline bomber by the Halifax and Lancaster. (Gordon Swanborough collection)

9. First jet to fly

On August 27, 1938, the Heinkel He 178 experimental aircraft becomes the first jet-powered aircraft to fly.

10. Bomber en-masse

The prototype Consolidated B-24 Liberator makes its maiden flight on December 29, 1939. Despite being a complex aircraft, it is the USAAC's most numerous bomber and holds the distinction of being the most produced American aircraft - at over

19,000 examples of all variants. (KEY collection)

11. Shturmovik

The development Ilyushin BSh-2, predecessor of the Il-2 Shturmovik, makes a successful first flight on December 30, 1939. The Il-2 goes on to become the Soviet Union's workhorse of World War Two, particularly in the low-level ground attack role. It is also built in more numbers than any other aircraft, with over 36,000 being delivered. (KEY collection)

1930-39

SEPTEMBER 10, 1938: Germany imposes strict flight restrictions on aircraft within its airspace - aircraft must keep to specified air corridors.

OCTOBER 22, 1938: A new altitude record of 56,046ft (17,083m) is set by Lt Col M Pezzi flying a Caproni 161bis biplane.

DECEMBER 21, 1938: One of the Luftwaffe's most famous and versatile aircraft, the Junkers Ju 88, makes its first flight. Almost 15,000 are eventually produced, to be used as bombers, fighters and reconnaissance aircraft.

DECEMBER 31, 1938: The Boeing 307 Stratoliner makes an historic first flight. Fully pressurised, the airliner is designed to cruise at up to 20,000ft (6,096m) and makes use of the wings and tail surfaces from the B-17 bomber.

JANUARY 27, 1939: The prototype Lockheed XP-38 makes its first flight. Destined to find fame as the P-38 Lightning, the twin-boom aircraft proves to be an exceptional long-range fighter, seeing action in both Europe and the Pacific during World War Two.

JUNE 1, 1939: The Focke-Wulf Fw 190, designed by Dipl Ing Kurt Tank, completes its maiden flight. The radial engine Fw 190 proves to be one of Germany's most outstanding fighters, especially in the hands of experienced pilots.

JULY 25, 1939: The Avro 679 Manchester completes its first flight. The bomber is powered by a pair of Rolls-Royce Vulture engines but these prove to be troublesome.

AUGUST 5, 1939: Imperial Airways begins a weekly airmail service from Southampton to New York using Short C-class flying-boats. Handley Page Harrows provide air-to-air refuelling - the first regular use of the technique by the airline.

SEPTEMBER 3, 1939: As a result of the German invasion of Poland, Britain and France declare war on Germany - World War Two begins, heralding a huge acceleration in aviation development.

SEPTEMBER 14, 1939: The Vought-Sikorsky VS-300 helicopter makes its first tethered flight. It features a single main rotor and two tail rotors.

NOVEMBER 19, 1939: First flight of the Heinkel He 177 Greif takes place. Designed as a long-range bomber, the He 177 was never a success due to continued technological difficulties, especially with its close-coupled Daimler Benz engines.

NOVEMBER 21, 1939: The Piaggio P.108B bomber makes its first flight and is to be the only Italian operational four-engine bomber of World War Two.

NOVEMBER 24, 1939: Imperial Airways and British Airways merge to form the British Overseas Airways Corporation (BOAC).

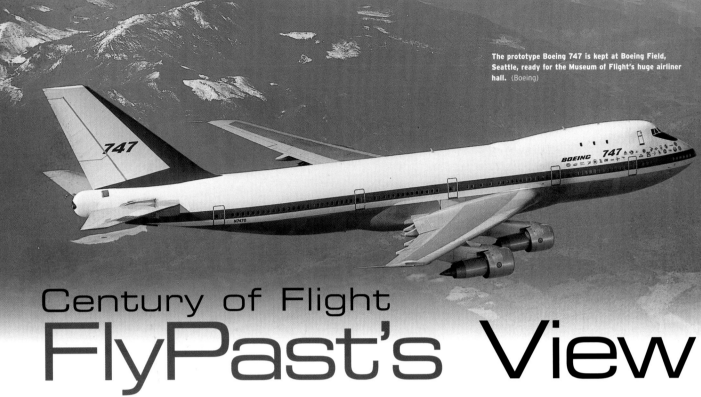

The prototype Boeing 747 is kept at Boeing Field, Seattle, ready for the Museum of Flight's huge airliner hall. (Boeing)

Century of Flight
FlyPast's View

FlyPast's KEN ELLIS LOOKS AT THE CHALLENGES FACING THE 20TH CENTURY'S AVIATION HERITAGE

A s *Flypast* is an aviation heritage magazine – and Britain's top-selling aviation monthly to boot – the pages of *Century of Flight* cover much of its 'territory'. That being the case, we shall take a look forward to some of the issues that face the world's aviation museums as they try to tell the story of the history of aviation and preserve for generations as yet unborn the gems of an amazing century.

With certain exceptions, the museums and collections of the world caught on quite late to the concept of preserving aviation heritage. Generalisations are always open to being shot at, but for the sake of argument, the widespread retention of airframes belongs to the late 1950s, the 1960s through to the 1980s being the 'golden era' - this especially applies to the UK and USA.

Consequently, a large number of very important pioneer and 'early' types escaped the net completely. Both World Wars saw some aircraft 'reserved' for preservation, with varying degrees of success in their survival. This has left it to craftsmen to create reproductions - both good and bad - to fill the 'holes' in collecting policies.

During the second half of the century a veritable explosion of museums - good and bad, large and small - appeared all over the planet. Lest this feature be seen as overly pessimistic, let's get something straight: the

scope, depth and spread of aviation museums on Planet Earth is exceptional - we are really blessed with countless items saved for the future. That said, we shall examine some trends.

On the Light Side

While many of the comments here can be said to reflect trends worldwide, we open with one that is very much a UK problem. Perhaps reflecting prevalent attitudes to the subject by the public in general (or is it the 'mandarins' in charge of major museums?) the vitally-important role of light and general aviation receives what is best described as a 'light dusting' in the nation's museums.

Irrespective of the era they come from, most light aircraft cannot be described as 'awesome' in the way that a supersonic fighter might be regarded - or as 'sexy' as something like Concorde could be labelled. But they are *very* 'people-friendly'. The public can actually relate to a Moth, an Auster, or a Vari-Eze.

There is no national policy to preserve light and general aviation artefacts. Those there are can be found spread across collections, having been acquired for a variety of reasons - some fairly chaotic. Some of the greatest initiatives in preserving such airframes in the UK have come from the 'private sector' and from amateur collections.

In Europe, particularly in France, Italy and Spain, the

preservation of light and general aviation is much more established and comprehensive, and the same is true of Australia and New Zealand. In the USA - where such flying is regarded as day-to-day - the situation is excellent, most collections making sure they have their quota of interesting types.

Top of the tree in this field is, of course, the incredible EAA Air Venture Museum at Oshkosh, Wisconsin. Here is proof - if any were needed - that this is an exciting and vibrant subject. I don't see the situation getting better in the UK. Bodies such as AOPA and the Popular Flying Association could well play a role in righting this potential deficiency.

Long Service Awards

The sector that is well catered for worldwide is military aviation. In the past, former military types have been released in abundance into the museum world - to the extent that globally there is a glut of some types that could really do with a 'cull' to prevent the waste of precious resources. (To name but two, de Havilland Vampire T.11s in the UK and Lockheed T-33As in the USA.)

The world of military aviation changed dramatically during the 20th Century. Gone are the days of gluts - in many cases a worryingly small number of warplanes is finding its way to museums upon retirement. Those which do find homes do so with the 'big boys' - the nationals - and it seems there is little chance of such types percolating to the regional and small collections.

This is true almost everywhere other than the USA, which continues to have an exemplary policy of filtering aircraft to collections, with the USAF and US Navy acting as 'guardians'. For example, Grumman F-14 Tomcats have found many homes, and the first phase of retirements of Rockwell B-1B Lancers in the autumn of 2002 means that these are also earmarked for spectators countrywide.

But for most countries - including much of Europe and certainly the UK - the percentage of recent major military

Above: **The UK has no overall policy for preserving its rich heritage of light and general aviation. A DH Tiger Moth visiting the Shuttleworth Collection in 2001.** (KEY - Nigel Price)

airframes being made available for preservation is worryingly small. 'Preservation' is not an assured state, attrition does happen within the museum world.

There are reasons for this paucity. Arms limitation treaties have played a part in reducing the McDonnell Douglas Phantom almost to an endangered species in the UK. While the reasoning behind the destruction of such types is noble, within a decade a UK museum wanting to acquire an F-4 will have to import to get one.

A much more prudent view of the disposal of airframes is also to blame, in the name of looking after taxpayers' interests by keeping a high residual value. This ensures that more airframes go to scrap merchants and to 'most favoured' disposal agencies rather than into the museum 'circuit'. Here again, only the USA realises that the true cost of letting a realistic number of, say, Grumman A-6 Intruders, is buttons in comparison to overall defence expenditure. (Besides, via the loan system, the airframes remain state property.)

Take a couple of near-term UK examples. Shortly, three at the most BAE Systems Sea Harrier F/A.2s will move to

One aircraft more than any other cries out for display at a host of museums – and not necessarily aviation collections, either. The Boeing 747 encompasses the concept of mass travel and could be equally at home in a museum devoted to social history, economic development, industrial and technological achievement....the list goes on.

The impact of the 'Jumbo' is such that there is a strong case for most countries of the world to have one in their national collection, at least. Depending on the background of the country in question, many other types of airliner also deserve preservation, from the 'first generation' onwards.

The 'traditional' way in which museums across the world have gained such large items is via donation by a 'flag carrier' airline or by the manufacturer handing on prototypes or development airframes. Long before September 11, 2001, the residual value of many older jetliner types was reducing to the point where museums could consider purchase if all else failed.

But while airliners are becoming easier to acquire and the need to display them more and more pressing, they have a drawback that presents the museums of the 21st

droves, such exhibits will ultimately become unsafe and will face scrapping.

There are two solutions. The first is to regard the 747 programme as so long and ongoing that, like a good bus service, 'another one will be along in a minute'. In other words, treat the 'Jumbo' as a 'consumer durable' and replace your -100 with a -400 in 25 years or so. Despite the downturn in production rates, who can say when Boeing's iconic 747 will become a finite resource?

The long-term answer would mean an incredible undertaking – putting all these aircraft under cover and into a controlled environment. During mid-2002, the Museum of Flight at Seattle, Washington, announced revolutionary plans to put its airliner collection (Boeing 247 to 747 and all points in between) under one roof.

Others will need to do the same. Museums which currently keep large aircraft of all kinds outside will need to find ways of quintupling their covered floor area to make this possible. Even a dome or similar structure for an Airbus A300 would cost much more than a 25-year conservation programme for the airframe. And by

The US has a fine record of making large numbers of retired USAF and US Navy aircraft, such as this F-14A Tomcat, available to a wide range of museums. (US Navy)

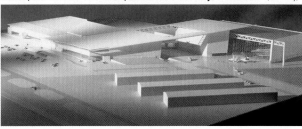

museums, following the premature decision to retire them from the Fleet Air Arm. The rest are likely to be melted down to rise again as Lockheed Martin JSFs. While the RAF Museum and the Imperial War Museum get out-of-service Sepecat Jaguars, the chances of a Norfolk or Scotland-based regional museum getting one are remote. Yet their claim to preserve aircraft which have flown in the local skies for decades is just as strong...

The nature of prototypes is helping this situation. Unlike their 1950s or 1960s equivalents, the prototype Tornados had limited flying lives and little application as test-beds. This is the same for the Eurofighter Typhoon and the Lockheed Martin/Boeing F/A-22 Raptor. The RAF Museum is not that far off getting a 'real' Typhoon, most probably three decades before they could expect an operational one.

Global Widebodies

While the military world – at least in terms of types – is contracting, another area of flight has grown exponentially since the 1960s and will continue to do so. Air transport has shrunk the globe and accordingly, examples of jetliners can be found in museums all over the world.

Century with major headaches. Jetliners may have helped to shrink the world, but nobody has discovered a way of making *them* shrink – quite the opposite!

Putting a Lid on It

Across the world a huge range of airliner types are preserved in a variety of museums. A quick scan through the reference books puts the figure at 300-plus and rising. Fewer than 10% of these are indoors and therefore they are decaying at an almost perceptible rate.

The first Boeing 747s have already joined, or have been earmarked for, museums, with examples in France, Germany, Japan, South Africa and the USA. Rumour has it that a 747 is there for the asking to a UK national museum.

The apparent impossibility of displaying a 747 at any museum that does not have access to a runway is not a major factor. In Germany, the collection at Speyer is preparing for the task of re-assembling the biggest of all kits – and putting a former Lufthansa 747-200 on display.

However, this aircraft – along with the others so far destined for public display – will be outside. Despite the best efforts by conservation staff and volunteers in their

introducing an Airbus type to the narrative, we can remind the reader that, unlike military aircraft, jetliners are getting *bigger*...

There is a tendency to believe that because the world has so many aircraft museums, with more on the way, everything is fine in the land of aviation heritage. In terms of the acquisition of meaningful airframes and other exhibits, this is probably so.

The challenge facing present-day curators and directors is to make sure that their 'star' exhibits, at least, survive to be gazed upon in the 22nd Century. Beam me up, Scottie...

Above: **The second prototype Tornado has been on show at the RAF Museum, Hendon, for some time. Retired GR.1s are now joining the UK nationals.** (Raytheon)

Above: **Seattle's Museum of Flight has unveiled plans for an enormous airliner hall. The hall is to the right: the model airliner gives an indication of the huge size of the project.** (Museum of Flight)

Air Power
DOMINANT

The military lessons of the First World War (see page 12) affected individual countries in different ways – the victorious Allied powers either returning to the colonial mentality or, as in the case of the United States, returning to isolationism. As far as aircraft and air power were concerned, the 1920s and early 1930s saw little development in terms of equipment and doctrine. Many of the combat types from the latter part of the war, such as the Bristol F2b, were still in front-line use with the RAF in the late 1920s.

Even where new types had been introduced they would, in many cases, have not seemed out of place in 1918 rather than the 1930s – the large and cumbersome RAF bombers such as the Virginia and the Heyford being prime examples. Even fighters were slow to develop, and biplanes armed with two or four machine-guns remained the standard into the 1930s.

As far as doctrine was concerned, and it is important to remember that it is doctrine that drives the development and procurement of new equipment, the dominant theory was that of 'the bomber will always get through'. Therefore the destructive power of the bomber force must be maintained – as both a deterrence to conflict and as a war-winning weapon when a conflict develops.

False sense of security

For European politicians the main focus in the late 1920s was disarmament conferences and a reliance on the League of Nations (forerunner of the United Nations) to prevent conflict. The growth of extreme nationalist parties in Italy and Germany in the early 1930s was to change this and lead to a new arms race. The withdrawal of Germany from the Disarmament Conference and League of Nations in October 1933 led British Prime Minister Baldwin to state that Britain would expand its air force to that of its rivals, the so-called 'One Power Standard'. This led to a series of Expansion Plans for the RAF, which called for a massive increase in both size and capability, although with the initial focus remaining on the bomber force.

In Germany development of the air force (Luftwaffe) was both rapid and impressive, with the introduction of new aircraft and tactics, both elements of which would give the Luftwaffe an initial advantage over its

THE SIX YEARS OF THE SECOND WORLD WAR SAW RAPID ADVANCES IN AVIATION TO SUCH AN EXTENT THAT AIR POWER BECAME A DECISIVE FACTOR IN THE CONFLICT, CULMINATING IN THE USE OF ATOMIC WEAPONS. KEN DELVE SUMMARISES.

Above: **Of all the combat aircraft from World War Two, the Spitfire is perhaps the best known. This superb fighter, with its classic lines, entered service shortly before the war and was in use in every theatre of operations to 1945 – and remained in service into the 1950s until replaced by jet types.** (KEY - Duncan Cubitt)

Above: **The Short Stirling was the first of the four-engined bombers to enter service, soon followed by the Halifax and Lancaster.** (Gordon Swanborough collection)

Chamberlain on his return from Munich, war was inevitable unless Britain and France continued to accede to German demands. The crunch came over Hitler's Polish claims. With the German invasion of Poland on September 1, 1939, the British and French governments stood by their guarantees to Poland and, two days later, declared war on Germany. Britain would receive sterling support from the Dominion and Commonwealth countries and relied heavily on this resource of manpower. The world was at war again.

Lightning War

The German *Blitzkrieg* (Lightning War) tactic of armoured forces combined with air power quickly devastated the Polish forces, aided by the fact that the Poles had to face a war on two fronts as Russia invaded from the east. The Polish Air Force was destroyed in a matter of days, most of it on the ground.

It is not possible in such a short article to even outline

opposition. The experience gained by German involvement in the Spanish Civil War from 1936 also proved invaluable. Italy had invaded Abyssinia in 1935 and aircraft had played a role in the campaign, albeit with few lessons for the forthcoming major conflict. America remained convinced that Europe's problems could be kept at a distance, and whilst new aircraft were under development, some of which would later become household names (such as the Flying Fortress) there was little new in the way of doctrine.

A new power had arisen in the Far East, as Japan created for itself an empire in Asia; however, as this expansion was at the expense of other Asian countries such as China and Korea, little attention was paid by the West to either Japanese imperial policy or its military potential – which included a significant development in the use of air power with the employment of aircraft carriers. True, other countries had carriers but the bold employment of this type of air power was developed by the Japanese.

Europe on the brink

Thus by early 1938 all the European states were re-arming as quickly as they could and whilst America was still on the sidelines, its industrial potential was being used by Britain and France, both countries sending purchasing missions in search of aircraft. The first British order was placed in June 1938 for 200 Hudsons and 200 Harvards – the first of what would become thousands of aircraft acquired by purchase or Lend-Lease.

With Hitler's continued brinkmanship in Europe – "this is my last territorial demand in Europe" – the Munich Crisis of September 1938, whereby Britain and France acquiesced to the German demand for a partition of Czechoslovakia, almost led to war. This appeasement gave Europe one more year of peace, a year in which each of the protagonists accelerated their rearmament programmes. For the RAF it was a vital year in which it not only increased the number of front-line squadrons but, more importantly, re-equipped from obsolete biplane types to modern fighters and bombers. The first of the modern bombers, the Wellington, was only introduced to squadron service in January 1939 and the first Spitfire had only entered service the previous June. Despite the 'peace in our time' statement by Prime Minister

Above: **Specialist aircraft such as the Ju 87 were an integral part of the German *Blitzkrieg* strategy of combined air and land operations but when faced with strong air opposition, as during the Battle of Britain, these aircraft proved very vulnerable.**

Above: **Air gunners prepare ammunition for loading into the rear turret of this Wellington. The .303 machine-gun was standard self-defence armament for the RAF's bombers, in this case a two-gun rear turret, although later types such as the Lancaster had four guns in this turret.**

the course of the conflict and so we will focus on various aspects of the war as they were influenced by or influenced air power.

With the Polish campaign, the conflict settled down into a phase often referred to as the 'Phoney War' as there was no significant ground fighting. The RAF had conducted its first operations on Day One of the war with Bomber Command Whitleys dropping propaganda leaflets over Germany. Billions of leaflets were dropped during the war, providing – according to one German report – better 'lavatory paper' for the people than they could buy; not quite the desired intention!

Bomber Command's war doctrine, developed in the 1930s, was for a series of knockout blows against German industry, especially in the Ruhr. However, there was reluctance amongst politicians to bomb a country that appeared to have the capability to hit back as hard, if not harder. Thus the bomber missions were confined to leaflet drips over Germany and attacks on German ships – but not when they were in port. The few daylight attacks on shipping that took place towards the end of the year were almost invariably disastrous with poor results and heavy losses to enemy fighters.

The pre-war belief that well-armed bombers flying in formation could fight-off enemy fighters was shown to be wrong, although this was a lesson that the Americans would re-learn in 1942. With the success of the night leaflet raids – success in as much as losses were light – there was a gradual change of RAF doctrine to the use of night bombing, this being formalised in April 1940 for night attacks on Germany as soon as political clearance was given for such attacks.

The Luftwaffe had made its first attack on Britain on October 16, 1939, the target being in the Firth of Forth, and two weeks later (October 28) a Heinkel He 111 was shot down near Dalkeith, the first German aircraft to be brought down on British soil in the war. 'Island Britain' relied on its sea lanes, from the Empire and the United States, for its very survival and as in World War One, the German strategy included cutting these lifelines – using submarine warfare as well as surface raiders. The U-boat started operations in late 1939 and for the first three years, the advantages lay with the submarines, although the RAF did score a few successes. Mining of ports and sea-lanes was undertaken by the Germans and British

using ships and aircraft; the first RAF mining (referred to as 'gardening') sortie took place on the night of April 13/14, 1940. By the end of the war thousands of mines had been laid by air and this type of operation was an important part of the naval war.

Technology growth

A three-word summary of air power developments during World War Two could be speed, range and weapons. Shortly before the outbreak of the war the average fighter aircraft had a top speed of 250-300mph, by the end of the war advanced piston types and the early jets had pushed this to nearer 500 mph. For both the Luftwaffe and the RAF one of the main problems with offensive operations was the range of their bombers and, more especially, the range of the fighters that acted as

escort to the bombers. By 1944 Allied fighters were able to escort bombers to the farthest reaches of Germany, whereas in 1941 they had barely been able to reach targets in the western part of Germany. There are two important aspects of attacking any type of target: finding/hitting it and the effect of the weapon. This applies to all aerial warfare from fighter combat to bombing of ground targets. World War Two was to be a technological war, the first such on this scale, with new weapons and other systems (such as radar and self-defence electronics) being devised to give an advantage, albeit often fleeting, over the enemy. It is this aspect of the air war that is perhaps the most interesting and deserving of some focus.

Finding the target

The fighter's prime task is preventing enemy aircraft from operating. To do this it has to be able to find the enemy and then destroy him. This requires a combination of agility (to manoeuvre to make the kill) and firepower (to effect the kill) – but first you have to find the target. The bomber's task is to find its target and deliver weapons of sufficient power to destroy the target. The same basic criteria apply to other air power tasks such as reconnaissance and air supply.

In 1939 the primary means of finding the enemy in the air or on the ground was through visual navigation followed by visual acquisition of the target. With good weather and no interference from enemy defences it was no real problem to find ground targets, especially if those targets were large cities. Pre-war RAF exercises used

Above: **Framed by the wing of a Spitfire on an airfield in North Africa, this Bf 109 had been abandoned by its previous owners. The fluid nature of the Western Desert campaign meant that airfields frequently changed hands.**

Above: **Mosquitoes of 139 Squadron at Marham; equipped with radio navigation aids such as Oboe and flown by experienced crews, the Mosquito played a significant role in RAF Bomber Command's Pathfinder Force.**

Hurricane of 42 Squadron in its dispersal at an airfield in the Far East. Groundcrew are positioning vegetation as camouflage against Japanese reconnaissance aircraft. For much of the war in this theatre the Hurricane was the RAF's main fighter and ground-attack aircraft.

marking, the accuracy of Bomber Command attacks dramatically increased. The Luftwaffe's bombers also employed such systems, the 'Knickebein' beam being one of the earliest such devices to enter service.

Trials on the use of airborne radar as a navigation/bombing aid commenced in late 1941 and was put into operation with the Pathfinder Force (PFF) by early 1943. The main advantage of radar was that it was independent of ground stations and was harder to jam. Its main disadvantage was that the Germans were able to 'listen' for the radar signal and so pinpoint the aircraft. As mentioned before, electronics in warfare proved to be a 'cat and mouse' game.

Radar was of far more significance to the fighter than the bomber and with ground-based and airborne radar, the chance of the fighter finding its quarry was greatly increased. It is often said that radar was one of the reasons for the RAF's victory in the Battle of Britain and to a large degree this is true, without the warnings given by radar the RAF's fighter resources could not have been marshalled as effectively. The main aim of ground-based fighter direction was to place the fighters in an advantageous position from which to attack the enemy and whilst this ideal may not have been achieve every time, the basic premise worked – and remained unchanged throughout the war.

With an increase in night attacks, the defending fighters had to rely on natural light (moonlight) or artificial light, from searchlights or flames from burning cities. These 'cats eyes' fighters met with some success, the Luftwaffe employing single-seaters such as the Focke Wulf Fw 190 in this role, but the use of airborne radar with which to locate the enemy proved far more successful. With such radar sets having limited range, the usual tactic was for the fighter controller to vector the fighter to the area of the target, ideally a few miles behind it, and for the radar operator in the fighter to then take up the final stage of the intercept. Both the RAF and Luftwaffe employed two-man (sometimes three-man) types for this task, the Bristol Beaufighter and de Havilland Mosquito proving adept on the RAF side and the Junkers Ju 88 and Messerschmitt Bf 110 equally so on the Luftwaffe side.

various cities, such as Bristol or Swansea, where the docks were designated as aiming points, as 'enemy targets', and with fighter squadrons tasked to defend the areas. Reports from such exercises invariably state that the bombers had no difficulty in locating and attacking their aiming points and that on most occasions no fighters were seen.

The real war scenario of the early 1940s was to prove very different. Whilst visual navigation was to remain very important, especially during day operations by bombers and fighter-bombers, the capability of attacking a target at night or in poor weather had to be developed. The Luftwaffe's attacks on London in late 1940 and early 1941 relied on visual navigation helped by using the Thames to lead the bombers to the target. However, the Bomber Command experience of 1941 was that targets were hard to find at night, a fact that was not truly appreciated until the advent of cameras that recorded the actual bombing. A report stated that only one in three bombers was dropping its weapons within five miles of the target.

With daylight bombing too costly, the solution was to develop new tactics and systems that would increase the accuracy of night bombing. This led to the development of radio/radar aids to navigation and bombing, the first of which entered service in 1942. On the night of March 8/9, Bomber Command attacked Essen using a ground-based aid called 'Gee'. The basic concept was simple in that the

aircraft fitted with the system received signals from ground stations that allowed it to pinpoint its position with reasonable accuracy, not enough as a blind-bombing aid but certainly to get the bomber into the target area. By August, the Germans were jamming the signal making it far less useful and highlighting one of the major problems with the 'electronic war' – for every device one side develops the other will come up with a counter. In December 1942 a more accurate system, 'Oboe', entered service and when combined with the new tactic of target

Without aircraft such as the Consolidated PBY Catalina, the maritime war against German surface ships and U-boats would have been far more difficult. Patrols of up to 20 hours duration were flown by these aircraft.
(KEY - Duncan Cubitt)

The navigator/radar operator directed the pilot to within a short range of the target, at which point the pilot would hopefully pick up the target's silhouette, or flames from the engine exhaust, and thus complete the attack. To make such an attack effective required sufficient firepower to destroy or cripple the enemy almost instantly, which leads us to a consideration of weapons.

Destroying the target

One of the most destructive of fighter weapons was the 'schrage musik' used by the German nightfighters, not so much because of the weight of its firepower but because this upward-firing cannon system was directed at short range into the vulnerable underside of RAF bombers. The ability to deliver destructive firepower in the shortest possible time is the key to a fighter's success and of all the lessons of the First World War, this is the one that was missed in the inter-war period.

With a belief that the fighter would be able to find and outmanoeuvre its bomber target, the RAF doctrine envisaged fighters taking it in turns to make attacks and to that end what was needed to knock down the enemy was weight of bullets. Thus in the 1930s the RAF standardised on the .303 machine-gun as its weapon of choice for aerial fighting, trials with cannon having proved less effective (see Air-to-Air Combat, p147). The Hawker Hurricane and Supermarine Spitfire, entered service and with wing-mounted guns harmonised for greatest effect at 250 yards (i.e. the point at which the streams of fire converge), while cannon armament found more favour with the Luftwaffe.

The nature of the target, its size, vulnerability, defences, etc, were factors in determining the effectiveness of the fighter weapon and as with all the other aspects alluded to in this overview, it is not possible to go into detailed discussion. One example that illustrates the point is the Japanese Zero fighter. This lightweight fighter was superbly manoeuvrable but poorly protected with armour plate or other defensive considerations. Once the Americans had better aircraft and gained combat experience, the seemingly invincible Zero lost its edge and a short burst of gunfire was often

enough to turn it into a fireball.

The argument over fighter armament continued throughout the war but in general terms there was an increase in the use of cannon. Later Allied fighter types tended to have a combination of two 20mm cannon and two 0.5in machine-guns, although the P-51 Mustang retained its machine-gun armament. German types acquired specialist weapons in addition to their cannon/machine-gun fit, air-to-air unguided rockets being used to break up the American bomber boxes, and towards the end of the war, the first air-to-air missiles.

The appearance of the German jet fighters, especially the Me 163 and the Me 262, added a new threat to the daylight battles over Germany and whilst there has been much debate on the German failure to capitalise on this superior technology, there is little doubt that whatever tactics had been employed, the overall result would have been the same. There simply were not enough pilots or aircraft to make a decisive difference. The first Allied jet to become operational, the Gloster Meteor, saw little service during the war, although 616 Squadron did have some success against the V-1 flying bomb.

The bombers went through a similar development of

self-defence guns, from having more guns to having heavier guns. However, as the main task of the bomber was to destroy ground targets, it is more relevant to look at the weapons used for this task. In the late 1930s, the number and type of bombs were limited and whilst the Germans had learnt some lessons from their campaigns since 1936, it was to take the RAF over a year of operations to realise that its bombs were, in general, not suitable.

In 1932 the Air Staff decreed that the 250lb bomb would be the RAF's standard weapon; in the same year it issued a requirement for its next bomber - and specified a max bomb load of 1,000lb. Ten years later, the RAF was developing bombs of almost 10,000lb (and a 22,000lb bomb, the Grand Slam, would eventually appear), while standard bomb loads were nearer 15,000lb. It was not simply a question of bigger bombs but rather one of weapon effect - does the 'bang' produced cause the right kind of damage. Delivering the bombs accurately and in concentration are also vital to success, we have already alluded to this within 'finding the target.'

In 1942 the new Commander-in-Chief of Bomber Command, Air Marshal Arthur Harris, decided to demonstrate the destructive potential of the bomber. On the night of May 30/31, he sent 1,050 aircraft to attack Cologne, the first time such a large bomber force had been gathered. Destruction in the city and its industrial areas was severe and Harris followed this up with similar raids on Essen and Bremen.

New bomber types, such as the Halifax, Stirling and Lancaster, were entering service with their longer range and heavier bomb loads, new weapons such as the 8,000lb blast bomb were available, and the first navigation/bombing aids had been tested. These factors, combined with the use of dedicated specialist aircraft to make the first attacks on the target and thus 'mark' it for the Main Force of bombers, were to be decisive in making the night bombers increasingly effective.

With the arrival of the heavy bombers of the United States Army Air Force (USAAF) - the first operation being flown on August 17 - the Combined Bomber Offensive

Above: **Coastal Command Beaufighters attack a German convoy in the North Sea as part of the campaign to disrupt lines of communication and supply. Armed with cannon, rockets and, in some cases, torpedoes, aircraft played a major role in the destruction of merchant shipping.** (KEY collection)

Above: **The Boeing B-17 Flying Fortress, along with the B-24 Liberator, equipped the 8th Air Force and undertook daylight missions over Germany from the UK, suffering very heavy losses.** (KEY - Duncan Cubitt)

became a central facet of Allied strategy. The bomber as a war-winning weapon had not gone away. In the Far East theatre, the Japanese attack on Pearl Harbor on December 7, 1941, had truly made this a world war – a new aspect of air power was to dominant the campaign, aircraft carriers.

For a more detailed consideration of air-to-ground weapons see the article 'Bombs on Target' on page 16.

Naval war

Whilst aircraft carriers are the most significant aspect of air power at sea, naval air war has a broader canvas, and World War Two brought aircraft and naval forces into

Above: **First Allied jet fighter to become operational was the Gloster Meteor and although it saw only limited action, the Meteor entered the post-war RAF in large numbers. This white Meteor was used by No 616 Squadron, the first RAF jet squadron, in early 1945.** (All Ken Delve Collection unless stated)

Above: **The Corsair was one of the most successful naval fighters and was used extensively in the Pacific Theatre of operations both as a carrier-based and land-based fighter and ground-attack aircraft.** (KEY - Duncan Cubitt)

such an operation with the assault, using gliders and paratroops, on the Belgian fortress at Eben Emal. This type of operation was favoured by planners for the ability to strike speedily and stealthily at targets beyond the front line. However, troops delivered in such a way had limited firepower and supplies, and relied on surprise plus support (air and ground) to achieve any long-term objective. The problems were demonstrated by the Germans during the air assault on Crete in 1941, a success but at a heavy cost, and the Allied air assault on D-Day and in Holland.

One of the greatest aircraft of the war was the Douglas DC-3 Dakota (C-47 Skytrain) – the thousands of aircraft that took part in supply missions in Europe and the Far East were often critical to land operations. Of all the air power roles, it was air transport that underwent most development during World War Two and yet it is all too often ignored.

conflict in what was a pivotal area, the Battle of the Atlantic.

Unrestricted submarine warfare intent on destroying Britain's sea communications almost succeeded and on more than one occasion, Churchill stated that victory in this battle was the "single most important factor in the conduct of the war." The threat was from surface raiders, including powerful battleships such as the *Bismarck*, U-boats and long-range aircraft.

By late 1940, Allied shipping losses had reached alarming proportions, 350,000 tons of shipping being sunk in October alone. The campaign was long and hard, with the balance of power changing from one side to the other. Final Allied victory was due to a combination of factors including American industrial might (building large numbers of, for example, 'Liberty ships'), instigation of the convoy system, increasingly effective escort forces and the use of aircraft. In 1942 the Allies lost 1,664 ships (nearly eight million tons) and although aircraft, such as the B-24 Liberator, were starting to have an effect, the advantage still lay with the U-boats. The following year the tide turned and at one stage, the U-boats were withdrawn from the Atlantic as losses were too high. Attacks on U-boat bases in France, improved tactics, weapons and equipment (such as the Leigh Light) kept the Allies in the ascendancy.

Although a number of countries had aircraft carriers at the outbreak of war, it is the American and Japanese operations in the Pacific Theatre that used this type of weapon to best effect. Without carrier battle groups, the Japanese campaign of conquest that began in 1941, and the American re-conquest of the subsequent years, would not have been possible. The failure of the sneak attack on Pearl Harbor to destroy the American carrier force is often seen as a decisive moment, whilst the Battle of Midway takes its place as one of the turning points of World War Two. This was the first great carrier versus carrier battle in which two naval forces used air power as their main offensive elements.

The island-hopping campaign by which the American stormed island after island relied on carrier air power to provide air support for the ground troops. As soon as a

foothold had been gained on a piece of land, one of the first actions would be to build an airstrip. Naval air power is covered in more detail on page 140 and those with an interest in carrier air war can still order a copy of our 84-page magazine 'Carriers' – contact .our Mail Order Department (+44 (0)1780 480404 or e mail orders@keypublishing.com).

Transport

The last aspect of air power that flowered in World War Two was that of the transport aircraft both for air supply and air assault. During the 1930s, the Russians had developed air assault using massed paratroop drops but it was the Germans that first demonstrated the surgical nature of

Atomic Age

The world entered the nuclear age on August 6, 1945, when an American B-29 *Enola Gay* dropped an atomic weapon on the Japanese city of Hiroshima. The destructive effect of this single bomb was greater than anything the world had seen and equalled that of many hundreds of bombers. A second bomb was dropped on Nagasaki on August 9 and it was without doubt, the effect of these two attacks that caused the Japanese to surrender. The war was over, the final act of air power had demonstrated its dominance and the new atomic world was one in which a single aircraft had the ability to destroy a city – little more than 50 years after the first manned flight at Kitty Hawk.

Above: **Transport aircraft such as the C-47 Skytrain (DC-3 Dakota) fulfilled many tasks including air assault and air supply. The part they played rarely gets the credit it deserves.** (KEY - Duncan Cubitt)

The skies over Oshkosh, USA, bring forth a gathering of historic aircraft (warbirds) every July, with pristine examples of fighters, bombers, trainers and transports to delight the crowds. Many of the colour images in this article are of preserved aircraft and we are fortunate that so many private individuals spend time (and vast amounts of money) preserving these rare aircraft. (KEY - Duncan Cubitt)

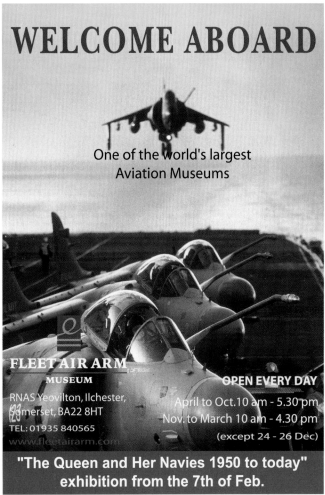

1

1940-49

2

3

1940-49

1. Tank killer
The Hawker Typhoon makes its first flight on February 24, 1940. The aircraft proves highly effective in the ground attack role, especially after the invasion of Europe in June 1944. (Gordon Swanborough collection)

2. Mitchell
What is to become one of the most famous and effective medium bombers of World War Two, the North American B-25 Mitchell, makes its first flight on August 19, 1940. (KEY - Ken Delve)

3. Ultimate fighter
Undoubtedly the most famous piston-engined American fighter ever built, the North American P-51 Mustang first flies on October 26, 1940. Originally designed to a British specification, when its Allison engine is replaced by a Rolls-Royce Merlin, it proves to be a highly effective long-range fighter. (KEY - Duncan Cubitt)

4. Wooden Wonder
Nicknamed the 'wooden wonder', the de Havilland DH.98 Mosquito was built as a

5

SIGNIFICANT DATES

FEBRUARY 22, 1940: The first British gun-camera film is taken by Squadron Leader D Farquhar of 602 Squadron while shooting down a Heinkel He 111.

APRIL 5, 1940: The Mikoyan-Gurevich MiG-1 makes its first flight, setting the stage for a long line of classic aircraft from the Soviet manufacturer.

APRIL 9, 1940: German forces overrun Denmark and invade Norway, making use of paratroops dropped by Junkers Ju 52s.

APRIL 29, 1940: The Empire Air Training Scheme is established by Canada, Britain, Australia and New Zealand to train crews for

operations in Europe. Some 29 pilot schools plus gunnery, observation, bombing and navigation schools are to be built in Canada.

APRIL 30, 1940: New Zealand airline Tasman Empire Airways commences services between Auckland and Sydney, Australia, using a Short C class flying-boat.

MAY 10, 1940: German forces invade the Low Countries, again making extensive use of airborne troops.

MAY 29, 1940: The Vought F4U Corsair makes its first flight. By the end of the war it has significantly contributed to the capabilities of Allied naval carrier operations.

JUNE 4, 1940: Measured and timely intervention by the RAF helps keep the Luftwaffe at bay as the evacuation of the British expeditionary force is completed from Dunkirk.

JUNE 11/12, 1940: In reaction to Italy's entry into the war, the RAF attacks the Fiat factory in Turin with 36 Whitley bombers.

JUNE 17, 1940: With the collapse of France, all British air routes to the Empire are cut.

JULY 8, 1940: TWA commences Boeing 307 operations between New York and San Francisco, shaving two hours off the time taken by a DC-3.

JULY 10, 1940: The Battle of Britain begins as RAF and Luftwaffe forces begin over two months of intense combat.

AUGUST 10, 1940: One of the most impressive Italian aircraft of World War Two is the Macchi MC.202, a development of the MC.200 powered by a Daimler-Benz DB 601A liquid-cooled engine, which makes its maiden flight today.

AUGUST 24/25, 1940: German bombers hit London due to a navigational error. The following night the RAF retaliates with a raid on Berlin.

AUGUST 8, 1940: The Italian Caproni-Campini N-1 makes its first flight using a piston engine to drive a turbine but its performance is disappointing.

private venture but its incredible performance could not be ignored after the prototype's first flight on November 25, 1940. Eventually 7,781 are built and serve in a wide variety of roles, notably as night fighters and reconnaissance aircraft. (Gordon Swanborough collection)

5. Avro's bomb truck
Developed from the under-performing Manchester, the Avro Lancaster four-engine heavy bomber makes its first flight on January 9, 1941. Some 7,377 are built and form the backbone of RAF Bomber Command's bomber fleet during the second half of World War Two. (KEY - Duncan Cubitt)

6. German jet
What is shortly to become the world's first operational jet fighter, the Messerschmitt Me 262, makes its maiden flight on April 18, 1941, albeit powered by a piston engine at the time. This example is preserved at Chino, California. (KEY - Mark Nicholls)

7. 'Jug'
Affectionately referred to by many as the 'Jug', the portly Republic P-47 Thunderbolt takes to the air for the first time on May 6, 1941. It soon proves itself both as an escort fighter and as a ground attack aircraft with the USAAF. (KEY collection)

8. British jet
Frank Whittle's jet engine, first patented in 1930, finally makes it into the air with the first flight of the experimental Gloster E.28/39 on May 15, 1941. (Gordon Swanborough collection)

9. German rocket plane
Arguably the most startling aircraft of World War Two is the rocket-powered Messerschmitt Me 163 Komet which flies for the first time on August 13, 1941. Very fast and with an amazing rate of climb, the Komet is primarily used against the large American daylight bomber formations. (KEY - Duncan Cubitt)

1940-49

SEPTEMBER 7, 1940: The Blohm und Voss BV 222 flying-boat makes its maiden flight. The six-engine craft is one of the largest flying-boats to see operational use during World War Two.

SEPTEMBER 17, 1940: Adolf Hitler postpones Operation Sea Lion, the invasion of the UK, due to the failure of the Luftwaffe to overcome the RAF.

NOVEMBER 10, 1940: Organised ferry flights of new American aircraft to Britain begins.

NOVEMBER 11, 1940: Royal Navy Fairey Swordfish torpedo bombers attack the Italian fleet in Taranto harbour, effectively neutralising the Italian Navy.

NOVEMBER 20, 1940: Fl Lt John Cunningham and his Airborne Interception operator Sgt J Phillpson of 604 Squadron achieve the first night kill using electronic airborne interception equipment. They succeed in downing a Junkers Ju 88 over Oxfordshire in their Bristol Beaufighter.

NOVEMBER 25, 1940: The Martin B-26 Marauder makes its first flight. The medium bomber sees extensive use, notably by the USAAF's Ninth Air Force in Europe.

DECEMBER 18, 1940: Germany completes a successful first flight of the Henschel Hs 293A radio-controlled guided bomb.

FEBRUARY 10, 1941: RAF Whitleys from Nos 51 and 78 Squadrons perform the first British paratroop drop of the war during an unsuccessful assault on the Tragino viaduct in Italy.

MARCH 11, 1941: US President Roosevelt authorises the Lend-Lease Act which permits huge amounts of American-built arms to be supplied to Britain and her allies.

APRIL 2, 1941: The Heinkel He 280 twin-turbojet fighter makes its first flight - it is fitted with a compressed air operated ejector seat. Despite being the world's first dedicated jet fighter it is not put into production, the Luftwaffe opting for the Messerschmitt Me 262 instead.

MAY 20, 1941: In the Luftwaffe's largest airborne assault to date, some 22,750 men are parachuted on to the island of Crete. Although the island is taken, losses are high and no such large-scale operations are repeated.

MAY 26, 1941: A Fleet Air Arm Swordfish from HMS *Ark Royal* succeeds in damaging the German battleship *Bismark* in the Atlantic leading to its sinking by Royal Navy battleships.

JUNE 16, 1941: Washington DC's National Airport opens for business.

JUNE 20, 1941: The United States Army Air Force (USAAF) is formed from the USAAC.

1. Italy's best
On April 19, 1942, the Macchi MC.205 makes its maiden flight and is considered to be the best Italian fighter of World War Two. It is seen here alongside its predecessor, the MC.200. (KEY collection)

2. Black Widow
The twin-boom Northrop p-61 Black Widow makes its maiden flight on May 26, 1942. The P-61 is the first American aircraft designed as a radar-equipped night fighter and proves to be highly effective in the European and Pacific theatres. (US National Archives)

3. Hellcat
Designed as a successor to the F4F Wildcat, the Grumman F6F Hellcat incorporates many improvements, such as a wider track undercarriage and better armour protection for the pilot, and first flies on June 26, 1942. Some 2,500 are built in 1943 alone, and the type is credited with 4,947 kills in air-to-air combat against the Japanese. (KEY collection)

4. Mighty Mars
When the Martin Mars makes its first flight on July 3, 1942, it is the largest flying-boat

SIGNIFICANT DATES

JUNE 22, 1941: Germany launches Operation Barbarossa, the invasion of the Soviet Union, with a huge air strike that claims almost 1,500 Soviet aircraft destroyed on the ground.

JULY 8, 1941: The first operational use of the Boeing B-17 Flying Fortress takes place when RAF examples attack Wilhelmshaven.

AUGUST 1, 1941: The Grumman Avenger prototype makes its maiden flight. The aircraft is destined to become the US Navy's primary torpedo bomber.

OCTOBER 1941: Heinkel flies the first He 111Z glider tug, a modified He 111 which has two

fuselages joined by an extra wing section carrying a fifth engine.

OCTOBER 2, 1941: Heini Dittman flies the third Messerschmitt Me 163 prototype to a record speed of 623.85mph (1,004km/h), though the feat remains unknown until after the war.

DECEMBER 7, 1941: The Japanese launch a surprise attack on Pearl Harbor, Hawaii, bringing the United States into the Second World War.

DECEMBER 22, 1941: The Fairey Firefly fighter/reconnaissance aircraft makes its first flight.

JANUARY 14, 1942: The Sikorsky XR-4 helicopter makes its first flight and becomes the world's first production helicopter.

JANUARY 18, 1942: Maiden flight of the Vought-Sikorsky VS-44A flying-boat. It is used by American Export Air Lines on a new New York to Foynes, Ireland, service on June 20.

FEBRUARY 19, 1942: Japanese aircraft attack shipping in Port Darwin, Australia, exposing the vulnerability of the southern continent.

FEBRUARY 27, 1942: The UK's Army Air Corps is established.

MARCH 3, 1942: The Avro Lancaster undertakes its first operational mission, mine laying by No 44 Squadron.

APRIL 18, 1942: A one-way raid against Tokyo is mounted by 16 B-25 Mitchells led by Lt Col J Doolittle flying from the USS Hornet. The raid is a propaganda exercise but has the desired effect, the B-25s continue to China where most force land.

MAY 5, 1942: RAF Mustang 1s perform their first operational mission with sorties over France.

MAY 16, 1942: Canadian airline CP Air is formed from ten independent operators.

Feb 27, 1942: Blackburn Firebrand **Mar 1942:** Messerschmitt Me 323 **Mar 20, 1942:** Mitsubishi J2M1 **Apr 12, 1942:** Miles Martinet **Apr 30, 1942:** Fiat G.55 **May 29, 1942:** CAC Boomerang **June 19, 1942:** Saab 18 **July 5, 1942:** Avro York

7

8

9

10

to have flown at the time. Only six are eventually completed but serve the US Navy well in the transport role. Survivors continue to be used as fire-fighting aircraft in Canada to this very day. (KEY - Ken Ellis)

5. Fast Hawker
When the Hawker Tempest makes its first flight on September 2, 1942, it displays a remarkable performance, thanks on no small part to its very thin wings. Powered by either a Napier Sabre or Bristol Centaurus, the Tempest was one of the few Allied piston-engine fighters able to attempt

combat with the Messerschmitt Me 262 jet. (KEY collection)

6. American jet
America's first jet-powered aircraft, the Bell XP-59 Airacomet, makes its first flight on October 1, 1942, using two General Electric built turbojets based on Frank Whittle's design. (USAF)

7. Beautiful Connie
Viewed by many as the most beautiful piston-engine airliner of all time, the Lockheed Constellation began life as the military C-69 which first flew on January 9, 1943. After the

war it became a firm favourite with the airlines and was developed into the Super Constellation and the Starliner. (KEY collection)

8. British Meteor
Britain's first operational jet aircraft is the Gloster Meteor, the prototype of which flies for the first time on March 5, 1943. The aircraft first sees combat, chasing and destroying German V-1 flying bombs. (Gordon Swanborough collection)

9. First jet bomber
The Arado Ar 234 Blitz makes its first

flight on June 15, 1943. The aircraft is the world's first jet bomber, making its first raid against Liège, Belgium, on December 24, 1944. (KEY collection)

10. Wooden jet
Following its tradition of making extensive use of wood, de Havilland flies its turbojet-powered Vampire fighter on September 20, 1943. The aircraft is too late to see action during the World War Two but becomes one of the RAF's primary fighters in the post-war years. (KEY - Duncan Cubitt)

1940-49

MAY 30/31, 1942: In a demonstration of the potential of the bomber, RAF Bomber Command launches a 1,000 bomber raid against Cologne.

JUNE 3/4, 1942: The Battle of Midway is fought in the central Pacific and results in Japan losing four aircraft carriers and with them the initiative in the Pacific War.

JULY 5, 1942: The Avro York prototype, a transport aircraft developed from the Lancaster bomber, makes its first flight.

AUGUST 15, 1942: The RAF's Pathfinder Force is established under the leadership of Air Commodore D C Bennett. Throughout

the remainder of the night bombing offensive pathfinder aircraft play a valuable part in marking targets.

AUGUST 17, 1942: The USAAF's Eighth Air Force carries out its first raid of the war when B-17s of the 97th Bomb Group attack the Rouen marshalling yards in France.

SEPTEMBER 21, 1942: The prototype Boeing XB-29 Superfortress makes a successful first flight in Seattle, Washington. The aircraft is set to dominate the heavy bombing offensive against Japan in 1945.

NOVEMBER 15, 1942: The Heinkel He 219 Owl night fighter makes its maiden flight. The

twin-engine aircraft proves to be an effective design and it is the first production aircraft to be equipped with ejector seats.

DECEMBER 1942: The Messerschmitt Me 264 prototype *Amerika Bomber* makes its first flight. The long-range aircraft is designed to fly bombing missions against the USA from Europe but it never goes into production.

1943: The Japanese Nakajima Ki-84 Hayate makes its first flight during 1943 but does not enter service until the summer of 1944. Had it been available earlier, it could have had quite an impact in the Pacific war due

to its excellent performance.

JANUARY 30, 1943: RAF Mosquitos of No 105 and 139 Squadrons carry out the first daylight attack against Berlin.

MARCH 13, 1943: Convair is formed with the merger of Consolidated Aircraft and Vultee Aircraft. The new company has a workforce of 100,000.

APRIL 18, 1943: In a decidedly one-sided encounter, RAF and American fighters decimate a German transport flight off the Tunisian coast, claiming some 59 Junkers Ju 52s and 16 Me 109s destroyed and dozens more damaged.

Sept 12, 1942: Miles Messenger   Sept 21, 1942: Boeing B-29   Nov 1, 1942: Westland Welkin   Nov 4, 1942: Latéoère 631   Nov 15, 1942: Heinkel He 219   Dec 7, 1942: Bell P-63   1943: Nakajima Ki-84   July 30, 1943: Saab 21

HEINKEL HE162A SALAMANDER

1940-49

1. Brigand

The Bristol Brigand makes its maiden flight on December 4, 1943. Designed as a replacement for the Beaufighters of Coastal Command, the aircraft arrives too late for the war but does see service as a light bomber in the Far East. (Gordon Swanborough collection)

2. New 'Lanc'

Originally designated the Lancaster IV, the Avro 694 became known as the Lincoln and was a long-range, high-altitude development of the earlier Lancaster. It first flies on June 9, 1944, and is the RAF's primary bomber in the immediate post war years. (Gordon Swanborough collection)

3. de Havilland's finest

De Havilland's sleek DH.103 Hornet, a single-seat and smaller development of the Mosquito, makes its first flight at Hatfield on July 28, 1944. The aircraft enters service with No 64 Squadron in 1946 and the type sees extensive service, notably in Malaysia, before being retired in 1955. (Gordon Swanborough collection)

4. Bearcat's brawn

Grumman's final piston-engine naval fighter is certainly its best – the type flies for the first time on August 21, 1944. The lightweight F8F Bearcat boasts amazing performance, thanks to its 2,100hp Pratt & Whitney R-2800 Double Wasp radial engine. (KEY - Duncan Cubitt)

5. Dedicated transport

Fairchild's C-82 Packet is the first transport in the world designed specifically to meet the needs of the military and flies for the first time on September 10, 1944. Featuring clamshell doors at the rear of its fuselage, it can carry a wide range of cargo for quick loading and unloading. (KEY collection)

6. People's Fighter

Faced with an increasingly desperate situation Germany built the first Heinkel He 162 Volksjäger (People's Fighter) in just 38 days from approval of the final drawings and flies on December 6, 1944. A simple turbojet aircraft with wooden wings, it is designed for rapid construction but arrives too late to have any effect on the outcome of the war. (KEY - Duncan Cubitt)

7. Swedish trainer

Saab flies its model 91 Safir for the first time in 1945, the prototype being fitted with a de

---

SIGNIFICANT DATES

APRIL 18, 1943: With the help of good code-breaking, USAAF P-38 Lightnings shoot down a Japanese Mitsubishi G4M Betty bomber carrying Admiral Isoroku Yamamoto over Bougainville. Yamamoto was the architect of the surprise attack on Pearl Harbor.

MAY 11, 1943: American aircraft production hits new heights with a fresh aircraft rolling off a production line somewhere in the country every seven minutes.

MAY 17/18, 1943: A daring low-level raid against three German dams in the Ruhr is made by specially-modified Lancasters of No 617 Squadron led by Wg Cdr Guy Gibson.

Using the Barnes Wallace bouncing bombs, they succeed in breaching the Mohne and Eder dams.

JUNE 11, 1943: The Italian garrison on the Mediterranean island of Pantellaria surrenders after a prolonged bombing offensive. This is the first known occasion whereby airpower alone has defeated an enemy.

JUNE 19, 1943: The crew of B-17F *Memphis Belle* returns home to a hero's welcome after completing 25 missions from England with the Eight Air Force. The crew, led by Capt Robert Morgan go on to make a recruiting tour of the USA with the aircraft.

JULY 9, 1943: Allied forces commence landings on Sicily, making extensive use of airborne assault techniques.

JULY 24/25: The RAF uses 'window' for the first time, dropping large quantities of aluminium strips so as to confuse enemy radar. The target is Hamburg and the result is one of the most devastating bombing raids of the Second World War.

AUGUST 17/18, 1943: The Henschel Hs 293-A1 guided bomb is used operationally for the first time against Royal Navy ships in the Bay of Biscay. This is the first ever use of an air-launched remotely guided weapon.

AUGUST 17, 1943: Heavy losses are incurred by Eighth Air Force B-17 formations during deep-penetration raids against Regensburg and Schweinfurt.

OCTOBER 26, 1943: The Dornier Do 335 makes its first flight. It is unusual in that it has both pusher and tractor propellers but it is very fast.

JANUARY 9, 1944: The Lockheed XP-80 Shooting Star prototype makes its first flight. In 1945 it becomes the first turbojet-powered single-seat fighter to enter service with the USAAF.

MARCH 10, 1944: The Blohm und Voss BV238

Aug 18, 1943: Sikorsky R-5 Oct 26, 1943: Dornier Do 335 Jan 9, 1944: Lockheed P-80 Mar 10, 1944: Blohm und Voss BV 238 June 25, 1944: Ryan Fireball 1945: Pilatus P-2 Jan 26, 1945: McDonnell FH-1 June 14, 1945: Avro Tudor

Havilland Gipsy Major engine. When fitted with a more powerful Lycoming flat six engine, it becomes a popular military trainer, serving with over 20 countries. (KEY -Malcolm English)

8. Timeless Yak
1945 witnesses the maiden flight of the Yakovlev Yak-18 trainer. Its simple but effective design makes it highly popular in the Eastern Bloc, and after the end of the Cold War it finds a new market in the West – it remains a common sight even today. (KEY - Stephen Bridgewater)

9. Definitive Hawker
The final piston-engine fighter from the Hawker factory and also the last to serve with the Fleet Air Arm is the Bristol Centaurus-powered Sea Fury. It makes its first flight on February 21, 1945, and proves to be a very fast and manoeuvrable fighter, also enjoying considerable export success. (KEY - Duncan Cubitt)

10. Natter
On February 28, 1945, the Bachem Ba 349 Natter rocket-powered interceptor makes its first flight. The German aircraft is launched vertically

and is designed to intercept Allied bombers but is never used in any numbers. (KEY - Mark Nicholls)

11. Take cover!
Probably the most potent single piston engine ground attack aircraft of all time, the Douglas AD-1 Skyraider flies for the first time on March 18, 1945. The aircraft sees extensive use during the long Vietnam War where its ability to carry a large weapons load is especially useful. (US National Archives)

12. Neptune
May 17, 1945, sees the first flight of the

Lockheed P-2 maritime patrol and anti-submarine warfare aircraft. The type is to see widespread use around the world and some 1,181 are built. (Lockheed)

13. Classic Cessna
Cessna flies its model 120 for the first time on June 28, 1945. It is a high-wing, single-engine monoplane with a two-seat cabin designed to meet the needs of the general aviation market. It is the first in a series of designs that have maintained their popularity to the present day. (KEY collection)

1940-49

flying-boat, the world's largest at the time, makes its first flight.

June 6, 1944: The D-Day invasion of occupied Northern Europe commences with a huge airborne assault by American, Canadian and British paratroops. On June 10, Allied aircraft begin operations from makeshift airfields in Normandy.

June 11, 1944: US Forces, led by 15 aircraft carriers of Task Force 58, commence operations to capture the Mariana Islands. In what becomes known as 'the Marianas turkey shoot' the American fliers decimate Japanese air resistance, destroying 402 enemy aircraft on June 19 alone.

June 13, 1944: The use of Germany's first 'terror weapon', the V-1 flying bomb, begins against targets in south east England.

July 17, 1944: Napalm incendiary material is used for the first time by P-38s in an attack on a fuel depot at Coutances, France. Napalm later becomes synonymous with the Vietnam War during the 1960s/70s.

July 29, 1944: A USAAF B-29 makes an emergency landing near Vladivostok, Russia, and together with others that subsequently land in Russia, forms the basis of the Tupolev Tu-4 bomber – almost identical to the American design.

August 4, 1944: The RAF's new Meteor jet scores its first success against a V-1 flying bomb when one is 'tipped over' using the jet's wing.

August 16, 1944: The Junkers Ju 287 four-jet prototype makes its maiden flight. The aircraft is unusual because it has forward-swept wings but it never sees production.

August 20, 1944: The devastating firepower of close support aircraft, such as the Hawker Typhoon, is demonstrated in the Falaise pocket where almost an entire German army is destroyed.

August 28, 1944: The USAAF's 78th Fighter

Group claims to have shot down a Messerschmitt Me 262 – the first jet downed in combat.

September 8, 1944: Germany commences V-2 ballistic missile attacks against Paris and the UK.

October 1944: The Japanese test fly the Yokosuka MXY-7 Ohka rocket-powered suicide plane, designed purely as a 'manned missile'.

October 25, 1944: The American escort carrier USS St Lo is sunk by Japanese Kamikaze suicide attacks, the first effective use of the technique.

1940-49

1. Atom bomb
On August 6, 1945, B-29 *Enola Gay* flown by Col Paul Tibbets drops the first atomic bomb to be used in anger on the Japanese city of Hiroshima. Three days later a second device is dropped on Nagasaki and shortly afterwards the Japanese agree to an unconditional surrender. (US National Archives)

2. Whirlybird
One of the most easily recognisable helicopters ever built, the Bell 47 is also one of the oldest, making its first flight on December 8, 1945. Popular with both military and civilian operators, it remains in production until 1976. (KEY collection)

3. Liftmaster
Designed as a long-range military transport to succeed the DC-4, the DC-6, or C-118 in military terms, first flies on February 15, 1946. It becomes very popular with airlines in the post-war years and can carry around 50 passengers. (KEY collection)

4. Thunderjet
Republic flies the prototype F-84 Thunderjet on February 28, 1946. The type is destined to become the mainstay of the USAF's fighter bomber fleet during the early 1950s, and also enjoys huge export success among NATO countries. Originally designed with a straight wing, the F-84F Thunderstreak introduced a swept wing and greater performance. (KEY collection)

5. Yak jet
The Soviet Union's first jet fighter to enter squadron service, the Yakovlev Yak-15, makes its first flight on April 24, 1946. Illustrated is the very similar Yak-23 which is preserved at the Monino museum in Moscow. (KEY - Stephen Bridgewater)

6. Supersonic Swallow
The experimental de Havilland DH.108 Swallow makes its maiden flight on May 15, 1946. The original prototype crashed on September 27, 1946, killing Geoffrey de Havilland Jnr but the third prototype became the first British aircraft to exceed Mach 1 on September 9, 1948, flown by John Derry. (KEY collection)

SIGNIFICANT DATES

NOVEMBER 15, 1944: The Boeing XC-97 Stratofreighter prototype makes its first flight. Effectively a B-29 wing with an enlarged fuselage, the 'Strat' is destined to be particularly successful with the USAAF after the war.

DECEMBER 14, 1944: The UK's largest military flying-boat, the Short Shetland, makes its first flight.

JANUARY 16, 1945: Allied aircraft, grounded by bad weather and fog, are finally able to attack German forces that have broken through in the Battle of the Bulge. Airpower is decisive and the enemy is forced to retreat.

MARCH 14, 1945: The RAF's 617 Squadron makes the first operational drop of the 22,000lb Grand Slam earthquake bomb on the Bielefeld viaduct in Germany.

MARCH 18, 1945: The USAAF mounts its largest daylight raid against Berlin, sending 1,250 bombers escorted by 670 fighters.

MARCH 23/24, 1945: Operation Varsity sees Allied forces cross the Rhine into Germany, aided once more by extensive airborne assault operations.

APRIL 7, 1945: Japan's largest battleship, the 71,000 ton *Yamato*, is sunk by US carrier based aircraft off Okinawa.

APRIL 23, 1945: PB4Y Liberators of the US Navy launch two ASM-N-2 Bat un-powered glide bombs against Japanese ships. This is the first use of fully-automatic guided weapons.

JUNE 14, 1945: The first post-war flight by a new British airliners takes place with the maiden flight of the Avro Tudor. This is closely followed on June 22 by the Vickers-Armstrong Viking.

JUNE 25, 1945: America's first cargo only airliner, National Skyway Freight Corporation (later called Flying Tiger Line Inc) is established.

AUGUST 1, 1945: The USAAF launches the largest conventional raids on Japan, consisting of 851 B-29 Superfortresses.

SEPTEMBER 20, 1945: Gloster flies a Meteor fighter powered by two Rolls-Royce Trent turboprop engines.

OCTOBER 24, 1945: Scheduled transatlantic land plane flights begin with the arrival of an American Overseas Airlines DC-4 at Hurn Airport, Bournemouth, from New York.

DECEMBER 2, 1945: The prototype Bristol 170 Freighter makes its first flight.

DECEMBER 3, 1945: The third de Havilland Vampire prototype becomes the first jet-

7. New Tiger Moth

The de Havilland Canada DHC-1 Chipmunk was viewed as the successor to the classic Tiger Moth trainer and indeed it fills the role admirably. The prototype first flies on May 22, 1946, the first of over 1,200 built - many of which are exported around the world. (KEY - Steve Fletcher)

8. Giant bomber

Powered by six piston engines and four turbojets, the Convair B-36 dwarfs all previous bombers when it makes its maiden flight on

August 8, 1946. Designed to meet a USAF requirement for an intercontinental bomber, the aircraft is impressive but already out-of-date in view of the arrival of jet fighters that can easily intercept it. (KEY collection)

9. Navy Banshee

McDonnell flies the prototype F2H Banshee on January 11, 1947. The aircraft is the successor to the FH-1 Phantom - it starts arriving with the US Navy's VF-171 in August 1948. (KEY collection)

10. US jet bomber

The North American B-45 Tornado makes its first

flight on March 17, 1947, and becomes America's first jet bomber. (US National Archives)

11. Legendary MiG

The Mikoyan MiG-15 prototype takes to the air for the first time on July 2, 1947. The aircraft is considered to be superior to the American F-86 Sabre in some respects but when the two eventually clash in combat during the Korean War it is the experience of the American pilots that makes the difference. (KEY collection)

12. Stratocruiser

The Boeing 377 Stratocruiser, a

development of the C-97 military transport, makes its first flight on July 8, 1947. Pan Am and BOAC are among the operators of the type, it being extensively used on the North Atlantic route. (KEY collection)

13. Jet flying-boat

The first of three experimental Saunders-Roe SR.A/1 jet-powered flying-boat fighters makes its first flight on July 16, 1947. It proves to be very fast, but doctrine of the time means the idea is dropped in favour of land-based jet fighters. (KEY collection)

1940-49

powered aircraft to operate from the deck of an aircraft carrier, HMS *Ocean*.

DECEMBER 22, 1945: The Beechcraft model 35 Bonanza makes its first flight. The single-engine monoplane features an unusual butterfly tail.

JANUARY 1, 1946: Three British state airlines are formed, British Overseas Airways Corporation (BOAC), British European Airways (BEA) and British South American Airways (BSAA).

JANUARY 10, 1946: A Sikorsky R-5 helicopter sets an unofficial helicopter altitude record of 21,000ft (6,400m) over

Stratford, Connecticut.

MAY 31, 1946: London's Heathrow Airport is officially opened.

JUNE 25, 1946: Northrop's XB-35 flying wing bomber prototype makes its maiden flight. The aircraft is designed to carry a 28 ton bomb load a distance of 10,000 miles.

JULY 5, 1946: The Mooney Aircraft Company is formed.

JULY 31, 1946: Scandinavian Airline System (SAS) is established with the joint assets of the national airlines of Denmark, Norway and Sweden.

SEPTEMBER 19, 1946: Portuguese national carrier Transportes Aéreos Portugueses (TAP) is established.

SEPTEMBER 24, 1946: Cathay Pacific Airways, based in Hong Kong, is formerly established.

SEPTEMBER 29 - OCTOBER 1, 1946: A US Navy PV2 Neptune establishes a world distance record of 11,235 miles (18,081km) with a non-stop, un-refuelled flight from Perth, Western Australia to Columbus, Ohio. The journey took 55 hours 15 minutes.

NOVEMBER 9, 1946: The four-engine Lockheed Constitution airliner makes its

maiden flight. The design was taken over by the military during the war as a transport able to carry over 200 troops. However, it is underpowered and never goes into production as an airliner.

JANUARY 30, 1947: TWA commences a transatlantic freight-only service.

MARCH 10, 1947: The Saab J 21R jet fighter makes its first flight. It is powered by a de Havilland Goblin turbojet but is the same airframe as the piston-engined J 21.

APRIL 4, 1947: The International Civil Aviation Organisation (ICAO) is set up with its head office in Montreal, Canada.

1940-49

1. Giant biplane
The Antonov An-2 Colt makes its first flight on August 31, 1947. Designed as a transport/ agricultural aircraft, the single-engine biplane is built in huge numbers, including licensed production, totalling over 15,000 examples. (KEY - Malcolm English)

2. Sabre!
One of the USA's classic jet fighters, the North American F-86 Sabre, makes its maiden flight on October 1, 1947. Destined to find fame during the Korean War, the Sabre provides the USAF and its NATO allies with a fast and agile jet fighter. (KEY - Duncan Cubitt)

3. Hughes' giant
With Howard Hughes at the controls, the gigantic Hughes H-4 Hercules eight-engine flying-boat makes its one and only flight on November 2, 1947. Dimensionally it is one of the largest aircraft ever built, with a wing span of 320ft. (KEY collection)

4. Swept wing bomber
On December 17, 1947, Boeing changes the face of strategic bombing when it flies its new sleek six-engine jet bomber, the B-47 Stratojet. (KEY collection)

5. Popular Piper
Developed from the original Taylor Cub, the Piper PA-18 Super Cub first flies in 1948 and gains a reputation for being a docile and easy aircraft to fly. (KEY - Duncan Cubitt)

6. Viscount turboprop
The prototype four-engine turboprop Vickers Viscount airliner makes its maiden flight on July 16, 1948. On July 29, 1950, it performs the world's first turboprop passenger flight. (KEY collection)

7. Swedish barrel
The tubby Saab J-29, commonly known as the barrel, makes its first flight on September 1, 1948. It is the West's first swept wing jet fighter to enter service, joining the Swedish Air Force in 1951. (Saab)

8. Tailless Cutlass
The Chance Vought F7U Cutlass makes a successful first flight on September 29, 1948. The aircraft has no conventional

SIGNIFICANT DATES

MAY 7, 1947: Italian national airline Alitalia begins scheduled operations.

JUNE 25, 1947: The Boeing B-50 makes its first flight. The bomber is effectively a B-29 re-engined with more powerful Pratt & Whitney Wasp Major powerplants.

JULY 27, 1947: The Tupolev Tu-12 makes its first flight – it is the Soviet Union's first jet bomber to enter production.

AUGUST 16, 1947: The de Havilland Canada DHC-2 Beaver makes its maiden flight. Designed as a STOL bush transport, the Beaver proves highly successful, equally at home operating from land or water.

OCTOBER 14, 1947: Charles 'Chuck' Yeager becomes the first man to fly faster than the speed of sound when he takes the Bell X-1 rocket-powered research plane to Mach 1.015 over the Rogers Dry Lake in California.

JANUARY 21, 1948: The diminutive D.9 Bébé Jodel lightweight monoplane makes its first flight.

JANUARY 23, 1948: The de Havilland Australia DHA-3 Drover makes its first flight.

MARCH 23, 1948: John Cunningham sets a new altitude record of 59,445ft (18,119m) in a de Havilland Vampire.

MAY 26, 1948: Charles 'Chuck' Yeager sets a new altitude record of 64,000ft (19,500m) in the Bell X-1.

JUNE 26, 1948: The Berlin airlift gets underway as USAF C-47s start flying supplies to the beleaguered city from Frankfurt.

JULY 14, 1948: Silver City Airways commences car ferry flights between Lympne, Kent and Le Touquet, France.

JULY 14, 1948: Six RAF Vampire fighters complete the first transatlantic flight by jet aircraft when they land in Labrador after staging through Iceland and Greenland.

AUGUST 16, 1948: The Northrop XF-89 Scorpion prototype makes its first flight. When it enters service in 1950 it is the USAF's first all-weather jet interceptor.

AUGUST 23, 1948: The McDonnell XF-85 Goblin parasite escort fighter makes its first flight. It is designed to be carried by the giant B-36 bomber for protection but the concept is eventually dropped.

SEPTEMBER 18, 1948: The Convair XF-92 delta wing research aircraft makes its first flight. The aircraft owes much to German wartime research and eventually leads to the F-102 and F-106 fighters.

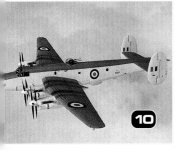

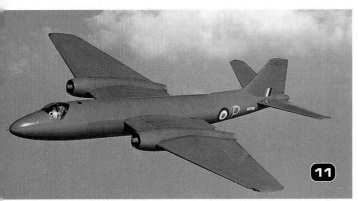

horizontal tail surfaces, thanks to German research and introduces a complex wing and many other new technologies to the US Navy, the type's only customer. (KEY collection)

9. Martin's loser
The experimental Martin XB-51 flies for the first time in 1949, it is designed to fill the need for an American medium jet bomber. However, it fails to attract orders, with the USAF opting for the licence-built Martin B-57 Canberra. (KEY collection)

10. Avro classic

The Avro Shackleton, developed from the Lancaster and Lincoln bombers, makes its maiden flight on March 9, 1949. Designed as a maritime patrol aircraft, it is subsequently modified to provide an AEW capability which the Shackleton AEW.3 continued to provide for the RAF until 1991. (Gordon Swanborough collection)

11. Classic Canberra
One of the most famous British jet aircraft ever built, the English Electric Canberra, makes its first flight on May 13, 1949. Still in service today with the RAF in the photo reconnaissance

role as the Canberra PR.9, variants of the Canberra have served with many air arms around the world and a few of these still retain the type. (Gordon Swanborough collection)

12. British giant
Designed to operate non-stop across the Atlantic, the huge Bristol Brabazon is powered by four pairs of coupled Bristol Centaurus piston engines and has a wing span of 230ft (70.1m). However, with the dawning of the jet age it is too slow and only the single prototype is completed, flying for the first time on September 4, 1949. (Gordon Swanborough collection)

13. Trojan trainer
Designed by North American as a replacement for the classic T-6 Texan, the T-28 Trojan makes its first flight on September 26, 1949. The aircraft is built in large numbers and is also used by a number of air arms for light attack missions. (KEY - Duncan Cubitt)

14. Douglas giant
The Douglas C-124 Globemaster II, developed from the earlier C-74 Globemaster I, makes its maiden flight on November 27, 1949. It goes on to provide the backbone of the USAF's heavy lift capability well into the 1960s. (KEY collection)

1940-49

NOVEMBER 15, 1948: Israel's national airline El Al Israel Airlines is established.

DECEMBER 1, 1948: Boeing perfects a new in-flight refuelling system using a flying boom to transfer fuel into a receiver socket on the recipient aircraft. The system is set to become standard for the USAF, though the US Navy prefers the hose and drogue system.

FEBRUARY 4, 1949: The American CAA grants the use of ground-controlled approach (GCA) radar as the first choice as a landing aid in bad weather.

MARCH 2, 1949: A USAF B-50 completes a

94 hour 1 minute round-the-world flight. The 23,452 mile (37,742km) flight includes four air-to-air refuellings.

MARCH 4, 1949: A US Navy Martin Mars flying-boat carries a record 269 passengers on a flight from San Diego, California to Alameda, Idaho. A journey in the other direction on May 19 carries 301 passengers.

APRIL 21, 1949: A French-built experimental aircraft, the Leduc 0.10, makes its first powered flight after being air launched. It is powered by a revolutionary ramjet which only works when sufficient velocity has been reached.

APRIL 26, 1949: A new endurance record is set by Bill Barris and Dick Reidel in an Aeronca Chief when they stay airborne for 1,008 hours and 1 minute. Fuel and supplies are hauled up from a speeding jeep four times a day during the flight.

JUNE 3, 1949: The Boeing 377 Stratocruiser is introduced on transatlantic services by Pan Am.

JULY 27, 1949: The world's first jet-powered airliner, the de Havilland DH.106 Comet, makes its maiden flight at Hatfield, England.

AUGUST 10, 1949: The Avro Canada C-102

jet-powered airliner makes its first flight, however, it does receive any airline orders despite being very similar to the British Avro Tudor.

SEPTEMBER 4, 1949: The first of four delta-wing Avro 707 research aircraft takes to the air as part of development work on the Vulcan bomber.

SEPTEMBER 19, 1949: The double-Mamba turbine powered Fairey Gannett makes its maiden flight. In service the aircraft is initially used by the Royal Navy Fleet Air Arm in the anti-submarine warfare role. Later versions serve as AEW platforms to protect the fleet.

Jet
Power

THE INVENTION OF THE JET ENGINE BEFORE WORLD WAR TWO WAS SET TO REVOLUTIONISE
AVIATION BEYOND MEASURE AFTER THE WAR WAS OVER. BILL GUNSTON OBE FRAeS CHARTS
THE DEVELOPMENT OF ONE OF THE MOST SIGNIFICANT TECHNOLOGICAL DEVELOPMENTS OF
THE PAST 100 YEARS.

Throughout the 19th Century would-be aviators could have got their flying machines into the air by using a rocket, or a small succession of rockets, reliable examples of which had been developed as weapons. Instead they beavered away at complex and heavy engines of many kinds, which after 1900 included massive gas turbines geared to propellers. Then in 1929 came the breakthrough.

Whittle's brainwave

The man who made the breakthrough was Frank Whittle. He was a young RAF fighter pilot, the last sort of person supposed to invent anything. He could see that a simple engine could be created by using a spinning centrifugal compressor to deliver compressed air to a combustion chamber where fuel was burned. The hot gas could then rotate a turbine driving the compressor. Such engines, called gas turbines, had been proposed for many years, with the turbine geared down to drive a propeller. Called turboprops, such engines tended to be bulkier and heavier than existing piston engines.

Whittle's brainwave was to see that the hot jet behind the turbine could propel an aeroplane by simply expelling

The impressive range of Snecma engines illustrates the diversity offered by the French manufacturer. Like all the key players in the jet engine market, it provides power for helicopters, regional airliners, combat jets and large airliners. (Snecma)

it at high speed through a nozzle. The big factor was that such an engine, called a turbojet, could drive aircraft to speeds far higher than the 500mph (804.5km/h) limit for heavy and complex engines driving propellers.

In 1930 Whittle showed his idea to a supposed expert, and later to the main British aero-engine companies, but nobody was interested. He took out a patent, which by 1932 had been published for all to read, but still nobody showed interest and when his patent expired he could not afford to renew it. But in 1935 a friend said he might be able to arrange a little money to make a jet engine, and in March 1936 a tiny company called Power Jets was formed. By scraping together £3,000 a turbojet was made and on April 12, 1937, testing began. It worked: indeed, when first started it ran away screaming out of control because a small pool of paraffin fuel had gathered at the bottom of the combustion chamber so that closing the throttle had no effect!

Sir Frank Whittle and his Power Jets Team outside their facility at Wetstone in 1945. (Alstec)

German developments

Still nobody showed interest, but by this time turbojets were being developed in Germany. One group, led by Max-Adolf Mäller and Herbert Wagner, were working at the mighty Junkers factory at Dessau and at a secret cell at Magdeburg. The other, led by young inventor Pabst von Ohain, worked at

the Heinkel factory at Rostock-Marienehe. While the Junkers team studied a mass of complex ideas, von Ohain had a simple scheme closely similar to Whittle's (von Ohain denied copying anyone, but his assistant Gundermann said they had studied Whittle's patent, among many others).

On a night in September 1937 the first von Ohain test apparatus was started. To avoid the problem of spraying liquid fuel, it ran on hydrogen gas, piped from the workshop supply. In 1938 the HeS 3 engine was on test, started on hydrogen but then run on paraffin vaporised by the flame in the combustion chamber. By May 1939 the HeS 3A could be started on liquid fuels, and it was tested under an He 118 dive bomber. Meanwhile, Heinkel had built the world's first turbojet aircraft, the He 178, powered by the HeS 3B, with an installed thrust of some 834lb. This flew on August 27, 1939. It made several brief flights, with the landing gear locked down, before being sent to a Berlin museum.

On April 2, 1941, Heinkel flew the first jet fighter, the He 280, powered by two 109-001 engines, but none of the later Heinkel and Heinkel-Hirth jet and turboprop engines achieved anything. In contrast, the Junkers team, from August 1938 led by Dr Anselm Franz, had decided to concentrate on the 109-

004, a turbojet with an axial compressor. Such a compressor comprises a succession of moving rotor blades like miniature radial wings interspersed with stator blades fixed to the casing. Compared with a centrifugal compressor, as had been used in superchargers, an axial compressor tended to be more complex, heavy, vulnerable to damage and far more difficult to develop. The big plus factor was that in the long term it might make possible higher pressure ratios, leading to engines of greater power and efficiency.

Jet fighters and experiments

For the 004 engine Franz chose a compressor with eight stages of blades, giving a pressure ratio of 3.1. On July 18, 1942, two improved 004A engines powered the third Messerschmitt Me 262 prototype twin-jet fighter, and by March 1944 the 004B, with a thrust of 1,984lb, went into enormous mass-production for the Me 262A, Ar 234B and other aircraft. Despite the facilities being heavily bombed, more than 6,000 004B engines were made before the factories were overrun.

In totally unrelated development, German engineers had

The Eurofighter Typhoon uses two Eurojet EJ200 afterburning engines yet has the ability to supercruise - flying faster than Mach 1 without the need to use the afterburners. The engines are also small and lightweight, and offer the potential to be fitted with thrust vectoring nozzles. (EADS)

Above right: **The engine that started it all, the Whittle W.1, seen here in the Alstec exhibit at the SBAC Farnborough Airshow.** (KEY - Dave Allport)
Above: **The General Electric J47-powered North American F-86 Sabre, in the hands of experienced World War Two pilots, was to prove more than a match for the Russian MiG-15 during the Korean War.** (US National Archives)

experimented with rockets. In 1928-29 simple gliders had flown propelled by cordite-fuel rockets. In 1937 a Heinkel He 112 fighter flew with a liquid-propellant rocket in its tail, by which time a wealth of fighters, bombers and other aircraft in the USSR were flying with pump-fed liquid rocket engines to boost maximum speed. Other Russian aircraft had ramjet engines, called stovepipes because of their simplicity. Not least, in Germany, Paul Schmidt was testing a pulsejet, a simple resonant duct with spring-steel flap valves admitting air in gulps at the rate of 45 per second to mix with fuel and create a propulsive blast down the tailpipe. In World War Two these deafeningly noisy but cheap engines powered 31,100 'doodlebug' flying bombs, most of which were aimed at London or Antwerp. In desperation, the Me 328 interceptor was designed around two such units, but such an idea was a non-starter. Another desperate last-ditch effort was the Ba 349 rocket interceptor which took off pointing vertically upwards and returned in pieces by parachute.

Britain plays catch up

In 1944 the existence of German jet aircraft came as a shock to the British, who finally realised how foolish it had been to ignore Whittle. His efforts began to be taken seriously in 1939. His engine could have been fixed on a flying test-bed in a matter of days, but what happened was that Gloster Aircraft was allowed to spend two years creating a special aircraft. The E.28/39 at last flew on May 15, 1941, apparently to the utter astonishment of most of the few observers. No official photographer was present on this historic occasion. Whittle was told to collaborate with Rover Cars. There followed two years of argument, until Lord Hives, boss of Rolls-Royce, simply said to Rover... "You can have our tank-engine factory in Nottingham and we'll take over the Whittle engine".

Overnight, British jet development got going, 12 years after the patent and five years after the start of testing. Thanks to Rolls-Royce's drive and resources, the first jet fighters in regular service in the world were Gloster Meteor Is, each powered by two Rolls-Royce Welland engines of basic Whittle design, operated by the RAF's 616 Squadron. On the other hand, for every Meteor I delivered, Messerschmitt was making over 100 Me 262s, and the Me 262 was a far superior aircraft.

In fact, the first Allied jet fighter was the Bell XP-59A Airacomet, flown on October 2, 1942. It was powered by two General Electric (GE) engines of pure Whittle design, because by chance US General 'Hap' Arnold had been in England when the Whittle engine first flew. He at once got GE to make the new invention, and while Whittle was frustrated in Britain, GE began making turbojets by the thousand. In April 1944 Rolls-Royce's Dr Stanley Hooker was astonished to find that GE was running two types of turbojet, one a Whittle-derived centrifugal and the other an axial, both rated at 4,000lb.

He hurried back and designed the Nene, to be rated at 5,000lb. Amazingly, little use was made of this engine in the UK, while over 100,000 were made in Australia and Canada, by Hispano-Suiza in France, by Pratt & Whitney in the USA, and by enormous factories in the USSR and China! It powered the swept-wing 670mph MiG-15, while the RAF's fastest fighters were 100mph slower.

Afterburners

Many Nenes, including the RD-45F and VK-1F derivatives in the USSR, were among the first to be fitted with an afterburner. This is a method of boosting thrust for short dashes at increased speed, and especially at supersonic speed. The jet pipe is enlarged and fitted with spray rings and flame-holders for burning additional fuel. When the afterburner fuel is turned on, the jet pipe propelling nozzle is made larger and changed in profile by adjusting 'petals' forming its periphery. Afterburning increases thrust by up to 50%, but it also burns fuel so quickly as to seriously reduce range and flight endurance.

Korea and split-compressors

The only fighter able to take on the MiG-15 in Korea was the North American Aviation (NAA) F-86 Sabre, powered by the General Electric J47 axial engine. Over 36,500 J47s were made, mostly for the F-86 and for the swept-wing six-engined Boeing B-47 strategic bomber. The B-47 was followed by the monster eight-engined B-52, for which Pratt & Whitney designed the J57. Together with Britain's Bristol Olympus, the J57 was a pioneer of the two-spool, two-shaft or split-compressor principle. The air is compressed in a large LP (low-pressure) axial compressor driven by a multi-stage LP turbine and then compressed further by a separate smaller HP (high-pressure) compressor driven at higher speed by a white-hot HP turbine via a tubular HP shaft surrounding the LP shaft. The greater compression means better fuel economy.

Pratt & Whitney and licensees made 21,226 J57s for the B-52, A-3, F-100, F-101, F-102, F4D and F8U. The commercial JT3C version powered the 707 and DC-8, the pioneer long-range jet airliners. By 1960 Pratt & Whitney had followed the JT3 by the JT4A, or J75, and also by the much more important JT3D.

Turbofans

This was a pioneer turbofan, in which the LP compressor is made larger, to send a greater flow of compressed air around the rest of the engine, called the core. This improves propulsive efficiency and reduces noise.

Early turbofans had a BPR (bypass ratio) of about 1, in other words half the airflow was bypassed around the core.

The first combat use of a jet-powered aircraft was made by the German Luftwaffe during the latter part of World War Two. The Messerschmitt Me 262 was powered by a pair of Jumo 004B turbojets, this Me 262 is one of a number taken to the USA after the war and is pictured at Chino in 1975. (MAP)

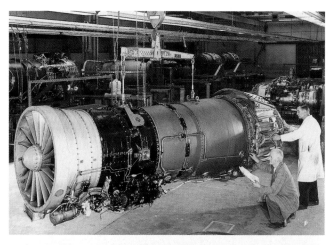

Top: **Although offering more power than the J47, eight Pratt & Whitney J57s were needed to get the huge B-52 Stratofortress off the ground. In its commercial JT3C form, the engine was fitted to the early Boeing 707 and Douglas DC-8 airliners.** (KEY collection)
Above: **The Mach 3 Lockheed SR-71A Blackbird relied on a pair of Pratt & Whitney J58 turbojets, each delivering 32,500lb (145.6kN) of thrust, to power it to such breathtaking speeds.** (KEY - Duncan Cubitt)

Top: **The first major British turbofan engine was the Rolls-Royce Conway which powered the Vickers VC 10.** (Rolls-Royce)
Above: **The Rolls-Royce RB211 high-bypass turbofan needed a lot of government support to make it a reality, initially for the Lockheed L1011 TriStar. Today it is still in production with thousands powering airliners around the globe.** (Rolls-Royce)

Gradually, as designers believed the arithmetic, they became bolder until in 1965 General Electric designed the TF39 as a true turbofan, with a slim core driving a giant fan of over 10ft (3.04m) diameter, the BPR being 8. This showed the way to go, and all of today's airline engines have a BPR of at least 4, the largest being the Rolls-Royce Trent, Pratt & Whitney PW4000 and, biggest of all, the GE90-115B. These have BPR of 6.5-8.6, and soon the norm will be about 12. Such engines generate almost all their thrust by the huge fan, and have much in common with turboprops.

Turboprops

The first turboprop, the Rolls-Royce Trent, was simply a fighter turbojet with a gearbox driving a small five-blade propeller. Two flew on a Meteor fighter in September 1945. Soon afterwards, Lionel Haworth designed the Rolls-Royce Dart, a properly schemed turboprop (like Rolls-Royce jet engines, it was named after a river). It had two centrifugal compressors in series, like a bigger edition of the two-stage superchargers. Starting life at 900hp, the Dart was

developed to give 3,245hp, and over 7,100 were made, mostly for the Vickers Viscount and Fokker F27 airliners.

Rolls-Royce followed with the totally different Tyne, with separate axial LP and HP compressors and rated at 4,800 to 6,100hp. At Indianapolis Allison designed the T56 (the civil version being the Model 501) with a single-shaft axial power section driving a remote propeller gearbox carried on struts ahead of the inlet duct. Rated at 3,750 to 5,250hp, some 15,500 were made for such aircraft as the C-130 Hercules, Electra, P-3 Orion

and E-2 Hawkeye. Allison is now Rolls-Royce Corporation, making a T56 successor named the AE2100, driving six-blade propellers for the C-130J and other aircraft.

In 1955 Western observers were astonished to see a gigantic bomber, the Tupolev Tu-95, fly over Moscow: it had swept wings and tail and propellers. Gradually they understood that the Kuznetsov NK-12 turboprop, putting 15,000hp through an eight-blade contra-rotating propeller, could combine turboprop economy with jet speed. Other NK-12 versions powered huge hovercraft, while Kuznetsov went on to develop giant afterburning engines for the Tu-144 supersonic airliner and the Tu-22 and Tu-160 supersonic bombers.

Turboshafts

At the other end of the propulsion spectrum, in 1948 Turbomeca in France began making small gas-turbine engines. In 1955 the 400hp Artouste powered a little helicopter named Alouette (Lark). Since then helicopters have increasingly used turboshaft engines, which dramatically reduce installed weight, burn jet fuel

●**Sectioned drawing of the International Aero Engines (IAE) V2500-A5 turbofan. This engine was introduced in 1988 and is a popular choice for the Airbus A319/320/321 family of airliners.** (IAE)

61

Top: **The General Electric CF6 has proved a highly-popular product and can be found on many of the larger airliners, such as the Boeing 747.** (General Electric)
Above: **One of the early turboprops, the Armstrong Siddeley Python, was used to power the Westland Wyvern. This example is seen at the Rolls-Royce Heritage Trust at Coventry, though the collection has since moved to Derby.** (KEY - Duncan Cubitt)

Top: **The latest version of the Lockheed Martin C-130 Hercules, the C-130J, is powered by four Allison AE2100 advanced turboprops driving new six-blade composite propellers.** (KEY - Steve Fletcher)
Above: **The Rolls-Royce Pegasus engine was the key to the success of the V/STOL Hawker P.1127 and its descendant the Harrier. Thrust is routed through four rotating nozzles enabling the aircraft to hover by balancing on the vertical thrust.** (Rolls-Royce)

instead of high-octane petrol, need no complex cooling system, and can run at full power for long periods.

GE delivered over 6,300 T58 engines in the 1,000hp class (with many more made by licensees) and have followed with an even greater number of T700s in the 2,000hp class and, in smaller numbers, the T64 of up to almost 5,000shp. Leader in the small-helicopter field is the Rolls-Royce (ex-Allison) 250, which began life with a six-stage axial compressor followed by a centrifugal example producing 250hp. Such is the progress with centrifugal compressors that today the most powerful RR 250 has no axial compressor and delivers 791hp, and total deliveries exceed 29,000.

Clear leader with large helicopters is Russia. The 5,500-6,500hp D-25V made possible the monster Mi-6 helicopter and Mi-10 crane version, while the Mi-26 is powered by D-136 engines rated at 11,400shp. The only Western VTOL (vertical take-off and landing) aircraft that comes anywhere near such capability is the V-22 Osprey, with tilting prop-rotors driven by Rolls-Royce T406 engines of 6,150hp.

Vertical jets

The term VTOL became common after 1955 when it was realised that gas-turbine engines opened up a previously unattainable spectrum of jet aircraft able to rise vertically and even hover. In 1960 Hawker Aircraft began

testing the P.1127, a small aeroplane fitted with a unique Rolls-Royce turbofan (originally designed by Bristol Siddeley) with four thrust nozzles. These nozzles, one on each side for fan air and one on each side for the hot jet, were able to swivel in unison through an angle of 98.5° to give lift, forward thrust or rearwards braking. From this small beginning came the Harrier, Sea Harrier and US Marine Corps AV-8, all multi-role fast-jet warplanes that

do not need a long runway.

In 1960 such an aircraft appeared essential, because nuclear missiles could by then wipe any airfield off the map. Strangely, the vulnerability of airfields seems today to have been forgotten, but at least the intention is that one version of the new F-35 Joint Strike Fighter (JSF) will have STOVL (short takeoff, vertical landing) capability. The Lockheed Martin F-35B version will have a Pratt & Whitney F135 or General Electric F136 engine with a downwards-vectoring nozzle, and a shaft drive to a Rolls-Royce contra-rotating lift fan well ahead of the aircraft centre of gravity. In hovering flight some 39,000lb (174kN) of lift is provided by this fan (48%), the down-vectored main engine nozzle (40%) and the rest by the hovering roll-control nozzles under each wing. Today the jet-engine scene is more varied and exciting than ever.

Gears, propfans and competition

One of the many causes for argument is the geared fan. In around 1920 designers began putting a gearbox - heavy, and a source of possible failure - between the crankshaft and propeller so that an engine could run at high rpm to generate more power yet drive a large propeller at lower rpm for better efficiency. In the same

The massive General Electric GE90 was designed to power the twin-engine Boeing 777, initially rated at 71,200lb (316.69kN) but later versions have produced well in excess of 100,000lb (448kN). (General Electric)

Turboshaft engines are the preferred choice for most modern helicopters and have been for over 40 years. The EH Industries EH-101 Merlin uses one of the latest derivatives of this form of power, in this case three Rolls-Royce Turbomeca RTM 322-01/8 turboshafts for the Royal Navy Merlin HM.1 variant. (EH Industries)

The new Lockheed Martin F-35B V/STOL variant of the JSF uses both direct engine lift as well as thrust provided by a shaft-driven lift fan. (Lockheed Martin)

way, it makes sense to use a gearbox so that a simple high-speed turbine can drive an efficient fan of large diameter. Put another way, the direct-drive PW4090 has a fan smaller than the optimum size yet still needs a turbine with seven stages to drive it. Such a turbine is heavy and expensive. Showing the way to go, Pratt & Whitney have studied the geared PW8000, and P&W Canada is now marketing the geared PW800 for smaller jetliners and long-range bizjets.

In the field of military airlifters, Antonov has developed the An-70 powered by outstandingly efficient D-27 propfans in the 14,000hp class. In contrast, the air forces of Western Europe have spent over 30 years doing little but talk. In the 1970s they began studying the design of a military airlifter to replace the C-130 and Transall C.160. In May 1994 it was decided that the engines should be turboprops. The problem was that, apart from the D-27, no engine exists. Eight years further on, the proposed

engine has been rejected, and Pratt & Whitney Canada has been allowed to offer competition.

This Canadian company has done rather better than the Europeans in building a mighty business from nothing. It began in 1960 with the PT6, a small turboprop in the 500hp class. Today PT6 power ranges up to over 1,600hp (the PT6C-67A for the BA609 tilt-rotor transport is close to 2,000hp), and the number delivered exceeds

Pratt & Whitney Canada's PT6 turboprop has enjoyed huge success, selling in excess of 30,000 units worldwide. (Pratt & Whitney)

30,000. A succession of small turbofans followed, all in mass production, and the PW100 turboprop was quickly created to replace the Rolls-Royce Dart. In around 1955 many observers derided the Dart because it had

centrifugal compressors. They would have been astonished to be told that in the new century the PW100 has exactly the same arrangement of two centrifugal compressors!

Jet legacy

Since the 1950s almost all fighter engines have been augmented (afterburning) turbofans of low BPR, slim enough to fit in fighter fuselages. They range from the Adour of around 5,000lb thrust to the F135 and F136 for the Lockheed Martin F-35 Joint Strike Fighter in the 40,000lb class. One measure of success is ratio of thrust to weight. The German axial turbojets of 1944 had a T/W ratio close to unity. The Nene of 1945 achieved 3.2, and it took another decade for afterburning fighter engines to get beyond 4. However, today the F100-229A and EJ200 comfortably exceed 8, and US research is aiming at T/W beyond 15.

There can be little doubt that the jet engine has revolutionised both military and commercial aviation. It enables the military to strike faster and it allows millions of people to travel around the world in speed and comfort. More than any other invention of the past 100 years, it has opened up the globe to business and commerce on a scale unimaginable before the 1950s.

Future fighter engines will use advanced composites and single-crystal metals, increased gas temperatures far beyond the melting point of ordinary uncooled metal alloys, new types of nozzle able to change shape and the direction of the jet, and contra-rotating machinery with the near-elimination of stators. And we may be sure that some of the most exciting advances are either secret or not yet even thought of.

The Lyul'ka-Saturn AL-31FP, which powered the first prototypes of Sukhoi's remarkably agile Su-30MK development of the *Flanker* is the world's first fully operational thrust-vectoring engine and will power the Su-30MKI currently being delivered to the Indian Air Force. Unlike the example shown here, the latest engines have two-plane vectoring nozzles, capable of vectoring the full 27,560lb (122.9kN) thrust in afterburner. (Yefim Gordon)

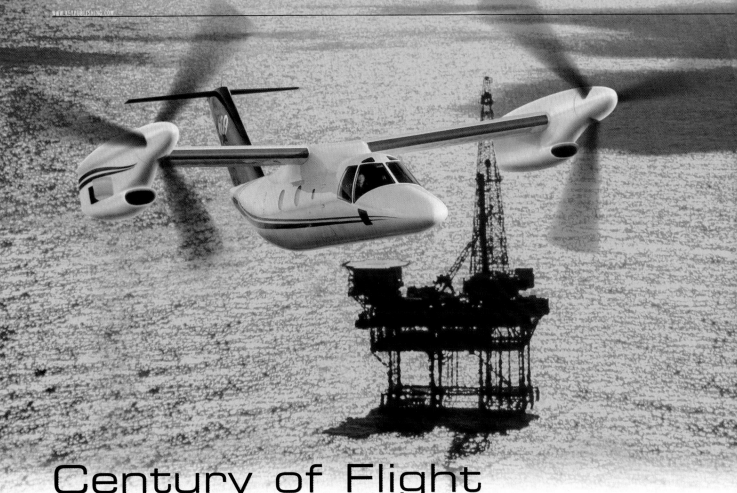

Century of Flight
AIR International's View

A LOOK AT 'A CENTURY OF POWERED FLIGHT' THROUGH THE EYES OF

AIR International EDITOR, MALCOLM ENGLISH.

A*IR International* celebrated its 30th anniversary in July 2001, a period which almost covers the latter third of the history of powered flight. During its lifetime, the monthly journal has reported on a number of major events, including Concorde's introduction into service, the emergence of low-cost airlines, the ending of the Cold War and more recently, the tragic events of September 11, 2001. Whilst all of these had a major influence on the future of aviation, they almost pale into insignificance when compared to earlier developments.

On a positive note, powered flight has provided safe and fast travel worldwide for the 'masses'; arguably less welcome is a new dimension in warfare. Allied to these developments in aeronautics, there have been countless indirect benefits, many of which are invaluable. These range from the global socio-economic improvements brought about by the ease with which people and cargo can be transported across continents, to technology spin-offs – particularly in materials and computer sciences – that have found applications in numerous fields, from space flight to home appliances.

As befits a magazine with a remit to educate as well as entertain its readers,

An exciting new concept for commercial transport is the Bell-Agusta BA609 tilt-rotor. Although its military forerunner is suffering from teething problems, the BA609 offers to combine the benefits of vertical take-off and landing with cruise speeds associated with conventional turboprop aircraft. (Bell-Agusta)

AIR International has published a number of features on aircraft design and operation. These have included a description of the technologies, such as aerodynamics, stability and control, structures and propulsion, that were mastered by Wilbur and Orville Wright, and still form the basis of academic studies for pilots and aeronautical engineers. Thanks to others, neither structures nor propulsion posed the challenges that had confounded so many of their predecessors. However, ensuring adequate lift, stability and control were daunting tasks. It is interesting to note that while huge advances have been made in aircraft design over the years, many current and future combat aircraft (and the futuristic Boeing Sonic

Cruiser) adopt the canard configuration chosen by the Wrights for their Flyer – albeit for different reasons.

Thanks largely to developments in computational methods, structural loads can now be predicted accurately, thus leading to much safer airframes than were possible in the early days of flying. Likewise, the introduction of computerised flight control systems allows an aircraft to be given 'artificial stability'. Consequently a modern combat aircraft, such as the Eurofighter Typhoon, has more docile handling characteristics than a World War One fighter, such as the Sopwith Camel. One of the hallmarks of *AIR International* is its monthly 'cutaway drawing' and over the years they have illustrated types as diverse as the Handley Page HP.42 and Boeing 757, and SE5A and Lockheed Martin F-22 Raptor. These graphically illustrate the changes in military and commercial aircraft design over the years.

The Wars

Step changes in the 'natural' evolution of aircraft occurred as a result of the two major World Wars and the Cold War. The direct and immediate effects were seen in military aircraft, as a result of which they were able to fly faster, further and higher, and carry increasingly sophisticated

AIR International prides itself on its monthly detailed cutaway drawings. This drawing of the Eurofighter Typhoon clearly illustrates its structure, configuration and weapons capability.

however, brought a penalty, as every airline passenger will know – airport congestion. Gone are the heady days of carefree flying from places such as Croydon Airport. That said, there are relatively far fewer delays due to aircraft unserviceability and weather. Furthermore, flying non-stop from London to destinations such as Hong Kong, or to New York from London in under four hours, were things undreamed of not that many years ago.

Faster, further, higher

During the early days of aviation, it was enough to aim to fly faster, further and higher. More recently, however, in response to finance and ecological pressures, engines have become more efficient, cleaner and quieter. Military engines have benefited from significant increases in thrust/weight ratios allowing 'supercruise' (supersonic flight with dry

Above: **Powerplant efficiencies have developed to an extent that aircraft, such as the F-22 Raptor, powered by two P&W F119-PW-100 turbofans are able to fly supersonically in dry power.** (Lockheed Martin)
Right: **Aircrew workload has been significantly reduced with the advent of glass cockpits and fly-by-wire flight control systems.** (Airbus)

weapons. Navigation aids and avionic systems allowed aircraft to operate safely at night and in all weather conditions, while radar enabled combat aircraft to fire missiles at targets beyond the pilot's visual range. Many of these advances in technology were subsequently applied to commercial aircraft thus increasing their efficiency and capability. Indeed, commercial aviation has become so competitive that it is often now the technology leader, with spin-offs going into military aviation.

Sadly, the advances made during wartime were tempered shortly afterwards by a reduction in aircraft manufacturing effort. The latest example of this was seen with the ending of the Cold War, which brought with it a price – the so-called 'Peace Dividend'. No longer facing a major 'conventional' threat, Western governments slashed defence budgets. Secondary effects were numerous company mergers, fewer military contracts being placed, a move toward multi-role

aircraft to minimise support costs and an increase in the number of aircraft upgrades to extend their operational life. Who could have foreseen the disappearance of such household names as Avro, Fokker, Hawker, McDonnell Douglas and Supermarine? In contrast, commercial aviation has seen extremely healthy growth and (with the exception of the reduction in output following the events of September 11, coupled with a downturn in the global economy), does not look like it will slow down in the longer term.

The tremendous growth in commercial aviation has,

power). When Concorde entered service, it was generally accepted that supersonic flight would shortly be available for 'the masses'. History has shown us that this was not to be the case; politics, environmental concerns and economics all combined to restrict its use to a privileged few.

Looking to the future, the two remaining commercial aircraft giants, Boeing and Airbus are polarised in their views of the future passenger market. With its giant A380, Airbus is intent on usurping Boeing's lead as the manufacturer of the world's largest commercial airliner – the 747. In contrast, Boeing believes that speed will be of more importance than capacity and is developing the Sonic Cruiser, an airliner designed to operate at high subsonic speeds.

Recognising the importance of keeping its readers informed on all aspects of aviation matters, *AIR International* prides itself on its extensive, up-to-the-minute news of worldwide military, commercial and industry events.

● **Reduction in defence budgets have resulted in more aircraft undergoing upgrades, rather than air arms purchasing new aircraft. A classic example is the venerable B-52 which first flew in 1952 and is predicated to remain in service until 2040.** (USAF)

Manufacturing
– 100 years of learning

TONY BUTTLER AMRAeS, LOOKS AT THE REMARKABLE ADVANCES MADE IN AIRCRAFT

MANUFACTURE OVER THE PAST 100 YEARS.

One of the most important parts of designing an aircraft, but perhaps the least known, is the method and choice of materials used to make it. The overriding factor is that the aircraft's structure has to be strong enough to stop it breaking apart during flight, which means the material used must have the strength to support the loads applied, but if that material is very heavy, let us say cast iron or bronze, then the aircraft will be so overweight that its engines might be incapable of getting it off the ground. Since the start of manned flight, the design and manufacture of aircraft has been dominated by a basic requirement of strength with lightness. However, this is complicated by other needs, some of them critical, such as stiffness, toughness, durability in unfavourable environments, ease of fabrication and cost, and the equation has become more complex as the performance and size of aircraft have increased.

Beginnings

The most attractive materials to the earliest aircraft constructors were wood, canvas and piano wire; birch and spruce being the most widely-used timbers in the first generation of powered aircraft. The first wings followed the established practice for making kites, with a typical example having two spars running the whole distance from root to tip. A series of ribs would be placed at right angles and shaped such that they would support a cloth covering to the correct aerodynamic shape (i.e. each rib had the shape of a wing section). The structure would then be strengthened and stiffened with wires which could withstand the loads experienced in the fore-and-aft direction. However, obtaining enough strength in the up-and-down direction was more difficult because the wing had its greatest dimension in the horizontal plane but its smallest in the vertical plane, so to obtain

sufficient 'depth' to prevent the wing from folding up, the biplane arrangement was used where two wings were kept apart by vertical struts with diagonal wire bracing.

The entire wing and fuselage skeleton would have a fabric covering bonded to it and the outside surfaces were then treated with dope to make the fabric shrink to give a tight, rigid structure. This method was standard during the First World War but natural wood gave some problems in that it would often absorb moisture which could affect the structure's dimensions and shape. The solution was to use plywood with new synthetic resin adhesives which brought great improvements in strength. However, wood presented another wartime problem to Britain because obtaining sufficient stocks required the import of considerable volumes of material.

The use of fabric-covered aeroplanes with wire-braced wooden structures continued to the Second World War

● **Aircraft production has come an awful long way in 100 years. Here the first production Eurofighter Typhoon has its three fuselage sections joined in an automated alignment facility. Laser alignment and computer controls are becoming standard in the modern aviation industry.** (Eurofighter GmbH)

but there was an increase in 'box' structures made of spruce and laminated plywood, the latter often forming the outer skin and contributing a good deal to the strength. This also eliminated internal and external bracing wires which removed the tedious process of 'rigging' – the need to adjust the tension of the wires to ensure that the wings and other surfaces maintained the correct angles and did not warp. The biggest snag to all-wood structures was that the glue used at the joints could be attacked by fungus growths.

The largest aeroplane to be built in wood was Howard Hughes' H-4 Hercules 'Spruce Goose' flying-boat, the

Above: **A Royal Aircraft Factory FE.2b ably illustrates early aircraft construction, which often left parts of the metal frame exposed. The amount of wire bracing required to strengthen the airframe is readily apparent.** (Gordon Swanborough collection)

construction of which began in 1942. However, by the time war arrived pretty well all frontline aircraft were being built in metal although there was one notable exception. The de Havilland DH.98 Mosquito light bomber, flown in 1940, was built entirely in wood to keep it light and to utilise the then very underused wood and furniture manufacturing industries. So successful was the Mosquito that de Havilland employed a mixture of wood and aluminium construction and Redux adhesives in its later Hornet piston and Vampire jet fighters.

A move to metal

Steel had been used as an aircraft material right from the start but it found more airframe applications during World War One. During the war Dutchman Anthony Fokker adopted a welded tubular steel structure covered with fabric for his German fighter aircraft and this form of construction was still used in 1950s Piper light aircraft.

The next phase was the choice between high tensile steel and heat-treated aluminium alloys. Steel offered high strength but it was about three times 'heavier' than aluminium and ten times the figure for plywood. To obtain the full benefits it was necessary to use steel in very thin form. During the 1930s most British constructors used some tubular and box-type spars made in thin gauge steel which had complex curve patterns to prevent buckling, but these found little favour outside the UK. Twenty years later, Bristol Aircraft began to build a Mach 2 research aircraft in stainless steel called the 188, the material's use here being to combat the build-up of kinetic heat caused by air friction. This aeroplane employed special welding techniques but proved so difficult to build that when it flew it was several years behind schedule; the more

successful Russian MiG-25 *Foxbat* also used a large amount of steel in its construction. Steel is still used today for parts needing very high strength or to protect areas that experience great heat, such as engine bays.

The cylinder block of the engine that powered the Wright brothers' aeroplane at Kitty Hawk was a one-piece aluminium casting but the first non-engine application took a little longer. Aluminium propeller blades appeared in 1907 while aluminium covers, seats, cowlings, struts and cast brackets were common by the beginning of the First World War. In 1910 Hugo Junkers patented an all-metal aerofoil section and by the end of the War both the Allies and Germany had employed aluminium alloys in the structural framework of fuselage and wing assemblies.

Alloys

In 1906 Alfred Wilm, while seeking to develop a stronger aluminium alloy to replace brass in cartridge cases, accidentally discovered that an alloy of 3.5% copper and

0.5% magnesium would harden spontaneously after rapid cooling from 480°C. Patent rights were acquired by Durener Metallwerke, which christened the new alloy Duralumin and for many years this material, or developments of it, formed a major element in the construction of aeroplanes. Other more complex alloys followed, culminating in the very strong aluminium-zinc-magnesium series first adopted in the 1930s. For designers and engineers the choice of which alloy to use depended on the intended role of their aircraft – for example the demands of civil types that were expected to fly in excess of 30,000 hours were more searching in terms of corrosion and fatigue than military aircraft whose service life would probably only last 10 to 20% of this figure.

The first time aluminium alloys were used for fuselage and wing skins came in 1919 when the Junkers F.13 airliner employed corrugated sheet to increase strength. The first British all-metal aircraft was the Shorts Silver Streak of 1920, which the manufacturers followed with the Springbok fighter, but these machines were years ahead of their time and it was the 1930s before stressed skin metal airframes were accepted for the RAF in types like the Spitfire and Bristol Blenheim bomber.

The improved design and construction methods available after the First World War promoted the development of a new generation of passenger aeroplanes in which the wing took an appreciable portion of the payload. Metal stressed skin structures contributed to the aircraft's strength and also, with a

● **The Sopwith Pup is a fine example of how fabric was used to enclose the aircraft's frame, though these early designs lacked much in the way of structural strength when compared to all-metal aircraft.** (KEY collection)

● **The Boeing Monomail has the distinction of being the world's first all-metal monoplane to feature a smooth metal fuselage and a strong unbraced single wing.** (KEY collection)

components joined by riveting. In America the Northrop wing, developed in the late 1920s, was the forerunner of modern multicellular construction and was composed of flat webs, extending from wingtip to wingtip, riveted to extruded angles at the top and bottom. Similar webs formed the ribs and divided the whole wing into a series of cells, while the skin was riveted to the extruded sections and rib flanges. In this arrangement there were no main members to take the load, instead it was distributed throughout the whole lightly stressed structure and the skin.

It must be noted that the engineers of the 1930s had a paucity of technical information regarding the properties of shell structures compared to the familiar braced alternatives, which made their progress and achievements in this area all the more impressive. As aircraft speeds increased, particularly in fighters which also needed to manoeuvre violently, a wing structure's stiffness became just as important as its strength.

Quality control

The demands of aircraft production effectively created a British light metal industry and one of the new firms was High Duty Alloys, established at Slough in 1928 by Wallace Charles Devereux to produce high-strength castings and

Above: **The longevity of metal aircraft can be no better illustrated than by the Douglas DC-3 Dakota. Developed from the DC-2, the all-metal DC-3 first flew in 1935 but some are still in use commercially today.** (KEY - Duncan Cubitt)

smooth exterior and thinner wings, helped to form the correct external shape. This brought a further advance in speed and economy and the first 'modern' airliner to use these techniques was the 1930s Douglas DC-3; the aerodynamic potential of the monoplane could at last be exploited. By the 1950s nearly all aircraft had stressed skins but the trend had moved towards shell-like structures where the skin took more of the stress than any inner arrangement of spars and stiffeners, most or all of the material being concentrated in the shell. These monocoque structures, usually employed for the fuselage or engine nacelles, solved the problem of how to absorb compression without the skin buckling.

Rivet, weld or bond

Methods also had to be developed to fit the metal skins to the airframe and the industry's in-house solutions were 'pop' rivets, explosive rivets (developed by Heinkel) and Avdel and Chobert blind rivets, all of which were adopted by other branches of industry. Spot welding was used before 1939 but adhesive bonding came later. The bonding of structural aluminium parts with synthetic resin adhesives eventually led to the development of aluminium honeycombed panels which gave a very high strength to weight ratio, great rigidity and excellent resistance to fatigue. These sandwich structures used corrugated metal between two 'slices' of thin sheet (in just the same way as corrugated cardboard) to increase strength without adding weight.

Most wing spars were 'made up' sections with their

forgings. Devereux realised the need for effective quality control – at the time casting was a black art without technical supervision, and component quality was variable to say the least. He realised that for aircraft applications quality had to be 100% at all times and he introduced techniques and standards for examining and establishing a component's integrity that set the level for the rest of the world. Some of the aluminium industry's WW2 products, such as the cast aluminium beam for the Lancaster's undercarriage and some of the other larger undercarriage forgings, were major achievements for their day.

In 1929 Devereux acquired the world rights to market a series of Rolls-Royce alloys which swiftly evolved into the Hiduminium RR range for airframes and engines. The development of one of these, RR.58, makes a classic story. It was first developed as a forging alloy with good high temperature properties specifically to make impellers for the first Whittle engines. A desire in the 1950s to build a supersonic transport (which became Concorde) meant that

● **The de Havilland Mosquito, perhaps the most famous of all wooden aircraft. This example is NS591, a PR.Mk.XVI, seen at Hatfield in 1946.**
(British Aerospace via author)

● **The Supermarine Spitfire is a fine example of how complicated early all-metal aircraft were to produce. It took three times as many man hours to build than its German equivalent, the Messerschmitt Bf 109.** (KEY - Duncan Cubitt)

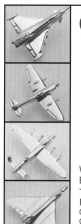

a skin material capable of resisting the high temperatures created by kinetic heat was now needed as the main structural material. Again the choice was RR.58 which, in a major development programme, now had to be modified and made available for the first time in sheet form.

Other important early developments in aluminium technology were the availability of extrusions in a great variety of light and strong sections, and the introduction of cladding in pure aluminium. Extrusions are made by forcing the metal through dies while it is hot, similar to toothpaste being squeezed from a tube. Alclad afforded effective protection to Duralamin or other base alloys against corrosion which can produce a serious loss of strength but with only a slight indication of deterioration; cladding also reduced the need for maintenance and gave rise to the profusion of aircraft in 'natural metal' finish.

Manufacturing processes

In the earliest days, aircraft were built by hand; even during the first war when machines were required in huge numbers they had to be fitted together manually. The advent of all-metal structures needed something better, and the amounts of jigging and tooling needed to assemble an individual aeroplane increased. A technique called split construction was introduced in the 1930s where several sub-assembly lines produced parts of a complete aircraft in a manageable size before they were brought together for final assembly.

After World War One the British Air Ministry provided just

Top left: **World War Two saw some quite astounding production totals emerge from the USA. This is the Consolidated B-24 Liberator and C-87 line at Fort Worth, Texas. Over 19,000 were built, despite being a highly complex design – proof, if any was needed, that the Americans pioneered the methods of aircraft mass production.** (KEY collection)
Top right: **The largest wooden aircraft ever to fly, indeed one of the biggest aircraft ever built, was the Hughes H-4 Hercules 'Spruce Goose' flying-boat.** (KEY collection)
Above right: **After World War Two Boeing was one of the best-placed manufacturers to make use of its mass production techniques. This 1960s image shows 727 and 737 airliners under assembly at Renton.** (Boeing)

enough work to keep the major design teams going but the limited number of orders available in the early 1930s meant that British companies worked on a small scale. Aeroplanes were still built hands-on but the job of working and shaping metal needed highly-skilled craftsmen. British designers tended to be less adaptable to 'designing' for ease of production and large numbers; for example a Mk.Vc Spitfire required 13,000 man hours to complete when the Messerschmitt Bf 109G needed just 4,000.

When the late 1930s expansion programme began, the industry had to make changes to adapt; manufacturing capacity was nowhere near sufficient but the 'shadow' factory scheme helped to improve this. However, World War Two brought an ever-growing need for more aircraft, a greater emphasis on improved production techniques and large production lines relying on a vast amount of

unskilled labour. In 1943 a Mission to America headed by Roy Fedden revealed a gap between US and UK manufacturing capability.

The achievements of the British aircraft industry in WW2 were remarkable but it was the Americans who fully developed the techniques of mass production, drawing on auto industry methods with moving production lines and specialised tools which reduced handwork to a minimum. Their ability to build huge numbers of aeroplanes in a very short time was impressive, although the US (and some British factories) did benefit from the efficiencies that accrue from long production runs. Britain produced a larger number of different aircraft types, suffered from limited manpower and, at times, a shortage of raw material imports, all of which helped to reduce the number of aeroplanes built compared to

Aluminium propeller blades and rotor hubs, and a pile of piston forgings, are seen in the heat treatment bay at High Duty Alloys Slough in 1937. (HDA via author)

The McDonnell Douglas developed AV-8B Harrier II was the first aircraft to see extensive use of carbon fibre composites, notably in the wings. (BAe)

Above: **Airbus Industrie also employs modern techniques in the manufacture of its range of airliners. Most single aisle production takes place at Hamburg with the A318, A319 and A321 all assembled on the same line, the A320 will join them shortly as production is moved from Toulouse.** (Airbus)

America. Between 1940 and 1944 the UK built 43,000 fighters, 12,000 heavy bombers and nearly 48,000 transports and trainers, the equivalent US figures were 48,000, 36,000 and 139,000 respectively. After the War, the fine-tuned American mass production system, with less man-hours per aircraft, proved ideal for the competitive manufacture of commercial aeroplanes and set the standards for others to follow.

Modern materials and methods

The design problem of keeping down weight was part alleviated during the 1950s by the arrival of the first titanium alloys. Titanium exhibited some impressive properties with strength approaching that of steel and weight not much more than aluminium, while its corrosion resistance at normal and moderate temperatures was outstanding (at 150°C titanium was also much stronger than aluminium). The one downside was the very high cost needed to separate the metal from its ore but the savings that were now possible in aircraft weight and fuel costs justified this expense.

American engineers were the first to recognise the metal's value. Douglas Aircraft ordered the first titanium for flight applications in 1949 for its X-3 Stiletto Mach 2 research aircraft, while North American used it on its F-100 Super Sabre fighter. British fighters, like the de Havilland Sea Vixen, used some of the first UK produced forgings but it was the Mach 2 English Electric Lightning that adopted the alloy in quantity. Titanium is used for high strength and heat resistant parts; it is not used

extensively on airframes, but the American Lockheed SR-71 could boast a fuselage built entirely in the material to allow it to fly at Mach 3.

The problem of distributing metal to the best advantage was solved by the use of integrally stiffened construction. This was made possible by advances in the production of thick aluminium plate which, before it is machined on automatic milling equipment, may be more than 5cm thick and anything up to 15m long and 4m wide. A thin skin with shaped stiffeners is formed out of the original solid and as much as 90% of the original plate can be machined away. Machining the skin and stringers together in one part also removes the need for many joints between components.

Today the manufacture of aircraft involves plenty of high technology. Carbon Fibre Composite (CFC), developed at RAE Farnborough in the mid-1960s, is probably the most valuable new structural material to become available in recent years and consists of very strong fibres set in a matrix of epoxy resin which is also mechanically and chemically protective. They offer outstanding stiffness and strength to weight (20% lighter than aluminium) but also give the chance to design a structure and its material at the same time, which benefits the aerodynamics and performance of the aircraft.

CFC is expensive but the development of the AV-8B Harrier II out of the original Harrier saw its first major application, although earlier types had tested smaller parts. The General Dynamics YF-16 fighter combined a mix of 'old' and 'new' materials – the upper and lower wing and mid-fuselage skins all employed conventional aluminium

alloys, while the vertical fin box skin was made of graphite-epoxy laminate, and the fin leading edge, the rudder and horizontal tail planes used graphite epoxy sandwich.

The metal industry's competitor to carbon fibre is aluminium-lithium which is about 10% lighter and 10% stiffer than conventional alloys and has high strength. The Eurofighter Typhoon uses forgings and thick plate which, combined with CFCs, has saved around 10 to 12% of the structure weight. These new materials are matched by advanced development and construction technology; for many years computers have been used to aid design and manufacture (CADCAM) while modern tooling employs lasers to ensure that parts are lined up accurately in their jigs.

The century of powered flight has seen the design of many superb aeroplanes. One of the reasons for their tremendous success in both civil and military fields has been the equally remarkable developments in materials and construction techniques.

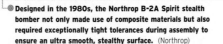

The early 1960s saw the construction of the Mach 3 Lockheed SR-71 Blackbird, the first aircraft to be built largely from Titanium. (Lockheed)

Designed in the 1980s, the Northrop B-2A Spirit stealth bomber not only made use of composite materials but also required exceptionally tight tolerances during assembly to ensure an ultra smooth, stealthy surface. (Northrop)

Modular construction, computer aided design, laser alignment, composite materials and exceptional stealth – the ultimate fighter under production, the Lockheed Martin/Boeing F-22 Raptor. (Lockheed Martin)

1950-59

1. Jet-powered Wing

The Northrop YRB-49A jet-powered flying wing prototype bomber makes its maiden flight on May 4, 1950. The USAF opts for the Convair B-36 and the revolutionary B-49 was dropped. (KEY collection)

2. Super Connie

Lockheed flies the stretched L-1049 version of its classic Constellation airliner on October 13, 1950. The increased length, from 95ft 2in to 117ft 7in, allows for up to 92 passengers to be carried. This example is one of a handful still airworthy. (KEY - Duncan Cubitt)

3. First Turboprop Service

On July 29, 1950, this aircraft, Vickers Viscount G-AHRF operated by BEA, performs the world's first turboprop-powered commercial flight on a scheduled service from London Northolt to Paris. (KEY collection)

4. Panther Strikes

The US Navy's Grumman F9F Panther is the first American jet fighter to be involved in air-to-air combat when the type downs two Yaks over Korea on July 3, 1950. (KEY collection)

5. Medevac Helo

During late 1950 the Sikorsky HO3S (S-51) becomes the first helicopter to be actively involved in medical evacuation and the rescue of downed pilots during operations in Korea. (US National Archives)

6. First V Bomber

The first of the RAF's three V-Bomber types, the Vickers Valiant, makes its maiden flight from Wisley on May 18, 1951. (Gordon Swanborough collection)

7. First Jet Trainer

The Fokker S.14 makes its maiden flight on May 19, 1951. It is the first jet aircraft from the Dutch company and it is also the world's first aircraft designed as a dedicated jet trainer. (KEY collection)

8. Hawker Classic

July 20, 1951, witnesses the maiden flight of the sleek Hawker P.1067, the prototype Hunter, designed by Sydney Camm. (KEY collection)

9. Adjustable Wings

Making use of German wartime research, the NACA-operated Bell X-5 performs the first ever in-flight variable wing sweep over Edwards AFB, California, on July 27, 1951. The aircraft can adjust its wings between 20 and 60 degrees, as illustrated here. (NASA)

10. Twin Boom Beauty

Maintaining its philosophy of twin-boom jet fighter design, de Havilland flies the prototype DH.110 Sea Vixen for the first time on September 26, 1951. The twin-engined naval fighter is one of the most powerful of its era. (KEY collection)

SIGNIFICANT DATES

MARCH 22, 1950: The RAF takes delivery of the first four of 70 Boeing B-29 Superfortresses, which it calls the Washington.

MAY 17, 1950: Transcontinental & Western Air retains its TWA initials but changes its name to Trans World Airlines to more appropriately reflect the growth in the company's international business.

JUNE 1, 1950: BEA introduces the world's first regular passenger helicopter service between Liverpool and Cardiff using Westland/Sikorsky S-51 helicopters.

JUNE 1, 1950: Frontier Airlines is formed by merging Arizona Airways and Challenger Airlines, thus making it one of the USA's largest regional carriers.

JUNE 25, 1950: The Korean War starts and becomes the first conflict to witness extensive jet combat.

SEPTEMBER 22, 1950: The first transatlantic jet flight, assisted by air-to-air refuelling, is completed by two USAF F-84E Thunderjets when they land at Limestone, Maine, after a ten-hour flight from Manston, Kent.

OCTOBER 1, 1950: The Danish Air Arm becomes the Kongelige Dansk Flyvevåbnet (Royal Danish Air Force).

NOVEMBER 8, 1950: The first ever air-to-air kill by a jet fighter over another jet fighter is achieved by Lt Russell J Brown when he shot down a MiG-15 in his F-80C Shooting Star.

FEBRUARY 5, 1951: The USA and Canada reveal that they are planning a distant early-warning (DEW) system for the North American continent to provide adequate notice of any Soviet attack. The work was completed by General Electric during October.

FEBRUARY 21, 1951: An English Electric Canberra B.2 is the first jet aircraft to fly non-stop and unrefuelled across the North Atlantic. The 2,072 mile (3,335km) flight from Aldergrove, Northern Ireland to Gander,

11. Delta Fighter

The world's first delta wing, twin-engine jet fighter, the Gloster Javelin, makes its first flight from Moreton Valance on November 26, 1951. It is set to become the primary interceptor fighter for the RAF until the advent of the Mach 2 English Electric Lightning during the 1960s.
(Gordon Swanborough collection)

12. Double Rotor

The maiden flight of the Bristol Type 173, Britain's first twin-engined, twin-rotor helicopter takes place at Filton on January 3, 1952. It was subsequently developed into the Belvedere for the RAF and was to se extensive service in the Far East.
(KEY collection)

13. B-52 Flies

The prototype eight-engine Boeing YB-52 makes its maiden flight on April 15, three days before the Convair YB-60 against which it is competing for a lucrative USAF strategic bomber contract. (KEY collection)

14. Monster Convair

The massive Convair YB-60 bomber prototype, a jet-powered derivative of the B-36 Peacemaker, featured eight J57 engines and a swept wing and tail. It first flies on April 18, 1952, but the USAF bomber contract was awarded to the Boeing B-52. (KEY collection)

1950-59

Newfoundland, is accomplished in 4 hours 37 minutes.

APRIL 18, 1951: A deal is reached for the licensed production by the Glenn L Martin Company of the English Electric Canberra bomber. Designated B-57 by the USAF, it is the first overseas design to be accepted by the Americans since 1945.

AUGUST 1, 1951: Japan Air Lines is formed with the help of aircraft and crews loaned by American carrier Northwest Airlines.

This is due to restrictions placed on Japanese pilots and aircraft implemented at the end of World War Two.

AUGUST 15, 1951: Two BEA DC-3s fitted with Rolls-Royce Dart turboprop engines begin the world's first turboprop cargo service, flying from Northolt, London to Hanover, Germany.

AUGUST 22, 1951: The Fleet Air Arm introduces the Supermarine Attacker into service with 800 Squadron. The aircraft is

the service's first jet fighter.

SEPTEMBER 21, 1951: For the first time helicopters are used to infiltrate troops into enemy territory when US Marine Corps Sikorsky HRS-1s are used to carry personnel to a strategic location near Kansong, Korea.

OCTOBER 3, 1951: The US Navy commissions its first anti-submarine warfare (ASW) helicopter squadron (HS-1) at NAS Key West, Florida. Many more squadrons are to be added in the coming years.

NOVEMBER 27, 1951: The first interception of an airborne target, in this case a drone aircraft, by a missile takes place at the White Sands test range.

DECEMBER 5, 1951: Eleven key airlines reach an agreement to introduce tourist (economy) class seats to transatlantic services, thus paving the way for a dramatic increase in passenger numbers.

DECEMBER 10, 1951: The first turbine-powered helicopter, the Kaman K-225,

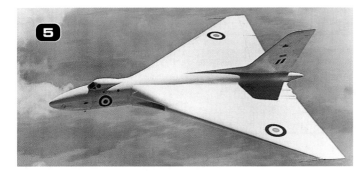

1950-59

1. Russian *Badger*

The Tupolev Tu-88 prototype, the forerunner of the Tu-16 *Badger*, makes its first flight on April 27, 1952. This Tu-16K-26 represents the type at the splendid Monino museum in Moscow, this variant being able to carry the large KSR-5P/K-26 missile.
(David Stephens collection)

2. Butterfly-Tailed Trainer

The diminutive and attractive butterfly-tailed Fouga CM170 Magister makes its first flight on July 23, 1952. The aircraft is to form the backbone of French Air Force jet training and is also popular on the export market. (KEY collection)

3. Britannia Takes Off

The turboprop Bristol Britannia prototype (G-ALBO) makes its maiden flight from Filton on August 16. It is seen here being rolled out prior to the first flight. (KEY collection)

4. Princess Flies

The world's largest all-metal aircraft, the ten-engined Saunders-Roe S.R. 45 Princess flying-boat makes its first flight from Cowes, Isle of Wight, on August 21, 1952. An ever-increasing price tag and the arrival of the jet transport, spells the end for the commercial flying-boat. (KEY collection)

5. Vulcan soars

August 30, 1952, sees the first flight of the prototype delta-wing Avro 698 Vulcan bomber

(VX770). It joins the Vickers Valiant, becoming the second of the three V-bombers destined for the RAF to take to the air. The third, the Handley Page Victor, makes up the trio when it performs its maiden flight on December 24. (KEY collection)

6. Flying Dart

On October 20, 1952, the Douglas X-3 Stiletto research aircraft makes its first flight at Edwards AFB, California, though it is significantly underpowered and never achieves the Mach 2 speed it was designed for. (NASA)

SIGNIFICANT DATES

makes its maiden flight at Windsor Locks, Connecticut. The move away from piston engines is set to revolutionise rotary flight.

JANUARY 5, 1952: Pan American introduces its first cargo-only transatlantic service, using Douglas DC-6 aircraft.

JANUARY 22, 1952: The de Havilland Comet 1 becomes the first turbojet-powered airliner to receive a certificate of airworthiness.

MARCH 18, 1952: The longest jet flight is completed by a pair of USAF F-84 Thunderjets when they arrive at Neubiberg, Germany, after a 2,800 mile (4,506km), 4 hour 48 minute flight from the USA.

APRIL 30, 1952: The US Navy reveals that after successful trials aboard HMS *Perseus* it will install steam catapults on its own carrier fleet.

MAY 1, 1952: Tourist class is introduced to scheduled transatlantic flights by BOAC, TWA and Air France.

MAY 3, 1952: The first landing by an aircraft at the North Pole is achieved by a ski-equipped USAF C-47.

JUNE 17, 1952: The world's largest non-rigid airship, the ZPN-1, is delivered to the US Navy at Lakehurst, New Jersey. The craft measures 324ft (98.7m) long and has a maximum diameter of 35ft (10.6m)

JULY 1, 1952: The Fôrça Aérea Portuguesa (Portuguese Air Force) is created following the amalgamation of the Portuguese Arma da Aeronáutica and the Aviacão Maritima.

JULY 29, 1952: A USAF B-45 Tornado light bomber completes the first non-stop transpacific flight by a jet aircraft, flying between Elmendorf AFB, Alaska and Yokota AB, Japan, with the aid of two in-flight refuellings.

AUGUST 9, 1952: A Royal Navy Hawker Sea Fury FB.11 flown by Lt Peter Carmichael scores the first British kill during the Korean War – downing a MiG-15.

Mar 2, 1952: Piper PA-23 **Apr 11, 1952:** Piasecki H-21 **Apr 27, 1952:** Tupolev Tu-88/Tu-16 **July 23, 1952:** Fouga CM170 **Aug 16, 1952:** Bristol Britannia **Aug 30, 1952:** Avro Vulcan **Oct 16, 1952:** Sud-Ouest SO 4050

1950-59

7. Powerful *Bear*
The Soviet Tupolev Tu-95 *Bear* makes its first flight on November 12, 1952. Driven by the most powerful turboprop engines in the world, the *Bear* is designed as a long-range strategic bomber and reconnaissance aircraft. (Anatoly Andreyev)

8. Sleek twin
The twin-engine Cessna 310 takes to the air for the first time at Wichita, Kansas, on January 3, 1953. Designed to compete in the lucrative corporate transport market, the fast six-seater is set to become very popular. (KEY collection)

9. Sea Jet
The strange and exhilarating sight of a jet aircraft taking of from water is witnessed for the first time on April 9, 1953, when the Convair XF2Y-1 Sea Dart makes its first flight. (KEY collection)

10. Super Sabre
North American successfully flies the YF-100 Super Sabre prototype for the first time on May 25, 1953 - it is the first jet fighter able to sustain level supersonic flight. Production examples are fitted with an enlarged tail fin to improve lateral stability. (KEY collection)

11. Flying Bedstead
Officially called the Rolls-Royce Thrust Measuring Rig (TMR), this extraordinary device is designed to study the practicalities of vertical jet lift. Powered by a pair of Nene turbojets, it makes its first (tethered) flight on July 3, 1953, and provides valuable research that will lead to the Harrier jump jet. (Gordon Swanborough collection)

AUGUST 11, 1952: BOAC commences weekly London-Colombo services with the Comet 1 jet airliner.

AUGUST 13, 1952: The Boeing B-52 is selected to fulfil the USAF's long-range strategic bomber requirement and is ordered into production. Including the two prototypes some 744 are built.

SEPTEMBER 18, 1952: Denmark and the USA announce that a massive air base has been completed at Thule, Greenland.

OCTOBER 14, 1952: BOAC introduces the Comet 1 on its London to Singapore route and halves the journey time.

OCTOBER 16, 1952: Australian carrier Qantas commences flights to Europe by extending it existing route to Cairo on to Frankfurt via Beirut.

NOVEMBER 19, 1952: The first unscheduled flights across the northern Polar regions are made by Scandinavian Airline System (SAS) Douglas DC-6s. Scheduled services did not begin until 1954 and it is not long before such flights become routine.

FEBRUARY 5, 1953: Royal Navy helicopters rescue over 600 people from severe flooding in the Netherlands - this is the first major use of the helicopter in a humanitarian relief role.

MARCH 27, 1953: The Koninklijke Luchtmacht (Royal Netherlands Air Force) is officially formed as a service in its own right.

MAY 2, 1953: Exactly one year after entering service, a BOAC Comet 1 crashes near Calcutta, India, killing 43 passengers and crew. This is the first of a series of accidents that are set to put the British jet airliner back several years, leaving the way open to competition from the USA.

MAY 18, 1953: American aviatrix Jacqueline Cochran becomes the first woman to fly faster than the speed of sound in a Canadian-built F-86E Sabre.

1950-59

1. Mother hen

It is revealed on August 25, 1953, that the giant B-36, in GRB-36J form, and its associated GRF-84K 'chick' can now offer the USAF more flexibility in reconnaissance missions with the small fighter able to be carried, launched and recaptured on long-range missions. (KEY collection)

2. Delta Dagger

Convair's exotic and fast F-102 Delta Dagger prototype makes its first flight on October 24, 1953. This early development YF-102A (53-1787) is currently preserved at the Louisiana Military Museum, Jackson Barracks, New Orleans.
(KEY - Duncan Cubitt)

3. Ultimate Flying-Boat

The huge turboprop-powered Convair R3Y-1 Tradewind flying-boat makes its first flight on April 18, 1950. It is one of the most impressive flying-boats ever built, but sadly the eleven examples enjoy only a brief service life with the US Navy. (KEY collection)

4. Mach 2 Missile

The incredible Mach 2 Lockheed XF-104 Starfighter prototype performs its official maiden flight on March 4, 1954, having achieved a brief hop during fast taxi trials on February 28. (Lockheed)

5. Helo Revolution

The Sikorsky S.58 makes its maiden flight on March 8, 1954. It is destined to be a huge success for the company, supplying the US Military and being exported to many countries as well as being built under licence in France and the UK (as the Wessex). (KEY - Duncan Cubitt)

6. Timeless Skyhawk

The prototype Douglas XA4D-1 Skyhawk takes to the air for the first time on June 22, 1954. Almost 3,000 A-4s are built and these serve with many nations as well as the US Navy/Marine Corps. (Boeing)

7. Jet Provost

The RAF's new jet trainer, the Hunting Jet Provost, makes its first flight on June 16, 1954, and is better placed to train pilots who will progress to jet fighter and attack types. (Gordon Swanborough collection)

SIGNIFICANT DATES

June 18, 1953: A USAF C-124 Globemaster II crashes while taking off from Tachikawa air base near Tokyo killing all 129 people on board - this is the first air crash to claim over 100 fatalities.

July 8, 1953: The USA's first scheduled helicopter passenger services are introduced by New York Airways between Idlewild, LaGuardia and Newark.

August 1, 1953: Indian Airlines is formed as a state-owned carrier when the Indian government buys out eight smaller, privately owned airlines.

August 26, 1953: Air France commences its first jet airliner operations by launching a regular Comet 1 service from Paris to Rome and Beirut.

September 1, 1953: The first air-to-air refuelling between two jet aircraft is performed by a USAF KB-47B tanker and a standard B-47 bomber.

September 11, 1953: A Sidewinder air-to-air infrared guided missile achieves its first successful aerial interception when it destroys a Grumman Hellcat drone during a test at the US Navy's China Lake weapons range. Through significant development, the AIM-9 Sidewinder is still in use today.

October 20, 1953: The first scheduled non-stop transcontinental flight across the USA is made by a TWA Super Constellation between Los Angeles and New York.

December 20, 1953: German airline Lufthansa is allowed to fly again following the relaxation of restraints imposed by the Allies at the end of World War Two.

December 29, 1953: Official figures released by the International Civil Aviation Organisation (ICAO) show that in 1953 over 50 million passengers were flown worldwide, excluding China and the USSR.

April 1, 1954: A photo reconnaissance Spitfire based in Malaya flies the last

May 18, 1953: Douglas DC-7   May 25 1953: NA F-100A   June 19, 1953: Piaggio P.149   Jan 5, 1954: MiG-19 (SM-9/1)   Mar 4, 1954: Lockheed F-104   Mar 8, 1954: Sikorsky S.58   June 22, 1954: Douglas A4D   June 26: Hunting Jet Provost

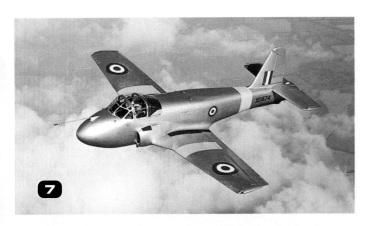

8. Revolutionary Jet Transport

Little is it realised at the time, but when the Boeing Model 367-80 makes its first flight at Boeing Field on July 15, 1954, history is being written. The aircraft is the prototype for a refuelling tanker (KC-135) for the USAF, but it also forms the basis of a new commercial airliner, the Boeing 707. (Boeing)

9. Lightning Prototype

The forerunner of the Lightning interceptor, the English Electric P.I.A makes its first flight on August 4, 1954. (KEY collection)

10. Herculean Transport

Unquestionably the most versatile airlifter ever built, the Lockheed YC-130 makes its maiden flight on August 23, 1954. Powered by four Allison T56 turboprops, the high wing design has a large cargo hold and can operate from short, austere airstrips. (KEY collection)

11. Tweety Bird Trainer

The XT-37 prototype makes its first flight on October 12, 1954. Affectionately known as the 'Tweet', the tiny Cessna T-37 jet trainer is still used extensively by the USAF

12. Classic Cessna

Set to become one of the most successful four-seat general aviation aircraft ever built, the Cessna 172 makes its maiden flight during 1955. (KEY collection)

today and some 1,268 have been built, many for the export market. (KEY collection)

13. Crusader Power

The mighty Vought XF8U-1 Crusader prototype completes its first flight on March 25, 1955. The aircraft, in F-8 production form and capable of Mach 1.8, proves to be a popular fighter with the US Navy. Additionally, it sees service with the Philippines Air Force and the French Navy. (KEY collection)

---

frontline RAF sortie by the classic Supermarine type.

APRIL 1, 1954: The US Air Force Academy is established at Lowry AFB, Colorado.

APRIL 12, 1954: Following another Comet crash on April 8 near Naples, the aircraft's airworthiness certificate is revoked.

JUNE 7, 1954: Pakistan International Airlines (PIA) commences international flights with three Lockheed Super Constellation aircraft. The airline is officially established on January 10, 1955, and remains the country's national carrier to this day.

AUGUST 26, 1954: A new altitude record of 90,440ft (27,566m) is set by Major Arthur Murray in the Bell X-1A over the Mojave Desert.

OCTOBER 17, 1954: The Sikorsky XH-39 helicopter establishes a new altitude record for rotary aircraft of 24,500ft (7,467m)

JANUARY 1955: The RAF's first V-bomber squadron, No 138 flying the Vickers Valiant B.1, is established at RAF Gaydon.

APRIL 17, 1955: The first commercial flight, a BEA service to Amsterdam, departs from the new London Airport Central at Heathrow. Unbeknown to those present, the new facility is set to become the world's busiest international airport.

MAY 27, 1955: French manufacturer Sud-Est flies its new SE 210 Caravelle jet airliner

for the first time. The aircraft differs from other jets by having its two Rolls-Royce Avon engines mounted at the rear of the fuselage.

JUNE 6, 1955: A new altitude record for helicopters of 26,934ft (8,209m) is set by a Sud-Est SE 313 Alouette II being flown by Jean Boulet.

JUNE 15, 1955: Russia enters the jet airliner business with the first flight of the Tupolev Tu-104.

1950-59

1. Fastest Flying-Boat

The amazing jet-powered, swept-wing Martin XP6M Sea Master flying-boat makes its maiden flight on July 14, 1955. Primarily designed for mine laying duties, the Sea Master remains the only supersonic (in a dive) flying-boat ever built. (US National Archives)

2. Dragon Lady

One of the most significant reconnaissance aircraft, the Lockheed U-2, makes its first flight from the top secret and very remote Groom Lake facility on August 4, 1955. (Lockheed)

3. Thud Flies

On October 22, 1955, the huge Republic YF-105A Thunderchief prototype lifts into the air for the first time. Best remembered for its strike role in the Vietnam War, the 'Thud' is the largest single-engine fighter/attack aircraft used by the USAF. (KEY collection)

4. Slick Saab

What is set to become one of the most recognisable shapes in Scandinavian skies takes to the air for the first time on October 25, 1955 - the Saab J-35 Draken. (KEY collection)

5. Fabulous Fokker

The prototype Fokker F27 Friendship first flies on November 24, 1955, and is set to see extensive use with airlines and the military, as illustrated here. (KEY collection)

6. Classic MiG

One of the most numerous jet fighters ever built, the MiG-21 *Fishbed*, illustrated here by a pair from the Hungarian Air Force, is still in front line use around the world. The development Ye-5 first flew on January 9, 1956. (I Toperczer)

7. Scimitar Flies

The Royal Navy's first nuclear capable strike aircraft, the Supermarine Scimitar, makes its first flight on January 19, 1956. (KEY collection)

8. Transport Giant

The latest military airlifter from the Douglas Company, the huge turboprop-powered C-133 Cargomaster, flies for the first time on April 23, 1956. Its high wing and blister housed multi-wheel undercarriage permits a large unhindered interior allowing the carriage of bulky loads. This example is preserved at the Pima County Air & Space Museum, Arizona. (KEY - Dave Allport)

9. NATO's Fighter

On August 9, 1956, the Fiat G91 makes its first flight. The design had won a 1954 NATO competition for a new light fighter/strike aircraft. (KEY collection)

10. Kaman Twin Rotor

Kaman's unique intermeshing rotor system makes its products easily identifiable. One of the most famous, the H-43 Huskie, first flies on September 27, 1956. (David Stephens collection)

SIGNIFICANT DATES

JUNE 16, 1955: Capital Airlines takes delivery of its first Vickers Viscount turboprop airliner, the first for any American airline.

AUGUST 1, 1955: Research into zero gravity begins in the USA using Lockheed T-33 jet training aircraft.

OCTOBER 13, 1955: Pan Am places the largest airliner order to date, worth $269 million, to buy 20 Boeing 707s and 25 Douglas DC-8 jet airliners. Neither aircraft has yet flown but the airline is committed to the idea that jet airliners are the way ahead - it is soon to be proved emphatically correct.

NOVEMBER 14, 1955: The first instance of an airliner being destroyed by a bomb planted in luggage befalls a United Air Lines DC-6B shortly after take-off from Denver, Colorado.

FEBRUARY 27, 1956: It is revealed by the UK Ministry of Transport that British airports have handled more than 5 million passengers during the previous 12 months.

MARCH 10, 1956: The Fairey Delta 2 high-speed research aircraft smashes the world speed record during two runs over a measured course with a speed of 1,131mph (1,820km/h). The previous record was set by an American F-100C in 1955 at 822mph (1,322km/h).

JULY 4, 1956: The first over flight of the Soviet Union by a CIA-operated Lockheed U-2 takes place with a flight over Moscow and Leningrad, originating from Wiesbaden AB in West Germany.

JULY 7, 1956: The Comet 2, the first jet transport aircraft to serve a military air arm, enters service with the RAF's Transport Command at RAF Lyneham. The aircraft incorporates design changes following investigations into the previous Comet 1 crashes.

AUGUST 31, 1956: The first production Boeing KC-135A refuelling tanker makes its maiden flight. The type remains the backbone of the USAF's refuelling fleet to this day.

Mar 25, 1955: Vought F8U   Apr 8, 1955: Dornier Do 27   May 27, 1955: Sud-Est SE 210 Caravelle   June 15, 1955: Tupolev Tu-104   June 25, 1955: Dassault MD.550 Mirage   June 25, 1955: Scottish Aviation Twin Pioneer

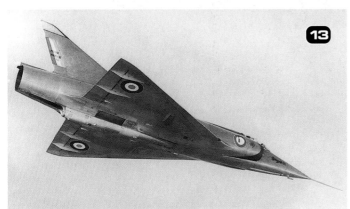

11. Bell *Huey*

On October 22, 1956, the Bell XH-40, prototype of the UH-1 Iroquois, makes its maiden flight. Better known as the 'Huey' during its service in the Vietnam War, the type is built in larger numbers than any other helicopter. (KEY collection)

12. Hustler!

Powered by four afterburning General Electric J79 turbojets, the Convair XB-58 Hustler supersonic bomber makes its first flight at Fort Worth, Texas, on November 11, 1956. (KEY collection)

13. Mirage Delta

Following the flight of the original Dassault M.D.550 Mirage prototype on June 25, 1955, the French company presents the true delta wing Mirage III on November 17, 1956. (KEY collection)

14. Ultimate Dart

The prototype Convair F-106A Delta Dart first flies on December 26, 1956. More advanced than the F-102, it goes on to serve the USAF until 1988 after which many were modified for target drone use. (KEY collection)

15. Vertical Short

On April 2, 1957, the Short SC.1 delta wing research aircraft makes its first flight. It is equipped with four Rolls-Royce RB.108 engines for vertical take-off and another for horizontal propulsion. (Gordon Swanborough collection)

1950-59

September 7, 1956: Test pilot Iven Kincheloe sets a new altitude record of 126,200ft (38,466m) in the Bell X-2 and is hailed as the first 'spaceman'.

September 27, 1956: Having established a new absolute speed record of Mach 3.2, the Bell X-2 research aircraft loses control, killing test pilot Milburn 'Mel' Apt.

October 24, 1956: British carrier BOAC orders 15 Boeing 707 jet airliners to offset delays with the de Havilland Comet 4.

January 18, 1957: In a display of global power, three USAF B-52Bs of the 93rd BW fly around the world to demonstrate their global bombing capability. The flight lasts 45 hours and 19 minutes, covers 24,325 miles (39,146km) and requires just three aerial refuellings.

February 1, 1957: BOAC introduces the Bristol Britannia on its route from London to Johannesburg, making it the first long-haul turboprop.

February 17, 1957: Bell's X-14 experimental aircraft, the first ever that is capable of performing vertical take off and landing (VTOL), makes its first controlled hover.

April 6, 1957: Greek carrier Olympic Airways is formed.

May 17, 1957: Westland flies the prototype Wessex helicopter for the first time. It is basically a Sikorsky S-58 but is powered by a Napier Gazelle turboshaft engine.

July 1, 1957: The Lockheed L-1649A Starliner enters service with TWA on the New York-Paris route. This is followed on October 2 by a direct Los Angeles-London flight lasting 23 hours 19 minutes non-stop.

July 16, 1957: US Major John Glenn establishes a new coast-to-coast speed record in a Vought F8U-1P reconnaissance Crusader. The 2,460 mile (3,958km) flight takes 3 hours, 23 minutes and 50 seconds at an average speed of 723mph (1,163km/h)

1950-59

1. Two-seat Cessna
Cessna flies its new model 150 two-seat general aviation light aircraft in September 1957. (KEY collection)

2. JetStar
The Lockheed CL-369 JetStar makes its first flight on September 4, 1957. It is designed to meet a USAF requirement for a fast light transport but predominantly finds a niche in the commercial market and is America's first executive jet.
(KEY - Malcolm English)

3. Huge Hook
On making its maiden flight in September 1957, the Mil Mi-6 *Hook* becomes the world's largest and fastest helicopter. The

shoulder-mounted wings give added lift in the cruise and can be detached when the helicopter is carrying out for heavy lift duties. (KEY collection)

4. Revolutionary Rotodyne
The Fairey Rotodyne is designed to combine the practicality of a helicopter with the speed of a conventional aircraft and provide direct city centre to city centre flights. Its first flight is on November 6, 1957, but the project is cancelled in 1960. (KEY collection)

5. Lockheed Electra
Design work on the Lockheed L-188 Electra began in 1954 and the first example makes its first flight on December 6, 1957. Powered by four Allison turboprops, the aircraft achieves moderate success, many eventually being converted to freighters. (Lockheed)

6. Boeing's Gamble
The first true Boeing 707, a 707-120 for Pan Am, makes its maiden flight on December 21, 1957, at Boeing Field, Seattle, Washington. Boeing had invested a huge

amount of money in the aircraft and is set be rewarded handsomely. (Boeing)

7. Antonov's Winner
The turboprop Antonov An-12 transport aircraft makes its first flight in 1958 and is destined to be a huge success, particularly among the communist nations. Today it remains in both military and commercial use, as shown by this example at Sharjah in May 1999. (KEY - Dave Allport)

8. Blackburn's Brick
Affectionately known as the 'Brick', the Blackburn B-103 Buccaneer makes its maiden flight on April 30, 1958. It is the world's first two-seat, low-level maritime strike aircraft, designed to penetrate hostile airspace beneath enemy radar cover. (KEY collection)

SIGNIFICANT DATES

AUGUST 28, 1957: Whilst performing test flights for the Napier Double Scorpion rocket engine, an English Electric Canberra sets a new altitude record of 70,308ft (21,429m).

SEPTEMBER 30, 1957: Austrian Airlines is officially formed by combining the assets of Air Austria and Austrian Airways – although neither had actually commenced operations.

OCTOBER 4, 1957: Russia sends the world's first satellite into space, called Sputnik (Fellow Traveller), using an Intercontinental

Ballistic Missile (ICBM) as the launch vehicle.

DECEMBER 3, 1957: The minuscule Tipsy Nipper makes its first flight. Designed to be Europe's 'people's aeroplane', the small aircraft finds favour among flying clubs and is designed to be assembled from kits.

FEBRUARY 1, 1958: Hot on the heels of the Russian Sputnik, America launches its first satellite, Explorer I from Cape Canaveral using a Jupiter-C rocket.

APRIL 8, 1958: A USAF KC-135A Stratotanker sets a new non-stop, straight line distance record of 10,229 miles (16,461km) during an 18 hour 48 minute flight between Tokyo and Lajes Field in the Azores.

APRIL 27, 1958: The new de Havilland Comet 4, modified after the earlier crashes involving the original Comet 1, makes its first flight from Hatfield. Despite a number of orders, the lead in the jet airliner business has already gone to the Americans and the Comet never fulfils its promise.

MAY 7, 1958: Altitude records continue to tumble, as Major H C Johnson reaches 91,243ft (27,811m) in a Lockheed F-104A.

MAY 30, 1958: The jet-powered Douglas DC-8, rival to the Boeing 707 jetliner, makes a flawless first flight from Long Beach Airport, California.

JUNE 9, 1958: London gets another airport when Her Majesty Queen Elizabeth II opens the new Gatwick Airport, some 35 miles (56km) south of London.

Apr 23, 1956: Douglas C-133A   May 24, 1956: Piper PA-24   July 24, 1956: Dassault Etendard IV   Aug 9, 1956: Fiat G.91   Aug 31, 1956: Boeing KC-135A   Sept 27, 1956: Kaman H-43   Nov 11, 1956: Convair B-58   Dec 26, 1956: Convair F-106A

9. Jet Legend
One of the most successful and potent Western jet fighters ever built makes its first flight on May 27, 1958, the McDonnell YF4H-1 Phantom II. Eventually 5,195 are built and serve with dozens of air arms, many still do. (KEY - Duncan Cubitt)

10. Naked Helicopter
June 15, 1958, witnesses the first flight of the Westland Westminster, a transport helicopter research aircraft. Early flights are accomplished with most of the bodywork panels removed, when added later they gave it a particularly streamlined appearance. (KEY collection)

11. Corporate Grumman
The first of what is to become a hugely successful range of executive/business aircraft, the Grumman G-159 Gulfstream I, makes its first flight on August 14, 1958. Powered by two Rolls-Royce Dart turboprops, the Gulfstream I can seat up to 14 passengers in a corporate layout. (KEY collection)

12. Carrier Monster
Arguably the most potent aircraft to serve aboard a Western aircraft carrier, the North American A-5 Vigilante was designed as a high-speed, all-weather attack aircraft able to deliver a nuclear device. The YA3J-1 prototype first flies on August 31, 1958, but in the event, the type spends most of its career as a reconnaissance asset, designated the RA-5C. (KEY collection)

13. Sabreliner Soars
The prototype North American NA-265 (T-39A) Sabreliner makes its maiden flight on September 16, 1958. The aircraft is to see great success in both military and civil markets and is still in widespread use. (KEY - Chris Penney)

14. Argosy Freighter
Armstrong Whitworth flies the prototype AW 650 Argosy for the first time on January 8, 1959. Used by the RAF and a number of civilian operators, including Australian freight carrier IPEC, the Argosy has an indifferent career, despite being a very practical design. (Gordon Swanborough collection)

15. Rapid Convair
The sleek Convair 880 performs its first flight on January 27, 1959, and is the world's fastest airliner with a maximum speed of Mach 0.89. Despite its higher speed, it fails to attract airline orders of the same scale as the Boeing 707 and Douglas DC-8. (KEY collection)

1950-59

JULY 4, 1958: Ghana Airways is established jointly by the government of Ghana and BOAC.

JULY 30, 1958: The short take-off and landing (STOL) capable de Havilland Canada DHC-4 makes its maiden flight. Eventually 307 are built, and serve with many air arms and also civilian operators, as they are able to carry cargo, troops and equipment into seemingly inaccessible landing strips.

SEPTEMBER 7, 1958: An unmanned Lockheed X-7 high-speed test vehicle achieves Mach 4 following an air launch from a modified B-50 bomber.

SEPTEMBER 30, 1958: UK commercial flying-boat services cease when Aquila Airways terminates its Southampton to Madeira service.

OCTOBER 1, 1958: A new organisation, the National Aeronautics and Space Administration (NASA), is formally established to oversee all US non-military space programmes, as well as absorb the duties of its predecessor, NACA.

OCTOBER 4, 1958: The first transatlantic jet airliner services are introduced by BOAC between London and New York with the new Comet 4.

OCTOBER 27, 1958: The Boeing 707 flies its first revenue earning flight when Pan Am 707-121 N711PA performs the carrier's first transatlantic jet service between New York and Paris.

OCTOBER 31, 1958: The US Federal Aviation Agency (FAA - renamed Federal Aviation Administration on April 1, 1967) is formed to regulate all commercial and military aviation across the USA.

FEBRUARY 12, 1959: Such is the pace of new aircraft development that after a very short service career, the last Convair B-36 Peacemaker is retired by the USAF. Sent for desert storage, the giant Convair bomber provides good pickings for the scrapman and only a handful survive today.

1950-59

1. High-Performance Helo
The Sud Aviation SE 3160 Alouette III first flies on February 28, 1959, and immediately astounds everyone with its exceptional high-altitude performance. Production exceeds 1,800, including licensed production, and the type serves with countries around the globe. (KEY collection)

2. Sea King
The Sikorsky S-61, better known as the Sea King or Jolly Green Giant, first flies on March 11, 1959, and becomes one of the most successful helicopters ever built. Both Sikorsky and licensed-built examples still serve dozens of air arms and civilian operators, including the Royal Malaysian Air Force (illustrated). (KEY - Alan Warnes)

3. STOL Grumman
Not the most beautiful aircraft but well equipped for its role as a battlefield surveillance platform, the Grumman OV-1 Mohawk completes its first flight on April 14, 1959. (KEY - Duncan Cubitt)

4. Magic Mirage
First flown on June 17, 1959, the Dassault Mirage IV is designed to carry the French nuclear deterrent. Today a handful of the type remain in service in the photo reconnaissance role, thus the chance of witnessing the amazing rocket-assisted take-off is slim. (KEY collection)

5. Freedom Fighter
Northrop's F-5 Freedom Fighter is developed alongside the T-38 Talon two-seat trainer (right) and made its first flight on July 30, 1959. Some 2,622 are eventually built and equip many air forces around the world, some are still in frontline service. (KEY collection)

6. Patrol expert
The Lockheed P-3 Orion, which makes its first flight on November 25, 1959, is still dominating the anti-submarine warfare and maritime patrol role, serving as it does with the US Navy and many other countries. Here a P-3C from VP-62 flies over its home base at NAS Jacksonville, Florida. (KEY collection)

SIGNIFICANT DATES

APRIL 5, 1959: Czechoslovakia's first indigenous jet aircraft, the Aero L-29 Delfin two-seat trainer makes its first flight. It is the first of a series of successful light jets from the company.

APRIL 6, 1959: Seven men are selected to become America's first astronauts. NASA picks them from the military and they are Virgil Grissom, Leroy Gordon Cooper, Donald Slayton (all USAF), Alan Shepard, Walter Schirra, Malcolm Scott Carpenter (all US Navy) and John Glenn (USMC).

JUNE 4, 1959: Max Conrad establishes a new light aircraft distance record of 7,683 miles (12,365km) in a time of 58 hours 38 minutes when he completes a flight from Casablanca, Morocco to Los Angeles in a Piper Comanche.

JUNE 8, 1959: The North American X-15 high-speed rocket plane makes its first unpowered flight after release from a B-52 mother ship. On September 17 it makes its first powered flight in the hands of test pilot Scott Crossfield.

JUNE 10, 1959: The Morane-Saulnier MS-880 Rallye makes its maiden flight. Designed as a three-seat touring aircraft, it sees considerable success under the Socata brand.

JULY 29, 1959: Qantas introduces the first jet service across the Pacific with a scheduled 707 flight between Sydney and San Francisco. On September 5 the service is extended past San Francisco to New York and London.

AUGUST 24, 1959: Thai Airways International is formed.

DECEMBER 14, 1959: Another altitude record is set, this time by USAF Captain J Jordan in an F-104C at 103,389ft (31,513m).

DECEMBER 16, 1959: China Airlines is formed in Taiwan, at first just providing domestic flights, though international flights follow in 1966.

July 30, 1958: DH Canada DHC-4 Jan 20, 1959: Vickers Vanguard Apr 5, 1959: Aero L-29 Apr 10, 1959: Northrop T-38 Apr 29, 1959: Dornier Do 28 June 8, 1959: North American X-15 July 2, 1959: Kaman H-2

The Designers

TONY BUTTLER AMRAeS LOOKS AT SOME OF THE FAMOUS AIRCRAFT DESIGNERS FROM THE PAST 100 YEARS WHO HAVE HELPED SHAPE THE FACE OF AVIATION.

Many of the world's great aircraft companies were dominated by the personalities and designers who either founded or worked for them, and in many cases it was these people who were to bring about the most important advances in aviation.

Within a few years of the Wright Brothers' landmark first powered flight, several countries had seen the formation of embryonic aircraft industries. The first European to fully grasp the potential offered by flight was Henri Farman in France, who fitted large ailerons to a Voisin aeroplane in 1908 and then proceeded to use it make the world's first cross-country flight. The following year Farman designed and built his first biplane, the Henry Farman III, which became one of the finest flying machines of the period.

Back in America, Glenn Curtiss, born in 1878, made his first flight in May 1908 and was soon building his own

aircraft. He was to pioneer the design of the floatplane and flying-boat, while in 1911 another Curtiss machine made the first successful take-off and landing from a Navy ship, starting the process that was to lead to naval air arms and aircraft carriers. Curtiss did more than anyone to establish the US aircraft industry and by the end of World War One his aircraft company was the biggest in the world.

In Britain the first flight by a Briton in an all-British aircraft was made in June 1909 by Alliot Verdon Roe. Roe's triplane designs became well known but, after establishing A V Roe and Co at Manchester in 1910, his groundbreaking aeroplane was the Avro 504, which first flew in 1913. Although used in World War One as a combat aircraft, it was to become the most famous wooden trainer ever built and many were used in civilian service long after the end of the conflict.

1914 to 1939

The First World War brought the first big acceleration in the pace of aircraft development taking it from those early and very basic designs to highly advanced machines with high performance. The type to benefit most was the fighter, and two designers - one British, one German - were to make the biggest mark. T O M Sopwith, born in 1888, had himself been a pioneer pilot before founding Sopwith Aviation at Kingston-upon-Thames in 1912. A series of successful fighters was produced which, in his words, were "all done off the cuff", but by far the most important was the Camel which became the most successful British single-seat fighter of the war and served between 1917 and the Armistice. Sopwith's company went into liquidation in 1920 but he then formed another, Hawker Engineering, and soon moved back into building aircraft, of which more later.

Major Frank Halford (de Havilland Engines), Frank Whittle, Sir Geoffrey de Havilland and C C Walker (de Havilland Aircraft) stand in front of the prototype Comet airliner in 1949. Between them they ushered in the age of commercial jet aviation and changed the world forever. (British Aerospace via author)

T O M Sopwith, responsible for World War One classics such as the Camel, also played a major part in British aviation during the 1920s and 1930s when he helped form Hawker Engineering. (British Aerospace via author)

of all transport aircraft and served for nearly 40 years.

More famous than the Ju 52 was the Douglas DC-3, the world's first 'modern' airliner. Donald Douglas started his company in 1920 and four years later, two of his 'World Cruisers' became the first to fly right around the world. But it was the DC-3, first flown in late 1935 and later universally known as the Dakota, that was his greatest achievement, primarily because it used an all-metal stressed-skin construction and a smooth surface which brought a big advance in speed and economy. The DC-3 was built in great numbers and many are still in revenue-earning service today.

These early airliners created a revolution within the world of travel across Europe and America but they could not take passengers between the two continents because there was nowhere in the Atlantic in which to put refuelling stations. The problem of finding a way to carry enough fuel to fly non-stop was finally solved in the 1930s by the use of very large flying-boats, which also offered the extra comfort needed for

Frenchman Henri Farman (right) and one of the Voisin brothers, pioneers of early aviation in France. (KEY collection)

Sopwith's contemporary in Germany was Anthony Fokker. Another long series of fighters came from his drawing boards of which undoubtedly the most well known was the Fokker Triplane of 1917 and this became the mount for Manfred von Richthofen, the most famous pilot in that conflict. Fokker continued to design and build fighters in his native Holland throughout the 1920s and 1930s. The 1914-1918 war also saw the arrival of the world's first heavy bombers, the Gotha designed in Germany and the 0/100, 0/400 and four-engined V1500 from the company founded by Frederick Handley Page. Page's company was to become a specialist in large bombers and civil airliners.

After the war designers turned to non-military types, and within a few years a network of airline routes had been established. Pioneers like Sir Alan Cobham began to make breakthrough flights to India, Africa and Australia and commercial routes to these countries quickly followed. The first types to be designed with the sole objective of carrying passengers were most uncomfortable but by the 1930s the art had matured. In 1919 the German firm of Hugo Junkers produced the single-engined F.13 airliner - its corrugated metal skinning making it one of the most advanced aircraft of its time. Continuous developments finally led to the Ju 52 conceived in 1930, which became one of the most famous

a long flight. The standards were set by the British C-Class Empire boats designed and built by the company established in 1908 by Albert, Horace and Hugh Short. The Short Brothers' boats were ahead of their time and no aircraft so large and complex had previously been built by a British manufacturer. Early examples entered service in October 1936 and the first Atlantic crossing, a survey flight, was made in July 1937. Besides carrying passengers, the C-Class also helped to expand the Empire's air mail routes and a service between London and Sydney was inaugurated in 1938.

The American answer to the C-Class was the Boeing Clipper, a luxurious flying-boat that eventually made the first ever scheduled transatlantic crossing. The company formed by William Boeing was well established by the mid-1930s and during and after the Second World War it built an enormous number of bombers, the most famous being the B-17 Flying Fortress, which was followed by a series of very successful civil jet airliners, including the 747 Jumbo.

The concept of private flying and flying clubs was born in Britain during the 1920s, the catalyst being the Moth series of light aircraft built in great numbers by de Havilland. Geoffrey de Havilland had formed his company in 1920 and its most famous Moth was the Tiger, which served as a primary trainer with the RAF. In 1940 de Havilland also flew the unique all-wood Mosquito, designed by R E Bishop, which was initially intended as a

fast unarmed light bomber but eventually became the world's first multi-role combat aircraft.

World War Two

The 1920s and 1930s saw big increases in aircraft speed but, for a period, take-off from water was the only way of getting ever-faster machines into the air - no ground strips were available for the very long take-off runs that were required. The catalyst was the Schneider Trophy competition for which designers from Britain, America and Italy designed the world's most advanced seaplanes. In 1934 an Italian Macchi seaplane recorded 440mph (708km/h) but it was the Supermarine S-series, designed by Reginald Mitchell, that left the greatest legacy. The final version, the S.6B, won the Schneider Trophy outright for Britain in 1931 while at the same time gathering for its designer an enormous amount of experience in high-speed flight. Born in 1895, R J Mitchell was a true genius who used this experience to produce the classic Spitfire fighter, perhaps the most famous of all British aeroplanes. But he was also very versatile and was responsible for many other types, ranging from small flying-boats to four-engined bombers (which actually never flew because the prototypes were destroyed in an air raid). A tragically early death in 1937 prevented Mitchell from getting his hands on the jet but he will forever be remembered for the *Spit*

Glenn Curtiss at the controls of one of his early aircraft. Curtiss is a name synonymous with the early years of American aviation and indeed his company was to build some classic aircraft well into the 1940s. (KEY collection)

Anthony Fokker stands on the bow of a Fokker B.4 flying-boat. Fokker is best remembered for the aircraft he designed for use by Germany during World War One. However, his company was to remain in the aviation business until March 1996 when it filed for bankruptcy. (KEY collection)

and by the Me 262 jet fighter, which was the most advanced jet aircraft to serve during the war.

Mention should also be made of George Carter who designed the first British jet aircraft - the Gloster E.28/39 research aeroplane and the Meteor fighter. Sir Frank Whittle has, quite rightly, received so much acclaim for inventing the jet engine and for designing and building the world's first practical power units, but Carter contributed a great deal to the story; his designs were relatively simple but they proved ideal as the first British vehicles to be powered by the jet.

Post-war developments

The jet did not remain just a fighter powerplant for very long - the first jet bombers were built and flown before the end of the war and in 1949 the world's first jet airliner, the de Havilland Comet, made its appearance. Once again de Havilland had applied genius, and taken risks, to produce an aeroplane which put Britain back in the lead of aircraft design; in fact so far ahead was the Comet that there was no competition in sight. Sadly it had a troubled early career which allowed American manufacturers like

Mitchell's great British rival was Sydney Camm who was born in 1893 and, after joining Sopwith's new Hawker Company in 1923, quickly became its chief designer. The most famous aircraft to come from the Camm stable has to be the Hurricane, the Spitfire's wartime partner, but it was followed by a several other fine piston- and jet-powered fighters. Unlike Mitchell, Camm was not a great innovator and, prior to the arrival of the Hawker P.1127 vertical take-off aircraft in 1960, tended to be more cautious with his designs. The P.1127 was developed into the highly successful Harrier, the first V/STOL aircraft to enter squadron service. Another great British designer was Roy Chadwick at Avro who gave the RAF the superb Lancaster, which served Bomber Command so faithfully during World War Two.

The first jet aircraft to fly was the Heinkel He 178 which took to the air just before war broke out in August 1939. Ernst Heinkel was also responsible for the He 280, the world's first jet fighter, but this only flew in small numbers and never entered service. However, Heinkel's

stature in the German aircraft industry was eclipsed by Willi Messerschmitt. Messerschmitt was responsible for some great aircraft including the Bf 109 flown in 1935, the most famous German aircraft of all time and a type built in greater numbers than any other aircraft bar one, the Russian Ilyushin Il-2. The 109 was followed by the remarkable Me 163 Komet rocket-powered interceptor

Boeing to recover lost ground and dominate the early generations of jet airliner design. In 1948 another de Havilland aircraft, the DH.108, became the first jet-powered machine to fly supersonically; chief designer for both DH.108 and Comet was R E Bishop.

An important British designer was W E W Petter who in the late 1940s and 1950s was responsible for the

R J Mitchell, the designer of perhaps the most famous fighter ever built - the Supermarine Spitfire. (Dr Gordon Mitchell, son of R J)

W E W Petter, responsible for such post World War Two classic British jets as the English Electric Canberra and Lightning. (Peter Green)

Roy Chadwick while working for Avro designed some quite exceptional aircraft, including the famous wartime Lancaster bomber and the memorable Vulcan V bomber. (British Aerospace)

Professor Dornier was responsible for a wide and successful range of flying boats as well as land based aircraft, many of which equipped the Luftwaffe during World War Two. (KEY collection)

The White House in 1935 as President Franklin Roosevelt presents the Collier Trophy to Donald W Douglas. Douglas was the father of the legendary DC-3 Dakota but also produced a wide range of military aircraft. (KEY collection)

One of the many aircraft to come from Willi Messerschmitt was the Bf 110. Messerschmitt was of course also responsible for the classic Bf 109 and later the jet-powered Me 262. (KEY collection)

The Cierva C.30 autogyro is one of many designed by Juan de la Cierva as an alternative to the helicopter. (KEY - Robert Rudhall)

Canberra (Britain's first and highly successful jet bomber), the Lightning Mach 2 fighter and the Gnat. The latter fulfilled Petter's concept of the lightweight fighter, an attempt to halt the ever-increasing size and complexity of modern military aircraft. Post-war the American Ed Heinemann produced for Douglas a series of naval jet-powered combat aircraft. Heinemann's genius was in solving engineering problems and again the need to keep down weight – his most famous design was the A-4 Skyhawk attack aircraft.

Towards the end of World War Two a completely different type of aircraft became established. In 1909 and 1910 Igor Sikorsky had built two helicopters but neither flew and progress in vertical take-off became stalled until Juan de la Cierva began experiments in the 1920s with autogyros that used freely-rotating rotor systems with independently-articulated rotor blades. Using one of his machines, in 1928 Cierva became the first rotary-wing pilot to cross the English Channel. Trial helicopters were flown before World War Two by Heinrich Focke and Herr Achgelis in Germany, and Weir in Britain, but it was Sikorsky who eventually brought together all of the best ideas to produce the first practical helicopter and in 1944 his R-4 performed the first recorded helicopter rescue.

The jet engine offered the opportunity for much higher speeds but the first aeroplane to break the sound barrier was actually powered by a rocket. In October 1947 the X-1, produced by Larry Bell's company in the United States, became the first supersonic aeroplane, passing through Mach 1 just 44 years after the first powered flight.

In Russia Andrei Tupolev's Design Bureau began to specialise in large bombers and airliners and has continued to produce superb aeroplanes to this day; in fact Tupolev can perhaps lay claim to being the greatest of all aircraft designers. Two more Russians, Artyom Mikoyan and Mikhail Guryevich, actually gave the world a new word – MiG. The first MiGs were piston fighters used during the World War Two but their most famous product has to be the swept wing MiG-15 jet fighter which burst onto the scene during the Korean War and gave the Allies a big shock. It was followed by many more MiG fighters, including the MiG-21 supersonic fighter manufactured in

greater numbers than any other post-war combat aircraft.

Today the design of a new aircraft needs big design teams with computers and other modern research tools. Gone are the days when a single brilliant mind can formulate the concept of a new aeroplane and even by the end of World War Two designers were backed up by many other staff as part of a team.

Perhaps the last in a long line of great designers was Clarence 'Kelly' Johnson of the American Lockheed company, who was responsible for two unique aeroplanes, both intended for top secret reconnaissance, a vital commodity during the Cold War with the Soviet Union. The first was the U-2, a subsonic jet first flown in 1955 and intended to fly at very high altitude and above the dangers of the new surface-to-air missiles designed to shoot them down. This was followed by the incredible SR-71 of 1964 which, with a top speed in excess of three times the speed of sound, was intended to be faster than any type expected to attack it.

This short piece has brought to life some of the great aircraft designers from the first half century or so of powered flight. There were more, including many in France, Italy and Japan, and all have contributed to the rich and varied history of aviation.

One of the USA's greatest designers is Lockheed's Kelly Johnson, seen here in the cockpit of an A-12. Among his creations are the U-2 high altitude spy plane, the Mach 2 F-104 Starfighter and the Mach 3 SR-71A Blackbird. (Lockheed)

Widely renowned as the father of the helicopter; Igor Sikorsky and his famous Fedora board one of his early designs, the S-51. (KEY collection)

Sir Barnes Wallis in 1976. Best remembered for the bouncing bomb used by the Dambusters, he also designed a number of aircraft, including the Vickers Wellington. (KEY collection)

From
Parachutes
to
Bang Seats

'WHAT GOES UP MUST COME DOWN' IS A
UNIVERSAL DEFINITION OF
INEVITABILITY, AND AIRCRAFT FLIGHT
IS GOVERNED BY THIS PRINCIPLE.
ALAN DAWES LOOKS AT THE
ALTERNATIVE – AND OFTEN
EXTREME – WAYS OF
'COMING DOWN' WHEN
AIRCRAFT GET INTO
DIFFICULTIES.

The successful achievement of powered flight in a heavier-than-air machine – the Wright brothers' Flyer – at Kitty Hawk, North Carolina on December 17, 1903, was the realisation of Man's centuries-old dream of conquering the 'fifth ocean' and of flying as freely as the birds. Unfortunately, manned flight is nowhere near as efficient or reliable as avian mastery of the air and as powered aircraft started to fly higher and faster, it became obvious that some method of safe escape from a malfunctioning aeroplane had to be devised. Fortunately, however, the invention of the parachute had predated the invention of the aeroplane by several centuries – the Chinese had produced a rudimentary, but workable, parachute design as far back as the 12th century. Later, in 1495, the great Italian artist, inventor and scientist Leonardo da Vinci came up with a design for a pyramid-shaped parachute, but the credit for the design of the parachute as we know it today is ascribed to a Frenchman, Louis Sebastien Lenormand, in 1783.

Early impetus

The impetus to develop a system to save the life of an aeroplane pilot or crew arose from the first fatality of powered flight, which occurred on September 17, 1908. Lieutenant Thomas Etholen Selfridge of the United States Army, flying as a passenger with Orville Wright at Fort Myer, Virginia, died after sustaining a fractured skull in a crash, following disintegration of the aircraft's propeller. (Orville Wright suffered several fractures, bruises and severe shock). Although the accident happened at only 125ft (38m) above the ground, too low to safely use a parachute, it did inspire serious thought about how pilots could escape from a crashing aircraft.

An important stage towards developing a workable parachute was reached with the successful first descent from an aircraft in flight by Captain Albert Berry of the United States Army on March 1, 1912. Flying in a Benoist Pusher biplane, Berry made his historic jump over Jefferson Barracks, Missouri, from a height of 1,500ft (457m) and at a speed of 55mph (88.5km/h), dropping 500ft (152.4m) before the parachute opened fully. The parachute itself was cumbersome, but it did prove the feasibility of using such a device to escape from an aircraft in flight. With aviation still in its early infancy when World War One broke out in 1914, parachutes were only issued to crews of tethered observation balloons, since they were still too bulky and impractical for use in aircraft. Nevertheless, only three years later, German pilots successfully used container-type parachutes from then until the end of the war to escape from their damaged aircraft.

First life saved in combat

One recorded incident involved a German pilot bailing out of his stricken fighter in 1917, using a Henicke seat-type parachute operated by an eight-foot static line, thereby reportedly becoming the first pilot to save his life by escaping from an aircraft via parachute. Further advances were made following the invention of the backpack parachute by Leslie Irvin and Floyd Smith. This parachute, which incorporated the now universally familiar 'ripcord'

Above: **A de Havilland DH.9 biplane fighter, similar to that from which Leslie Irvin jumped in 1919 to test the first ripcord-operated parachute designed by himself. It is often difficult to comprehend the phenomenal pace of aviation development in the 100 years of its existence, with aircraft and escape systems now representing some of Man's most advanced engineering achievements.** (KEY collection)

Below: **Benny Lynch in the rear cockpit of the converted Meteor F.3 (inset) and successfully clearing the tail of the aircraft in the first UK live ejection from a jet aircraft on July 24, 1946. Much is owed to men like Lynch, who helped to advance the physiological understanding of high-speed ejections by selflessly risking their own lives.** (KEY collection)

Bottom: **The only known operational application of an encapsulated ejection seat was on the supersonic Convair B-58 Hustler bomber. The three crew positions can be identified by the familiar red warning triangles alongside their seat locations.** (KEY collection)

Illustrating the dual benefit of the parachute and the ejection seat as a life-saving component of the modern jet fighter, this test of the American Advanced Concept Seat II (ACES II) shows the dramatic exit of a dummy from the cockpit section of a Boeing F-15 Eagle fighter. (McDonnell Douglas)

saving role came with the introduction of jet aircraft, where the high speed of flight made it necessary to eject the pilot away from the aircraft, since he could not just simply step over the side in an emergency.

The parachute is not enough

This requirement led to the invention of the ejection seat and since Germany had been working on the development of a number of jet and rocket-powered aircraft before World War Two, it was the first to develop a workable propulsive escape system. The Heinkel He 219 was the first production aircraft to be equipped with an ejection seat, but the first emergency use of such a device was made from a He 280 on January 13, 1942. The Heinkel-designed seat used a compressed air propulsion system, and around 60 successful ejections are believed to have been made by German pilots during World War Two using Heinkel compressed air systems. Sweden was another European country which was involved in early ejection seat work – SAAB carried out experiments in 1942 which involved propellant-powered seats. SAAB's first successful in-flight ejection of a dummy took place on January 8, 1942, and the first successful live ejection was made on July 29, 1946. In the United Kingdom, in 1944, the Martin Baker Aircraft Company, founded originally to build aircraft, began pioneering work in the field of aircrew escape systems and went on to become the world's most renowned manufacturer of ejection seats.

Exploiting the experience of both the Germans and the Swedes, Martin Baker refined their designs by developing a two-cartridge propellant gun, which met human physiological limitations whilst still providing the peak G-acceleration required to clear the aircraft safely. The company's Mk.1 seat was sufficiently developed for the first English live ejection test to be carried out by Bernard 'Benny' Lynch from a modified Gloster Meteor F.3 on July 24, 1946. This event was followed on August 17, when Sergeant

method of opening the canopy, was used for the first time on April 28, 1919, when Irvin jumped from a de Havilland DH.9 biplane while flying at over 100mph (161km/h) at 1,500ft (457.2m) over McCook Field, Dayton, Ohio. More than 1,500 successful experimental jumps were made from aircraft before the seat pack-type parachute was issued to the US Army in 1919, and in 1922 the use of parachutes in military aircraft became mandatory. The Royal Air Force adopted the US-type of seat pack parachute in 1925.

Before this, on October 20, 1922, Lieutenant Harold Harris, Chief of the Flight Test Section of the US Army Air Service Engineering Division, had become the first American pilot to save his life by jumping from his disabled aircraft (a Loening W-2A fighter) with a ripcord-operated parachute (Interestingly, he was also flying from McCook Field in Dayton). Harris's experience inspired the creation of the Caterpillar Club, which celebrated the saving of life by the use of a parachute – so named because the parachute canopy and shroud lines were made of silk spun by the silkworm caterpillar. The Irvin Air Chute Company, founded by Leslie Irvin in 1919, started the Caterpillar Club in 1922 and initiated the practice of awarding a small gold caterpillar pin to anyone who had saved their life by parachuting from a disabled aircraft. By the end of World War Two there were around 34,000 members of the Caterpillar Club and it is estimated that there have been more than 100,000 recipients of these cherished pins since its inception.

Airborne assault

The military did not take long to realise the potential of the parachute as a an additional tool for the infantryman, and the former USSR became the first nation to deliver its troops into combat by dropping them by parachute during its

winter campaign against Finland in 1939-1940. By April 1940, the German Army (Wehrmacht) had used paratroops in its assault on Norway and the US Army set up its first training course for paratroopers in the same year. Today, most of the world's larger armies have paratroop units and members of these formations are usually regarded as the élite of the soldiering profession. However, the military has always considered the parachute more as a life-saving device than a 'flying machine' in its own right, despite the fact that some modern parachutes can effectively be described as flexible-winged gliders. Today, of course, parachutes have evolved into sporting accoutrements, and sky-diving enthusiasts willingly throw themselves out of fully-serviceable aircraft for the sheer exhilaration of falling freely through the air before opening the canopy. However, a major challenge in the use of the parachute in the life-

Below: **Dramatically illustrating why the ejection seat is so essential on military jets, the pilot of this US Navy Crusader fighter abandons his crashing aircraft just before it plunges into the sea. Most modern ejection seats can also be operated under water in extreme emergencies.** (Martin Baker)

The Russian Kamov Ka-50 Hokum fighter-helicopter is currently the only rotary-winged craft equipped with an assisted escape system. Often referred to as an ejection seat, the helicopter's Zvezda K-37 seat is actually an extraction seat, which pulls the pilot out of the cockpit using a small rocket pack. The co-axial arrangement of the rotors of the Ka-50 complicate the escape procedure for the pilot, but Zvezda and Kamov have perfected a system which uses explosive bolts to blow the rotors off first. (Artur Sarkisyan)

Lawrence L Lambert made the first manned test of an ejection seat in the United States from a Northrop P-61 Black Widow over Dayton, Ohio. By June 1947 the Royal Air Force had decided to fit the Martin Baker Mk.1 seat in all British tactical military aircraft of the day. By the mid-1950s, Martin Baker ejection seats had attracted the attention of air forces around the world which were becoming increasingly interested in providing adequate emergency escape systems for their new high-performance jets. Today, the name Martin Baker is synonymous with ejection seats and is the most experienced manufacturer of such assisted escape systems in the world, with almost 7,000 lives saved to date. Sweden continued to refine its own ejection seat designs for the revolutionary SAAB J35 Draken supersonic fighter, which had a very compact cockpit layout, requiring the seat to be tailored to its dimensions. SAAB-designed seats were used on all Swedish post-war jet fighters up to the J-37 Viggen, although the latest SAAB fighter, the JAS-39 Gripen, uses the Martin Baker Mk.XL seat.

American ejection seats diverged, the USAF preferring to support indigenous programmes whereas the US Navy maintained its preference for Martin Baker's products. As a result, many American companies became involved in producing US-designed ejection seats as sub-contractors. The largest escape system development programme ever undertaken in the United States, NACES (Navy Aircrew Common Ejection Seat), has also involved many US companies, Government Agencies and Service personnel, even though the UK's Martin Baker was selected to supply the NACES seat to the US Navy.

Other solutions

In addition to the normal 'open' type of ejector seat, a number of other solutions have been exploited to save the lives of aircrew, including the radical separation of the pilot's cockpit from the aircraft, which would then descend separately under a large parachute canopy. This concept was pioneered by the Germans on a number of unrealised

style ejection seats capable of saving pilots in high-altitude, high-speed ejections, from ground level to more than 60,000 feet. These modern seats can be used at zero speed and zero altitude, and for that reason are known as 'zero-zero' systems. They can also function underwater.

Passengers not so lucky

For a variety of practical reasons, airline passengers have always been unable to escape from a disabled aircraft by parachute and the only realistic system for their evacuation in an emergency (on the ground, or water) is the escape chute. Passenger escape chutes are now mandatory on all large commercial passenger aircraft and they must, additionally, be capable of acting as a stable life raft in the event of ditching. The first escape chutes were designed by an American balloon specialist, James Boyle, and the first usable system was installed on President Eisenhower's Lockheed L1049 Constellation 'Columbine' (the first 'Air Force One') in the 1950s. The most recent innovation in the application of parachute technology is the fitting of a 'ballistic' parachute recovery system as standard on the Cirrus SR20 light aircraft, the first such system in the history of aviation. The first actual use of the system was recorded on October 3, 2002, when a solo pilot used the airframe parachute system to bring his Cirrus SR22 four-seat light aircraft safely to the ground after experiencing control difficulties over Dallas, Texas. A similar system is now available as a retrofit on the Cessna 172 Skyhawk, and in Germany it is mandatory for all microlight aircraft to be equipped with a ballistic recovery system. This is a particularly fitting point on which to end, since the concept was first mooted in the infancy of aviation, in the early part of the last century and thus embraces almost the entire century of aeronautical endeavour. It not only emphasises the principle that 'what goes up must come down', but also that 'what goes around, comes around'.

Worldwide ejection seats

In the United States, ejection seat design was influenced by study of the Heinkel seat captured at the end of World War Two and by Martin Baker's work in the United Kingdom. In the early days of American work on ejection systems, Lockheed began development of its own seats, along with pioneering work on jet aircraft, whilst other major aircraft manufacturers also started to produce seats for aircraft designed by themselves. These included such famous (and some forgotten?) names as North American, Grumman, Republic, Northrop, Vought and Douglas. The same procedure was used in the former Soviet Union, where design bureaux like MiG, Sukhoi and Tupolev produced KM-1, KS-1 and KT-1 ejection seats for their aircraft, where the letters (in reverse) stand for 'MiG Seat' (i.e. Kreslo MiGa), 'Sukhoi Seat' and 'Tupolev Seat' respectively. All Russian ejection seats, including the first system for use on helicopters, are now built by Zvezda, and equip virtually all the Russian Air Force's combat aircraft and the Ka-50 helicopter. After initial studies, the development of

projects and taken up by the Russians on the unflown Su-17(R) prototype in 1949. On these aircraft, the entire nose section and cockpit was designed to be blown off explosively and on the Su-17(R) the pilot had the choice of ejecting normally, or by jettisoning the cockpit. The ejectable capsule concept was successfully realised on the General Dynamics F-111 swing-wing tactical bomber and was designed into the original Rockwell B-1A strategic bomber, though not adopted for the series-produced B-1B. An interesting compromise between the open ejection seat and the ejectable cockpit module was the Stanley Aviation Capsule, designed for the Convair B-58 Hustler supersonic bomber. This system, provided for all three crewmembers of the B-58, was like a standard ejection seat, but had a clamshell protective hood which came down over the occupant just before the seat left the aircraft on ejection. All B-58s, with the exception of the pilot-trainer version, were upgraded with the Stanley capsule. With advances in aircrew protective clothing, helmets and rocket propulsion of seats, Martin Baker and Zvezda in Russia have perfected a range of normal 'open'

The General Dynamics F-111 is one of the few combat aircraft to use an escape capsule system. The USAF has long since retired its F-111 fleet but the Royal Australian Air Force still operates the type. (RAAF)

The Russian Zvezda K36D ejection seat is rated as one of the best in the world, featuring many innovations not found on Western designs. (KEY collection)

WOMEN PILOTS HAVE MADE A SIGNIFICANT CONTRIBUTION TO AVIATION FROM THE EARLIEST TIMES, YET, DISAPPOINTINGLY STILL ACCOUNT FOR AS LITTLE AS 2.5% OF ALL COMMERCIAL PILOTS AND ONLY 6% OF PRIVATE PILOTS. CLARE WALKER CHARTS THE HISTORY OF WOMEN IN AVIATION.

Women in Aviation

It could be argued that the first women to fly were those who jumped from balloons - one of these early parachutists, Briton Dolly Shepherd - even earned a place in the Guinness Book of Records for having made the first air rescue in 1908.

This phenomenal feat occurred at over 11,000ft (3,352m) when Dolly Shepherd succeeded in transferring novice parachutist Louie Law from her parachute, after she got into difficulties. The pair reputedly fell to earth like a stone - Dolly injured her back, temporarily paralysing her and leaving her unable to speak. She did, however, recover and went on to make many more jumps before retiring in 1912.

However, women are known to have taken to the air as early as 1798 when Jeanne Labrosse made a solo balloon flight in her native France. After the first manned powered flight by the Wright brothers in December 1903, women were soon eager to take to the skies, although they had to battle accusations that they were 'temperamentally unfit' to fly because they were prone to panic.

Early achievements

The honour of being the world's first licensed female pilot went to Frenchwoman Raymonde de Laroche when she gained her licence on March 8, 1910. Only four months later she was seriously injured in a flying accident during an air race, but recovered to race again two years later.

The year 1911 represented a considerable milestone for women in aviation. In the UK, the little-known Hilda Hewlett entered the record books when she became the first British woman to gain her Private Pilot's Licence at Brooklands Museum - the spiritual home of today's British Women Pilots' Association.

Across the Atlantic, renowned lady pilot Harriet Quimby was learning to fly with Matilde Moisant - America's first two licensed women pilots. A year later, Harriet Quimby became the first women to cross the English Channel in 1912 - a feat accomplished in a Blériot monoplane. Sadly,

she was killed later that year when her aircraft crashed into Dorchester Bay in America.

Belgium's first licensed lady pilot, Hélène Dutrieu, impressed the world by flying non-stop from Ostend to Bruges in 1910, a distance of some 28 miles, capping that achievement in 1911 by competing against 14 male pilots in the Italian King's Cup race, which she won. Later in the year, the 'Girl Hawk' as she was known, set a new world non-stop record for women by flying 158 miles (254km) in 2 hours and 58 minutes.

Germany's first female pilot, Melli Beese also gained her licence in 1911, later opening a flying school in Berlin where she taught men to fly. Not to be outdone, Britain's Hilda Hewlett ran a flying school as well, instructing trainee pilots during World War One, as well as teaching her own son, Francis, to fly.

Russia's first female pilot, Lidia Zvereva, soloed in 1911, with women from other countries following suit - Tadashi Hyodo from Japan in 1922, Anesia Pinheiro from Brazil in 1922, Millicent Bryant from Australia in 1926, and Ruthy Tu from China in 1932. The world's first black female pilot, Bessie Coleman, had to leave her native America to learn

Amy Johnson, probably the most famous name in women's aviation in the UK. (KEY collection)

A well-known face among UK display pilots is Caroline Grace, the world's only female Spitfire pilot. Before her, women pilots of the ATA regularly ferried Spitfires to RAF squadrons during World War Two. (KEY - Duncan Cubitt)

to fly in France, having been rejected by US flying schools because of her race. She achieved her pilot's licence in June 1921.

More than a pilot

A notable feature of these early women pilots was that many were skilled engineers – Hilda Hewlett founded the aircraft company Hewlett & Blondeau Ltd, which built many aircraft for use in World War One, while Melli Beese built her own monoplane, the Melli Beese Dove, which was used as a training aircraft at her flying school.

America's best-known aviatrix of the 1920s and 1930s was Amelia Earhart who mysteriously disappeared over the Pacific while attempting a round-the-world flight in 1937. (KEY collection)

Amy Johnson, one of aviation's legendary pilots, became the first licensed ground engineer in December 1929, shortly after gaining her pilot's licence with the London Aeroplane Club at Stag Lane. Her engineering skills proved invaluable when she flew from London to Australia in *Jason*, her Gipsy Moth, as she was able to repair the aeroplane when it sustained damage during the course of several landings.

However, despite losing two days to repairs, she made it to Australia in 19 days – and became the first woman to fly solo from England to Australia. Amy Johnson and her American contemporary Amelia Earhart – the first woman to fly cross the Atlantic – were also the first female aviators to use sponsorship to help fund their flying exploits.

Golden age

With sponsorship came massive media attention, making the 1920s and 1930s a golden age for aviation and, particularly, for women in aviation. Although countless women throughout the world notched up world records in the following decades, no other era has been as notable,

with, perhaps the exception of the 1940s when women made a significant contribution during World War Two. As we shall see later, the 1990s may also be judged, in hindsight, as another golden era for women in aviation.

Unlike Amy Johnson, who worked as a secretary, many of the early aviatrix were well-to-do and often titled, such as Lady Mary Bailey – the first woman to fly solo from England

Left: **As with the ATA in the UK, in America women also ferried combat aircraft from the factory to front-line units, including those across the Atlantic.** (KEY collection)

Lettice Curtis, one of the many ATA women pilots who ferried aircraft to front-line RAF units, thus freeing up other pilots for combat. (KEY collection)

to South Africa, Lady Heath and the Hon Mrs Victor Bruce.

The latter set out to fly around the world in 1930, taking five months to fly 20,000 miles (32,186km) over 23 countries – a feat recorded in her book 'The Bluebird's Flight'. During her journey she achieved several records: the first solo flight from England to Japan, the longest solo flight and first solo flight from India to French Indo-China.

Amy Johnson's lack of personal fortune meant sponsorship was a necessity. As a result, Lord Wakefield of Wakefield & Castrol Oil, owned a 50% share in *Jason*. Through sponsorship, including that of the Daily Mail newspaper, Amy made many other record-breaking flights, including England to South Africa, England to India, and England to Tokyo.

In 1940, she joined the Air Transport Auxiliary (ATA), along with many other women pilots to ferry aircraft from their place of manufacture to the airfields, playing a vital role in helping the Allies to eventually achieve air supremacy.

Jacqueline Cochran probably set more women's world speed records than any other female pilot. She is seen here in the company of her good friend Charles 'Chuck' Yeager – the first supersonic man. (KEY collection)

One of the earliest aviation-related job opportunities for women was to become a stewardess. Often – and unfairly – called 'trolley dollies', cabin crew are crucial to the smooth operation of any commercial airline. Although the public image may be that they simply keep passengers comfortable, fed and watered, they are primarily there to ensure the safety of passengers. (KEY Collection)

repeated solo in 1932, earning herself a ticker-tape parade through New York City.

But the flight that she most wanted to complete was a circumnavigation of the world via the Pacific, which she began in 1937. Tragically, it ended near Howland Island in the South Pacific Ocean after her Electra aircraft failed to make contact with the Coast Guard ship, *Itasca*.

Her disappearance spawned a series of rumours and conspiracy theories, none of which have been proved to this day, although there are still claims being made that bones have been found or that her aircraft has been spotted in Pacific waters.

Amelia Earhart has at least one other claim to fame: as one of the original 99 women pilots who founded the now international organisation, the Ninety-Nines, in November 1929. Although it remained the only international body for women pilots for many decades, the Ninety-Nines has been gradually overtaken by Women in Aviation

Left: **Many European countries allowed women into combat jet cockpits far earlier than in Britain or America. This is Pilot Officer Anne-Marie Jansen of the Belgian Air Force at Brustem Air Base in September 1992.** (KEY collection)

Triumph and tragedy

Amy Johnson's last – and least desirable – record was to be the first member of the ATA to be killed when she bailed out of an Airspeed Oxford over the Thames Estuary in 1941. The mystery surrounding the circumstances of her death – possibly the result of friendly fire, according to recent investigation – only enhanced the legend, something else she had in common with Amelia Earhart.

Amelia Earhart earned her place in the record books in June 1928 when she was one of a three-strong crew to fly across the Atlantic, landing at Burry Port in Wales. Although she did not fly the aircraft herself, she became the first woman to cross the Atlantic – a feat she later

International, a highly influential group whose 7,000-plus members include Colonel Eileen Collins, the first woman to command a space shuttle mission.

Famous names

Another famous aviatrix of the 1930s was New Zealand pilot Jean Batten, known as 'The Garbo of the Skies' because of her glamorous appearance. In 1934, she set a women's solo record of 14 days, 22 hours and 30 minutes for flying from Lympne in England to Darwin in Australia.

A year later, she repeated the feat in reverse, taking 17 days, 16 hours and 15 minutes – becoming the first woman to fly solo from England to Australia and back. In 1935, she set world absolute records (for pilots of either sex in any

type of aircraft) for flying from Lympne to Natal and for the 1,900 mile (3,057km) South Atlantic crossing from Thies in Senegal to Natal in Brazil. The latter made her the first woman to fly herself from England to South America.

Jean Batten's most famous achievement, however, was her flight from England to New Zealand in her Percival Gull 6, which set a world absolute record for flying 14,224 miles (22,890km) in eleven days.

Remarkably, for a woman who pushed so many boundaries, Jean did not share the fate of several other women pilots in those pioneering early decades – a premature death in an air accident – indeed, she lived until 1982. However, even then her death was shrouded in mystery as her body was not found until several years later in a pauper's grave in Majorca.

Other pioneers

While women pilots in the rest of the world were busy setting and breaking records, German aviatrix were held back by legislation that prohibited Germany from having aircraft that could be used for military purposes. Instead they had to confine their activities to gliders and small sport aircraft.

Hanna Reitsch, a skilled glider pilot, was undoubtedly one of the most capable of the female pilots, serving as a test pilot for the Luftwaffe, as well as becoming the first woman to pilot a helicopter, demonstrating its hovering abilities in Berlin's giant 'Deutschlandhalle' stadium.

World War Two provided a rare opportunity for British, American and Canadian women to prove their aviation abilities. British women pilots such as Pauline Gower, who commanded the women's section of the ATA, Joan Hughes, Lettice Curtis, Ann Welch, Diana Bernato-Walker, Monique Agazarian, Jackie Moggridge and Freydis Sharland (first chairman of BWPA), fully expected to be able to continue their work as commercial pilots when the war ended.

Kara Hultgreen has the distinction of being the US Navy's first female F-14 Tomcat pilot after combat restrictions on female American pilots was lifted in 1991. Sadly she was killed while attempting to land on the USS Abraham Lincoln in October 1994 – but she paved the way for many female combat pilots. (AP)

Jo Salter was the RAF's first female Tornado pilot – the service now has a number of women pilots flying a wide range of aircraft. (RAF)

Forgotten Pilots

However, they were disappointed to discover that they were expected to return to the kitchen and became 'The Forgotten Pilots' as detailed in the book of the same name by Lettice Curtis. A few managed to continue flying commercially, but usually only so long as they were not seen and not heard.

By the 1970s, a handful of women were working as pilots for commercial airlines, most notably Yvonne Sintes, who joined Dan-Air in 1969, becoming the UK's first female pure-jet airline Captain flying a BAC 1-11 out of Gatwick.

However, the credit for captaining Britain's first all-female crew goes to Captain Caroline Frost, who flew for British Air Ferries (BAF). The date was October 31, 1977, on BAF's inaugural flight from Southend to Düsseldorf.

The 1960s and 1970s were a period of achievement for former actress Sheila Scott, who had won over 50 flying

Above: **Polly Vacher MBE recently flew a Piper PA-28 around the world to support the charity Flying Scholarships for the disabled. Evidence, if ever any was needed, that women today still have that pioneering spirit.** (KEY - Steve Fletcher)
Below : **In recent years women have found themselves in other combat roles, as illustrated by USAF HH-60G gunner Vanessa Dobos.** (USAF)

trophies by 1976 and was the holder of 94 World Class Air Records, including London to Cape Town and the South Atlantic and Brazil to West Africa.

By the 1980s, women were at last beginning to break through the barriers that had prevented them from becoming commercial pilots, although it wasn't until 1987 that British Airways appointed its first female pilot - Lynn Barton, who now captains Boeing 747s for the airline. Later, the airline even appointed its first female Concorde pilot, 1st Officer Barbara Harmer.

Breakthrough

But it wasn't until June 1991 that Julie Gibson became the first full-time RAF operational woman pilot, progressing through the ranks to become the first woman

transport captain, in command of a C-130 Hercules flying out of Lyneham. Once the principle that women could fly had been accepted, it was not long before they started flying fast jets, such as Tornados, Jaguars and Harriers, as well as military helicopters. There are now very few military or commercial aircraft that women do not fly.

The 1980s and 1990s heralded another golden era for women in aviation. During this period an increasing number of American women took part in space shuttle missions, following the examples set by Sally Ride, the first American female astronaut, Shannon Lucid, who flew five missions, and Colonel Eileen Collins. Their achievements and their willingness to be role models are inspiring other young women to follow in their footsteps. In the UK, Dr Helen Sharman became Britain's first female astronaut in 1991 when she took part in the Anglo-Russian *Juno* Mission.

New aviation records were also set during the 1980s/1990s - with Eve Jackson becoming the first woman to pilot a microlight from England to Sydney in Australia, Jennifer Murray flying the first female solo circumnavigation of the world in a single-engine piston helicopter, and Polly Vacher earning a record for the smallest aircraft flown solo by a woman around the world via the Pacific.

Looking ahead to the future, it is easy to predict that women will play an increasingly important part in the development of aviation, not just as pilots, but also in the world of aircraft and aerospace design and manufacture. More women will run airlines, like Go's former CEO Barbara Casani, and there will be many more - like June Maule of Maule Air Inc and Eileen Collins who is pushing forward the boundaries of space as an astronaut. ■□

Author: Clare Walker is the recently retired chairman of the British Women Pilots' Association, the joint author of a 'Career in Aviation' (published by the BWPA) and a member of Women in Aviation International and Whirly-Girls Inc.

Patty Wagstaff is a competent aerobatic pilot in the USA and also does test flying for Raytheon. The USA has more women pilots than any other nation, both in military and commercial employment. (KEY collection)

The world's airlines are finally realising that women can help fill their needs for pilots and more and more women are now either captains or co-pilots with many carriers. (Air Jamaica)

A Century of
Private
Flying

THE ASPIRATION TO FLY HAS GRIPPED THE PUBLIC IMAGINATION FOR CENTURIES. HOWEVER, TODAY NOT EVERYBODY WANTS TO – OR IS ABLE TO – FLY EITHER FOR THE MILITARY OR AS AN AIRLINE PILOT. AS STEPHEN BRIDGEWATER ERXPLAINS MANY THOUSANDS OF PRIVATE PILOTS FLY SIMPLY FOR THE LOVE OF IT.

Since the earliest days of flight, pilots have flown because of their love of being in the air. To leave the ground far behind and climb into the sky like a bird is a remarkable feat and never ceases to give a pilot a feeling of awe which cannot be explained to those who have not tried it for themselves.

Over the last 100 years, the aeroplane has been greatly developed as a method of transport and a machine of war, but alongside this, the popularity of flight for its own sake has never waned. A love of flying is infectious and many people find a small taste of passenger flying is enough for them to want to learn to fly.

Just as the Wright brothers dedicated themselves to the achievement of flight, countless individuals around the world still pursue the same aim today. These pilots fly purely as a hobby – they fly because they love flying. Whether they hire an aeroplane from a flying school or are lucky enough to possess their own machines, pilots like these finance their own flying – and even today flying does not come cheap. Aeroplanes need to be fuelled, oiled, maintained and insured, but so strong is the will to fly that somehow the money is found.

Still, it has to be said that flying can be as expensive as the individual chooses to make it. Purchasing the latest airframe is always going to be expensive, but as aviation has advanced the options available to pilots have increased. In 1909, when five British gentlemen decided they wanted to fly, they had little option but to design their own machines or acquire proven Wright Flyer aeroplanes. They each chose the latter and paid a cool £1,000 each for the privilege.

Today a brand-new Cessna 172R costs around £103,500 from the factory in Wichita, Kansas, but the modern pilot has more options open to him than the aviator of 1909. The second-hand market is buoyant, with aircraft of all ages, sizes and shapes available: a single-seat Volkswagen Beetle-engined Evans VP-1, for example, can be acquired for as little as a few thousand pounds, with running costs similar to a family car.

Private individuals conducted the earliest powered flights and this desire for private flying drove the development of the aeroplane until the outbreak of World War One. Designers such as Anthony Fokker and A V Roe, who were later to make their name in military circles, began their careers producing private aircraft, and the pre-Great War era saw many weird and wonderful designs achieving varying degrees of success.

War itself, as is so often the case, drove tremendous

Above: Featuring composite construction throughout, side-stick controllers and a Ballistic Recovery System parachute to bring you and the aircraft down safely in the event of an in-flight emergency, the Cirrus SR20 (and similar SR22) look set to change the face of light aviation in the 21st century. (All KEY - Duncan Cubitt unless noted)

technological advances, and by 1918 the aeroplane was far more capable than it had been in pre-war days. Methods of control had been perfected and engine performance and reliability was also much improved – but more important as far as the growing private flying movement was concerned was the fact that aircraft were now being produced in large numbers.

The end of the Great War brought about a massive disposal of military aeroplanes which had become surplus to requirements. The Royal Air Force had 22,000 aircraft by 1918, and while many of these now-redundant machines were scrapped at the end of the conflict, others found their way into private hands. Public perception of flying increased and the 1920s saw the creation of flying clubs across the UK.

This was also the era of the Barnstormers, a band of aviators who travelled the country performing daredevil aerial stunts and offering the public the chance to take short pleasure flights. The Barnstormers increased public awareness of flying and some with the available income considered learning to fly. Although aviation was now incredibly popular and almost every town wanted its own airport, it was still very much a recreation for the wealthy and there was a need for affordable aeroplanes that the humbler enthusiast could fly.

In 1923, the British Air Ministry, in association with the *Daily Mail* newspaper, held a light aircraft competition at Lympne airfield in Kent. It attracted 23 entries from the leading manufacturers of the day and prizes were awarded for speed, altitude and landing accuracy. The

As we move into the 21st century, many pilots are looking back on the first century of flight with fondness, and consequently the number of restored classics is increasing. However, there is another way to get your hands on a classic design – by having a new example built. Aviat Aircraft in the USA includes this reproduction Monocoupe in its range of aircraft. (Aviat Aircraft)

principal award, however, was for fuel economy: consequently, the aircraft entered had engines so tiny they were barely capable of lifting them off the ground. First place in the award was shared by an English Electric Wren and an ANEC monoplane, both of which flew 73 miles on a single US gallon of fuel! Other entries included the de Havilland DH53 Hummingbird and the Hawker Cygnet.

Lessons learned from these trials were incorporated into all manner of later aircraft, the most noteworthy being the de Havilland DH60 Moth. Aware that the flying public needed a cheap and reliable aeroplane in which to learn to fly recreationally, Geoffrey de Havilland designed this aircraft to be light and strong, with good fuel capacity for touring and folding wings for storage and transport. Originally powered by a 60hp Cirrus engine, the aircraft later evolved to take a host of more powerful powerplants, all offering reliability. As a result, the Moth became the aircraft which really brought affordable private flying to England. Throughout the 1920s and 1930s, the Moth series continued to evolve to include enclosed cockpits and monoplane designs, many used for route proving and record-breaking flights.

By the 1930s, ever more specialist aircraft were being designed to cater for the growing ranks of private pilots. In 1931 William Piper invested $400 in Taylorcraft's E-2 Cub design. Although initially under-powered, the aircraft evolved quickly, and when more powerful engines were used it became a world-beater. By the time production ended in 1981, more than 34,500 Cubs – and later Super Cubs – had been constructed.

In 1932 Bernie Pietenpol flew his first Aircamper, a two-seat parasol machine that remains in production today, and in 1934 the first flight of the Bücker Bu131 Jungmann ushered in a new era of aerobatic flying.

By the mid-1930s flying had become more popular than ever, a fact demonstrated in 1936 when aerobatics was given the status of a sport at the Berlin Olympics, in which the Jungmann and the single-seat Jungmeister excelled.

When Henri Mignet first flew his HM.14 Pou du Ciel ('Flying Flea') in 1935, he could justifiably claim to have launched the homebuilding movement which thrives today. His book *Le Sport de l'Air* (also published in the UK as *How to Fly and Build the Flying Flea*) inspired many to begin constructing flying machines in their sheds and garages.

The 1930s was a decade when aviation was seldom out of the public eye, though as the world hovered on the brink of war in the latter part of the decade, development of GA types was slowed down in favour of machines of war.

The Beech D17 Staggerwing was essentially the Learjet of its day. Designed in the early 1930s, the aircraft exuded the elegance and styling associated with that era. The unusual backward-staggered wing was selected to aid visibility from the cockpit and provide a clean aerodynamic profile while maintaining a strong airframe. (KEY Collection)

Above: With a Blackburn Tomtit twin-cylinder engine producing just 26hp, the DH53 Hummingbird was entered in the Lympne aircraft trials in 1924. Because of its economical performance and light weight, the aircraft was used for airship launching experiments by the RAF, though only eight were subsequently built. One, G-EBHX, remains airworthy at the Shuttleworth Collection at Old Warden, Beds. (KEY Collection)

Once again, conflict brought tremendous advances in technology and by the time the fighting ended in 1945, the world of aviation was a very different place. The low-powered biplanes of the 1920s and 1930s had been replaced by fast all-metal aircraft with vastly increased horsepower from both piston and turbojet powerplants. As had happened at the end of World War One, peace brought a glut of spare aircraft available for disposal - along with large numbers of qualified pilots seeking new adventures and occupations.

Not surprisingly, these pilots bought up some of the redundant aircraft and used them in a variety of commercial applications. While transport and bomber aircraft found a home with the fledgling airlines and air taxi companies, retired training aircraft were snapped up

Above: **The first Pitts Special was designed in 1945, though the type remains a favourite with aerobatic pilots. Homebuilt examples continue to offer cheap entry to aerobatic competitions and the latest factory-produced two-seat machines offer unlimited performance.**
Below: **During a 50-day endurance flight, Bill Burkhart and Jim Heth picked up fuel for the Cessna 172 in containers passed from a truck speeding down the runway. The fuel was then lifted into the cabin and poured into the auxiliary tank from where it was pumped into the main tanks. Over the first 100 years of flight, private flying has included many record-breaking flights, proving its usefulness in the overall development of aviation.** (Cessna Aircraft Company)

by flying clubs, which were now starting to open up again.

With so many retired military pilots keen to retain their flying skills, the need for cheap and easy-to-fly light aircraft was huge, and consequently a number of pre-war civilian types were put back into production. In America, Luscombe returned its Model 8 Silvaire to production in 1945, refining the 1937 design with more power and a metal wing in place of the original fabric-covered unit. Similarly, the Aeronautical Corporation of America (Aeronca) refined its pre-war Chief into the Model 7AC Champ, first flight taking place in 1944 in readiness for the end of fighting.

Although returning aircraft to production was a quick and cheap option for some aircraft manufacturers, others chose to start afresh with new designs. In the UK, FG Miles designed the twin-engined Miles Gemini, which became a capable and popular four-seat touring aircraft, while in the USA a number of important light aircraft made their first flights. These included a small biplane designed by Curtis Pitts - the Pitts Special - and the Beech Model 35 Bonanza, two types which remain in production nearly 60 years later.

Perhaps one of the most important aircraft of the decade, in terms of its effect on private flying, was the Bell Model 47, the first helicopter in the world to achieve

private helicopter training and operations for many decades and the type is still a common sight today.

Throughout the 1940s, light aircraft continued to develop apace, though it slowed down a little as the next decade began. However, two of the most important light

aircraft of all time first took to the skies in the mid-1950s, both the product of the same manufacturer. In 1955 the Cessna Aircraft Company first flew its Model 172 four-seater, followed by the two-place Model 150 two years later. Since then, a combined total of more than 60,000

Above: **Taking its initial inspiration from research by the US military, the sport of microlighting has resulted in more affordable flying for all.**

Above: **The 1930s saw a tremendous increase in the popularity of aerobatics. The 1936 Berlin Olympics included it as a sport, attracting participants such as this Bücker Jungmeister.**

examples of the aircraft and their derivatives have been produced. The Model 172 remains in production and there can be few private pilots who have not sampled at least one of these machines during their careers.

The Cessna duo enjoyed unrivalled success until the early 1960s when the Piper Aircraft Company launched its PA-28, an aircraft which was to become a flying club workhorse, vying with Cessna's 150 and 172 for the title of 'most popular light aircraft'. Today more than 30,000 PA-28s have been built, in a number of versions, and around 1,000 fly in the UK alone.

Early 1962 saw the first flight of the helicopter which would change the face of rotary aviation. With a sensible selling price of well under a million dollars and reasonable running costs, the Bell 206 JetRanger made a four or five-seat turbine-powered helicopter affordable to the private pilot for the first time.

In the mid-1960s the US military commissioned a series of trials in which motors of increasing sizes were mated to a modified hang-glider wing developed by Francis Rogallo. While the proposed military applications (reconnaissance, and a freight carriage system to be towed behind a helicopter) were never realised, the research formed the basis for the first flex-wing microlight. Today microlighting affords a cheap and easy entry into private flying and the sport is becoming more and more popular.

Although the demand for – and consequently the development of – new light aircraft designs continued to slow into the 1970s, the homebuilding movement was taking off as new designs began to appear on drawing boards around the world. One of the most radical of these designs was Burt Rutan's Vari-EZ, a two-seat design with a canard foreplane and all-composite construction. In fact, the kit plane industry has remained vibrant beyond the turn of the century, even though sales of certificated aircraft are once again experiencing a slump.

One of the most important aircraft to emerge from the 1970s was Frank Robinson's two-seat R22 helicopter. First flying in 1975, this piston-powered machine became the basic trainer used by almost every private helicopter pilot during the 1980s and 1990s – a role it continues to

Piper's PA-34 Seneca was developed from the single-engined PA-32 Cherokee Six in the mid-1960s. Today the aircraft remains in production and is one of the most numerous twin-engined designs available to the private pilot.

Above: The two-seat Rans S6 is a popular choice for first-time kitbuilders as it comes with a high level of pre-finished parts, reducing the build time to some 500 hours. Powered by the ubiquitous Rotax 912 water-cooled engine, the S6 can cruise at around 85kts.

fulfil today.

Considering the economic boom of the 1980s, it is perhaps surprising to find that so few new GA designs were launched. Those which were, such as Richard Noble's ARV Super 2, an assortment of Britten Norman designs and the Trago Mills SAH-1, met with limited response from pilots.

In late 1980s many American manufacturers were affected by the draconian California Product Liability Law, which essentially brought to a halt the construction of single-engined light aircraft for fear of law-suits in the

event of a potential accident. Fortunately, the law was changed in the early 1990s and in 1995 Cessna restarted its Model 172, 182 and 206 production lines.

It was not until the 1990s that significant new designs began to appear on the GA market. March 1995 saw the first flight of an aircraft which was to send GA kicking and screaming into the 21st century – the Cirrus SR20. Built of composite construction, with side stick controllers and an extensive avionics suite, the aircraft has a Ballistic Recovery Systems parachute in the upper fuselage which can be deployed should it become unflyable.

Today, as powered aviation moves rapidly towards its centenary, the Cirrus, along with the Austrian-designed Diamond range of aircraft, remains the leading light of GA. In the USA, aircraft development appears to be focused on the higher end of the market, with corporate jets and aerial taxis receiving vast amounts of investment. However, this is slowly changing. Aircraft such as the new Liberty XL-2 are aspiring to become the Cessna 152 equivalent for the 21st century. The kit plane market remains active, new designs seeming to appear almost monthly.

The first century of powered flight produced some interesting aircraft – what will the second bring? Flying cars, strap-on helicopter backpacks and even personal tilt rotors have been discussed for some time, and in workshops across the world designers are working feverishly to make them a reality. The designs which will take us forward to the next 100 years may already be on the drawing board.

Above: When the affordable Robinson R22 first flew in 1975, it brought helicopter flying within the reach of more pilots than ever before. (KEY - Steve Bridgewater)

The Diamond Katana DA20-C1 Eclipse, one of many types flown by Dave Unwin for the flight test series in *Today's Pilot*.
(KEY - Steve Fletcher)

Century of Flight
Today's Pilot's View

DAVE UNWIN, EDITOR OF TODAY'S PILOT MAGAZINE,

APPRAISES THE CENTURY OF POWERED FLIGHT FROM THE

GENERAL AVIATION PERSPECTIVE.

Left: **'Going Places' is a continuing series of articles covering specific airfields and the services they provide. Sherburn certainly leaves the intrepid flyer in no doubt regarding the distance to his destination!** (KEY collection)

The history of flight is in many ways a considerable paradox. Indeed, were the Wright brothers able to view any modern light aircraft it is extremely unlikely that they would be particularly fazed by its appearance, at least externally. Indeed, such an aircraft would almost certainly be propelled by a piston engine turning a propeller, just as the earliest Wright Flyers were!

The new science of aviation proved almost irresistible to the Edwardians, and the early pioneers, such as Cody and Roe, became household names. This tremendous interest was not only prevalent in the UK, but also in many parts of Europe. In 1909 more than 500,000 people attended an aviation meet at Reims in France, what would airshow organisers give for figures like that today?

As is so often the case, it was the exigencies of war that really drove the development of the aeroplane. In 1914 the aeroplane was a flimsy contraption of very limited use, yet barely four years later it had been developed into a formidable weapon of war for both offence and defence. The cessation of hostilities saw many thousands of aircraft being sold as surplus on the civil market, where they were

Derby airfield is one of many UK airfields visited by the *Today's Pilot* team. Air-to-ground imagery is incorporated into several features and includes numerous sites of historic interest. (KEY - Stephen Bridgewater)

operated by the many pilots who had also found themselves out of a job at the end of the war. The war had also generated a huge amount of interest in aviation, with the top-scoring fighter aces becoming celebrities in their own right. Now everyone wanted to fly, and redundant military aviators were soon barnstorming surplus aircraft such as the Avro 504 all over the UK and North America. During this time the public's interest in both range and speed was almost insatiable, and pioneering flights such as Alcock and Brown's transatlantic crossing or the Smith brothers' flight to Australia were followed avidly, as were the great air races of the time, such as the Schneider Trophy.

Perhaps one of the most significant events for General Aviation in the UK during the 1920s was the introduction of the de Havilland Moth. With its reasonable speed, endurance and range, combined with folding wings and a modern, reliable engine, this aircraft more than any other made private flying a viable proposition. During this time great advances were also made in the field of gliding, most notably by the Germans who had been banned from developing any new powered aircraft by the Treaty of Versailles.

In the 1930s private flying made another quantum jump with the introduction of the Piper Cub, while interest in long-range races, such as the MacRobertson Race from the UK to Australia, was also very strong. It is interesting to

Above : **Today's Pilot editor Dave Unwin (centre) discusses GA issues at the 2001 AOPA exhibition in Fort Lauderdale, Florida.**
(KEY - Stephen Bridgewater)

Above right: **Today's Pilot reports on all of the major GA aerospace shows, such as Aero 2002 at Friedrichshafen, in order to bring you all the latest news from the GA scene.** (KEY - Ken Delve)

note that, for probably the only period in the history of aviation, many of the fastest aircraft were actually designed and built for the civil market! At the other end of the speed scale, Henri Mignet launched the 'homebuilt' movement with the publication of his book 'How To Fly and Build the Flying Flea'.

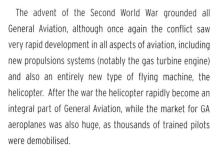
The advent of the Second World War grounded all General Aviation, although once again the conflict saw very rapid development in all aspects of aviation, including new propulsions systems (notably the gas turbine engine) and also an entirely new type of flying machine, the helicopter. After the war the helicopter rapidly become an integral part of General Aviation, while the market for GA aeroplanes was also huge, as thousands of trained pilots were demobilised.

This very exciting period saw the design of such timeless classics as the Beech Bonanza and Cessna 172, two GA types that are still in production today. At the other end of the GA spectrum, the first jet-powered business jets were beginning to take shape on the drawing board, with perhaps the Lear 23 being the most famous. The

helicopter also continued to make considerable progress, particularly when it was fitted with a gas turbine engine.

Although the next three decades saw a protracted period of apparelled growth, two unrelated events were to have a very profound effect on General Aviation. The first was the 1973 oil crisis, which, perhaps for the first time, forced both manufacturers and operators to look at the real costs of fuelling GA aircraft as oil prices quadrupled practically over night. The second was the Product Liability issue, which forced virtually every US aircraft manufacturer to cease production of light aircraft. However, as the production of certificated types slowed from a torrent to a trickle, the 'homebuilt' market expanded in leaps and bounds as innovative designers such as Burt Rutan created radical new types for this flourishing market.

Despite changes to US legislation, few of the major manufacturers got back into the light end of GA aircraft production in a significant way. However, the 'kitplane' market continued to go from strength to strength with companies such as Vans and Europa producing thousands of airframes. Although a modern GA aircraft is externally

essentially the same as its counterpart from the mid-1950s, there have been significant advances in both propulsion systems and avionics. Indeed, it is in the area of avionics that we have seen the most significant changes, with some remarkable innovations (such as all-glass cockpits) being found in some GA aircraft. Propulsion systems have also seen a sea change, with a move away from the classic air-cooled direct drive aero-engine to lighter, liquid-cooled geared engines and the first of the new breed of aero diesel engines. Another innovation in propulsion has been the very light jet engine, such as the Williams FJ44. This development has made it possible for designers to begin work on small, personal jet aircraft, while the ubiquitous Pratt & Whitney PT6 turboprop continues to be the engine of choice for a wide variety of airframe manufacturers.

So much for the first century of General Aviation, but what about the next? For a variety of reasons it seems likely that the propeller will continue to be the preferred method of propulsion at the light end, although it is possible that efficient electric motors, driven by a combination of ultra-modern batteries and fuel cells will become viable. The cockpit will continue to evolve rapidly, as systems currently under test by NASA come to fruition. Whether we will see affordable VTOL aeroplanes (such as a scaled-down V22 Osprey) widely available is a moot point, although the gyrocopter has certainly enjoyed resurgence in interest lately. Within the UK, one of the biggest GA stories of recent years has been the introduction of the NPPL, a subject covered in some depth by Today's Pilot. Whether this initiative will regenerate interest in GA within the UK remains to be seen, although it is a fact that the new breed of 450 and 750kg light aircraft are already proving to be more capable than earlier types in just about every way.

The GA sector of the aviation world is just as fascinating today as it was in those heady days of the 1930s and every aspect of the subject is covered regularly by Today's Pilot.

1960-69

1960-69

1. Canadian Tutor
The Canadair CL-41 prototype makes a successful first flight on January 13, 1960. The type, better known as the CT-114 tutor, goes on to serve with the Canadian military for more than 30 years. (KEY collection)

2. Piper four-seater
On January 14, 1960, Piper flies its new PA-28 four-seat touring aircraft. Thirty-two years on, the aircraft is still in production, albeit in a modernised form. (KEY - Steve Fletcher)

3. All-weather attack
Grumman's A-6 Intruder makes its first flight on April 19, 1960. The aircraft is set to provide the US Navy with an all-weather attack capability before eventually being retired in December 1996. (KEY collection)

4. Hawkeye
Yet another product for the US Navy emerges from the Grumman stable – the E-2 Hawkeye carrier-borne AEW aircraft, which flies for the first time on October 21, 1960. The aircraft goes on to serve with a number of air arms around the world, though the principal customer is the US Navy. (US Navy)

5. Vertical jet
The Hawker P.1127, prototype of the famous Harrier jump jet, makes its first flight on October 21, 1960. Today the aircraft remains the only practical VSTOL jet aircraft in regular service. (KEY collection)

6. Ilyushin's largest
The Ilyushin Il-62 four-engine jet airliner makes its maiden flight on January 3, 1961. The aircraft is designed as a long-range transport and is remarkably similar to the British VC 10 which flies over a year later. (David Stephens collection)

7. Turbo Porter
The Pilatus PC-6 Turbo Porter, illustrated here by an Austrian Air Force example,

SIGNIFICANT DATES

JANUARY 23, 1960: The first ski-equipped Lockheed C-130D Hercules lands at Byrd Station, Antarctica, on the first of what will become regular supply flights.

FEBRUARY 20/21, 1960: The first non-stop flight between London and Bombay, India, is accomplished by an Air India Boeing 707 on a delivery flight.

MARCH 23, 1960: Westland absorbs the helicopter division of Bristol Aircraft and on May 2, acquires the Fairey aviation, part of an early trend in consolidation amongst British aerospace companies.

APRIL 6, 1960: The Short SC.1 VTOL research aircraft completes the first transition from vertical to forward flight by a jet-powered aircraft. The aircraft has four lift engines and one for forward flight.

APRIL 9, 1960: A world speed record for propeller-driven aircraft of 545.07mph (338.07km/h) is set by a Soviet Tupolev Tu-114 airliner. The aircraft is a commercial development of the Tu-95 bomber and is powered by four massive turboprop engines.

MAY 1, 1960: An American U-2 high altitude reconnaissance aircraft is shot down by a surface-to-air missile over Sverdlovsk, USSR. Pilot Garry Powers is sentenced to ten years hard labour for spying but is traded for Soviet spy Colonel Rudolf Abel on February 10, 1962.

JULY 1, 1960: British United Airlines commences operations.

OCTOBER 31, 1960: Today sees the last piston-engine scheduled service to use London Heathrow, a BEA DC-3 flight to Birmingham. It is also BEA's final DC-3 flight.

NOVEMBER 16, 1960: A freight version of the Canadair CL-44 (CL-44D-4), the first freighter to feature a completely hinged tail section to enable rear loading, makes its first flight.

makes its first flight on May 2, 1961. The aircraft has an astonishing STOL performance and proves highly popular in the Alpine regions. (KEY - Alan Warnes)

8. Utility Mil
Probably the most common Soviet utility helicopter is the Mil Mi-8 *Hip*, which flies for the first time in June 1961. It is extensively used by the Soviet Bloc countries and also enjoys good export sales around the world. (David Stephens collection)

9. Carvair
The Aviation Traders' Carvair was a unique cargo design, using surplus Douglas DC-4 airframes, which made its first flight on June 21, 1961. It features an elevated flight deck allowing direct loading through a hinged nose section. (KEY collection)

10. Maritime Atlantic
The Dassault-Breguet Atlantic maritime patrol and ASW aircraft makes its first

flight on October 21, 1961. The aircraft is used extensively by France and Germany, but is also exported - illustrated is one operated by the Pakistan Navy.
(KEY - Alan Warnes)

11. Mach 3 jet
Originally designed for operation by the CIA, the Lockheed A-12 Mach 3 capable reconnaissance aircraft makes its first flight from the secret Groom Lake facility in Nevada on April 26, 1962. Illustrated is

one of two A-12s modified to carry the D-21 drone under Project Tagboard. (Lockheed)

12. British trijet
The de Havilland DH.121 Trident makes its first flight on January 9, 1962. The company is soon absorbed by Hawker Siddeley, but the Trident's sales potential is restricted due to its limited capacity and short range. (KEY collection)

1960-69

FEBRUARY 28, 1961: The Cessna 336 makes its maiden flight. The aircraft features a pusher and puller propeller arrangement and finds fame as the O-2 observation aircraft during the Vietnam War.

MARCH 30, 1961: NASA's Joe Walker establishes a new altitude record of 169,600ft (51,695m) in the North American X-15, the first of a series of astounding records achieved by this incredible aircraft.

APRIL 12, 1961: Soviet astronaut Yuri Gagarin becomes the first man into space when he is carried into orbit by a the Vostoc 1 rocket.

MAY 26, 1961: A USAF Convair B-58 Hustler completes a flight from New York to Paris in 3 hours, 19 minutes and 41 seconds - an average speed of 1,103mph (1,775km/h)

JUNE 1, 1961: United Air Lines becomes the western world's largest airline when it absorbs over Capital Airlines.

JUNE 17, 1961: First flight of Hindustan Aircraft's HF-24 Marut, designed by German Kurt Tank who also designed the Focke-Wulf 190 of World War Two.

OCTOBER 14, 1961: For a 12-hour period, all commercial aircraft in American airspace are grounded while the USAF undertakes a massive air defence exercise called Operation Sky Shield II.

OCTOBER 16, 1961: Air Afrique is established

by 12 independent African states to provide domestic and international flights.

JANUARY 12, 1962: Defoliation operations in Vietnam to expose Vietcong trails are begun by the USAF using low flying aircraft spraying defoliating herbicides.

FEBRUARY 1962: The Central Flying School at Little Rissington, Gloucestershire, commences operations with the new Folland Gnat jet trainer.

Cessna336 **May 1961:** SOKO G2 Galeb **May 2, 1961:** Pilatus PC-6 **June 1961:** Mil Mi-8 **June 17, 1961:** Hindustan HF-24 **Aug 15, 1961:** Beagle Basset **Sept 21, 1961:** Boeing Vertol CH-47 **Oct 21, 1961:** Breguet Atlantic

1960-69

1. Sky Crane
The ungainly, but highly practical, Sikorsky S-64/CH-54 Sky Crane makes its maiden flight on May 9, 1962. This example is still operated by Erickson Air-Crane, seen in use fighting forest fires. (KEY - Dave Allport)

2. VC 10
The Vickers VC 10 makes its maiden flight on June 29, 1960. It is the final large airliner to be built solely by a British company. (Gordon Swanborough collection)

3. Super Frelon
Sud Aviation successfully completes the first flight of the Super Frelon helicopter on December 7, 1962. Eventually 99 are built in France, though the type is also produced under licence in China as the Changzhou WZ-6. (French Navy)

4. Jet Ranger
The Bell 206 Jet Ranger prototype (HO-4) made its first flight on December 8, 1962. The first proper 206 flew on January 10,

1966, and is to prove popular with both military and commercial operators the world over. (Bell)

5. STOL Skyvan
The Short Skyvan makes its maiden flight on January 17, 1963. It is small but rugged and its high aspect ratio wing gives it excellent short field performance. Eventually 153 are built and prove particularly popular in countries with little transport infrastructure. (Gordon Swanborough collection)

6. Bold Boeing
Seeing the need for a jet airliner to replace piston engine types still used on domestic routes, Boeing flies its three-engine 727 on February 9, 1963. The company anticipates sales of about 300 - eventually 1,832 are built. (Boeing)

7. Euro transport
The C-160, built by the joint Franco-German Transall group, makes its first flight on February 25, 1963. The aircraft is ordered

SIGNIFICANT DATES

FEBRUARY 28, 1962: The first ejection of a human using an escape capsule is performed by Weapons Officer Edward Murray from a USAF B-58 Hustler at 20,000ft (6,100m) during a test of the system. It works perfectly and he lands safely.

APRIL 14, 1962: The Bristol 188 high-speed, high altitude research aircraft makes its maiden flight. Its primary objective to research the effects of kinetic heating on airframes.

APRIL 30, 1962: NASA's Joe Walker takes his world altitude record to dizzy new heights when he reaches 246,000ft (75,195m) in the X-15A.

JUNE 27, 1962: The X-15A, flown by Joe Walker, sets a new speed record of 4,159mph (6,693km/h) - in excess of Mach 6.

AUGUST 13, 1962: The de Havilland DH.125 executive jet makes its first flight at the company's Hatfield facility. However, the company is soon absorbed by Hawker

Siddeley, and the aircraft becomes known as the HS 125 and eventually, as the British Aerospace 125.

SEPTEMBER 19, 1962: First flight of the Aero Spacelines Inc Guppy, a Boeing 377 Stratocruiser airframe modified with a huge, bulbous fuselage to carry outsize items.

OCTOBER 14, 1962: USAF U-2 reconnaissance aircraft discover Soviet SS-4 ballistic missiles on Cuba. This sparks the Cuban missile crisis

and until the Soviets back down and withdraw the missiles on October 28, the world hovers on the brink of an all-out nuclear war.

OCTOBER 12, 1962: The Dassault Balzac, capable of vertical take-off and landing, makes its first flight. However, it requires eight small Rolls-Royce RB.108 lift jets to achieve this, plus a separate engine for forward flight. The weight and fuel penalties make the concept impractical.

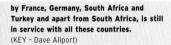

by France, Germany, South Africa and Turkey and apart from South Africa, is still in service with all these countries. (KEY - Dave Allport)

8. Dassault Exec jet
Dassault's first executive jet, the twin-engine Falcon 20, makes its maiden flight on May 4, 1963. It is the first in a long line of executive/business jets from the French manufacturer. (Dassault)

9. Saab jet trainer
The Saab 105 twin-engine jet trainer makes its first flight on June 29, 1963. The aircraft is supplied to Sweden and Austria, both of whom still operate the type. (Saab)

10. Starlifter
The USAF's latest strategic airlifter, the Lockheed C-141A Starlifter, makes its first flight on December 17, 1963. Some 270 of the 284 built are subsequently lengthened to produce the C-141B. Today the type is gradually being retired by the USAF as its replacement, the C-17A Globemaster III, is delivered. (Lockheed)

11. RAF giant
A new large transport aircraft able to carry heavy equipment and cargo, the Short Belfast, makes its maiden flight on January 5, 1964. Only ten aircraft are built and all serve with the RAF's No.53 Squadron. Following retirement by the military, a handful continue to be operated for many years by cargo carrier HeavyLift Cargo Airlines. (Gordon Swanborough collection)

12. King twin
On January 20, 1964, Beech flies the prototype Model 90 King Air twin-engine turboprop utility transport. The aircraft proves to be a huge success, and thousands are built to a multitude of specifications for both military and civil operators. (Beech)

1960-69

FEBRUARY 11, 1963: Test pilot Bill Bedford lands and takes off from the Royal Navy aircraft carrier HMS Ark Royal in the prototype Hawker P.1127.

APRIL 18, 1963: The Northrop X-21A, a modified Douglas WB-66D, makes its maiden flight. The aircraft features a revolutionary laminar airflow wing designed to eliminate boundary layer air turbulence over the wing and convert it into thrust by channelling it through thousands of tiny holes and ducts in the wings.

MAY 27, 1963: The first USAF variant of the McDonnell Douglas F-4 Phantom, the F-4C. In USAF service the Phantom goes on to fly fighter, reconnaissance, fighter-bomber and wild weasel missions until 1996.

JUNE 5, 1963: US President John F Kennedy pledges to give government funds to aid the development (estimated at $1billion) of an American supersonic transport (SST) in response to the efforts being made in Europe. Eventually America pulls the plug on its efforts and then causes the European Concorde a great deal of trouble getting access to US airports.

AUGUST 22, 1963: NASA pilot Joe Walker sets a new world altitude record at an amazing 354,200ft (107,960m) - 67 miles up! The record has never been broken.

OCTOBER 7, 1963: A new sleek executive jet takes to the air today - the Learjet 23. William Lear's vision is spot-on: the family of Learjet aircraft which follow becomes one of the most lucrative in the business jet field.

OCTOBER 30, 1963: In an extraordinary feat of flying, a US Marine Corps KC-130 Hercules makes a successful landing aboard the aircraft carrier USS Forrestal without the aid of an arrestor hook. This is the largest fixed wing aircraft to ever land on a carrier.

FEBRUARY 1, 1964: Eastern Airlines is the first carrier to introduce the new Boeing 727.

1960-69

1. Ultimate MiG
The MiG-25 *Foxbat* prototype makes its maiden flight on March 6, 1964. The Mach 3 aircraft is designed to intercept the anticipated fleet of American B-70 Valkyrie Mach 3 bombers. In the event, the MiG-25 serves mostly as a high speed reconnaissance aircraft. (KEY collection)

2. Mach 3 Valkyrie
The mighty North American XB-70 Valkyrie

prototype makes its first flight on September 21, 1964. The Mach 3 aircraft is designed to penetrate Soviet defences at high speed and high altitude. Powered by six General Electric J93-GE-3 engines producing a combined 180,000lb (806.4kN) of thrust, it is one of the loudest and most impressive aircraft ever flown. (NASA)

3. TSR.2 promise?
The advanced BAC TSR.2 makes its first flight on September 27, 1964. After initial

testing, the project is cancelled and although many consider this folly on the part of the British government, evidence emerges of more technical difficulties with the programme than the public realise. (KEY collection)

4. Sikorsky giant
The large and impressive Sikorsky S-65/CH-53 Sea Stallion makes its maiden flight on October 14, 1964. The helicopter is developed for the US Navy, US Marine Corps

and USAF, as well as being exported to a number of customers. (KEY – Duncan Cubitt)

5. Swinger!
Affectionately known by a number of nicknames, including 'Swinger' and 'Ardvark', the General Dynamics F-111 variable geometry strike aircraft takes to the air for the first time on December 21, 1964. It becomes a potent weapon, especially when equipped with the Pave Tac laser designation system. Another variant

SIGNIFICANT DATES

APRIL 9, 1964: The de Havilland Canada DHC-5 Buffalo takes to the air for its first flight. The aircraft is seen as a larger successor to the DHC-4 Caribou and can carry a considerably larger payload, though retaining a good STOL performance.

APRIL 17, 1964: Jerrie Mock is the first woman to fly solo round-the-world when she touches down at Port Columbus, Ohio. Her trip takes 29 days and covers 23,103 miles (96,497km) with 21 stops en route.

MAY 11, 1964: Jacqueline Cochran establishes a new speed record for women of 1,429.246mph (2,300.14km/h) in a Lockheed F-104G Starfighter.

DECEMBER 22, 1964: The Lockheed SR-71A Blackbird, a two-seat reconnaissance development of the A-12, makes its first flight. The Mach 3 Blackbird goes on to become the ultimate high-speed reconnaissance aircraft until its 'premature' retirement in the 1990s.

DECEMBER 22, 1964: US President Johnson approves funding for the development of the CX-HLS heavy transport aircraft for the USAF. Lockheed wins the contract and the aircraft becomes known as the C-5 Galaxy.

DECEMBER 26, 1964: A Piper twin Comanche, flown by Max Conrad, completes a 7,878-mile (12,678km) journey from Cape Town, South Africa, to St Petersburg, Florida – a new record distance for this class of aircraft.

JANUARY 11, 1965: The experimental tilt-wing Ling-Temco-Vought-Hiller-Ryan XC-142A aircraft completes its first transition from vertical to horizontal flight. The entire wing, housing four engines and propellers, tilts through 90 degrees. Although not put into production, the programme provides vital data for use in the V-22 programme of the 1990s.

FEBRUARY 25, 1965: The short-haul Douglas DC-9 twin-engine jet airliner makes its first flight at Long Beach, California. It is a huge

is the EF-111A ECM aircraft, illustrated.
(KEY - Duncan Cubitt)

6. Giant of the skies

Antonov's giant An-22 *Cock*, powered by four 15,000shp Kuznetsov turboprops driving contra-rotating propellers, flies for the first time on February 27, 1965. The large transport can operate from rough surfaces and a 724-seat, two-deck passenger version is also proposed but never built. (KEY - Duncan Cubitt)

7. Purposeful Puma

The Sud Aviation SA.330 Puma makes a successful maiden flight on April 15, 1965. The aircraft is used by a large number of countries and is further developed into the Super Puma and Cougar, the latter is still in production today. (KEY - Duncan Cubitt)

8. Tactical twin

The de Havilland Canada DHC-6 Twin Otter STOL light transport aircraft makes its first flight on May 20, 1965, and goes on to

enjoy great success . A total of 844 are supplied to customers around the world.
(de Havilland Canada)

9. Bronco

The North American OV-10 Bronco, designed to fulfil a US Marine Cops requirement for a light armed reconnaissance aircraft, makes its first flight on July 16, 1965. The aircraft is also supplied to the USAF and sees extensive use during the Vietnam War.
(US National Archives)

10. Huey Cobra

The Bell AH-1 Cobra is developed from the Bell UH-1 as an armed attack helicopter dedicated to providing close support to ground troops. It makes its first flight on September 7, 1965, and sees extensive service in Vietnam from late 1967. Illustrated is a US Marine Corps AH-1W which forms the attack element of any Marines Expeditionary Unit (MEU).
(KEY - Alan Warnes)

1960-69

success and is continually developed over the next 25 years. Today its descendant, the Boeing 717, continues the legacy of the Douglas design.

MARCH 6, 1965: A US Navy SH-3A completes the first non-stop transcontinental flight between the USS *Hornet* in San Francisco, California, and the USS *Franklin D Roosevelt* in Mayport, Florida.

APRIL 6, 1965: In what is the largest airliner

order so far placed, United Air Lines commits itself to a $750 million order for 144 Boeing 727s and 737s and Douglas DC-8s, made up of a mixture of lease, buy and options.

JUNE 9, 1965: The first telephone link between an aircraft and the ground is achieved via a communications satellite between the crew of a Pan Am 707 and the company's head office in New York.

JUNE 10, 1965: The first completely

automatic landing by a passenger-carrying airliner is made by a BEA Trident at London Heathrow.

JUNE 13, 1965: Britten-Norman flies the first Islander multi-role transport aircraft at its Bembridge facility on the Isle of Wight. The ten-seat aircraft proves popular and finds military as well as commercial customers.

OCTOBER 28, 1965: The International Air Transport Association (IATA) clears the way

for in-flight movies to be shown aboard aircraft.

NOVEMBER 15, 1965: A Flying Tiger Line Boeing 707 completes the first round-the-world flight via both poles.

DECEMBER 2, 1965: For the first time, a nuclear-powered aircraft carrier launches offensive air strikes: the USS *Enterprise* commences air strikes against Viet Cong targets in South Vietnam.

1960-69

1.Corsair II

The Vought A-7 Corsair II makes its first flight on September 27, 1965. Originally designed to meet a US Navy strike aircraft requirement to replace the A-4 Skyhawk, the A-7 is ordered by the USAF and supplied to Greece: refurbished examples have also been exported to Portugal and Thailand.

2.Skyservant

Originally developed from the earlier Do 27, the Dornier Do 28, which makes its first

flight on February 23, 1966, is an altogether different aircraft. A twin-engine light transport aircraft, it is widely used by the Germany military and is exported to a number of nations. (David Stephens collection)

3.New Swiss trainer

Although the original prototype Pilatus PC-7 first flew on April 12, 1966, it is not until August 18, 1978, that the first production aircraft flies. Over the years, the aircraft has enjoyed considerable export success,

serving with at least 14 different countries. A Royal Netherlands Air Force example is illustrated. (KEY - Dave Allport)

4.Versatile Yak

The Yakovlev Yak-40 three-engine airliner makes its first flight on October 21, 1966. It is designed to operate from rough airstrips

SIGNIFICANT DATES

JANUARY 17, 1966: A USAF B-52 and KC-135 collide over the Spanish Mediterranean coast, with the loss of seven crew. Four hydrogen bombs being carried by the B-52 are lost, but after an extensive land and sea search they are recovered.

APRIL 1, 1966: The British Airports Authority (BAA) is formed to look after the UK's airports, a role it still maintains.

APRIL 13, 1966: Pan Am commits itself to

purchasing 25 of the new Boeing 747 Jumbo jet in an order worth $525 million.

APRIL 20, 1966: The North American Air Defense Command (NORAD) combat operations centre moves into the extensive underground complex at Cheyenne Mountain, Colorado. In the 26 years that follow, the mountain is only sealed once - on September 11, 2001.

JUNE 8, 1966: The darkest day in the history of the Edwards Air Force base, California - the

Mach 3 Valkyrie bomber collides with an F-104 Starfighter flown by NASA's Joe Walker during a photographic sortie. Walker, who had set numerous records in the X-15, is killed, as is the co-pilot of the XB-70. Its pilot, Al White, ejected and survived.

JULY 12, 1966: The Northrop/NASA M2-F2 lifting body research aircraft makes its first successful un-powered flight after being dropped from a B-52. The wingless, bulbous shape of the aircraft generates considerable

lift and provides valuable data for use on the Space Shuttle in the 1980s.

SEPTEMBER 24, 1966: The women's world speed record is increased to 1,270mph (2,044km/h) by the Soviet Union's Marina Solovyeva, flying a MiG-Ye-76.

NOVEMBER 14, 1966: A USAF C-141 becomes the first jet aircraft to land in Antarctica when it touches down at McMurdo Sound.

Apr 21, 1964: HFB 320 Hansa Jet   July 15, 1964: SIAI-Marchetti SF.260   Aug 29, 1964: Piaggio PD-808   Sept 4, 1964: HAL Kiran   Sept 21, 1964: NA XB-70 Valkyrie   Sept 27, 1964: BAC TSR.2   Sept 29, 1964: Hiller-Ryan XC-142A

and can carry up o 32 passengers: more than 800 are eventually built. (Mark Stanton)

5. Mirage evolution

The Mirage F1, which first flies on December 23, 1966, follows on from the success of the Mirage III but abandons the proven delta wing configuration in favour of a shoulder-mounted conventional swept wing. However, it is a highly effective fighter/attack and reconnaissance aircraft and enjoys buoyant sales. (Dassault)

6. Mighty Viggen

One of the most distinctive aircraft ever built, the Saab Viggen takes to the air for the first time on February 8, 1967. The Swedish Air Force has been the only customer for the type, though only now is it finally being phased out of service. (Saab)

7. Flogger

The Mikoyan MiG-23 *Flogger* tactical fighter makes its maiden flight on April 3, 1967.

The aircraft, and its ground-attack derivative the MiG-27, form a vital part of Soviet Air Force tactics and remain in service with many air arms. (Artur Sarkisyan)

8. Brilliant Boeing

The most successful airliner ever built, the Boeing 737, makes its first flight on April 9, 1967. Designed for short-haul domestic routes, it is snapped up by the airlines and remains in constant development. Still in production today, more than 4,000 have been sold. (KEY - Dave Allport)

9. Comet reborn

Based on the de Havilland Comet airframe, the Hawker Siddeley Nimrod maritime patrol and ASW aircraft makes its first flight on May 23, 1967. The aircraft is still in service with the RAF, and 18 examples are currently being upgraded to MRA.4 specification with new avionics, wings and turbofan engines. (RAF/Sgt Rick Brewell)

1960-69

JANUARY 2, 1967: Boeing and General Electric are awarded the contract to build America's SST - but the project is eventually cancelled, due to technical difficulties and mounting costs.

JANUARY 13, 1967: America's fourth largest aerospace company is created with the merger of Douglas and McDonnell, forming the McDonnell Douglas Corporation.

FEBRUARY 10, 1967: The Dornier Do 31 VSTOL

research aircraft flies for the first time at Oberpfaffenhofen, Germany. Designed as a medium-size transport, it features eight Rolls-Royce RB.162-4D lift jets housed in large wing tip pods to provide vertical lift.

APRIL 6, 1967: TWA dispenses with the last of its piston-engine aircraft to become the first American carrier operating an exclusively jet fleet.

MAY 9, 1967: Fokker's first jet airliner, the

65-seat F28, makes its first flight at Amsterdam Schiphol airport.

JUNE 5, 1967: The Six-Day War commences with pre-emptive strikes against Egypt by the Israel Air Force. Barely four hours after the operation begins, Israel has destroyed half the Egyptian Air Force. Strikes are also made against Syria and Jordan.

JUNE 5, 1967: British charter carrier Monarch Airlines is formed to offer

exclusive charter flights to tour operators.

JUNE 28, 1967: French aerospace consolidation takes another step as Dassault merges with Breguet.

OCTOBER 3, 1967: The North American X-15A-2 sets a new outright world speed record for an aircraft when NASA's Pete Knight takes the aircraft to an astonishing 4,534mph (7,297km/h) or Mach 6.72 - 75 miles (120km) per minute!

1960-69

1. Water bomber
The Canadair CL-215 amphibian makes its maiden flight on October 23, 1967. Its primary role is as a fire-fighting water bomber and 125 are built and sold to many customers, including the Royal Thai Navy (illustrated). A retrofit kit to add turboprop engines is made available from 1990. (KEY collection)

2. Galaxy
The largest aircraft so far built in the West, the Lockheed C-5 Galaxy, takes to the air for the first time on June 30, 1968. Eighty-one C-5As and a further 50 C-5Bs are delivered to the USAF and these form the backbone of its airlift capability, able to carry tanks, helicopters and vast amounts of military equipment. The type is now commencing a series of major upgrade programmes which will keep it effective for many years. (KEY - Mark Nicholls)

3. Jaguar pounces
The first example of the Anglo-French Sepecat Jaguar takes to the air for the first time at Istres, France, on September 8, 1968. The attack aircraft remains a vital part of RAF strategy, though it is gradually being retired by the French Air Force. (KEY collection)

4. Bandeirante!
A new Brazilian-built light transport aircraft takes to the air for the first time on October 26, 1968. The programme is taken over by Embraer and the aircraft becomes known as the EMB-110 Bandeirante, becoming a popular design with both military and commercial operators. This Brazilian Air Force C-95 version is seen in Rio de Janeiro with Sugar Loaf Mountain in the background. (KEY collection)

5. Aero winner
The Aero L-39 Albatros first flies on November 4, 1968, and is to set to equip many Soviet Bloc air arms. After the end of the Cold War, it also finds numerous markets

SIGNIFICANT DATES

October 5, 1967: The Japanese Shin Meiwa SS-2 ASW flying boat makes its maiden flight. An amphibious version is subsequently introduced to service with the Japanese Marine Self Defence Force.

December 1967: The ultra-quiet Lockheed QT-2PC surveillance aircraft - a Schweizer SGS 2-32 glider fitted with a silenced Continental O-200-A engine - begins night operations over Vietnam. It is designed to gather intelligence on enemy troop movements without being detected, and is an unqualified success.

November 18, 1967: France flies the Dassault Mirage G, Europe's first variable geometry aircraft, but it does not go into production.

February 20, 1968: A Learjet 25 establishes a new climb-to-height record in its class, reaching 40,000ft (12,192m) in 6 minutes and 29 seconds.

March 1968: The Douglas DC-3 returns to combat missions with the USAF in the form of the AC-47 gunship fitted with three 7.62mm miniguns. Its success prompts the development of the far more capable AC-130 gunship.

May 5, 1968: A Grumman Gulfstream II becomes the first executive jet to cross the Atlantic non-stop with a 3,500 mile (5,633km) flight from Teterboro, New Jersey, to London Gatwick, which takes 6 hours 55 minutes.

September 5, 1968: The US Navy takes delivery of the 3,000th McDonnell Douglas F-4 Phantom - a further 2,195 are subsequently built.

December 21-27, 1968: NASA's Apollo 8 spacecraft undertakes a six-day mission taking the first men to orbit the moon - astronauts Frank Borman, Jim Lovell and William Anders.

December 31, 1968: The Soviet Tupolev Tu-144 supersonic airliner makes its maiden flight.

in the West and is popular as a private jet, notably in the USA. (KEY collection)

6.Boeing's Jumbo
Unquestionably the most easily-recognised Boeing airliner ever, the massive 747 Jumbo jet takes to the skies for the first time on February 9, 1969, changing the face of commercial air travel for ever. (Boeing)

7.Mach 2 airliner
The Anglo-French BAe/Aerospatiale Concorde makes its maiden flight on March 2, 1969. After a turbulent first few years, the aircraft settles down to provide the world's only regular supersonic passenger flights: it still does so on transatlantic flights between Britain, France and the USA. (Air France)

8.LET twin
The LET 410 light transport aircraft makes its first flight on April 16, 1969, and is originally designed as a small airliner for feeder routes. It also finds favour with the military and well over 1,000 are built.
(KEY - David Stephens collection)

9.Citation jet
Cessna flies its new Citation 500, appropriately registered N500CC, for the first time on September 15, 1969. The twin-engine executive/business jet proves a hugely popular design and is continually updated. This example is a Citation X, sporting a very attractive paint scheme.
(KEY - Ken Delve)

1960-69

Although it beats the European Concorde into the air, it does not enjoy the commercial success of the Anglo-French aircraft .

APRIL 30, 1969: The RAF's Bomber and Fighter Commands are united to create RAF Strike Command.

JUNE 4, 1969: Cuban Armando Socarras survived temperatures of -35 Celsius when he stowed away in the undercarriage bay of

an Iberia DC-8 during a flight from Havana to Madrid, Spain.

JULY 20, 1969: After a successful 'flight' from Earth, astronauts Neil Armstrong and Buzz Aldrin land on the moon. Armstrong then becomes the first human to walk on another world, thanks to the engineers who built the Apollo 11 craft that took him there.

JULY 21, 1969: The British Government pulls out of the European Airbus project,

but Hawker Siddeley continues to privately fund its efforts to develop and build the wings for the new European airliner, a decision which will subsequently be seen as both a wise and lucrative move.

AUGUST 6, 1969: The giant Mil V-12 (MI-12) helicopter sets a new payload record when it lifts 88,636lb (40,205kg) to an altitude of 7,398ft (2,254m)

NOVEMBER 7-10, 1969: A new closed-circuit

distance record for piston engine aircraft is set by James Bede in the BD-2. Un-refuelled, the aircraft flies a distance of 8,973.4 miles (14,441.26km).

DECEMBER 1, 1969: Federal Air Regulation (FAR) 36 comes into effect in the USA - the first legislation to tackle the problem of aircraft noise near airports. Similar measures are introduced over the next 33 years so that today's aircraft are far quieter than those of the 1960s.

Key Publishing Mail Order Service

Airport Specials - £17.95 each

90 minutes of take-offs and landings from a variety of perspectives. More than 100 different aircraft and airlines from the world's favourite airports.

Vol 26
Bangkok vh329
(running time 60mins)

Vol 24 Kai Tak-
Final days vh320

Vol 3 Heathrow
vh252

Vol 8 Palma De
Mallorca vh257

Vol 14 New York
JFK vh263

Vol 15
Paris CdG vh271

Vol 25 Chek
Lap Kok vh321

Also available:

Vol 1	Hong Kong Kai Tak	vh250	Vol 13	Vienna	vh262
Vol 2	Frankfurt	vh251	Vol 16	Chicago	vh276
Vol 4	Dusseldorf	vh253	Vol 17	Barcelona	vh277
Vol 5	Munich	vh254	Vol 18	Amsterdam	vh278
Vol 6	Berlin	vh255	Vol 19	Gran Canaria	vh290
Vol 7	Zurich	vh256	Vol 20	Brussels	vh291
Vol 9	San Francisco	vh258	Vol 21	Sydney	vh311
Vol 10	Los Angeles	vh259	Vol 22	Tampa	vh312
Vol 11	Miami Int.	vh260	Vol 23	Phoenix	vh313
Vol 12	Dubai	vh261			

Airliners of the World - £17.95 each

Each video features: 90 minutes of action from international airports around the world. With 150 taxi, take-off, approach and air-to air from more than 150 different aircrafts and airlines.

737 Special
vh282

747 Special
vh283

A320 Special
vh284

A340 Special
vh285

Mouse Mats

This practical range of civil aviation mouse mats is a must for all aviation enthusiasts. The 23cm x 18cm size affords plenty of surface to show off the high quality images. Protected by a scratch resistant, washable vinyl surface these images sit upon a non-slip natural rubber base.

BOEING 737-300
LUFTHANSA
MM3103

CATHAY PACIFIC -
BOEING 747-400
MM2873

AIRBUS 320
COCKPIT
MM3105

Only £4.50 each (plus P&P)

NEW! BRITISH AIRSHOWS 2002

The biggest and best aviation video of the year, featuring action from all the top British airshow events of 2002 and exclusive behind-the-scenes footage. From Spitfires and Lancaster bombers to the new Eurofighter and the Red Arrows aerobatics team, every great display of the year is here! Also available in DVD - includes an extra 30 minutes of exclusive material.

VIDEO 125 mins 05522	£14.99
DVD 125 mins 05523	£15.99

BIGGIN HILL AIR FAIR 2002

The annual Biggin Hill Air Fair, yet again features a fabulous display of fast jets, classic warbirds, and a few unusual performers such as the microlight and the group of Virgin Lightships. Surrounding them were the Tornado, Jaguar and Red Arrows, the Battle of Britain Memorial Flight, an F-16, the rare Grumman Albatros seaplane and many more.

VIDEO 90 mins 05423	£14.99

RAF WADDINGTON AIR SHOW 2002

Fast jets from no less than 10 countries wowed the huge crowds with breathtaking low fast passes, aerobatics and displays of awesome power provided by: F-16s, F/A 18s, Marine Tornado, a Mig 29 and F4 Phantom, a full range of RAF jets and national display teams. Features unrivalled behind the scenes and interview material.

VIDEO 05520	£14.99
DVD 05521	£15.99

FARNBOROUGH INTERNATIONAL AIRSHOW 2002

This official video (and DVD) brings you the action from all seven days of the show - including the five 'trade' days closed to the public. Highlights include an unprecedented flypast by no less than FOUR new Eurofighters, the F/A-18F Super Hornet, the Joint Strike Fighter, Harrier GR9 and UAV projects for the future plus much more!

VIDEO VHS/PAL (05629) & NTSC FORMATS (D05629) £14.99	DVD IS DVD10 AND WILL PLAY IN BOTH REGION 1 & 2 (05217) £15.99

BRITISH AIRSHOWS 2001

The only way to see all the action and highlights from Britain's best airshows of the year! This unique, extra-length tape features action from 13 top shows including the Kemble Hunter Anniversary Show and Delta Jets Open Day, Mildenhall, Biggin Hill, Cosford, Duxford, Flying Legends, Shuttleworth, Sunderland RIAT and much more.

VIDEO 146 mins 04724	£12.99
DVD 04725	£13.99

DUXFORD BATTLE OF BRITAIN 60th ANNIVERSARY AIRSHOW

The best-selling video of one of the greatest airshows ever! See all the action as 24 vintage Spitfires and Hurricanes take to the skies!

VIDEO 92 mins 03795	£14.99
DVD 04042	£15.99

RIAT 2002

Back at its traditional home of RAF Fairford, RIAT is the biggest and most spectacular airshow in the world, featuring more than 400 aircraft in 18 hours of display action, including: the B-2 stealth bomber and an F-15 as it flies with historic World War II fighters, and there's formation aerobatics from five national display teams as well as the crash of an Italian G-222. Also available in DVD featuring an extra 30 minutes of material.

VIDEO 90 mins 05794	£14.99
DVD 05795	£15.99

FLYING LEGENDS 2002

Flying Legends is a feast of propeller-driven nostalgia, and this year's show features several aircraft new to Duxford. They include a unique A-26 Apache a beautifully restored P-51 and more. The display ends with the sight of 34 immaculate warbirds in formation for the traditional Flying Legends 'Balbo'.

VIDEO 75 mins 05792	£14.99
DVD 05793	£15.99

NEW Aviation Videos & DVDs

Experience flights from the cockpit from all over the Globe including takeoffs and landings, great approaches and spectacular scenery on the World Air Routes. Most videos also take you inside the cabin during the flights, include views of the many Airports and other surprises. Each video/DVD runs 75 to 180 minutes.

Videos — Only £17.95 each

AIR NAMIBIA B 1900 VNMB1

AIR ATLANTA L1011 VABD1

AIR GEORGIA TU 154 VGEO1

STERLING B737-300 VSNB1

ISLANDSFLUG Atr 42 VICB1

AIR NAMIBIA B747SP VNMB2

DVDs — From £17.99

 £19.99

 £17.99

 £19.99

BRITANNIA 757-200, 767-300 DVDBRIT757

NOVAIR AIRBUS A330-200, BOEING 737-800R DVDNOVAIR

AIR TAHITI ATR 42, ATR 72 DVDTAHITI

 £17.99

 £23.99

 £23.99

SCENIC AIRLINES FOKKER 27 DVDFOK27

INT AIRPORTS 67 DVDINT67

AIR CONTRACTORS - AIRBUS A300F, C130 HERCULES DVDAIRCON

Visit www.keypublishing.com for further DVDs and videos in this series

VULCAN - A FAREWELL TO ARMS

Another deeply moving video for many people. The video is a historic film record of the last few days in the operational life of XH558 - the last flying Vulcan - and the effect of that final 'farewell'. Of course there are plans well underway to re-fly XH558.

VIDEO 52 mins approx. 00580 £12.99

RED ARROWS BEYOND THE HORIZON

The new Official Red Arrows video is 57 minutes of pure action and precision, captured in over a year of exclusive filming with the RAF Aerobatic Team with an abundance of previously unseen footage and air-to-air sequences.

NEW

The Spectator's Out With The Red Arrows

VIDEO 57 mins 05218 £12.99

CONCORDE

Concorde is the most famous aircraft in the world. This programme, packed with especially shot footage, puts you on the flight deck, behind the stick and in the air with this stunningly beautiful and awesomely powerful aircraft.
120 mins approx. Also available in DVD - includes extensive special features.
150 mins approx.

VIDEO 05634 £14.99
DVD 05635 £15.99

CONCORDE
The Worlds Greatest Airliner

NEW

CREATURE
comforts?

Y ou have just finished your cup of tea in bed, and there's time to enjoy a refreshing shower before sitting down to a hot breakfast in the restaurant - at 37,000ft (11,277m) somewhere over the North Atlantic. Customer service did not quite reach these dizzy heights during the first 100 years of flight (although true 'passenger' flight, via an airline, is only some 80 years old) - but innovations like these may now be only some three years away.

In-flight luxuries like these have been the subject of discussion between Airbus and airlines over the past year, ever since the launch of the manufacturer's giant A380 airliner.

In 1919 six European airlines formed IATA, the International Air Traffic Association, (today's International Air Transport Association) as a way of bringing some order to the rapidly-growing private airline ventures which sprang up at the end of World War One. Ex-military aircraft and pilots were readily available and there was a booming industry in the transport of people and goods by air. However, many of these aircraft were less than ideal for passenger travel! Flying from Berlin in an AEG aircraft in 1919, the 'passenger' sat

HAS AIR TRAVEL GONE FROM BEING THE HEIGHT OF LUXURY FOR THE FEW TO A LESS-THAN-ENJOYABLE EXPERIENCE FOR THE MASSES? MANY WOULD ARGUE THAT IT HAS. CHRIS PENNEY LOOKS BACK ACROSS THE CENTURY.

Above: **For *real* luxury, the business jet must be the ultimate - the interior design can be based on customer's requirements. Who says air travel has to be uncomfortable?** (KEY collection)

Above: **Gone are the days when airliners flew for no more than a few hours at a time between overnight stops and when your fellow passengers could be counted on the fingers. International mass air travel means being packed into a modern airliner with hundreds of other people for up to 20 hours.** (KEY - Tony Dixon)

astride a wooden plank, wrapped in a leather coat, woollen blanket, fur gloves, helmet and goggles for protection against the elements, having been served a tot of brandy before embarkation. You could fly from London to Paris in around 2¹/₂ hours depending on the wind: if the weather was bad, aircraft flew at 200ft to avoid the clouds and navigated by following the names painted on railway station roofs. From time to time, aircraft flying in opposite directions collided with others following the same navigable feature. In Europe, where the pilot or captain (a term derived from the shipping industry) was seated on the left, the way to avoid this kind of mishap was to keep roads, railways, or waterways on the left. Passengers were issued with handbooks allowing them to map-read their way along the route. Long-distance flights showed that aircraft were opening up world travel. For example, in 1919 two Australians flew a Vickers Vimy flew over 11,000 miles from London to Darwin in 28 days – the same journey today takes under 28 hours. More significant, perhaps, was the 1927 crossing of the Atlantic by Charles Lindbergh.

In the 1920s, the UK was ideally placed to take advantage of the new phenomenon of passenger air travel, which needed better speed, reliability and comfort if it was to rival transport by rail and ocean-going liner. Indeed, many would argue that the years between the two world wars were the best years of all in which to experience the airline industry. In 1924 Imperial Airways was formed as a 'national' airline with the aim of improving communication with the rest of the British Empire – with passengers being warned that tribes could prove hostile as they took exception to any aircraft. In the same year, Imperial commenced the Silver Arrow service from London to Paris, which included the novelty of gourmet meals served by a steward. Aboard the French airline Lignes Farman, flying Farman F300s with four large cabin windows that could be opened, a sign warned passengers against throwing litter over the side. However, there were those who saw the airship as a superior means of transport and still enthusiastically supported this mode of air travel. A wooden-panelled, carpeted cabin was an integral part of the German Zeppelin airships, which included such luxuries as toilets, showers, a bar, smoking room and dining room, as well as

The Douglas DC-2 was one of the world's first purpose-built airliners and the passengers who occupied its 14 seats were assured every luxury, in this case by TWA. (KEY collection)

separate crew quarters – comforts completely unknown in the aircraft of the day. Passengers sat in wicker chairs or on couches, with windows angled slightly downwards to provide a better view. Twin-cabin berths were located on an upper deck for those wanting to relax during a night flight – an important consideration, as a crossing of the Atlantic could take three days.

Many consider that the golden era of air travel is represented by the Short C-class flying boats, which introduced a new level of airborne comfort. Such was their stately pace that the atmosphere throughout the journey resembled that of a private members club, an impression that some airlines are now trying to re-create for their First Class passengers. The deep hull permitted a double deck design with a promenade cabin which incorporated smoking, midship and aft cabins, as well as toilets and a kitchen. Passengers could borrow items such as sunglasses, playing cards, books and games from the steward, although alcohol and cigarettes had to be paid for. Imperial introduced the adjustable seat, while on its rival American airline Pan Am's Clipper Class flying-boats passengers could experience reclining flat sleeper seats. There was little overnight flying and night stops were made in a series of first-class hotels down-route.

More passengers, lower standards?

The post-war jet era brought travel to a wider audience and increased both the desire to travel and the destinations available. It could also be said to have

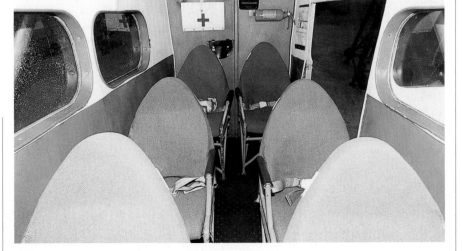

Above: **Basic seats in a Dragon Rapide – adequate for the trip from London to Paris and certainly much more of a 'pure' flying experience than a seat in a modern Jumbo Jet.** (KEY – Duncan Cubitt)

Above: **The cocktail bar in a Short Sandringham flying boat. The decline of the luxury interiors seen in airships and flying boats led to the adoption of a more basic passenger facilities in most aircraft.** (KEY collection)

Same concept but 60 years apart – the bar on a Douglas DC-2 in the late 1930s and the same idea as operated today by Virgin Atlantic's 747s. (KEY collection)

highlighting of medical problems such as DVT (Deep Vein Thrombosis), often referred to as 'economy class syndrome'.

When jets were introduced in 1959, a ticket surcharge was levied for jet passengers to allow those airlines without jets to compete. Similarly, with the arrival of Concorde and supersonic travel a surcharge was levied to allow subsonic operators to 'compete' on the same route. As air travel flourished, the Advanced Purchase Excursion (APEX) fare was introduced to enable airlines to attract business off-peak. If non-IATA airlines (such as Icelandic Loftleidir across the Atlantic in 1952) bucked the trend and created 'instability' by offering low fares, later entrants, such as Laker, caused positive meltdown. The growth of the Inclusive Tour/charter/seat only markets has been further complicated by the development of tour operator airlines, and most recently by low-cost no-frills airlines.

Feed me

In recent years, passenger expectations of in-flight catering have risen to the point where a hot and edible meal is the very least that is expected. However, in the early years of air travel, with the exception of the luxury airships and flying boats, catering standards were at best frugal, and more often non-existent. Traditionally, airline food has been categorised alongside railway sandwiches – verging on the inedible – though in recent years the major carriers have spent much time and effort in persuading passengers that the dining experience is now a plus point rather than something to be dreaded. This does, of course, depend on the airline and the type of ticket you have purchased – spend more money and you will get better service and better food. On a long-haul flight, a modern 747 or A340 can expect to carry around 1,500 meal servings, each with at least three courses. Ever more ingenious ways of adding to the onboard culinary experience are being introduced, the in-flight Sky Chef being just one such recent development. Airlines now cater for special dietary requirements, although the basic food type depends on the nationality of the airline, as will the range of dietary options. Low-cost carriers have adopted a 'pay and dine' system offering a limited range of snack-type food. As with the other comfort elements, such as entertainment and seat space, the basic premise is 'you get what you pay for". For those lucky enough to travel First Class, the in-flight catering can match the finest restaurants, while for those

ushered in a lower set of standards than those enjoyed by the more elite travellers of the 1930s. In an attempt to prevent cut-price competition, IATA organised annual tariff conferences to resolve the differences of its airline members. For instance, until 1953 a standard fare was charged across the Atlantic, and when economy class fares were introduced in 1958 the airlines made a number of restrictions, including the measured distance between each row of seats and the type of food to be served (cold sandwiches). The 'seat pitch' debate – in particular how much leg-room each passenger enjoyed – was not a matter of great concern in the early years. However, the debate has heated up in recent years with the

Above: **The seating layout depends on the route and the airline, but most scheduled carriers operate a two (Economy and Business) or three (same two plus First Class) arrangement. This is business class aboard a Boeing 777.** (Boeing)

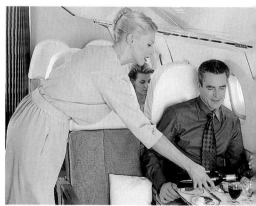

Above: **The luxury end of in-flight catering and service aboard an Air France Concorde.** (Air France)

at the back of the aircraft the dining experience can be far more variable.

Entertain me

Reading a newspaper or book and conversing with fellow passengers used to be the standard in-flight entertainment options until the advent of TV screens on aircraft. Although reading is still a popular way of passing time on a flight, the majority of passengers now expect visual entertainment. This aspect of air travel has certainly advanced greatly in the last 30 years, although there is wide variation between carriers, aircraft types – and seat price. The usual minimum standard is for a shared TV screen in the cabin roof, and depending upon where you are sitting, the view will be either poor or terrible. Audio is fed via earphones (which you may have to hire) via the seat and everyone has to watch the same programme. In the more expensive seats, individual viewing was introduced, each seat with its own small screen. On some airlines, the latter option is now available in Economy, though it depends on the aircraft type. At best a passenger will have his own display screen and a selection of programmes that include current blockbuster movies, as well as radio channels, computer games and, in the latest systems now being tested, internet access. No time to be bored – and, sadly, for many people even less reason to talk to the person sitting next to you

Make me comfortable

The number of cabin crew members is now regulated. One per 50 seats is a benchmark figure, which means that if you are the only passenger aboard a 90-seater regional jet today you will receive the attention of two cabin staff. As manufacturers have stretched their product lines to incorporate more seats within the same basic airframe, so the number of exit doors has been increased accordingly. This is directly related to the emergency evacuation time specified for any type of passenger airliner, which in the UK is 90 seconds.

Most people, perhaps, recall the air passenger experience in terms of the comfort – or otherwise – of their seat. "Air travel has gone from being the comfort class of the Comet to the cattle class of today," a seasoned traveller once remarked. Certainly airlines have realised that the average person is not only getting heavier, but also wider. US domestic low-cost airline

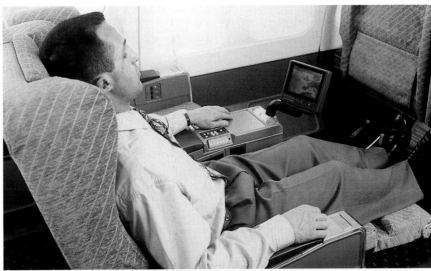

Individual IFE is a standard feature in most Business and First Class cabins – along with more leg space and reclining seats with foot-rests. The basic principle is you 'get what you pay for', as in this Gulf Air Airbus A340. (Airbus)

Southwest has stated that nine out of ten passenger complaints it receives are on the subject of seat space infringement and has introduced a policy of charging oversized people for two seats. Swiss International Air Lines is looking at ways of trying to make its aircraft's seats wider. On certain busy routes airlines often configure their aircraft differently, in a high-density layout with a subsequent closing of the gap between rows of seats. An aircraft's seating capacity is a dilemma for airlines – the search for the right aircraft to fly the right route has led to purchasing mistakes in the past.

The cabin temperature is likely to be set at the optimum which best reflects the climate of the carrier's home country – a point seldom considered by non-nationals when booking. One problem airliner manufacturers have not managed to crack is the subject of fresh air, which is still recycled throughout the flight – without the advantages of those opening windows in pre-war airships! So are we more comfortable and better looked-after in 2002 than we were in 1932? The basic answer is both yes and no, depending on how much you are prepared to pay for your seat. Pay enough and you can be pampered to First Class hotel and restaurant standard. However, in general terms the major long-distance carriers now provide better food and entertainment than was the case even 20 years ago.

Will the next 100 years of air travel see the same kind of dramatic changes as the first 100 years? I doubt it. As for taking your shower in-flight, the water would, of course, have to be recycled and it is doubtful whether airlines will want to carry the dead weight around. However, the development of the 555-seat A380 holds out the prospect of the world's first triple-decker, with sleeping accommodation downstairs.

Watch this space. ■

Above: Business class meal courtesy of British European (now FlyBe). Although the quality of in-flight catering was the subject of jokes for years, more recently it has shown considerable improvement. (British European)

Above: When in-flight entertainment (IFE) was introduced, it was based on shared screens fitted to the cabin ceilings, as in this MD-11. (McDD)

Above: The business and first class passenger aboard the new Airbus A380 can expect the luxury of a flying hotel when the aircraft enters service in 2006. (Airbus)

Century of Flight
Airliner World's View

The modern airport - such as Munich - offers visitors a wide range of amenities. (Flughafen München GmbH)

Charter operators can offer far more reliable services these days, although congested skies still mean that delays are commonplace. (KEY - Ken Delve)

TONY DIXON, EDITOR OF AIRLINER WORLD, SUMMARISES THE CHANGES IN COMMERCIAL AIR TRAVEL THAT HAVE BENEFITED THE PASSENGER DURING THE PAST CENTURY.

Charting the evolution of commercial aviation through the last century is a daunting task. Just skimming over the numerous milestones that have occurred in the last 100 years would provide enough material to fill an entire book and indeed many have been published. Airliner development, the jet engine, expansion at airports, passenger figures, supersonic transport...the list of chapter headings is almost endless.

Of course some of the most radical changes during that time have had direct bearing upon how passengers are carried. To be accurate, the first passenger took to the air long before the Wright brothers' mastered powered flight in December 1903. Balloon and airship flying dates back to the Mongolfier brothers in the late 1700s, when passengers were taken aloft in a variety of lighter-than-air machines.

In the early days of powered, heavier-than-air flying, it was

difficult enough to get the 'flying machine' airborne with just one person on board - let alone two; but early aviators soon found that they could earn extra cash by taking interested parties for a joyride. After the First World War, ex-military machines were converted into passenger-carrying aircraft,

but the cost of a ticket was prohibitive for all except the very rich. Nor did it help that the lucky few expected to travel with a full wardrobe, further limiting the already limited carrying capacity of early aircraft!

Conditions for those early passengers were cramped to say

the least and it was not until the early 1930s, with the arrival of the Junkers Ju 52 and the early Douglas models that some form of creature comforts were introduced, such as air ventilators, oxygen masks and the widespread services of stewards and stewardesses.

In-flight catering was available from the outset, with the first regular airline passenger service serving game sandwiches and cream teas during the two-hour flight from England to France in 1919. Aircraft were unpressurised and airlines did not have the benefit of today's accurate weather forecasting, so flights were often undertaken in less than ideal conditions, which tended to be quite uncomfortable for the passengers.

Trying to operate a financially successful airline was difficult. Early flights by the Irish airline Aer Lingus utilised a seven-seat de Havilland DH.84 Dragon biplane, which in 1936 operated services between Baldonnel (Dublin) and Liverpool - via the Isle of Man, and Baldonnel to Bristol - to connect with the railway services to London. There was not the public interest in flying as there is today - with only 171 passengers flying on the Baldonnel - Isle of Man route out of the 490 seats available and 49 on the route to Bristol with 400 seats available - an average load factor was around 20%!

By the end of the 1930s, air routes had been opened from Europe to Central and South America, across Africa and to the Far East and Australia. Many of the national airlines of today were already in existence, such as Air France and Lufthansa in Europe, American and Delta in the USA, and Qantas in Australia. Travelling to the far-flung limits of the British Commonwealth, such as Australia, was not something

that could be undertaken as part of a two-week summer holiday - the very first flights to Australia took as long as 28 days. By 1934, that time had been reduced to 13 days, with several refuelling and crew rest stops en route. Flying-boats took over from the conventional aircraft on the route in the late 1930s, with Imperial Airways using seaplanes from 1937. Their large size provided space for sumptuous cabins and full sleeping accommodation - something rarely seen on conventional aircraft of the time.

The Second World War obviously reduced the amount of civilians travelling by air - but advances in aircraft technology in the late 1940s heralded the introduction of long-range, ex-military aircraft, such as the Douglas DC-4, -6 and -7 and the Lockheed Constellation. In the UK developments of wartime bombers, like the Lancastrian, gave way to purpose-built passenger aircraft, such as the Avro York - basically Lancaster wings and engines mated to a

different fuselage - until the introduction of the turboprop engine resulted in the development of the Vickers Viscount and Handley Page Herald.

Air travel was becoming more accessible to the general public, with greater emphasis being placed on comfort, even at airports, where more substantial buildings were replacing the wooden huts of pre-war days. The newer pressurised airliners provided a greater measure of comfort, although the aircraft still had to fly through most of the weather as the technology to climb above it did not occur until the early 1950s with the advent of jets, such as the de Havilland Comet and the Boeing 707. Passenger numbers increased as reduced flying times, better reliability on routes and greater comfort made air travel more appealing.

As more and more jet aircraft were introduced, the piston-engined and turboprop types that they replaced became

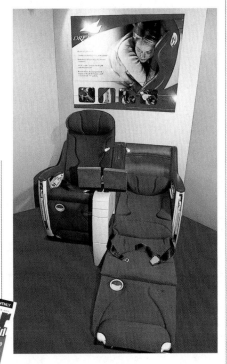

available for sale at reduced prices. This encouraged entrepreneurs to set up 'charter' airlines to carry the public on 'package holidays' making air travel available to an even greater cross-section of the general public.

The reliability of some of these early charter airlines was not as high as that of scheduled operators and package-tour passengers often had to endure delays and cramped seating. As the package-tour boom gathered pace, jet aircraft replaced the earlier turboprops, reliability and efficiency improved.

Passengers today, flying Tourist or Economy Class, might feel slightly irritated by the curtain that separates them from the better service available in Business or even First Class - certainly in the very early days there was no need for such blatant separation because First Class passengers were actually put on separate aircraft. As you would expect, the standards in Business are a great deal higher than in Economy, with extended legroom, more comfortable seats, better meals and individual TV/video screens (it is only in the last five or so years that this luxury has extended to

Economy), and these are combined with better facilities at airports, including executive lounges and 'fast-track' security queues. However, passengers pay dearly for the extra comforts, with Business tickets often double or treble the price of Economy.

One aircraft revolutionised air travel - the Boeing 747. At the time of its introduction in the 1970s, many people thought that its increase in passenger-carrying capability would cause insurmountable handling problems at some airports, but although there were some initial difficulties, airports soon became accustomed to handling 350 plus people for a single flight. The same problem is arising prior to the proposed introduction of the 550-seat A380 'Super Jumbo' in 2005. Again the level of comfort will increase and more people are likely to be attracted to air travel.

However, as we enter a new era of low-cost operations with carriers such as easyJet and Ryanair in the UK, and Southwest and JetBlue in the USA, the range of services available to passengers has actually been reduced. Now complimentary meals, in-flight entertainment and Business and First Class seating are regarded as unnecessary 'extras'. Low-cost operators have changed the whole ethos of air travel for the passenger, and reduced the journey to the equivalent of taking the train or bus. Whereas until recently air travel was still seen as an adventure by many, the low-cost carriers have made it routine - just another way of getting from A to B.

Airliner World has for the past two years published a range of features covering all aspects of commercial air travel. Each month it provides an in depth and impartial news service coving the latest developments among the airlines, the manufacturers and the rest of the commercial aerospace sector.

Passengers from the 1930s could never have imagined what luxuries would be available to today's travellers - this is the latest Upper Class reclining seat on offer from Virgin Atlantic. (KEY collection)

The level of facilities, shops and restaurants at most international airports is bewildering - this is Dubai. (Dubai Airport)

Aircraft such as this Boeing 767 have helped to make the world a much smaller place during the past 20 years, though commercial aviation has been around for most of the century of powered flight. (Mark Stanton)

Air Travel
the boom

Although the history of flight dates back to the first airships in the late 1700s, the Wright brothers' first powered flight in December 1903 marked the beginning of winged flight. However, as early aircraft designs were limited by the technology then available, opportunities for carrying passengers were restricted, owing to the weight and power of the aircraft. This did not stop some entrepreneurs, though, and early aviators are known to have taken interested parties on experience flights for money, becoming the pioneers of today's booming commercial market.

Slow beginnings

Initial growth in the sector was slowed by the outbreak of World War One and then accelerated during the 1920s and 30s. The effect of World War Two was to stifle this growth, although after its conclusion significant developments

Air travel saw a resurgence after World War Two with piston-engine transport aircraft such as this Avro York being employed by the airlines. (KEY collection)

were made as the knowledge gained from military experience was brought into the civilian world. Advances in technology heralded the introduction of longer-range piston models, many of them purpose-designed for civilian operation. These aircraft provided greater comfort for passengers and helped open up the market still further.

In the early 1950s, the world's airlines were beginning to introduce types such as the Boeing Stratocruiser, the Lockheed Super Constellation and the Douglas DC-7. BOAC and US giants Pan American World Airways and Trans World Airlines had begun transatlantic services – the fare for a return BOAC ticket to New York was £217.18.0.

Jet revolution

However, it was with the introduction of the first jet-powered aircraft, the de Havilland DH.106 Comet 1, in May 1952 that the industry started to experience its strongest growth.

The first production Comet 1 of BOAC departed London Heathrow Airport on its first commercial service to Johannesburg, South Africa, on May 2, 1952. The British-

significant benefits to customers, bringing down journey times from London to Rome to just two hours and London to Cairo to five hours.

Although this was a significant breakthrough, the Comet still had many operational pitfalls, principally concerning its range. The aircraft's first intercontinental service between London and Johannesburg had still taken a little less than a day (23 hours 34 minutes) due to enforced fuel stops at Rome, Beirut, Khartoum, Entebbe and Livingstone.

The general euphoria that supported the introduction of the Comet 1 had made the world sit up and take notice, and it was clear that de Havilland was never likely to hold its monopoly of the jet arena for long, especially after the well documented crashes that befell the type. The manufacturer was joined by US giants Boeing and Douglas in a race to develop a new longer-range aircraft aimed at opening up new markets. The two US companies wanted a lucrative slice of the commercial market 'cake' and both were to become household names in the field before the end of the 1950s.

Only weeks after the Comet 1 entered service, Boeing announced the launch of the Model 367-80, a project

The US major took delivery of its first 707-121 in the autumn of 1958 and the 12,500lb-thrust Pratt & Whitney JT3C-6 turbojet-powered aircraft entered service on October 26, 1958, serving the New York-Paris route. The first DC-8, a -10 variant, took to the air with US carrier Delta Air Lines in September 1959 and subsequent variants were to follow over the years.

However, it was de Havilland that led the intercontinental revolution, with the Comet 4, a stretched and more advanced development of the Comet 1, making the first transatlantic crossing by a commercial jet. The aircraft departed London on October 4, 1958, arriving in New York some 10 hours and 22 minutes later after a fuel stop in Gander. With the prevailing winds allowing the return journey to be completed without the need for a fuel stop, it was made in a revolutionary 6 hours 11 minutes.

The advent of the long-range models meant that less than ten years after the first jet aircraft took to the air, seating capacity had increased around five-fold, the baseline domestic variant of the DC-8 seating 176 in a high-density configuration. The long-haul operations of the Boeing 707 and Comet 4 had convinced many that air

ng years

THE INTRODUCTION OF THE JET AIRLINER IN THE 1950S WAS ONE OF THE MAJOR FACTORS BEHIND THE GROWTH OF THE CIVIL MARKET. *Airliner World's* RICHARD MASLEN LOOKS BACK AT THIS AND OTHER KEY DEVELOPMENTS AND AT HOW THEY PAVED THE WAY FOR FURTHER EXPANSION.

designed aircraft, which seated 36 passengers, was the first turbojet-powered commercial transport to see airline service and its introduction brought about a revolution in the industry, eventually bringing air travel to all social classes, rather than simply a privileged few.

Journeys were long and arduous before the introduction of the Comet. Through the advent of new technology – the turbojet engine – flight times were reduced considerably. Travelling at almost double the speed of contemporary transport aircraft, this offered

which brought together the aerodynamic designs of the B-47 and B-52 bombers for initially a military application, the KC-135 refuelling tanker and then the commercial Model 707 airliner. Douglas, meanwhile, was discussing a family of jet aircraft for domestic US, and longer-range, services. When the leading US airline Pan American World Airways announced an order for 20 Boeing and 25 Douglas aircraft in October 1955, the two projects, the 707 and DC-8, had been refined and the age of intercontinental jet air transport was born.

travel was a safe form of transport, and the 1960s proved to be the decade of growth for the commercial industry as significant new aircraft helped to mould its future.

Boeing domination

Although the 1960s saw an abundance of new designs, including the Sud-Aviation SE.210 Caravelle, Convair 880 and 990, Douglas DC-9, Hawker Siddeley Trident and the Vickers-Armstrong VC10, it was Boeing which took the lead in revolutionising the industry.

The Douglas DC-6 was a stalwart of the airline industry immediately after World War Two. (KEY collection)

After rectifying the design flaws of the original Comet 1, de Havilland produced the Comet 4 which offered intercontinental range. (Gordon Swanborough collection)

The Boeing 707 was already a success as the 1960s began, but the introduction of the turbofan engine was to take all jet airliners a significant step forward. The first high-bypass turbofan 707 customer was BOAC, which purchased Rolls-Royce Conway-equipped examples known as the 707-420. Pratt & Whitney responded with the more efficient JT3D-3 engine, giving the aircraft further customer appeal. Although the variants of the larger 707 (and later the 720) and the DC-8 met the requirements for longer-range travel, Boeing felt there was a clear need for smaller capacity aircraft to serve medium-range routes.

The arrival of the jets had led to the withdrawal of many

type, albeit a much advanced design, remains in serial production.

As the world's best-selling commercial jet aircraft, the Boeing 737 has operated in almost all global markets and has helped to support the development of new second and third tier airlines. As next-generation variants continue to roll off the production line at regular intervals, the early production aircraft are still plying their trade, principally in the African, Asian and Latin American markets. In fact, the second production aircraft (c/n 19014) still remains in commercial operation with Peruvian operator AeroContinente, some 35 years after first entering service with German national carrier Lufthansa.

it was the aircraft's own vast size that presented the main problem. The span and length of such an aircraft meant that it occupied much more apron space and at some airports, such as London Heathrow, additional gates has to be opened to support the aircraft.

The introduction of the 747 into commercial service on

Below: **An aircraft and airline synonymous with the development of commercial air travel - the Boeing 707 and Pan Am.** (Boeing)

Below left: **The Douglas DC-9 made an important contribution to the domestic air travel sector during the 1960s and 1970s. This TWA example is seen at Toronto in May 2001, shortly before the airline finally folded.** (KEY - Steve Fletcher)

larger propeller-driven types from long-haul services for use on shorter domestic routes: Boeing set about designing a jet replacement to substitute these ageing models. The resulting Boeing 727 and 737 programmes were to make a prominent impact on the industry, generating further demand for air transport.

The Boeing 727 entered commercial service on February 1, 1964, and achieved significant sales success, particularly in the booming US market for which the aircraft had primarily been designed. This stalwart was a major force behind the development of air transport, and only in the last couple of years have the US majors retired them from operation. Many second tier carriers still operate them.

With demand still growing, Boeing looked again at its options and in February 1965 announced the launch of the 737 programme, a family of aircraft aimed at the short and medium-haul markets. The first 737-100 entered service on February 10, 1968, and - quite amazingly - the

The Jumbo era

As this short-haul revolution continued, the larger capacity early jet models were no longer able to meet the growth in demand for long-haul travel. In 1966 Pan-American issued a requirement for an aircraft capable of carrying 400 passengers over 5,000 miles (8,000km). Clearly, developing an aircraft with this capability was going to be a risky venture under any circumstances and Boeing staked its very existence to build the Boeing 747. This turned out to be a worthy risk as the Boeing 747 made a massive impact on the industry.

Airport infrastructure had to be modified to take into account the continuing growth in passenger numbers. The introduction of the 400-seat 747 brought new problems for airports, forcing many to spend millions of pounds upgrading their facilities. Although 400 passengers disembarking one aircraft at the same time would place capacity pressures on any terminal building,

January 21, 1970 - and later the Douglas DC-10 and Lockheed L.1011 TriStar trijets - continued the expanding nature of the industry. The aircraft not only increased the number of passengers flying, but also necessitated a big change in baggage handling, in-flight catering and ground handling, simply because of their size and passenger loads.

European hopes

Alongside the development of the Boeing 747, plans for a collaborative effort between Aérospatiale and BAC to launch the first commercial supersonic airliner were under discussion. In October 1962, the French President Charles de Gaulle made a passionate plea for the British and French aviation industries to co-operate in building commercial aircraft in order to counter what was becoming an American colonisation of the skies.

One month after de Gaulle's speech, the British and French Governments signed an agreement to develop a

Boeing introduced the three-engine 727 in the early 1960s for use on medium-haul flights. Eventually 1,832 were built and many remain in service today with smaller airlines. (Boeing)

supersonic transport, aptly christened 'Concorde'. By the close of the decade, the prototype Anglo-French Concorde and the Soviet-designed Tupolev Tu-144 had made their first flights and the future of supersonic passenger travel looked secure.

Many believed the introduction of Concorde would have a similar impact on the market to the 747. However, this was not to be the case. Although it is true to say that entry into the supersonic age was a key breakthrough for the aviation industry, its development was stifled by the lack of orders for the aircraft. Only Air France and British Airways acquired Concorde, and although the type continues to play an important role in the transatlantic

Deregulation allowed airlines to introduce competitive fares as they wished, thereby saving the passenger money and providing a system which would make it easier for new airlines to start up.

Although passenger demand for short-haul models had slipped during the early 1970s the deregulation of the market, offering a level platform for free open competition, enhanced it. In 1978 Boeing secured some 145 new aircraft sales, a significant development compared to its average of just 40 aircraft per year during the six previous years.

Through the 1980s Boeing catered for the continuing demand by expanding the 737 family to take into effect

with fares significantly below those previously charged by the major carriers in the regulated market.

Low cost bonanza

One of the forerunners of this new sector was Southwest Airlines, which was established at Dallas/Love Field Airport in June 1970 with just two Boeing 737-200s. The airline had a 'no frills' marketing ploy to attract passengers, and by cutting costs to a bare minimum it was able to make a profit while still offering cut-price fares. The early 737 models were to become the backbone of these airlines' fleets and later, following deregulation in Europe, they played an important role in

Above left: **For over 25 years Concorde has been the world's best known and only truly viable supersonic airliner.** (KEY - Steve Fletcher)

Above right: **Low-cost pioneer airline Southwest now has a huge fleet of Boeing 737s, including a number of older -200 models, such as this one.** (KEY - Tony Dixon)

business market it never made the commercial impact on the industry that it might have done.

Deregulation

While the giant 747 and supersonic Concorde were generating further interest in the sector, the decision by the US Congress to pass the Airline Deregulation Act in 1978 provided an important fillip to the industry.

The US government supported the idea of a less-regulated airline industry, one which would allow it to move away from its responsibility of assigning air routes to airlines and approving the fares to be charged.

advances in technology. The development of these new, more powerful, fuel-efficient, short-haul models helped open up the world to air travellers. Air travel, once only available to the privileged few, had become more generally affordable - but the jet revolution significantly reduced travel times and, as a result, brought down costs even further, leading to even greater demand.

During the late 1970s and 1980s, attitudes to air transport changed. With more and more people keen to travel, airlines added additional aircraft to their fleets and direct or one-stop air connections were soon available between most cities in the developed world.

During this time, much of the air transport demand was from business travellers, though as the deregulation of US skies led to a continued drop in the cost of travel, the leisure market was beginning to grow. The introduction of dedicated no-frills operators in the US, offering low-cost domestic services, further strengthened demand,

the further growth of the no-frills market, with Ryanair, easyJet and its soon-to-be-absorbed subsidiary Go.

The low-cost segment is now one of the most fluid markets, having seen tremendous growth, particularly in the early years of the new century. In fact, since its launch in 1970, Southwest has expanded its fleet to over 350 aircraft, representing an average 17.5% capacity increase per annum. With airlines like Ryanair now even offering free flights, the low-cost sector really can be said to have opened up air travel to the mass market.

Charter factor

Alongside the no-frills sector, the 737 was well-suited to the maturing package holiday charter market in Europe. With an upturn in the global economy, disposable household income increased significantly during the 1970s and demand for foreign holidays rose. As one of the pioneers of the charter market in Europe, UK-based

The 737 is the popular choice for most low-cost carriers. Luton-based easyJet operates a fleet of -300 models and is taking delivery of the Next Generation -700 model as it continues to expand its operations. (KEY - Tony Dixon)

Above: **The giant Boeing 747 made a significant impact on the future of air travel when it was introduced in 1970. The 747-200, illustrated here by a Virgin Atlantic example, and its subsequent sub-variants represent probably the ultimate development of the design.** (KFY - Duncan Cubitt)

Left: **Charter airlines, such as Britannia, have operated a wide variety of aircraft over the years but today demand has seen an increasing use of larger types, such as this Boeing 767.** (KEY - Ken Delve)

Britannia had offered inclusive tour packages to the Mediterranean in the mid-1960s, using turboprop aircraft, but it was not until it introduced its first 737-200 in July 1968 that it experienced its main growth in international tourism.

Air transport is now one of the main forces driving tourism growth and development. In Europe, approximately one third of all international tourists arrive at their destination by air, according to World Tourism Organisation (WTO) statistics. This growth in the market has seen the Airbus A330 and Boeing 757 replace the 737 as the principal charter type, offering additional capacity and even cheaper seat mile costs.

Big twins to regionals

As further advances in technology led to more powerful engines being designed by the major aerospace manufacturers General Electric, Pratt & Whitney and Rolls-Royce, a series of twin-engine designs were developed to meet mid-sized demand. These aircraft were designed to carry between 150 and 400 passengers on medium-haul or short-distance trunk routes and thus opened up a new market.

Boeing entered the new generation with the 757 and 767 models, which both featured a state-of-the-art glass cockpit which was later to become standard on all its new models. Meanwhile, the A300 and A310 models were the first aircraft to be produced by the European Airbus consortium, which had brought together the aerospace expertise of France, Germany, Spain and the UK to form a strong competitor to Boeing in the commercial market.

By the end of the 1980s, Airbus had made some important breakthroughs in the short-haul sector with the fly-by-wire Airbus A320, the first aircraft to be designed solely through Computer Aided Design. The manufacturer has since added the shrunk A319 and the stretched A321 to the family, and is currently completing flight certification trials on the A318, the smallest variant, developing a family of short-haul aircraft providing credible competition to the 737.

Above: **The arrival of the single-aisle Airbus A320 during the 1980s heralded an era of stiff competition with Boeing and its 737. Designed by computer and featuring fly-by-wire avionics, the A320 family represents a new generation of airliners rather than just an upgrade of a 1960s design.** (Airbus)

At the upper end of its scale the manufacturer has developed the A330 and A340 models, and earlier this year it rolled out its prototype A340-500, the longest-range aircraft in production, and placed its largest aircraft, the A340-600, into commercial service with Virgin Atlantic Airways.

As the commercial market has matured, the past five years have seen a significant growth in the regional sector, and despite the recent closure of BAE Systems' regional aircraft business and Fairchild Dornier's insolvency, the sector remains strong.

Building on the previous successes of the BAC One-Eleven, Fokker F28/70/100 and British Aerospace 146, manufacturers such as Bombardier Aerospace and Embraer have become established names in the marketplace.

Regional airlines have seen some quite astonishing growth in recent years, helped in no small part by aircraft such as the Embraer ERJ-145s which are extremely efficient and therefore cheap to operate. (Embraer)

Market forces and the future

After generating such strong demand during the 1960s and 1970s, the industry has changed somewhat over the past ten years. When the first jet aircraft emerged in the 1950s, manufacturers were quick to take advantage of the technological advances and many new designs were brought to fruition. In the early years of jet aviation, demand was certainly driven by supply, but today the industry is much more cautious and is driven directly by customer demand.

As the aviation industry has matured, significant changes have occurred in its structure. In the 1980s and early 1990s, the main emphasis was on privatisation, though by the end of the decade, as regional economies began to suffer the early winds of an economic storm, operational alliances became the answer as airlines looked to gain some market stability.

This situation has led to the formation of global airline

Above: **The huge Airbus A380 is set to replace the Boeing 747 as the world's largest airliner. It is likely to have as big an impact on the industry, as the 747 did in 1970.** (Airbus)

groupings such as Star, **one**world and SkyTeam, as airlines look to strengthen their activities by working together with international partners. As a tool for extending or reinforcing competitive advantages during an economic recession, alliances provide a safety net in difficult times and they began to play a more important role in the development of the industry on a daily basis.

With the dawn of a new century on January 1, 2000, the commercial aviation industry anticipated a continuation of the growth and expansion which had typified the previous decades. However, this has so far not been the case. The industry has suffered at the hands of an economic crisis and the world has seen two of the darkest days in air transport history - the loss of the first Concorde at Paris on July 25, 2000, and the terrorist atrocities in the US on September 11, 2001.

Although the industry recovered from a market downturn following the 1991 Gulf War and emerged in a much stronger form, it is difficult to predict the lasting impact of such an unexpected event as occurred on September 11, 2001. In the meantime, although the aviation industry has been significantly restructured, the world's manufacturers continue to develop new models to meet future demand.

In 2004 Airbus plans to unveil the world's largest airliner when the first prototype Airbus A380 is rolled-out of the manufacturer's Toulouse facility. After launching the project in December 2000, the A380 (formerly dubbed the A3XX) has secured just short of 100 firm orders and is due to enter commercial service in 2006. The standard version

of the aircraft, the A380-800, will be available in both freight and passenger configuration, seating 555, although a smaller and a larger variant are both being discussed.

Boeing has taken on a different outlook and as well as competing with Airbus in the ultra-large capacity market, with its improved 747-400ER and -400QXLR variants, the company is planning to build a revolutionary airliner, designed to enter service towards the end of the decade and flying at just below the speed of sound.

Featuring a unique airframe design, the Sonic Cruiser is intended for fast city-to-city routes popular with the business traveler, on which it would offer time savings of two or more hours compared to a conventional aircraft by flying at speeds of around Mach 0.98.

While this new innovative model remains on the drawing boards, many of the early jet aircraft types are now no longer in commercial service and can now only be seen in museums. The Comet flew its last commercial service on November 9, 1980, with Dan-Air of London and operations of such aircraft as the Boeing 707, BAC One-Eleven and Douglas DC-8 are now severely limited.

However, not only the famous aircraft types are no longer with us. Pan American World Airways and Trans World Airlines, pioneers of transatlantic flights, ceded their long-haul operations to other US majors long ago and other famous brands, such as Douglas, Fokker, Sabena and Swissair, have all disappeared.

Looking back over the past 100 years, it becomes clear that the commercial aviation industry has come a long way, and although this growth is expected to continue during the years ahead, consolidation is now becoming the key word for the industry. When the Wright Brothers took to the air in December 1903, nobody could have imagined the impact their flight would have on transportation during the 20th century.

Currently the Airbus A340-600 is the largest design from the European manufacturer. This example was handed over to launch customer Virgin Atlantic during the Farnborough 2002 airshow. (KEY - Dave Allport)

Boeing is canvassing the airlines with its proposal for the Sonic Cruiser, an aircraft of radical design intended to fly at Mach 0.98, just below the speed of sound. (Boeing)

Rotary Flight

HELICOPTERS WERE PIVOTAL TO PROGRESS IN POWERED FLIGHT.

ROBERT F DORR EXAMINES THE DEVELOPMENT OF ROTARY AVIATION.

Recently, a 'trivia question' on an Internet message board asked, simply: "What was the first helicopter?" In a world where American culture often seems to dominate, almost everyone answered with the Vought-Sikorsky VS-300, the rotorcraft designed, built and flown by the great Igor Sikorsky in 1939. Sikorsky's contribution to helicopter aviation was both early and enormous. But in truth, the Russian immigrant to the US – whose name still adorns one of the world's premier helicopter companies – was neither first nor foremost.

First helicopters

The principles behind the helicopter, a logical development from the autogiros that enjoyed brief popularity in the 1930s, were well known to numerous pioneers in at least half a dozen countries. So while the answer to the 'trivia question' was wrong, the question actually was not trivial and the answer certainly is not easy.

According to no lesser source than the American Helicopter Society, on November 13, 1907, the French pioneer Paul Cornu lifted a twin-rotor helicopter into the air entirely without assistance from the ground for a few seconds. Subsequently, France's Etienne Oehmichen became the first to fly a helicopter a kilometre in a closed circuit in 1924, staying aloft for this purpose for 7 minutes and 40 seconds.

France's Louis Breguet (who, with René Dorand, established the Breguet-Dorand Gyroplane Laboratoire), Britain's Austria-born Raoul Hafner, and the USA's Russian-born Igor Sikorsky carried out their initial experiments in the 1930s, a decade ahead of Soviet designers Ivan Bratukhin, Nikolai Kamov and Mikhail Mil. The first, successful British helicopter flew in 1938. The Weir W.5, designed by C G Pullin, weighed only 860lb fully loaded and attained a maximum speed of 70mph during 80 hours of test flying. In 1939, the W.5 was followed by a scaled-up version, the W.6, which was the first two-seater helicopter in the world. The Second World War prevented further progress on this model.

Still, most observers say that if a claim to be 'first' requires a truly practical helicopter, the distinction should belong to Doctor Heinrich Karl Johann Focke, whose Focke-Wulf Fw 61 made its first free flight on June 26, 1936. By most accounts, that flight lasted just 28 seconds although Focke jotted in his logbook that

The arrival of the Boeing Vertol CH-47 Chinook gave the US Army a huge boost in its mobility. Able to carry troops and heavy cargo, the Chinook also serves with many other nations around the world. (KEY collection)

The Piasecki H-21 was one of the first twin-rotor helicopters, equally at home on land or water, and saw extensive use during the 1950s. (KEY collection)

126

1936: Focke-Wulf Fw 61 1938: Weir W.5 1939: Vought Sikorsky VS-300 1942: Sikorsky XR-4 1947: Bristol Sycamore 1948: Mil Mi-1 1949: Sikorsky S-55 1952: Bristol Belvedere 1952: Piasecki H-21 1954: Sikorsky S-58 1956: Bell UH-1

the duration was 45 seconds. With a tiny propeller on its nose to cool its 160hp Bramo Sh.14A seven-cylinder radial engine, the Fw 61 could easily have been mistaken for an autogiro, but it was a true helicopter, the only lift was provided by the Fw 61's twin, 23ft main rotors. In the year Nazi Germany hosted the Olympic games, the Fw 61 was duly adorned with the swastika on its tail.

Why Focke had to struggle for funds is another difficult question. Just as historians wonder why Adolf Hitler and the Third Reich never grasped the importance of nuclear weapons research, they also wonder why the Nazis never appreciated the significance of the helicopter. Germany's Focke-Achgelis Fa 223 Drache (Kite) and Flettner Fl 282 Kolibri (Hummingbird) were practical machines that performed military tasks well in tests and evaluation efforts - although Flettner's facility

American pioneers

Lawrence Bell, who hated to fly and held no special love for rotary wing aviation, deserves enormous credit as a helicopter pioneer with the Model 47, which in military form became the H-13 of M*A*S*H fame and, very late in life, was named the Sioux. Charles Kaman, the only one of the great helicopter pioneers still alive, equally deserves credit for his twin-rotor K-225 that evolved into the Vietnam era H-43 Huskie. But no one in any country contributed more than Sikorsky. Its designer Igor Sikorsky piloted the initial flight of the VS-300 on September 14, 1939, in Stratford, Connecticut. While Germany was ignoring rotary-wing talent in its midst, Britain and Russia were yet to develop a practical helicopter, and Japan was not seriously trying, Sikorsky followed up with his VS-316, which became the R-4 (later H-4) for the US Army Air Corps.

Sikorsky was already well along with its next design, the S-51 or military R-5 (later H-5), first flown August 18, 1944, and later widely used in the Korean War. Powered by a 450hp Pratt & Whitney R-985 with 48ft rotors, the S-51, manufactured in Britain by Westland as the Dragonfly, became one of the first practical civilian helicopters. In 1948, Congressman Lyndon B Johnson, campaigning for re-election, used an S-51 to transport him all over Texas. More than 500 S-51s were built. They had limited load-carrying capacity and limited range - a fully-loaded H-5 tipped the scales at less than 5,000lb (2,268kg) and had a range of only about 140 miles (225.3km). But the H-5, otherwise the HO3S-1 in US naval terminology, was possibly the first aircraft to bring rotary wing aviation to thousands of passengers.

Utility helicopters

Although the usefulness of the helicopter as a rescue

Above: **The Bristol Sycamore is a fine example of a successful early British helicopter. As well as commercial and military operators in the UK it was also exported to Australia, Belgium and West Germany.** (KEY collection)

Right: **Built in larger numbers than any other helicopter, the Bell UH-1 Huey is perhaps the most recognised helicopter in the world. It found fame during the Vietnam War and is still in widespread use today.** (KEY collection)

was too centrally located to avoid being pounded by the Allied bombing campaign.

There is no easy answer as to why Nazi Germany never funded or fielded a squadron of helicopters. In terms of scientific advances, Germany was well ahead of Britain and Russia in the rotary wing field, and at least the equal of the US. Evaluations of the helicopter for a variety of missions, including maritime surveillance and rescue, showed unmistakable promise. But the helicopter remained largely a curiosity in German, except in the Hollywood version of the war - the film *Where Eagles Dare*, features a 'German' helicopter, actually a Bell 47.

Powered by a Warner R-550 offering 200hp, the boxy R-4 is often called the world's first production helicopter, as well as the US Air Force's first service helicopter. The XR-4 made its initial flight on January 13, 1942 and the Air Corps ordered 30 more, one each of which went to Burma and one to Alaska, while others were assigned to the US Navy, US Coast Guard and the Royal Navy as the Hoverfly I. They showed such promise that the USAAF ordered 100 R-4Bs. An R-4B pulled off history's first combat rescue in Burma in May 1944, prompting Col Philip G 'Flip' Cochran of the 1st Air Commando Group to write, "Today the 'egg-beater' went into action and the damn thing acted like it had good sense."

machine seems obvious today, in the 1940s helicopters were used first for general utility work. Several countries developed fine utility helicopters, including the Soviet Union, where the Mil Mi-1 was first flown in September 1948 and the US, where the Sikorsky S-55 (military H-19) was first flown in November 1949. One aircraft that made a contribution but rarely receives credit was the British Type 171 Sycamore, the first post-war British commercial helicopter.

Hafner, who had been working on autogiro and helicopter designs since the 1930s, led the team that began work on the Sycamore in June 1944 and turned out two prototypes powered by 450hp Pratt & Whitney 11-985

One of the earliest British helicopters was the Weir W.5 which first flew in 1938. The German Focke-Wulf Fw 61 was of a similar configuration. (Gordon Swanborough collection)

The Sikorsky R-4 was the world's first production helicopter and saw limited service during World War Two. (US National Archives)

Wasp Junior radial engines. The first of these took to the air on July 27, 1947, and the type earned the first airworthiness certificate ever awarded to a British helicopter just two years later. On September 3, 1949, Bristol flew the four-seat Sycamore Mk.2 powered by a 550hp Alvis Leonides 71 piston engine. Numerous production variants followed.

The Sycamore was one of the first helicopters pressed into commercial service. Although used mainly by the military, Hafner's Sycamore had been designed as an air taxi. BEA began an experimental service with these helicopters between Eastleigh and Heathrow Airport in

1954. Altogether, 177 Sycamores were built.

In the US, experiments with the Sikorsky S-51 and S-55 and the Piasecki 174 were short-lived. Helicopter airlines appeared briefly in the 1950s, re-appeared in the mid-1960s, and then vanished, the economics never quite right, despite the convenience of helicopters and the difficulty of getting to the airport any other way.

The Fairey Rotodyne of the mid-1950s, a remarkably handsome aircraft that looked like a transport aeroplane without full-sized wings, won a contract from New York Airways and was to be built in a 54-65 seat version – roughly double the passenger load of a Douglas DC-3 – but the economics of the airline industry, coupled with technical delays, killed it. The Sikorsky S-61 performed well in San Francisco, Los Angeles and elsewhere as an intra-city airliner but, again because of economics, had largely disappeared from the scene by 1970.

As late as 1950, there were still only about a dozen production helicopters in the world and a next generation of larger, more useful rotorcraft was slow in coming. Men who flew helicopters still needed an adventurous spirit. Accident figures showed that if it had rotors rather than wings, it was significantly more likely to kill the operator.

Combat Rescue

The Korean War provided an impetus for helicopter development. In Korea, the H-5 (the US Air Force dropped 'R' for rotorcraft and shifted to 'H' for helicopter in July 1948) became the first helicopter used regularly for combat rescue missions, carrying a single pilot and up to three men on a bench seat.

Of 1,690 US Air Force members shot down behind enemy lines in Korea, rescue forces saved 170, or 10%. The H-5 is credited with about two dozen of these, but veterans of the Korean conflict remember the figure as higher. By the end of the Korean War, larger helicopters were performing rescue, transport, anti-submarine and

other missions and newer types like the Sikorsky S-58 (H-34) and S-61 (H-3) were coming along. Tandem, twin-rotor types such as the Piasecki Model 42 (H-21) and Vertol 107 (H-46) began to make a mark. Today highly complex helicopters, such as the Sikorsky MH-53M and the HH/MH-60G, perform the USAF's combat search and rescue missions.

Under direct orders from Josef Stalin who took a personal interest in such things, Aleksandr Yakovlev's design bureau developed the giant Yak-24 Letayushchaya Vagon (Flying Wagon), or 'Horse', helicopter which first flew on July 3, 1952. It appeared at a Moscow airshow two years later, and frightened the daylights out of Western observers, but it was a false alarm. Like the Piasecki YH-16 to which it was remarkably similar, the Yak-24 never entered large-scale service.

Pre-Vietnam

In the 1950s, believing nuclear war with the Soviet Union to be just around the corner, US Army officers vowed never again to be caught flat-footed. They launched a period of experimentation that did not initially yield practical results, but did much to advance knowledge.

De Lackner Aircraft gave American soldiers an individual helicopter, the HZ-1 Heli-Vector, on which an infantrymen stood above a pair of 15ft, contra-rotating rotor blades. Though the craft flew successfully, the psychological hang-up of standing in the open above a pair of thrashing rotor blades was something no buck private was going to endure.

The Army tested five single-seat XH-26 helicopters between 1952 and 1954, but proceeded no further. A similar fate befell the Chrysler XV-6 and the Piasecki VZ-8 Sky Car, two ducted-lift aircraft that were meant to be flying Jeeps. By the end of the 1950s, a more traditional helicopter was opted for. By then, the US Army was fielding the most famous helicopter of all time, the Bell UH-1 Iroquois, better known as the *Huey*.

Vietnam years

In the 1960s, the American Army operated more helicopters than any other user on the planet, military and civil, combined. In 1968, the US Army had more aircraft than the US Air Force. The majority were *Hueys*, the US Army purchased more than 9,440 *Hueys* from 1958 to 1980. After years of experimentation, the *Huey* was a symbol of orthodoxy – a conventional helicopter with an all-metal fuselage, single main and tail rotors, and tubular skid-type landing gear. The crew of a *Huey* consisted typically of two pilots and a crew chief, with other specialised personnel on board as required. A typical configuration was for ten passengers. The *Huey* was powered by a single small, lightweight gas turbine engine. The first practical such engine in the US, developed by Dr Anselm Franz, was introduced in 1953 as the Avco Lycoming T53. It was the perfect match for the *Huey*, originally known as the XH-40, which first made its first flight on October 22, 1956. Two

The world's most advanced helicopter is the Boeing/Sikorsky RAH-66 Comanche reconnaissance/scout/attack helicopter. It features stealth, fly-by-wire avionics, a ducted fan tail-rotor and a host of other new technology features. (Boeing/Sikorsky)

Currently the world's largest helicopter, the Mil Mi-26 is roughly twice the size of its nearest rival and can carry an enormous payload. (KEY collection)

The massive Soviet Mil V-12 (MI-12) never went into production but is a good example of the attitudes of the time. The huge helicopter is today preserved at the Monino museum in Moscow. (David Stephens collection)

years later, as the Army introduced a new naming system, it became the HU-1 – the source of the *Huey* appellation. In 1962, another change in nomenclature took place and the *Huey* became the UH-1.

Once the Army began flying the *Huey*, it devoted a major effort to helicopter doctrine. In August 1962 a report by the Howze Board, led to the creation of the Air Assault Division. Defense Secretary Robert McNamara authorised extensive testing of the air assault concept and in 1963 the 11th Air Assault Division was formed to continue large-scale tests.

By then, the first *Huey* helicopters had arrived in Vietnam. In 1963, Lt Gen Harry Kinnard took command of the 11th Air Assault at Fort Benning, Georgia, described by one member as a "grand experiment" in which *Hueys* replaced ground-based transport and weapons systems, giving soldiers true, three-dimensional mobility for the first time.

By the time Kinnard's division was renamed the First Cavalry and sent to Vietnam in 1965, it was one of the best-trained formations the US Army has put into the field. Under the new 'airmobile' concept, the *Huey* became the servant of the ground soldier and the means of getting to the right place quickly and reliably. In Vietnam, some *Hueys* were 'slicks', plain transport ships while others were gunships. Fewer in number, but never to be forgotten, were the 'dust-offs' – the medical evacuation *Hueys* that gave many American soldiers their lives.

Combat lessons

A considerable amount was learnt from the war in Vietnam. Manufacturers strove to produce more effective battlefield helicopters and the results include the Sikorsky UH-60 Black Hawk, which has replaced the *Huey* in the US Army. The first dedicated gunship, the Bell AH-1 Huey Cobra was used in Vietnam but it has since led to a thriving attack helicopter revolution. Leading the way was the Hughes (then McDonnell Douglas and now Boeing) AH-64 Apache – still the world's most feared attack helicopter. Elsewhere the likes of the Eurocopter Tiger, Agusta A 129 Mangusta and Denel Rooivalk are just some of the competitors in the attack helicopter market.

Bigger, better

By 1970, helicopters were ferrying crews to oil rigs on a daily basis, carrying out research in the polar regions, recovering astronauts returned from space missions, and

equipping virtually every nation's army, navy, and air force. According to Sergei Sikorsky, who flew aboard helicopters as a child in the early days, his father Igor predicted "an absolute, finite limit" to the size and weight a helicopter could reach. The elder Sikorsky may have had a point as far as US rotary flight is concerned, the size of craft like the Boeing Vertol CH-47 Chinook and Sikorsky CH-53E Sea Stallion has not increased for decades, but the situation in Russia was quite different.

From Bratukhin to Mil, in Russia bigger often meant better. Described by one expert as "by far the largest helicopter ever built," the Mil V-12 with its twin, side-by-side rotors having an overall span of 219ft (66.75m) made its first flight on July 10, 1968. Again, as with the Yak-24 a decade earlier, Western observers were in awe. Again, the awe was premature. The 230,000lb (104,328kg) V-12 was a muscular brute but it did not become a production aircraft.

The same cannot be said of the Mil Mi-26 *Halo*, which is today the largest helicopter routinely operating in both military and civil service - and can be found from Moscow to Mexico. About 115ft (35m) in length (including rotors) weighing 124,000lb (56,246kg) when loaded, the Mi-26 can haul outsized cargoes unable to fit aboard any other

rotorcraft. This type first flew on December 14, 1977, and is still in production.

Russia's design experts seem to have shown little interest in developing an aircraft able to take off like a helicopter and transition into level flight. In the 1950s, such an aircraft would have been called a convertiplane, and numerous experimental versions were tested in the US. Today, the only such aircraft being seriously developed are the Bell/Boeing V-22 Osprey for military users (primarily the US Marine Corps) and the Bell 609 for executive travel. Both are 'tilt rotor' aircraft. A 'tilt wing' under development by McDonnell Douglas in the mid-1990s has now been abandoned.

Rotary future

The future of helicopter aviation may be determined by what happens to the V-22 and Bell 609. The former is in serious difficulty in Washington because of delays and crashes during the flight test programme, while orders for the latter stagnated following appearance of a full-scale mock-up at the 1997 Paris airshow. Supporters say that the ability to transition from vertical to horizontal flight, in a craft that can fly as fast as a fixed wing aeroplane, must be the way of the future. Detractors argue that development of new helicopters, using 21st century digital technology, composite materials, and other new techniques, is being held back by the emphasis on tilt-rotors. If the Osprey fails, the US military will instead buy large numbers of a conventional helicopter, such as the Sikorsky S-92 or EH Industries EH-101.

Thus, rotary wing aviation is at a crossroads. It's likely that one road or the other (tilt rotor or conventional helicopter) will have become a clear choice by the time the 100th anniversary of controlled, powered flight is celebrated on December 17, 2003. In the second century of flight, the helicopter is certain to be a full-fledged partner with the aeroplane.

● **The way ahead for rotary flight? The Bell/Boeing V-22 Osprey tilt-rotor is currently under development for the US Marine Corps and the US Air Force.** (Bell/Boeing)

Among the world's leading attack helicopters is the Eurocopter Tiger – now entering production with orders from France, Germany and Australia. (Eurocopter) ●

1970-79

1970-79

1. Tomcat purrs
On December 21, 1970, the prototype Grumman F-14 Tomcat makes its first flight. Designed to fulfil the role as an air superiority fighter for the US Navy, the Tomcat is set to become one of the all-time classic carrier-based aircraft. (US Navy)

2. Douglas Trijet
The maiden flight of the McDonnell Douglas DC-10 takes place at Long Beach. The aircraft is designed to rival the new Lockheed TriStar and, to some extent, the huge Boeing 747. (KEY - Tony Dixon)

3. Lockheed Trijet
Powered by three Rolls-Royce RB211 turbofan engines, the first Lockheed L-1011 TriStar makes a successful maiden flight on November 16, 1970. This example, operated by ATA, is pictured on final approach to Orlando, Florida, in May 2000. (KEY - Tony Dixon)

4. Strange shape
One of the most unusual aircraft to take to the skies makes its first powered flight on March 19, 1970. The Martin Marietta X-24A lifting body is dropped from a B-52 and is designed to explore the flight characteristics of such a vehicle during research for a reusable spacecraft. (NASA)

SIGNIFICANT DATES

JANUARY 22, 1970: Pan Am flies the first passenger service with the new Boeing 747 between New York and London, heralding a new era in mass travel.

MARCH 4, 1970: Cargolux Airlines International is created to provide a specialised scheduled cargo service. In November 1993, the airline becomes the first to use the 747-400F freighter.

APRIL 17, 1970: Apollo 13 astronauts Jim Lovell, John Swigert and Fred Haise splash down safely in the Pacific after a major emergency during their outbound flight to the moon. An oxygen tank exploded in the service module, forcing NASA personnel to improvise in order to get the men home alive.

JULY 17, 1970: Walk-through metal detectors are introduced at New Orleans International Airport in an attempt to prevent weapons being taken aboard aircraft.

AUGUST 22, 1970: With the aid of air-to-air refuelling, a pair of USAF HH-53 helicopters arrive at Da Nang, South Vietnam, following the first non-stop helicopter flight across the Pacific Ocean.

OCTOBER 24, 1970: The North American X-15 high-speed research aircraft makes the last of its 199 flights in the hands of NASA's Bill Dana.

NOVEMBER 4, 1970: Prototype Concorde 001 attains a speed of Mach 2 for the first time during a test flight.

NOVEMBER 12, 1970: The Kawasaki C-1 short-range transport aircraft makes its first flight. Powered by two license-built Pratt & Whitney JT-8D-9 turbofans, the aircraft looks very much like a scaled-down Lockheed C-141 Starlifter.

NOVEMBER 12, 1970: During trials at Edwards AFB, California, a Boeing 747 takes off with an all-up weight of 820,700lb (372,263kg), a little over a staggering 366 tons.

DECEMBER 18, 1970: The European consortium Airbus Industrie is formed to develop the new A300 airliner. Many see this as the only way ahead for european aerospace comapnies.

JANUARY 6, 1971: The first Hawker Siddeley AV-8A Harrier for the US Marine Corps is officially handed over at Dunsfold, Surrey. The aircraft enters service with VMA-513 at MCAS Beaufort, South Carolina.

JANUARY 22, 1971: A US Navy P-3C Orion establishes a new turboprop distance record of 7,010 miles (11,281km) after a flight from Atsugi, Japan, to NAS Patuxent River, Maryland.

Feb 1970: Mil Mi-24 **July 18, 1970:** Aeritalia G222 **Aug 29, 1970:** McDD DC-10 **Sept 11, 1970:** B-N Trilander **Nov 12, 1970:** Kawasaki C-1 **Nov 16, 1970:** Lockheed TriStar **Dec 21, 1970:** Grumman F-14 **Mar 21, 1971:** Westland Lynx

5. Mach 2 Tupolev
May 26, 1970: the Tupolev Tu-144, which first flew on December 31, 1968, becomes the first commercial transport to exceed Mach 2. (NASA)

6. Westland Lynx
The Westland W.G.13, the prototype Lynx, makes its first flight at Yeovil on March 21, 1971. The helicopter, which is still being developed today, proves a major success for Westland. (Gordon Swanborough collection)

7. Soviet look-alike
Bearing more than a passing resemblance to Lockheed's C-141 Starlifter, the Ilyushin Il-76 transport makes its maiden flight on March 25, 1971.

8. Aviocar
CASA's versatile 212 Aviocar makes its first flight on March 26, 1971. Powered by two Garrett TPE331 turboprops, the aircraft has superb short field performance and is a popular choice with many operators, both military and commercial. (CASA)

9. Japanese jet trainer
The first indigenous supersonic Japanese jet aircraft, the Mitsubishi T-2 advanced trainer, on its maiden flight on July 20, 1971. A single-seat close support version, the F-1, makes its first flight in June 1975. (KEY collection)

10. Sleek Agusta
Italian helicopter manufacturer Agusta flies its new A 109 for the first time on August 4, 1971. Initially designed for commercial use, military versions are also developed and the helicopter proves to be a huge success. (KEY - Duncan Cubitt)

11. Versatile Viking
The Lockheed S-3A Viking makes its first flight on January 21, 1972, and is designed to perform the anti-submarine warfare role. During its career it is constantly updated, though today, in its S-3B form, it is primarily used as an air refuelling tanker. (Lockheed)

1970-79

January 31, 1971: The UK's London Air Traffic Control Centre at West Drayton, near Heathrow, is declared operational.

March 24, 1971: By the margin of one vote, the US Senate decides not to fund the development of an American supersonic transport, dealing a death-blow to the proposed Boeing 2707-300.

April 25, 1971: BOAC begins Boeing 747 operations on its London-New York route.

July 26, 1979: Cameroon Airlines is established by the Cameroon government, enabling it to withdraw from the multinational Air Afrique, itself formed on March 28, 1961.

August 5, 1971: The British Civil Aviation Authority (CAA) is formed to oversee all commercial and private flying in the UK.

September 3, 1971: The first jet aircraft to be built by the Brazilian aerospace industry, the Embraer/Aermacchi EMB-326GB Xavante jet trainer, makes its maiden flight.

September 13, 1971: The tiny Bede BD-5 Micro, a kit-built jet aircraft designed for construction by amateurs, makes its first flight.

November 23, 1971: The first set of wings for the new Airbus A300B is delivered from Chester to Toulouse.

November 30, 1971: The Boeing 747-200F Freighter, on order for Lufthansa, makes its first flight at Seattle, Washington. The freighter version of the 747 revolutionises the cargo sector of commercial aviation.

December 8, 1971: Clearance is given by the French government for the joint development by SNECMA and General Electric of the CFM56 turbofan engine, destined to become one of the world's most successful jet engines.

January 5, 1972: President Richard Nixon authorises a $5.5billion programme to develop the NASA Space Shuttle.

January 24, 1972: Singapore Airlines is established after Malaysia-Singapore Airlines is dissolved.

April 1, 1972: The British Airways board, formed in 1971, merges BAE and BOAC under one banner, British Airways.

April 29, 1972: An experimental McDonnell Douglas F-4 Phantom II is the first American aircraft to fly with the aid of computer controlled 'fly-by-wire' technology.

1970-79

1. Warthog!

The winner of the USAF's A-X programme, the Fairchild A-10A Thunderbolt II, makes its maiden flight on May 10, 1972. The A-10 is designed as a ground attack/close support aircraft, with particular emphasis on killing tanks. Over 700 are built and during the 1991 Gulf War, the 'Warthog' causes carnage among Iraqi tank divisions. (KEY collection)

2. Eagle soars

The McDonnell Douglas F-15 Eagle air superiority fighter makes a successful first flight on July 27, 1972. The type has also since been developed for the strike role (F-15E) but in air-to-air combat it has an amazing success rate of over 100 kills without a single loss. (USAF)

3. Airbus arrives

On October 28, 1972, the European consortium Airbus Industrie marks its arrival on the world commercial airliner scene with the first flight of its A300 wide-body, twin-engine airliner. Twenty years later, the type is still in production as the A300-600. (Airbus)

4. 1,000 727s

On September 22, 1972, Delta Air Lines places an order for a further 14 Boeing 727s, pushing Boeing's order book for the type past the 1,000 mark. (Boeing)

SIGNIFICANT DATES

MAY 30, 1972: The Northrop A-9A makes its first flight at Edwards AFB, California. It is competing for the USAF's A-X programme, but loses out to the Fairchild A-10.

JUNE 21, 1972: A new helicopter altitude record of 40,820ft (12,442m) is set by Jean Boulet, flying an Aérospatiale SA 315 Lama.

JULY 1972: Air Botswana is formed by presidential decree. Initial services are with Fokker F27s and Britten-Norman Islanders.

JULY 26, 1972: NASA confirms that Rockwell International has been selected as prime contractor to build the Space Shuttle.

OCTOBER 1, 1972: Originally set up on April 3, 1971, Malaysian Airline System commences operations.

JANUARY 24, 1973: Agreements which will end the Vietnam War are signed in Paris, leading to a ceasefire at midnight GMT on January 27. However, in one form or another, hostilities and advances by the North Vietnamese continue for another two years.

APRIL 17, 1973: Federal Express, formed in June 1971, commences flight operations with Dassault Falcon 20s, to distribute cargo. Using a hub and spoke system - the hub being at Memphis, Tennessee - FedEx is set to become the world's largest freight and overnight package carrier.

MAY 22, 1973: National airline Aero Peru is established by the Peruvian government.

JUNE 1, 1973: Some ten years after the initial order was placed, the first six examples of a 24-aircraft order of General Dynamics F-111Cs are handed over to the Royal Australian Air Force.

JUNE 3, 1973: The Mach 2 Tupolev Tu-144 crashes at the Paris Airshow, killing 14 people. The incident was a serious blow to Soviet plans for the airliner.

JULY 25, 1973: A new altitude record of 118,898ft (36,240m) is set by A Fedotov in the Soviet Union, flying a Mikoyan Ye-266.

JULY 26, 1973: The Sikorsky S-69 Advancing Blade Concept (ABC) experimental helicopter makes its first flight. It uses two contra-rotating rotors to cancel out the usual torque produced, enabling it to fly without a conventional tail rotor.

OCTOBER 6, 1973: The Yom Kippur war breaks out in the Middle East, with an Egyptian attack on Israel. After initial setbacks, Israeli air power gets the upper hand, helped by a massive airlift of supplies from the USA by

1970-79

5. New UK airline
British Caledonian Airways officially adopted this name on September 1, 1972, after the merger of Caledonian Airways and British United Airways in November 1970. (David Stephen collection)

6. Linebacker II
On December 26, 1972, during the Linebacker II offensive, a force of 117 USAF B-52s carry out a huge bombing raid on Hanoi, North Vietnam. (US National Archives)

7. New French trainer
The Dassault-Breguet/Dornier Alpha Jet makes its first flight on October 10, 1973. The aircraft is a great success, both as a trainer and a light attack jet, and sees good export orders as well as serving the French and West German Air Forces. (Dassault)

8. Tiny twin
Undoubtedly the world's smallest twin-engine aircraft, the Colomban Cri-Cri makes its first flight on July 19, 1973. Power comes from two chain-saw engines and the aircraft is aimed at the kit-build market.

9. X-24 evolution
Following the success of the original X-24 in 1970, Martin-Marietta redesigned the aircraft as the X-24B, enabling much higher speeds and improved lift-drag ratios to be reached. (NASA)

10. Supercritical wing
As part of ongoing research into reducing wing drag at near-supersonic speeds, NASA has modified this F-8A Crusader with a supercritical wing, invented by Richard Whitcomb. (NASA)

---

the new MAC C-5A Galaxy. A ceasefire finally holds on October 24.

OCTOBER 21, 1973: The world's first electrically-powered aircraft, the Militky Brditschka Electric 1, flies at Linz, Austria. It is a modified sailplane powered by two battery-driven electric motors.

NOVEMBER 1, 1973: Air Niugini is formed by the Papua New Guinea government as part of efforts to help the third world country develop.

DECEMBER 1973: In the aftermath of the Yom Kippur war, Arab oil-producing nations inflate oil prices by 70% while cutting production by 5%. The result has a direct financial impact on global airliner operations.

MARCH 1, 1974: The Sikorsky YMH-53E Super Stallion makes its first flight. The helicopter is a larger, heavy-lift three-engine variant of the original CH-53 Sea Stallion.

MARCH 13, 1974: The new Paris Charles de Gaulle airport, just north of the city, opens its doors for the first time.

APRIL 1, 1974: Air Malta, formed in March the previous year, commences flight operations.

MAY 23, 1974: The Airbus A300 enters service with an Air France flight between Paris and London.

JUNE 4, 1974: Breaking through the sex discrimination barriers, 2nd Lt Sally Woolfolk becomes the US Army's first female pilot.

JUNE 9, 1974: The Northrop YF-17, a contender for the USAF's lightweight fighter competition, makes its first flight. It loses the battle but is eventually developed by McDonnell Douglas into the F/A-18 Hornet and is used in large numbers by the US Navy.

JUNE 17, 1974: In an astonishing demonstration of speed, an Air France Concorde leaves Boston Logan airport bound for Paris at the same time as an Air France 747 sets off from Paris for Boston. The Concorde lands at Paris, refuels and sets off over an hour later, returning to Boston, where it lands 11 minutes before the 747!

JULY 20, 1974: Turkey invades Cyprus, aided by extensive use of its airpower assets. The move prompts a rapid airlift of British nationals and tourists out of Cyprus by the RAF.

1. 737 military trainer

On April 10, 1973, the first military T-43A, a derivative of the Boeing 737-200, makes its maiden flight. It serves primarily as a navigational trainer, though a number, including this one, are eventually passed on to EG&G at Las Vegas to ferry personnel to the top-secret Groom Lake/Area 51 facility. (KEY - Steve Fletcher)

2. Turbo Mentor

Following the huge success of the original Beech Mentor, the company equips the aircraft with a Pratt & Whitney Canada PT6A-25 turboprop engine. The resultant YT-34C first flies on September 21, 1973, and goes on to equip many air arms, including the Indonesian Air Force, an example of which is illustrated. (KEY - Alan Warnes)

3. Fighting Falcon

The General Dynamics YF-16 Fighting Falcon makes its first flight on February 2, 1974. It subsequently wins the USAF's lightweight fighter competition and goes on to become the most successful jet fighter of the last 30 years with over 4,000 being built. (Lockheed Martin)

4. Flying Squirrel

The Aérospatiale AS 350 Ecureuil (Squirrel) makes its maiden flight on June 27, 1974. Now under the Eurocopter umbrella, the AS 350 has evolved into many variants and over 3,000 have been delivered. (Eurocopter)

5. Tri-nation Tornado

The Panavia Multi-Role Combat Aircraft (MRCA), now known as the Tornado, makes its first flight at Manching, West Germany, on August 14, 1974. Developed by the UK, Germany and Italy, the design initially serves as a strike aircraft but is later adapted to the air defence role as the Tornado ADV. (KEY collection)

6. Hawker's Hawk

The Hawker Siddeley HS.1182 Hawk prototype completes its maiden flight in the hands of chief test pilot Duncan Simpson. Under the auspices of British Aerospace and then BAE Systems, the Hawk becomes one of the UK's most successful aerospace products. (British Aerospace)

SIGNIFICANT DATES

SEPTEMBER 1, 1974: En route to the SBAC Farnborough Airshow, a SAC SR-71A Blackbird establishes a new transatlantic speed record, covering 3,490 miles (5,616km) in 1 hour 55 minutes and 42 seconds.

OCTOBER 17, 1974: The Sikorsky YUH-60A or S-70 prototype makes its maiden flight at Stratford, Connecticut. Designed to replace the ubiquitous Bell UH-1 Huey, the UH-60 is named the Black Hawk by the US Army, but also serves with the US Navy and many other military operators worldwide.

NOVEMBER 1, 1974: The government-owned Royal Brunei Airlines is established.

DECEMBER 23, 1974: The impressive Rockwell International B-1A bomber makes its first flight at Palmdale, California. It is subsequently cancelled by President Jimmy Carter, but later resurrected as the B-1B by President Ronald Reagan.

JANUARY 12, 1975: Europe's first no-booking, guaranteed seat shuttle service is introduced by British Airways between London Heathrow and Glasgow.

JANUARY 13, 1975: The General Dynamics YF-16 is announced as the winner of the USAF's lightweight fighter competition by Secretary of the Air Force, John McLucas. Much developed and now part of the Lockheed Martin stable, over 4,000 F-16s have been built - including those assembled under licence - and it is still in production.

FEBRUARY 1, 1975: A specially-prepared McDonnell Douglas F-15 Eagle, appropriately called the Streak Eagle, sets some astonishing new climb-to-height records at Grand Forks AFB, North Dakota. It soars from a standing start to 98,425ft (30,000m) in just 3 minutes 27.8 seconds.

MARCH 27, 1975: The de Havilland Canada Dash 7 regional airliner makes its first flight. With the help of Fowler flaps, reversible pitch propellers and an amazing approach angle of 7 1/2 degrees, the aircraft has an impressive STOL performance.

APRIL 1, 1975: The Republic of Singapore Air Force is established, though many of its assets are eventually located in the USA due to space restrictions.

AUGUST 26, 1975: As part of the USAF's advanced medium short take-off and landing transport competition, McDonnell Douglas flies its YC-15 four-jet demonstrator aircraft. The aircraft uses a revolutionary high-lift wing with 'blown flaps' to enable an excellent STOL performance to be achieved.

1970-79

1. Sherpa
Often referred to as the Short Sherpa (military variant), the SD3-30 (later Shorts 330) is, in fact, an enlarged version of the popular SC.7 Skyvan. The SD3-30 makes its first flight on August 22, 1974. (KEY collection)

2. AWACS
February 1975 sees the first flight of the Boeing E-3A AWACS (Airborne Warning And Control System). The E-3A uses its AN/APY-1 radar to operate as an airborne tracking station to monitor the battle space and direct fighter aircraft to intercepts. (USAF)

3. Yak transport
A new Soviet medium-range airliner, the Yakovlev Yak-42, makes its maiden flight on March 7, 1975. First envisaged as a replacement for the Tupolev Tu-134, it has enjoyed considerable sales success in Eastern Europe. (Mark Stanton)

4. Finnish trainer
On July 1, 1975, a new Finnish-built training aircraft, the Valmet L-70 Vinka, makes its first flight. Thirty are subsequently delivered to the Finnish Air Force. (KEY - Alan Warnes)

5. Baby Jumbo
A shortened, but longer-range, version of the Boeing 747, the 747SP (Special Performance), first flew on American Independence Day, July 4, 1975. (Boeing)

6. Low-cost helo
The American Robinson Helicopter Company successfully flies its R22 two-seat helicopter on August 28, 1975. Designed to compete on cost with small fixed-wing aircraft, the R22 will prove popular, with over 3,300 being delivered by the end of 2002. (KEY - Duncan Cubitt)

7. Tank killer
The prototype Hughes YAH-64 Apache attack helicopter makes its first flight at Mesa, Arizona, on September 30, 1975. Armed with laser-guided missiles, rockets and a chain gun and designed to survive at low level over the battlefield, the Apache is set to revolutionise army tactics. (KEY collection)

SIGNIFICANT DATES

SEPTEMBER 1, 1975: Concorde becomes the first aircraft to fly two transatlantic return flights in a single day.

NOVEMBER 28, 1975: Evergreen International Airlines is established.

DECEMBER 18, 1975: The US House of Representatives votes by a margin of one to prohibit the European Concorde supersonic transport (SST) from landing at US airports for six months. Clearly, the failure of the USA to produce its own SST had some bearing on the decision and it delays the introduction of Concorde on the route for which it was intended .

JANUARY 21, 1976: After years of development, the joint Anglo-French Concorde enters service with simultaneous departures from London and Paris to Bahrain and Rio de Janeiro respectively.

MAY 3, 1976: The longest non-stop passenger flight is made by a Pan Am Boeing 747SP which covers 8,088 miles (13,016km) in 13 hours and 31 minutes. This was one leg of an equally record-breaking round-the-world flight.

JULY 28, 1976: A new absolute speed record for an air-breathing aircraft of 2,193.17mph (3,596.56km/h) is set by a USAF SR-71A Blackbird flown by Capt E Joersz and Maj G

Morgan Jr. Their record still stands today - or as far as we know it does?

AUGUST 9, 1976: The Boeing YC-15, the other participant in the USAF's advanced medium short take-off and landing transport competition, makes its first flight.

SEPTEMBER 6, 1976: Soviet pilot Lt Viktor Belenko defects to the West, landing his prized Mikoyan MiG-25 Foxbat at Japan's Hakodate airport.

DECEMBER 22, 1976: A new Russian wide-body turbofan-powered airliner, the Ilyushin Il-86, makes its first flight in Moscow. It is

designed to carry up to 350 passengers and is the largest passenger aircraft ever built in the Soviet Union.

JANUARY 22, 1977: Kenya Airways is established, initial services being flown by two leased Boeing 707s.

FEBRUARY 1977: US President Jimmy Carter clears the way for deregulation of America's airline industry in an attempt to increase competition, reduce costs and reduce fares. The US Senate gives its approval on October 27.

MARCH 23, 1977: The USAF takes delivery of the first production E-3A AWACS aircraft at

Sept 17, 1975: MiG-31 **Sept 30, 1975:** Hughes YAH-64 A **Aug 12, 1976:** Aermacchi MB339 **Oct 10, 1976:** Embraer EMB-121 **Nov 7, 1976:** Dassault Falcon 50 **Dec 22, 1976:** Ilyushin Il-86 **Feb 23, 1977:** SOCATA TB 10 **May 3, 1977:**

8. Italian flair
The Aermacchi MB339 advanced jet trainer makes its first flight on August 12, 1976. Utilised heavily by the Italian Air Force, the type also becomes an export success and can be used as a light attack aircraft.
(KEY collection)

9. Smooth Bell
The streamlined Bell 222, the world's first twin-turbine commercial helicopter, makes its maiden flight on August 13, 1976. Incorporating a great deal of the latest technology, the 222 proves popular as a fast executive transport.
(KEY - Duncan Cubitt)

10. Embraer Xingu
The latest product from Brazilian manufacturer Embraer, the EMB-121 Xingu, completes its first flight on October 10, 1976. Eventually, 111 are built, a quarter of these serving with the French Navy.
(Embraer)

11. Dashing Dassault
Following the success of its earlier Falcon executive jets, Dassault flies its first variant with a transatlantic capability, the three-engine Falcon 50, on November 7, 1976. (Dassault)

12. Shuttle carrier
The first flight of the modified Boeing 747 Space Shuttle carrier with the Shuttle Enterprise attached takes place at NASA Dryden, Edwards AFB, California, on February 18, 1977. The first free flight of the shuttle launched from the 747 occurs on August 13. (NASA)

13. French Tobago
The SOCATA TB 10 Tobago, a four or five-seat light aircraft, makes its maiden flight on February 23, 1977. It spawns a family of light aircraft still in popular demand today.
(SOCATA)

14. Out-Flanked
A new Soviet fighter, the Sukhoi Su-27 *Flanker*, makes its first flight (the T-10 prototype) on May 20, 1977. Built as an escort fighter and long-range interceptor, the Flanker can be directly compared to the American F-15 Eagle air superiority fighter.
(KEY - Duncan Cubitt)

1970-79

Tinker AFB, Oklahoma. The use of Airborne Early Warning takes on a whole new meaning with the arrival of this aircraft because as well as warning of hostile or suspicious aircraft, it can also direct fighters to intercept.

March 24, 1977: A stretched version of the Lockheed C-141A Starlifter, the YC-141B, makes its first flight at Marietta, Georgia. Subsequently, almost the entire C-141A fleet is modified to the B model, which also includes an in-flight refuelling probe.

March 27, 1977: The world's worst air disaster, at Los Rodeos airport, Tenerife,

Canary Islands. A communications misunderstanding in foggy conditions results in a KLM Boeing 747 colliding with a Pan Am 747 on the runway, killing 583 people.

March 31, 1977: The UK government gives approval for the development of an AEW variant of the Hawker Siddeley Nimrod.

May 3, 1977: A revolutionary tilt-rotor aircraft, the Bell XV-15, makes its first hovering flight. The wingtip-mounted engines and rotors are tipped forward once airborne to transit the aircraft to conventional flight.

August 31, 1977: A new altitude record for an air-breathing aircraft is established at 123,524ft (37,650m) by Soviet pilot Alexander Fedotov in a Mikoyan Ye-166M.

September 26, 1977: Freddie Laker begins his Laker Airways Skytrain low-cost service between New York and London. Almost immediately, six established airlines lower their fares in response.

November 22, 1977: Concorde at last lands at New York's John F Kennedy International Airport, enabling full transatlantic services to commence on the route for which it was built.

May 5, 1978: Capt Matthew Webb becomes the first person to cross the English Channel in a microlight, in this case a powered VJ-23 hang-glider.

May 20, 1978: The 5,000th McDonnell Douglas F-4 Phantom II is delivered to the Turkish Air Force some 20 years after the flight of the prototype. Turkey remains one of a number of nations still flying the Phantom today.

June 1, 1978: Following the fatal crash of a non-passenger-carrying Tupolev Tu-144, the Soviet supersonic transport is withdrawn from service by Aeroflot.

Bell XV-15 **May 20, 1977:** Sukhoi T-10 (Su-27) **June 27, 1977:** CASA 101 **Oct 6, 1977:** MiG-29 **Dec 22, 1977:** Aérospatiale TB 30 **Dec 22, 1977:** Antonov An-72 **Mar 10, 1978:** Dassault Mirage 2000

1970-79

1. Mighty MiG
Another new Soviet fighter made its debut on October 6, 1977, the Mikoyan MiG-29 *Fulcrum*. It eventually enters service with the Soviet Air Force in 1985 and is also snapped up by many Soviet Bloc air arms and other air forces around the world. (KEY collection)

2. Curious *Coaler*
The strange-looking Antonov An-72 *Coaler* makes its maiden flight on December 22, 1977, a feature of the aircraft being the positioning of its two D-36 turbofans. Their high-wing location, coupled with multi-slot flaps, give the aircraft superb STOL performance. (Cliff Knox)

3. British Aerospace
Consolidation of the UK's aerospace manufacturers reached a new level on April 29, 1977, when BAC, Hawker Siddeley Aviation, Hawker Siddeley Dynamics and Scottish Aviation merge to create British Aerospace. This is Europe's largest aerospace company, employing 67,000 staff and with a turnover of around £800 million. Illustrated is the Harrier GR.3, previously a Hawker Siddeley product. (KEY - Duncan Cubitt)

4. New Mirage
Dassault's latest fighter, the Mirage 2000, makes its first flight in the hands of company test pilot Jean Coureau. It is powered by a single SNECMA M53 engine and has advanced avionics, including a fly-by-wire flight control system. (Dassault)

5. Challenging jet
A new executive jet, the Canadair Challenger, makes a successful maiden flight in Montreal on November 8, 1978. The aircraft is the first of a series of derivatives which are set to become one of the world's best-selling business jets. (Canadair)

6. New Harrier
A new version of the British Aerospace Harrier developed by McDonnell Douglas, the AV-8B Harrier II, makes its first flight on November 9, 1978. Making use of new composite materials and featuring various avionics and other improvements, the new aircraft has more endurance and can carry twice the payload of its predecessors. (McDD)

7. Hornet stings
McDonnell Douglas took the losing design in the USAF's lightweight fighter competition, the Northrop YF-17, and developed it to meet the needs of the US Navy's VFAX programme. The result is the YF-18 Hornet, which makes its first flight on November 18, 1978. (McDD)

SIGNIFICANT DATES

AUGUST 20, 1978: The British Aerospace Sea Harrier FRS.1 makes its first flight at Dunsfold, Surrey. The Sea Harrier is to serve the Royal Navy aboard its new through-deck cruisers, better known as the Invincible class carriers. It is also exported for use by the Indian Navy.

SEPTEMBER 13, 1978: The multi-role Aérospatiale AS 332 Super Puma makes a successful first flight. The Super Puma offers significant performance improvements over the original AS 330 Puma and is set to see service with many nations, eventuallu leading to the AS 532 Cougar.

NOVEMBER 26, 1978: Orion Airways is set up by tour operator Horizon Travel to fly package tour holidaymakers from East Midlands airport.

DECEMBER 19, 1978: The British Solar One becomes the world's first aircraft to fly using solar power when it makes a short flight at Lasham, Hampshire. Basically a glider airframe, the aircraft uses solar panels to power a small 1hp electric motor which drives a propeller.

JANUARY 6, 1979: The first production F-16A Fighting Falcon for the USAF is delivered to the 388th Tactical Fighter Wing at Hill AFB, Utah. Eventually around 2,000 in a variety of variants are delivered to the USAF.

JANUARY 24, 1979: Pilatus takes control of Britten-Norman, the resultant company becoming known as Pilatus Britten Norman Ltd.

MARCH 9, 1979: The twin-engine Dassault Mirage 4000 makes its first flight. Effectivrely it is a larger twin-engine version of the Mirage 2000 but it is not ordered into production. However, some work from the project was to prove beneficial to Dassault's subsequent Rafale programme during the 1990s.

MARCH 25, 1979: For a while Qantas becomes a Boeing 747-only airline after retiring its last 707 model.

MAY 11, 1979: Boeing Vertol's CH-47 Chinook receives a facelift with the first flight of the upgraded YCH-47D Variant. Almost all US Army CH-47A/Cs are subsequently modified to the D specification.

JUNE 6, 1979: Following a crash at Chicago O'Hare airport on May 25 after an engine becomes detached on take-off, the entire US Douglas DC-10 fleet and many overseas aircraft are grounded on the orders of the FAA. A total of 279 people are killed, and the

8. Euro-Japanese helo

On June 13, 1979, the joint MBB/Kawasaki-developed BK 117 utility helicopter makes its first flight. Able to carry up to seven passengers, the helicopter can be used for a variety of roles including law enforcement, medical evacuation, fire-fighting and general cargo transport. (Eurocopter)

9. ADV Tornado

The Air Defence Variant (ADV) of the Panavia Tornado makes its maiden flight on October 27, 1979. The type goes on to serve the RAF, Royal Saudi Air Force and, in the late 1990s, the Italian Air Force. (BAe)

10. Latest Gulfstream

Making use of a new wing fitted with winglets, the Gulfstream Aerospace Gulfstream III makes its first flight on December 2, 1979. This example is one of a number operated by the USAF for VIP/communications work in Europe. (KEY - Dave Allport)

Oblique wing

NASA's AD-1 oblique wing research aircraft flies for the first time at the Dryden Research Centre, California. The concept aims to determine whether drag can be reduced by pivoting the entire wing in this way, instead of using the more usual swept-wing configuration. (NASA)

1970-79

possibility of faulty maintenance is seen as the most likely cause of the engine pylon failure. The grounding was lifted on July 13 but at the time the safety of the type is under the spotlight, much to the anger of the manufacturer.

June 14, 1979: An experimental aircraft designed to investigate a new low-drag wing, the Dornier Tragflügel Neuer Technologie (TNT - new technology wing), makes its first flight. The data learnt from the programme will see considerable use in subsequent aircraft from the German manufacturer.

June 27, 1979: The McDonnell Douglas F-15 Eagle makes its first air-to-air kills when Israel Air Force examples shoot down four Syrian MiGs.

July 1979: Air Seychelles is established after the national government bought up the assets of Air Mahe and Inter Island Airways.

July 1979: The UK's new Conservative government makes strides towards selling off the country's publically-owned nationalised industries with two announcements setting out the privatisation of the airline British Airways

and the manufacturer British Aerospace. In both cases the government retains approximately half the shares.

July 2, 1979: Swiss airline Crossair is formed, specialising in regional flights within the country and to other European destinations..

July 24, 1979: The Bell XV-15 makes the type's first in-flight transition from vertical lift to conventional wing-borne horizontal flight.

August 14, 1979: A new speed record for piston-engine aircraft is set at 499mph

(803km/h) by Steve Hinton in a modified North American P-51 Mustang.

August 23, 1979: No.201 Squadron at RAF Kinloss takes delivery of the first upgraded Nimrod MR.2 maritime patrol aircraft. Twenty-three years later, the type is again upgraded, this time to MRA.4 specification.

December 14, 1979: The unusual Edgley Optica observation aircraft makes its first flight. With excellent STOL performance, the aircraft is aimed for use by the police or in powerline inspection and forestry patrol work.

May 30, 1979: Cessna 650   **June 13, 1979:** MBB/Kawasaki BK 117   **Aug 1979:** Bell 412   **Oct 19, 1979:** McDD MD-80   **Oct 27, 1979:** Panavia Tornado ADV   **Dec 2, 1979:** Gulfstream III   **Dec 14, 1979:** Edgley EA-7 Optica

Airpower at Sea

COMMANDER DAVID HOBBS, CURATOR OF THE FLEET AIR ARM MUSEUM, EXAMINES THE RISE OF NAVAL AIRPOWER, IN PARTICULAR THE STRENGTH OFFERED BY THE AIRCRAFT CARRIER.

During the 20th century, only three navies - those of Britain, the United States and Japan - demonstrated the ability to design, build, man, equip with aircraft and take into action a significant carrier force. Other navies operated carrier fleets but relied to some extent on purchases and training from overseas. The arrival of the aeroplane in December 1903 meant that it was not long before the military asked how this new-found ability might be put to use at sea. The flimsy aircraft of the time were not suited to operation from ships, and indeed methods of launching them and landing them safely were, to say the least, basic. But within 40

Above: **The nuclear-powered carriers of the US Navy represent the pinnacle of naval air power during the past 100 years. With over 80 aircraft in a typical air wing they can project force around the globe at very short notice.** (US Navy)

Above: **The first successful landing aboard a ship was made by Commander E Dunning in a Sopwith Pup aboard HMS *Furious* on August 8, 1917.** (KEY collection)

Right: **Grumman F6F Hellcats prepare to launch from the USS *Essex* (CV 9) in June 1944 off Tinian. By this time the US Navy effectively had control of the skies wherever it operated in the Pacific due to its overwhelming aircraft numbers.** (US National Archives)
Below: **During World War Two MAC-ships provided much-needed assistance to the escort carriers protecting the Atlantic convoys. Here a Swordfish gets airborne from MAC *Amastra*.** (Gordon Swanborough collection)

years, which encompassed World War Two, naval aviation made its presence felt across the globe and left an indelible impression on naval planners.

First experiments

The US Navy was the first to both launch and recover an aircraft, using platforms built onto warships. However, as in Germany, early British interest centred on airships since their endurance, radius of action and potential load-carrying ability far exceeded that of contemporary aircraft. HM Rigid Airship Number 1 was ordered in 1909 but broke up on being extracted from its shed in September 1911. This setback led to trials with seaplane-carrying ships and to the procurement of *Ark Royal* in 1914 for the operational fleet.

At first, the tasks assigned to aircraft were not new and they performed functions which Nelson's captains would have understood. Spotting for long-range gunnery was expected to be important. Thus, preventing enemy aircraft from providing their fleet with a similar service grew in importance as the war progressed. Aircraft carriers developed because aircraft could not operate where they were needed without them. Nothing has changed.

When Royal Navy seaplanes proved ineffective against German Zeppelins, wheeled fighters capable of taking off from small platforms were embarked on seaplane carriers and light cruisers. These were 'one-shot' weapons that could not land back on their parent ship and they had to ditch near the fleet if they could not fly to a friendly shore.

This was not really acceptable and Admiral Beatty demanded a more aggressive use of aircraft to attack the German High Seas Fleet in its defended home ports. To achieve this, an aircraft capable of taking off from a carrier deck, with an 18in torpedo weighing nearly a ton, and of landing back on board after the mission was needed. The aircraft that evolved was the Sopwith T1, representing an altogether more sophisticated approach which needed flush deck carriers and large numbers of aircraft, not just the handful needed for 'one shot' defence. By late 1918 *Argus*, the world's first true carrier,

and the converted cruisers *Furious* and *Vindictive* were in commission and a new *Hermes*, the first ship built from the keel up as a carrier, was under construction.

Between-the-wars progress

In the UK the newly-formed Royal Air Force controlled all military flying, including that used for naval purposes. In the USA, similar ideas did not survive open public scrutiny, but the debate did force the US Navy to formalise the status of aviation within the Service. Funds to convert the collier *Jupiter* into an experimental carrier, renamed the *Langley*, were approved in 1920. Equally important, a Bureau of Aeronautics under Rear Admiral William Moffett was authorised in 1921, charged with "all that relates to designing, building, fitting out and repairing naval and marine corps aircraft".

Progress in the USN stemmed from the driving force of men such as Commodore Joseph Reeves, who was instructed in 1925 to develop 'strategy and tactics of the air in its relation to the fleet'. Reeves doubled the number of aircraft aboard the *Langley*, improved their sortie generation rates and gave her an operational capability.

In Japan, the important role foreseen for aviation led to

the light carrier *Hosho* being commissioned in 1921, before her contemporaries *Hermes* and *Langley*. Helped by a British Training Mission, the Imperial Japanese Navy made rapid progress and thought of carriers as forming part of a raiding force with fast battleships, a concept well suited to warfare in the vastness of the Pacific Ocean.

The German Navy is an example of a failed carrier force. The projected *Graf Zeppelin* was actually launched, but plans to complete her were first delayed by Luftwaffe opposition and then by a wrong appreciation of the vulnerability of carriers by the naval staff after the sinking of the British *Courageous* and *Glorious* in the early days of World War Two.

Whilst the US and Japanese Navies made progress throughout the 1930s, the British did not fully appreciate how far they had slipped behind their rivals. The lack of a Reeves or Moffett was only realised in the late 1930s when Sir Thomas Inskip, an eminent lawyer, was appointed Minister for Defence Co-ordination. In a judgement subsequently known as the 'Inskip Award', he stated that naval aircraft and their crews were "a great deal more than passengers in a convenient vehicle". In May 1939, two months early, the Admiralty resumed full control of embarked aviation and its shore support.

Above: **The Royal Netherlands Navy also operated a few aircraft carriers, including the *Karel Doorman* (ex-HMS *Venerable*) illustrated here with Grumman Avengers on deck.** (Royal Netherlands Navy)

One of the most influential naval aircraft of World War Two was the Vought F4U Corsair. The large gull-wing fighter earned the name 'whispering death' from the Japanese – it completely outclassed any opposition sent against it. (KEY - Duncan Cubitt)

Above: **The first US Navy jet fighter to see combat was the Grumman F9F Panther during the Korean War. This example is seen about to be catapult launched from the USS *Antietam* (CV 36) off Korea in January 1953.** (US National Archives)

World War Two

The first Axis aircraft to be destroyed by the British in World War Two was shot down by a fighter from HMS *Ark Royal* on September 25, 1939, and the last by fighters from HMS *Indefatigable* on August 15, 1945. Between these two dates, British carriers fought in every theatre of war in every conceivable role. Far from fearing land-based air attack, they proved able to dominate battle space and spread sea power inland to attack strategic as well as tactical targets.

The Norwegian campaign highlighted the reality, rather than the theory, of modern war and the brunt of air support for the Army fell first upon carrier-borne aircraft from *Furious*, and then *Ark Royal* and *Glorious*. The campaign saw the first major warships sunk by air attack: the British destroyer *Gurkha* on April 9 and the German cruiser *Kongisberg* on April 10. Skua fighter/dive-bombers showed versatility and Lieutenant Lucy, CO of 803 Naval Air Squadron, became one of the allies' first 'aces' on this unlikely mount.

The attack, by aircraft from *Illustrious*, on the Italian Fleet in Taranto harbour in November 1940 demonstrated the power of naval aviation for all to see. Half the battle fleet was sunk or disabled by a handful of biplanes bravely flown by men determined to prove their cause. The power of a fleet at sea had been brought to bear on an enemy

who would not leave harbour for a conventional action.

To say that the Japanese 'learnt' from Taranto underestimates the progress that had been made by the Imperial Japanese Navy. The December 7, 1941, attack on Pearl Harbor was a well-thought-out plan that represented Japan's best hope for a decisive blow.

The Battle of the Atlantic was the longest-running campaign of the war and escort carriers proved one of the decisive factors in winning it. They had been considered and rejected in Britain before the war because the scale of likely open-ocean U-boat warfare had been underestimated. Wartime plans to build or convert such ships based on mercantile hulls failed, at first, because of opposition from the Ministry of War Transport which would not release hulls from the merchant building programme. HMS *Audacity*, a former German prize converted to the first escort carrier, showed the dramatic impact of such a ship on the protection of a convoy. In Britain, MAC-ships supplemented the escort carriers on Atlantic convoy routes.

Midway and the Pacific

The Pacific War provided the most powerful demonstration that aircraft had come to dominate naval warfare. Fought across an ocean covering nearly half the earth's surface, it involved logistic support distances vastly in excess of those in the European war. The six Japanese carriers that attacked Pearl Harbor embarked 450 aircraft: against this, the US Navy had seven carriers capable of embarking up to 600 aircraft. Japanese fighters such as the Mitsubishi A6M Zero had a distinct edge at the outbreak of war, although US industry rapidly produced a number of excellent designs against which the enemy could not hope to compete. Nor could Japanese shipbuilders rival the dozens of superb Essex class carriers and over 100 escort carriers which began to leave builders' yards from 1943.

But it was June 4, 1942, and the Battle of Midway, which was to have an indelible effect on naval airpower. In a matter of minutes, US Navy Dauntless dive-bombers decimated the Japanese carrier force, sinking four, and changed the balance of power in the Pacific. Japan would never recover, and the way was open for an American advance west towards Japan itself.

Fast carrier task forces, together with the 'Jeep' carriers that supported amphibious assaults, made the 'island hopping' campaign possible. American aircrew and sailors learnt quickly in action and their leaders rose

Above: **For the past 20 years the UK's carrier capability has fallen to the three Invincible class carriers, equipped with a mix of Sea Harriers and Sea King, or more recently Merlin, helicopters.** (Royal Navy)

Above: **The helicopter has found itself to be a valuable asset for naval commanders and today it fills a number of roles including anti-submarine warfare, search and rescue, communications, re-supply and amphibious assault. Here two CH-53Es land aboard a US Navy carrier during an exercise.** (US Navy)

swiftly to command on their merits. The quality of the whole fleet rose with dramatic speed in consequence and the US Fifth/Third Fleet, with its associated Marine Corps formations, was probably the most efficient and effective instrument of war in the pre-nuclear age.

Postwar development

After 1945, the British and US Navies rapidly ran down their wartime carrier fleets, though Canada, Australia and other nations created carrier fleets of their own, leaning heavily on British experience. Ships were exported to Canada, Australia, France, India, the Netherlands, Argentina and Brazil. Britain saw difficulty in operating the postwar generation of jets from its relatively small carriers but overcame the problem with the invention of the steam catapult, angled deck and mirror landing sight; ideas subsequently adopted by every carrier navy.

The advent of atomic weapons led many to claim these to be the catalyst that would make strategic bombing effective and that now, bombers really would make fleets obsolete. However, the Korean War of the early 1950s was to prove the theorists wrong yet again. The American *Philippine Sea* and the British *Triumph* were both in Far Eastern waters, and were able to bring tactical aircraft to bear. They brought their own logistic train with them, were

Apart from American, British and Russian types, the only other country to build carrier-capable fixed wing aircraft is France. Its latest is the Dassault Rafale which is now in service with the French Navy aboard the nuclear-powered carrier *Charles de Gaulle*. (French Navy)

able to find their own good flying weather, and concentrate force when and where it was required. One-third of all tactical air missions in the three-year war were flown from the decks of American, British and Australian carriers.

After Korea, US and British carriers maintained their strike potential. At Suez in 1956, RN fighters flew two-thirds of the strike sorties and helicopters carried out the first British 'vertical assault'. There have been many instances, such as Kuwait in 1961, where the presence of a carrier has deterred aggression, negating the need to resort to the use of force.

Spiralling costs

The value of the West's strike carrier forces was, perhaps, best appreciated by the Soviets who expended considerable resources in trying to counter their potential though by the 1970s, western attention was focused on the cost of defence, with carriers and their air groups attracting particular study. As a result, nations such as Canada and the Netherlands opted out of the carrier business. In Britain the cost of ownership was at first held down by the modernisation of wartime hulls such as *Victorious* and *Eagle*. Successive attempts to

build new ships culminated in the cancellation of CVA01, which was to have been named *Queen Elizabeth*, in 1966.

Fortunately for the Royal Navy, it was able to build three small carriers of the Invincible class capable of operating a few V/STOL (vertical or short take-off and landing) Sea Harrier fighters as well as helicopters although, short-sightedly, they lacked AEW (airborne early warning) capability. Together with the former CVA *Hermes*, *Invincible* made the 1982 Falklands Campaign possible.

American resolve

Only the US Navy has continued to operate a credible carrier force and in conflicts such as Vietnam, the Gulf War, Kosovo and, more recently, Afghanistan, their faith in the flexibility offered by a mobile naval air force has been vindicated. At present the US Navy has 12 operational

carriers, all but three of them nuclear-powered. A further nuclear example, the USS *Ronald Reagan*, is almost complete. A next-generation carrier, the CVN 77, is at the design stage and will feature much new technology: it is due to enter service in 2008.

Aircraft types aboard the US Navy's carriers have been significantly reduced in recent years, mostly as cost-cutting measures as newer, more reliable aircraft are delivered. Even the legendary F-14 Tomcat is now in its twilight years and is being replaced by the F/A-18E/F Super Hornet.

Another new aircraft set to make its mark with the US fleet is the Lockheed F-35C Joint Strike Fighter (JSF). The carrier-capable F-35C variant will replace the F/A-18C Hornet and will work closely with the Super Hornet as a multi-role aircraft, though primarily in the attack role.

Participation in intervention operations after the end of the Cold War has re-awakened British interest in large carriers and has led to British investment in the F-35 Programme as a full partner. However, the RN has many hurdles to cross before the two new carriers recommended in the Strategic Defence Review become a reality.

The change of government in France during 2002 has rekindled interest in a second nuclear carrier, and funding is to be sought for this vessel between 2003-08 to join the *Charles de Gaulle*.

Naval airpower at sea has proved itself to be an increasingly important part of modern warfare, and any nation which can afford the capability of the aircraft carrier is in a very strong position indeed.

Above: **The former Soviet Union was slow to establish a carrier force and by the end of the Cold War its only effective carrier was the *Admiral Kuznetsov* equipped with Sukhoi Su-33s.** (via Yefim Gordon)

Above: **The carrier capable F-35C variant of the Lockheed Martin Joint Strike Fighter is to equip US Navy squadrons beginning in 2008. The STOVL F-35B is to equip US Marine Corps squadrons and can operate from its assault carriers, replacing the AV-8B Harrier II.** (Lockheed Martin)

Century of Flight –
AirForces Monthly's View

ALAN WARNES, EDITOR OF *AirForces Monthly*, LOOKS AT THE CURRENT WAYS OF DEPLOYING AIR POWER, AND CONSIDERS ITS EFFECTIVENESS.

AIR POWER really proved itself in 1999 when NATO aircraft bombed Serbia's President Slobodan Milosevic into submission and peace was achieved without sending ground troops into Kosovo (see Kosovo - Air Power Wins, AFM July 1999, p4-5). Aided by fighting in countryside they knew well, Serb troops would have held a big advantage over NATO troops had there been combat at ground level. The evolution of the military aircraft has now allowed troops to be sent in only as a last resort. The two World Wars, fought at a time when air power was in its infancy, resulted in the loss of millions of lives on the battlefield. Thankfully, most modern countries deem it no longer politically acceptable to lose such large numbers of combatants. To prove once again that air power can defeat the enemy, bombers from the US-backed forces were used to defeat al-Qaeda and Taliban positions in Afghanistan without having to send in combat troops to do the job. For two months, TV viewers the world over watched

as B-1s, B-2s, B-52s, F-14s, F-15Es, F/A-18s and F-117s bombed the enemy. Eventually the Taliban and al-Qaeda positions capitulated sufficiently to let local troops make the advances with support from Special Forces on the ground (On The Run, AFM January 2002, p4-5).

However, few of today's air forces have the capability to gain air superiority in the manner of the Allies or, more accurately, the US. Once a country does acquire it, though, it has more chance of winning the war. Today, the US and the UK are preparing for war against Iraq – and you can bet your bottom dollar that the basic strategies employed to beat Mr Milosevic and the al-Qaeda troops in Afghanistan will be used again to defeat Saddam Hussein.

Hot spots

Smart weapons make combat slicker, and they are now being introduced into many air forces. Two countries on a constant state of war alert are Pakistan and India, which have already fought each other twice - in 1965 and 1971. Over the past year, the India-Pakistan situation has deteriorated to such an extent that the two countries

only narrowly avoided war again earlier this year (see Closer to War, AFM June 2002, p4). With both sides possessing nuclear bombs – which could have been dropped by aircraft – and Surface to Air Missiles, many diplomats trod the well-worn path to Islamabad and Delhi in an effort to avert conflict, and this effort eventually paid off.

Both countries are involved in an arms race. India's defence budget is now so huge that many aerospace companies, particularly from France, Israel and Russia, are courting the country (see Aero India 2001 Report, AFM April 2001, p18-21). French Mirage 2000s, slick Israeli weaponry and Russian Su-30MKIs will form the backbone of the future Indian Air Force. None of these countries dare deal with Pakistan for fear of losing their slice of a lucrative market, a situation which means that Pakistan has to rely on China, its old ally in the east. 2002 saw the introduction into service of the Chengdu F-7PG (see Farewell to the F-6, AFM June 2002, p40-45), while the Super 7, a Chino-Pak collaboration, is set to make its first flight in June 2003. A Beyond Visual Range (BVR) missile is another main priority for Pakistan in its attempt to

The most recent combat aircraft to join the ranks of the Pakistan Air Force is the Chengdu F-7PG. Within weeks of entering service, the aircraft was almost sent to fight against India. (All KEY-Alan Warnes)

A Sri Lankan Air Force MiG-27 with a full load of FAB-500M54 general-purpose, high-explosive bombs taxies to the runway for another mission against the Tamil Tigers in February 2001. A ceasefire now exists in Sri Lanka.

keep up with its old adversary.

In Sri Lanka, the Government battles against the Tamil Tiger terrorist organisation, which had gone on for more than 20 years, finally stopped in December 2001 (*Ceasefire in Sri Lanka*, AFM March 2002, p4). The ceasefire finally came about not through air power, but rather because the Tamil Tigers knew that the War on Terrorism being waged by the USA could result in them being targeted. The Sri Lankan Air Force is hardly recognisable now from the one it was ten years ago, as government after government of the country has sought a military solution. However, the conflict in Sri Lanka is similar to the one waged by the USA in Vietnam, with the terrorists fighting either from the depths of the dense jungle or underground. As one senior Sri Lanka Air Force (SLAF) officer told the author in 2001: "We are fighting a Vietnam-style war but without civilian casualties". Even today, 27 years after the USA pulled out of Vietnam, it is difficult for air forces to see beneath a canopy of jungle. Kfirs were acquired from Israel and MiG-27s from Ukraine in an effort to bomb the Tigers into submission (see *Sri Lanka's Fighter Bombers*, AFM April 2001, p30-34), a strategy which never really succeeded. The war in Sri Lanka showed that air power is not always the key to success.

Israel has the best-trained air force in the world – hardly surprising as it is the most combat-proven air force, the result of over 50 years of conflict with its Arab neighbours. Since the start of the Palestinian intifadah in October 2000, the IDF/AF has once again been at the forefront of offensive operations against the Palestinians and the groups that support them. On TV, we have regularly seen TOW-equipped AH-1s (see *Israeli Vipers in Action*, AFM August 2002, p80-82) and F-16s of the IDF/AF firing laser-guided weapons into buildings, cars and streets in an attempt to stem the violence against Israel, but to no effect. In any war against those who believe passionately in a cause, air power is not the answer – diplomacy is a better option.

RAF

The first national air force was founded in 1918. The United Kingdom's Royal Air Force (RAF) began with the creation of four squadrons - 1, 2, 3 and 4 Squadron which celebrated their 90th anniversary this year. The Army of the early 20th century relied largely upon hardware such as tanks to win battles, while the Royal Navy called upon ships and submarines. This system has changed and today most of the developed countries have 'air forces' operating in the other services. The UK's Army Air Corps, for instance, calls upon attack, scout and transport helicopters to assist its troops, while the Navy flies Sea Harriers (or will until 2006 – see *Sea Harrier Axed*, AFM May 2002, p56-61) and other helicopters to protect its ships.

Today the RAF is preparing to move into a new era. Over the next few years we can expect to see the Eurofighter joining its ranks, along with the Airborne Stand Off Radar (ASTOR) which will be mounted on the Bombardier Global Express. Smart weapons such as ASRAAM (Airborne Short Range Air-to-Air Missile) and the Enhanced Paveway are currently being introduced into service – aircrews will be able to 'fire and forget' these weapons, without seeing the targets.

No longer does the air power of the UK's three services exist purely to defend the state as it was originally, but in UN and other peacekeeping operations. The RAF is currently involved in a number of permanent overseas detachments, at locations such as Ali Al Salem in Kuwait where Tornado GR.4s deploy as part of Operation *Southern Watch* (see *GR.4s Kuwait bound*, October 2001, p48-49). The basis of this mission is to stop Iraqi aircraft from flying below the 33rd Parallel. A similar situation exists in the north of Iraq, where Iraqi aircraft are not allowed to fly south of the 36th Parallel. RAF Jaguar squadrons deploy to Incirlik, Turkey, every three months for this mission, known as Operation Northern Watch (see *Operation Northern Watch*, AFM December 2002, p20-23), and at Prince Sultan Air Base in Saudi Arabia, a squadron of RAF Tornado F.3s is present to fly combat air patrol for fighters patrolling these no-fly zones (NFZs).

Two Israeli Air Force F-16Ds of the Scorpion Squadron prepare to depart Hatzor. The IDF/AF continues to play a major part in the two-year intifadah.

Tornado GR.4s now operate with all the front line squadrons, and are deploying to Ali Al Salem in Kuwait for Operation Southern Watch. The RAF now deploys more squadrons overseas for exercises and operations than it has ever done.

Air-to-Air

Combat

AIR-TO-AIR COMBAT HAS BEEN PART OF AVIATION FOR 90 YEARS OF THE CENTURY OF POWERED FLIGHT. LON NORDEEN EXAMINES THE DEVELOPMENT OF THIS ASPECT OF WARFARE.

The fighter aircraft is designed to find, intercept, deter and/or destroy opponent aircraft and, thus attain air superiority. A fighter pilot has several ways of achieving this:

1) Through aggressive manoeuvres, threat of attack and/or direct action.

2) Hitting the target with a bullet or other projectile having enough energy to damage an aircraft's structure, propulsion system, flight control, fuel system or crew.

3) Igniting an aircraft's fuel, hydraulics and structure and detonating armament.

Early days

On June 2, 1912, a Wright B aircraft, flown by US Army Lt Thomas de Witte Milling, took off armed with a Lewis machine-gun which was fired by Capt Charles de Forest Chandler. The first successful air-to-air engagement took place on August 25, 1914, when the crews of three British BE2s from No. 2 Squadron forced down a German aircraft. Two months later on October 5, the crew of a French Voison 'pusher' from Escadrille VB-24, Lt Joseph Franz (pilot) and Cpl Quenalut (observer) shot down a German Aviatik aircraft using a Hotchkiss machine-gun, the first confirmed air combat victory.

In the summer of 1915, Germany fielded the Fokker E1 monoplane with synchronisation gear to allow the firing of a Maxim MG08 machine-gun through the propeller arc. German fighter pilots flying the Fokker monoplane inflicted heavy losses on British and French aircraft until they were countered by machine-gun armed British Vickers FB.5 Gunbus plus French Newports armed with Lewis guns mounted on the top wing. The Allies had to wait until 1916 for Newport 17s and Sopwith $1\frac{1}{2}$ Strutters with synchronisation gear and Vickers Maxim machine-guns.

Tactics at the start were pretty basic, get in close and fire away until the enemy goes down. Pilots used the sun, clouds and dive and climb tactics to surprise unsuspecting adversaries. As the number and size of aircraft formations increased, large scale air battles,

Above: **The Fokker Dr.1 Triplane was the most feared German fighter of World War One. The use of synchronised machine-guns firing through the propeller arc was a huge advantage.** (David Stephens collection)

One of the most fearsome air-to-air weapons so far built, the AIM-54 Phoenix is only carried by the F-14 Tomcat and has an exceptionally long range. (US Navy)

The British SE.5 made use of a Lewis gun fixed to the top wing, it was to prove highly effective. (Gordon Swanborough collection)

control, and pilots to employ co-ordinated air tactics.

The Spanish Civil War (July 1936-March 1939) pitted the last of the biplane fighters such as the Fiat CR.32, Heinkel He 51 and Hawker Fury against the I-16, Bf 109D/E and Fiat G.50 monoplanes. The German fighter contingent led by Werner Molders, who achieved 14 victories flying the Bf 109, developed new air tactics and techniques which took advantage of the improved speed and firepower of the monoplane fighters.

During the summer of 1939 Japanese and Russian air and ground forces fought a bitter series of battles in Mongolia known as the Nomanhan Incident. The Japanese pilots were well trained and experienced as a result of air actions over China. On June 27, JAAF Warrant Officer Hiromichi Shinohara reportedly claimed eleven air victories during an intense day of air fighting, the highest by a single pilot in one day up to that date.

World War Two

During World War Two thousands of aircraft were shot down in air combat on many diverse fronts. Aircraft technology advanced at an incredible pace and every few months changes in aircraft propulsion, weapons and sensors shifted the balance of airpower. One of the early lessons of air combat was the need to fit both fighters and bombers with self-sealing fuel tanks, armour for the crew and vital areas plus hardened windshields for improved survivability. Another significant advance was the introduction of the gyro gunsight by the RAF and Americans. This reduced the pilot's challenge in computing rapidly changing lead requirements during a dogfight enabling improved gunnery.

With years of day-to-day fighter operations, the Luftwaffe experts achieved unbelievable combat scores; Eric Hartman downed some 352 aircraft, most on the Russian Front, while Lt Gen Adolf Galland achieved 103 kills against Allied adversaries. The top Japanese aces were Navy Lt Tetsuzo Iwamoto with 94 victories and Army WO Hiromichi Shinohara with 58, while for the Allies Sqn Ldr Pattle (UK) scored 40+, Maj Richard Bong 40 (USAAF) and Ivan Kozhedub (Russia) 62.

Toward the end of the war, German airframe and engine technology was in the lead resulting in the fielding of innovative new fighters such as the rocket-powered Me 163 and jet-propelled Me 262. The Me 262 was more than

known as dogfights, became more common. After 1916 formations of fighters and observation aircraft regularly clashed in the skies over Europe, the Middle East, Russia, Italy and Turkey. By the end of the conflict, nearly all fighters were armed with two machine-guns, could fly at a speeds of 120-140mph (193-225km/h) and reach altitudes of up to 25,000ft (7,620m). The leading pilots of the various air arms built up considerable scores led by German Manfred von Richthofen with 80 air victories, French Capt Rene Foch with 75 and Major E Mannock with the RAF who was credited with 73 victories.

Between the wars

During the 1920s and 1930s aircraft and engine technologies surged forward and by the late 1930s, biplanes fighters were being replaced with all-metal monoplanes capable of flying in excess of 300 miles per hour. This new generation of fighters were well armed with four to eight machine-guns or a mix of cannon and machine-guns, they were also equipped with enclosed cockpits and improved backlit reflector gunsights. The leading fighters of the late 1930s included the British Hurricane (eight machine-guns) and Spitfire (eight machine-guns), Messerschmitt Bf 109E (two 20mm cannon, two machine-guns), Russian Polikarpov I-16 (two 20mm cannon) and Japanese Ki-43 (two machine-guns). The firepower of these new fighters ranged from the

Japanese Ki-43 with two 7.7mm machine-guns that fired a puny .75 kg/sec, to the Bf 109E with two 20mm cannons and two 7.9mm machine-guns that could fire 2.5kg/sec. The impact of high explosive cannon shells was far more destructive than lead bullets.

One of the major advances of the late 1930s was the development and fielding of radar and addition of radios to fighter aircraft. The US Navy and other air arms also developed identification friend or foe (IFF) transmitters so that radar operators could distinguish friendly aircraft from adversaries. These advances significantly improved the ability of air commanders to maintain command and

Above: **Specially-designed machine-guns were needed to fit inside the thin wings of the World War Two P-51 Mustang. However, this superb aircraft with its six machine-guns proved to be one of the greatest fighters of its time.** (KEY - Duncan Cubitt)

Above: **The F-86 Sabre was initially fitted with the same armament as the P-51 Mustang. Later models, such as this Australian example, replaced the machine-guns with two cannon and air-to-air missiles.** (KEY collection)

100mph faster than Allied piston engine fighters and its four 30mm cannon fired 12.5kg/sec which was deadly against both fighters and bombers.

Jet combat

The Korean War saw the start of jet fighter air combat. The two primary fighter aircraft employed were the American F-86 and Russian MiG-15 which both relied on short range cannon and machine-guns armament. The F-86 Sabre had a battery of six 0.5 inch Colt-Browning machine-guns firing a small 1.6oz bullet which could destroy structure and/or ignite fuel. Offsetting the small size of each projectile was the large number fired per second (99).

The MiG-15 was designed to intercept bombers and thus was armed with slow-firing, but hard hitting, armament comprising two 23mm cannon and one 37mm cannon. The three cannon of the MiG-15 fired seven 1.6lb 37mm and 20 7oz 23mm projectiles per second. However, it was difficult to make a hit because of the slower rate of fire and the dynamic nature of air combat. Due to superior experience, USAF pilots were able to shoot down more than 700 Chinese, North Korean and Russian flown MiG-15s while losing about 100 Sabres during the Korean War.

Better firepower

During the Korean War American pilots complained that many MiGs had been repeatedly hit by machine-gun fire to little effect. The next generation of American fighters was armed with 20mm cannon having greater punch and range than machine-guns.

The US Air Force funded the development of a unique 20mm cannon, known as the M-61 which had six barrels and operated on the Gatling-gun principle. Each of the guns six barrels fired once during a single revolution of the barrel cluster. The barrels were driven by electric or hydraulic power. The M-61, first used on the F-104 fighter fired at a rate of 4,000 shots per minute. Later models including improved versions which arm the F-14, -15, -16 and F/A-18 fire some 6,000 shots per minute.

France and the United Kingdom upped the firepower of their 1950s era fighters through the addition of 30mm DEAF and Aden cannon. The British Hawker Hunter had heavy firepower from four 30 cannon which put out 160 shells in a one second burst. Soviet designers followed this trend and armed its new 1954 era MiG-19 with the Nudelman-Richter (NR-30) cannon. This gun had a slower rate of fire than

Western types but its projectiles were heavier.

Air-to-Air missiles

During the 1940s and early 1950s efforts were undertaken in a number of countries to develop the guided air-to-air missile. The Germans developed a wire-guided air-to-air missile which was tested at the end of World War Two but was not used in action. America developed the radar-guided Sparrow 1, radar and infrared-seeking Falcon and IR homing Sidewinder during the 1950s. Britain developed the heat seeking Firestreak, and France the radar-guided Matra 511, while Russian designers produced the radar-controlled AA-1 *Alkali*.

Air-to-air missies are generally divided into two basic groups; short-range missiles designed for close-in use against tactical targets and longer range missiles intended for use against bombers and other targets at night or in poor weather conditions.

Historically, short-range air-to-air missiles have employed heat-seeking or infrared guidance. The IR seeker and flight control section was situated behind a clear nose window in the forward section of the missile. A contact and proximity fuse, warhead and solid rocket motor were fitted aft of the guidance section.

The seekers of these early missiles had limited sensitivity and were optimised to detect and track jet engine exhaust plumes. These limitations required the fighter pilot using these early missiles to attack from the rear of the target where the jet exhaust is most intense, thus limiting his attack options. As a defence measure fighter pilots learned to fly low over the ground, quickly climb toward the sun or release a decoy flare to escape from missile attack. Since these missiles had only a modest warhead (10-20lb) and low sensitivity fuses, a direct hit or very close detonation was necessary to disable the target aircraft.

Medium-range air-to-air missiles are generally larger, have a longer range and are more complex (and expensive). Most early radar-guided missiles required continuous illumination from the radar of the launching aircraft in order to perform a successful attack. A receiving antenna in the nose of the missile detected and tracked the reflected energy from the target and flew a proportional lead collision course to intercept the target.

Semi-active radar guidance has several advantages over early IR-guided missiles. Attacks could be made from all aspects, not from just behind, and in all weather conditions. A negative aspect of semi-active radar missiles was that the attacking aircraft had to maintain radar illumination of the target until missile impact – early radar systems were very susceptible to electronic countermeasures. Early radar guided missiles also had limited utility against low-flying targets due to ground clutter.

Early radars required a great deal of space, power and weight, thus fighters equipped with these systems were usually large and complex, such as the F-4 Phantom II, and they also required a second crew member or weapons systems officer.

Results in combat

Military planners in the 1950s were so sold on the capability of air-to-air missiles that many postulated the end of close-

Above: **The British Hawker Hunter retained the use of the cannon, in this case four 30mm Adens, but could also carry unguided rockets, though these were seldom effective.** (KEY collection)

Above: **During the 1950s the Gloster Javelin armed with Firestreak missiles provided the RAF with its first line defence against Soviet bombers.** (KEY collection)

Left: **The most powerful gun ever fitted to a fighter/attack aircraft must be the 30mm Avenger cannon as used by the A-10A Thunderbolt II. Primarily used to destroy enemy armour, the gun can be used against airborne targets, and during the Gulf War at least one Iraqi helicopter fell to the Avenger's awesome rate of fire.** (USAF)
Below: **The mighty M-61 cannon, here exposed for maintenance, packs a fearsome punch and has seen continuous development.** (KEY collection)

in fighter combat. So great was the confidence that several fighters designed in the 1950s carried no cannon armament. The American F-4, Russian MiG-21PF and British Lightning only carried missile armament.

The AIM-9B Sidewinder was the first air-to-air missile to be used in combat. Republic of China Air Force F-86F Sabre jets downed four Peoples Republic of China MiG-15s in 1958 during combat over the South China Sea with these missiles.

The arrival of missiles prompted the development of tactics to defeat them. The key element to countering a missile was adequate warning time. With sufficient warning, a pilot being attacked by an air-to-air missile could make a tight turn or fly up into the sun and escape.

Vietnam experience

The first full-scale, long-term conflict to see the use of air-to-air missiles by both opponents was the Vietnam War. American F-4s, F-8s and F-105s faced North Vietnamese MiG-21s and MiG-17s. Soviet-built MiG-21s were armed with AA-2 *Atoll* Sidewinder-like IR guided air-to-air missiles and cannon, while the MiG-17 initially only had cannon. American fighters carried the AIM-9B Sidewinder or the improved AIM-9D which had a nitrogen-cooled seeker and a larger 22lb warhead. The F-4 was armed with the radar-guided AIM-7 Sparrow, only the F-8 and F-105 had cannon.

Combat experience demonstrated that military planners had greatly over-estimated the effectiveness of air-to-air missiles. During one period early in the war, US Navy F-4s fired more than 50 Sidewinder and Sparrow missiles without scoring a single victory. Complicated aircraft fire control systems, poor missile reliability under the rigors of combat and limited missile firing envelopes considerably reduced the probability of success when fired against small, highly manoeuvrable MiGs.

Between 1965 and 1968 US fighter aircraft downed some 120 North Vietnamese MiGs while losing some 55 aircraft. About 85% of US victories were made with Sidewinder, Sparrow and Falcon air-to-air missiles. Due to a number of factors (political restrictions, poor training, firing out of the envelope and poor reliability), missile probability of kill per launch was only about half that achieved by the North Vietnamese who used the AA-2.

When the limitations of early missiles became evident, massive efforts were undertaken to improve their performance. More effective models of the Sparrow and

Sidewinder were rushed into production, such as the AIM-9E and AIM-9G/H Sidewinders with cooled seekers and enhanced performance. USAF and US Navy F-4s also fielded the improved Sparrow E with better electronics, a large rocket motor and warhead.

The most effective effort was intensified air combat training by American forces. The US Navy initiated a specialised course known as Top Gun which stressed manoeuvring combat and a thorough knowledge of tactics and missile firing envelopes.

These efforts paid off. During the second phase of air combat over North Vietnam, which took place during the Linebacker Operation in 1972, US Navy F-4s downed 23 MiGs while losing only two Phantoms. This 11 to 1 kill ratio was the result of intensified training, new Sidewinder

missiles and improved tactics. US Air Force fighters downed 51 North Vietnamese MiGs while losing 20 aircraft. Air Force jets had to fly across Vietnam from their bases in Thailand and thus were more vulnerable to attack for a longer period than US Navy aircraft.

Arab-Israeli air battles

Between 1967 and 1973 Arab and Israeli jets fought hundreds of air engagements. All of the victories (about 40) achieved by Israeli pilots during the 1967 War were made with cannon. The Egyptians, Syrians and Iraqis shot down 8-12 Israeli jets during this conflict. These were achieved with cannon, Atoll air-to-air missiles and at least one with 57mm rockets.

During the period of 1967-1970 fighting continued in the region and Israeli pilots achieved some 100 air combat victories. Most of these fell to Mirage pilots who used their 30mm cannon, but a third were with AIM-9B/D Sidewinders or similar IR homing Israeli-made Shafrir air-to-air missiles.

The 1973 Arab-Israeli War saw the largest air engagements since the Korean War with more than 400 aircraft being shot down during a two and a half week period. This conflict pitted Israeli Mirage, Nesher and F-4 Phantoms armed with cannon, Sidewinder, Shafrir and Sparrow missiles against Egyptian, Syrian, Iraqi and Algerian Missile armed MiG-21s and Mirage Vs, plus cannon-armed MiG-17s and Su-7s. Israeli pilots shot down about 275 Arab aircraft while losing about a dozen IAF planes to MiGs, a kill ratio in favour of the Israelis of some

23 to 1. Israeli pilots said they owed much to the good performance of the Shafrir air-to-air missile, which reportedly had a 56% success rate and late model Sidewinders were credited with similar effectiveness.

Improvements of the 1970s-1990s

The lessons of the Vietnam and Middle East air wars influenced the design of a new generation of aircraft, fire control systems and weapons. The fighters designed in the late 1960s and 1970s were optimised to have superior performance in dogfights and more capable weapons. The F-15, F-16, F/A-18, Mirage 2000, MiG-29 and Su-27 all have high thrust to weight ratios and excellent agility.

Above: **Takhli, Thailand in September 1972 as dozens of USAF F-4 Phantoms await their next missions over Vietnam. More than any other conflict in recent years, the Vietnam War played a major part in weapons and tactics development.** (US National Archives)

These aircraft were equipped with improved fire control systems, which can detect and guide missiles against low-flying aircraft, they were also armed with an internal cannon plus short and medium-range air-to-air missiles.

A number of new missiles were developed and fielded during the 1980s. These included the AIM-9L/M Sidewinder, Matra 550 Magic, Python 3, AAM-3, Sky Sword and AA-8. These short-range dogfight missiles featured improved electronics, more sensitive cooled seekers and enhanced performance. The AIM-9L was the first short-range IR-guided air-to-air missile to have true all-aspect capability. Its sensitive seeker allowed for head-on and beam shots which considerably changed the nature of air combat tactics.

A new category of air-to-air missiles fielded during the 1980s was those carried by helicopters. USMC AH-W Cobra attack helicopters were the first to carry AIM-9L Sidewinders and many Russian helicopters can use the R-60. Because of weight, many helicopters are also armed with derivatives of shoulder-fired surface-to-air missiles. This includes the Stinger, SA-7, SA-14 and Mistral.

Medium- and long-range air-to-air missiles were also upgraded during the 1970s and 1980s. Among the widely deployed types were the AIM-7F/M Sparrow, AIM-54A/C Phoenix, AA-7 *Apex*, Aspide, Super 530 and Skyflash.

These missiles employed larger motors, improved seekers and semi-active radar homing guidance, which allowed for flight ranges in excess of 10 miles. The AIM-54 Phoenix was designed to reach out more than 70 miles and destroy Russian bombers before they could fire their anti-ship missiles. Initially this missile flew via semi-active radar homing but in the terminal phase an active radar seeker in the missile took over guidance. This expensive and large missile is only be carried by the US Navy F-14 Tomcat. Russian interceptors also carried missiles of similar size and performance such as the AA-6 fired from the Su-15 *Flagon*, which shot down Korean Air Lines' Flight 007 on September 2, 1983.

Experience with new generation weapons

The new generations of fighters and weapons have demonstrated their improved combat utility. The Falklands Conflict (April 2-June 14, 1982) included many aerial engagements between Royal Navy Sea Harriers and Argentine Mirages and A-4 Skyhawks. The Sea Harriers, which served as the first line of defence for the British fleet, were credited with downing 31 Argentine aircraft, 24 with AIM-9L Sidewinders, and seven with 30mm cannon without air combat losses to themselves. Sidewinder

effectiveness was excellent; 27 missiles fired and 24 aircraft shot down, a probability of kill per launch of 88%. Argentine Mirage/Neshers were armed with Matra 530 and Shafrir air-to-air missiles but British pilots had the upper hand due to good radar vectoring, better weaponry and excellent training.

Air combat over Lebanon between Israeli and Syrian fighters in June 1982 pitted some of the latest American Israeli-built fighters and systems flown by very combat-experienced pilots against Syrian pilots with Russian fighters. Eighty-five Syrian fighters were shot down by Israeli F-15s, F-16s and F-4s with no Israeli losses in air combat. The star performers were the American AIM-9L Sidewinder and Israeli Python 3 IR guided air-to-air missiles. The Israeli success was due to effective command and control, superior weaponry, sound Israeli training and highly experienced pilots.

The 1991 Gulf War was the most recent large-scale opportunity for new-generation fighters and air-to-air missiles to demonstrate their success. During Operation Desert Storm (January16 - February 8, 1991) US and Allied fighters shot down some 35 Iraqi aircraft with only one suspected air combat loss of Allied aircraft, possibly an F/A-18 lost to an Iraqi MiG-25. Two thirds of the air combat victories were achieved with radar homing AIM-7 Sparrow air-to-air missiles, many of these were fired from beyond visual range. The remaining Iraqi planes fell to Sidewinders, cannon and one to a 2,000lb bomb!

Much of the credit for this lopsided score must go to the superior situation awareness Allied pilots enjoyed due to orbiting E-3 and E-2 AWACS, good IFF systems and tight rules of engagement. Even though the Iraqi Air Force fielded good systems like the French-built Mirage F1s with Matra 550 missiles and the Russian MiG-29 with AA-11 (R-73) and AA-10 (R-27) missiles, Iraqi pilots and radar controllers were poorly trained.

Air-to-air missiles today

The USAF F-16 achieved its first air combat victory on December 27, 1992, against an Iraqi MiG-25 with an AIM-120 Advanced Medium Range Air-to-air Missile (AMRAAM). The AMRAAM has considerably enhanced the ability of any fighter, even German Luftwaffe F-4Fs have shown that with the AIM-120 they can match the manoeuvrable MiG-29 with the eye-watering AA-11(R-73) missile which has a helmet-mounted sight for excellent close-in attack capability. When the AIM-120 was added to the F-15, F-16

Primary weaponry carried by the French Air Force Mirage 2000C comprises a mix of the Super 530 medium-range missile and the Mica IR short-range missile. (KEY - Alan Warnes)

Above: **Israel's Python 4 gives the Israel Air Force a distinct advantage over potential opponents, as it is a highly agile short-range missile used in conjunction with an Elbit helmet-mounted sight.** (KEY collection)

Above: **An RAF 43 Squadron Tornado F.3 displays the standard fit of Skyflash and Sidewinder missiles. Recently the F.3 became operational with the AIM-120 AMRAAM.** (RAF/Sgt Rick Brewell)

The American Sidewinder is one of the most successful air-to-air missiles of all time. It has witnessed constant development and is used by numerous countries, including the UK. (RAF)

and F/A-18 tests showed that the combat potential of these jets was magnified by several hundred percent. While the AIM-120 has only slightly longer range than the AIM-7 Sparrow, it is faster, and can seek out its target autonomously. This allows a pilot to attack multiple targets and then turn away to improve his survivability.

For the near term, the American AIM-120, Russian R-27, R-77 and French MICA are the missiles which set the standard in the medium-range arena of air combat. The R-27 is a semi-active radar homing missile similar in performance to late model AIM-7M Sparrow but an IR-guided variant of this missile also is fielded. The slightly smaller and shorter range French MICA also follows this pattern, having both active radar and IR versions. The Russian R-27RE had a larger rocket motor which gave it greater speed and reach than the Sparrow. The R-77 *Adder* is a Russian system with similar fire and forget performance to the AIM-120. US, European and Russian designers are developing even higher performance medium-range missiles today which will enter service early in the 21st century, like the ramjet-powered European Meteor destined to equip the Eurofighter Typhoon.

Latest missiles

The close-in combat arena has seen even a greater advance during the past decade due to the introduction of the Russian MiG-29/Su-27 with the R-73 aimed by a helmet-mounted sight. With the fall of the Soviet Union and unification of German (where the MiG-29s could be tested extensively), Western military planners had widespread access to the Russian technology that demonstrated the uncomfortable lead this system had over the American AIM-9L Sidewinder. A pilot of a MiG-29 with R-73s could acquire a target up to 60 degrees off the centreline of his aircraft, while the AIM-9L had only a 27.5

degree field of view and 40 degree tracking capability. With the helmet-mounted sight, the R-73 can be cued, by head movement, to hit a target within 180 degree of the centreline. This is the most capable all-around short-range missile in service today.

Israel has fielded a system of similar capability on IAF F-16s and F-16s in the form of an Elbit helmet and the Python 4 agile missile. This system has reportedly been exported to a number of customers including Chile, which has it on upgraded F-5s. The Royal Air Force has recently fielded the ASRAAM which, when combined with a helmet-mounted sight, will match the performance of Russian systems. American fighter pilots still rely on the AIM-9M as their close-in missile but the new AIM-9X and an advanced helmet sighting system are just now starting to be deployed on the F-15 and F/A-18 and is in development for the F-16.

Future combat

It would appear that the trend toward beyond visual

range air combat will increase due to the proliferation of early warning aircraft (E-2, E-3, Israeli Phalon and similar systems) ground-based detection systems and space sensors. Programs now in process in the US and Europe are aimed at fusing together data from many sources and rapidly supplying this information to pilots and battle commanders. This data fusion network will allow pilots to fight while operating in an emission control environment – with all radars and radios turned off to enhance the opportunity for surprise. Passive Forward Looking Infrared (FLIR) sensors and other systems will be used to maintain operational utility and covert action.

Stealth and signature reduction will have a major impact in the future battlefield. The Lockheed/Boeing F-22 with its super cruise capability and similar advanced aircraft such as the F/A-18E/F, Rafale, Eurofighter Typhoon and the JSF will have a major advantage over current and earlier generation systems because of their integrated systems and reduced visibility. Further in the future Laser, particle beam or similar energy weapons could replace the cannon and short-range missile. While deployment of an operational system is expected to be many years away, these systems would dramatically change the nature of air warfare. It would place further emphasis on stealth, deception techniques and innovative tactics, for if you were detected you could almost immediately come under attack by a weapon moving at the speed of light.

Success in air combat since 1914 has been achieved through the complex interweaving of many factors, many of which are beyond the control of the fighter pilot. The quantity, quality and performance of weapons, ranging from machine-guns to air-to-air missiles, are just elements of the air combat equation; however they are important ones. Frequently it has been demonstrated during the air wars of the past decades that skill, determination, effective battle planning and tactics have allowed the pilots of an outnumbered force of inferior aircraft to overcome the odds and emerge from an air battle the winner. One must not forget that for every advance in weaponry, an adversary eventually develops a defence or countermeasure. Advantage, parity, disadvantage; like a chess game rival factions have always manoeuvred to restore the balance. ■

Above: **One of the most potent Russian missiles is the R-77 Adder, seen here in front of the MiG-21 I-93 upgrade which has been adopted by the Indian Air Force.** (KEY collection)

Above: **The Eurofighter Typhoon will feature the new ASRAAM (shown here) among its weapons, together with the European Meteor ramjet-powered beyond-visual-range missile.** (BAE Systems)

1980-89

1

2

3

4

5

6

1. Powered glider

On March 14, 1980, the Grob 109 powered glider makes its first flight. The aircraft proves very popular and is used by the UK's volunteer gliding schools. (KEY collection)

2. Brazilian winner

Embraer performs the first flight of its new EMB-312 Tucano turboprop trainer on August 16, 1980. The aircraft is purchased in large numbers by the UK and France and also serves with many other nations. (Embraer)

3. Civil Chinook

Boeing Vertol successfully flies a civilian version of its CH-47 Chinook heavy-lift helicopter on August 19, 1980. This Model 234 is operated by Helikopter Service AS of Stavanger, Norway, and is seen lifting ventilation equipment on to a shipping complex roof. (Helikopter Service)

4. French delight

The Socata TB 20 Trinidad makes its maiden flight on November 14, 1980. The

SIGNIFICANT DATES

JANUARY 7, 1980: Pan Am buys out Miami-based National Airlines, acquiring with it a number of new domestic routes..

JANUARY 16, 1980: Air UK is formed following the merger of Air Anglia and British Island Airways.

MARCH 28, 1980: Gates Learjet announces the delivery of its 1,000th aircraft.

JUNE 1980: European Helicopter Industries (EHI) is established by Westland and Agusta to produce the EH 101.

JUNE 1, 1980: Braniff International ends its lease of Concordes from British Airways and

Air France, due to rising fuel costs.

JUNE 13, 1980: The 16th and final Concorde is delivered to British Airways.

JULY 1, 1980: The first RAF Tornado strike aircraft are delivered to the newly-formed Tri-national Tornado Training Establishment (TTTE) at RAF Cottesmore, Leics.

JULY 12, 1980: First flight of the first McDonnell Douglas KC-10A Extender refuelling tanker for the USAF.

JULY 17, 1980: A heavily-modified Nimrod AEW aircraft makes its first flight. However,

the project is dogged by technical difficulties and high costs eventually force the cancellation of the project in December 1986.

SEPTEMBER 19, 1980: Iraq carries out extensive air attacks on Iran, beginning a long-drawn-out conflict.

NOVEMBER 12, 1980: Delta Airlines places the largest-ever order for a single commercial airliner type when it orders 60 of the new Boeing 757s to the value of $3billion.

NOVEMBER 30, 1980: The Solar Challenger, built by Dr Paul MacCready, makes the world's first solar-powered flight.

DECEMBER 26, 1980: Soviet carrier Aeroflot introduces the Ilyushin Il-86 to service.

JANUARY 7, 1981: A CAAC Boeing 747 completes a flight from Beijing to New York, the first scheduled flight from China to the USA since 1949.

JANUARY 26, 1981: Pan Am retires its last Boeing 707-320C airliner, 22 years after becoming the first operator of the type.

MARCH 2, 1981: Japan Air Lines is the first to use a flight simulator (747) featuring computer-generated imagery.

June 23, 1980: Mudry CAP 21 Nov 14, 1980: Socata TB.20 Jan 1, 1981: Lear Avia Lear Fan 2100 Mar 28, 1981: Dornier Do 228 June 1, 1981: Short 360 Nov 5, 1981: McDD AV-8B Dec 19, 1981: Tupolev Tu-160 Jan 30, 1982: Enaer

four-seat GA aircraft is set to prove very popular and is continually developed over the next 22 years. (KEY - Duncan Cubitt)

5. S.211 trainer
The SIAI-Marchetti S.211 jet trainer makes its first flight on April 10, 1981. However, its sales success is rather limited. (KEY collection)

6 Reusable spacecraft
NASA realises a dream on April 12, 1981, with the first launch of the Rockwell Space

Shuttle reusable orbiter as *Columbia* lifts on the first test mission. The Shuttle has continued to serve NASA for 21 years, and a replacement is still some way off. (NASA)

7. Stealth delivered
Lockheed successfully flies the first production F-117A Nighthawk stealth fighter on June 18, 1981. Its unique faceted shape is designed to reflect radar waves, while a coating of radar absorbent material further enhances the aircraft's low radar signature. (USAF)

8. Quiet jet
British Aerospace flies its four-engine 146 regional airliner for the first time on September 3, 1981. The aircraft is a huge success - as well as being quiet, it is efficient and has excellent short field performance. (BAe)

9. Boeing wide body
The Boeing 767, a twin-engine, twin-aisle, wide body airliner makes its first flight on September 26, 1981. It is not long before it

is selling in large numbers and by the 1990s it is the most numerous transatlantic airliner. (Boeing)

10. *Blackjack*
The Soviet answer to the USAF B-1B is the Tupolev Tu-160 *Blackjack*, which makes its first flight on December 19, 1981. It has more powerful engines and a higher top speed of Mach 1.88. Its four Kuznetsov NK-321s each produce 50,926lb (228kN) of thrust with reheat. (KEY collection)

1980-89

MARCH 28, 1981: The Dornier 228 15-passenger turboprop airliner makes its maiden flight.

APRIL 20, 1981: The production Sukhoi Su-27 *Flanker* makes its first flight.

MAY 8, 1981: The first updated Dassault-Breguet Atlantic 2 maritime patrol aircraft makes its first flight.

JUNE 7, 1981: Israeli F-16s, supported By F-15 Eagles, attack the Iraqi nuclear reactor at Osirak, near Baghdad.

JUNE 26, 1981: The General Dynamics EF-111A Raven, specially modified for the tactical jamming role, makes its first flight.

AUGUST 3, 1981: Boeing delivers its 4,000th jet airliner - a 727 for Australia's Ansett Airlines.

AUGUST 19, 1981: The F-14 Tomcat claims its first air-to-air kills when two aircraft from the USS *Nimitz* are fired upon by two Libyan Air Force Su-22s over the Gulf of Sidra. Both the Su-22s are shot down.

SEPTEMBER 15, 1981: The USAF's 494th TFS, based at RAF Lakenheath flying the F-111F, is declared operational with the Pave Tack

laser designation precision bombing equipment.

DECEMBER 17, 1981: An experimental, modified Hughes 500 flies as the NOTAR (no tail rotor) research aircraft. The tail-rotor is replaced by a controlled jet air flow to counter the main torque of the rotor.

JANUARY 10, 1982: A Gulfstream III called *Spirit of America* completes a round-the-world flight in 43 hours, 39 minutes and 6 seconds to establish a new record for business jets.

JANUARY 22, 1982: NATO accepts the first

of 17 Boeing E-3A AWACS aircraft, which will be based at Geilenkirchen, West Germany.

JANUARY 27, 1982: Cessna delivers its 1,000th business jet, a Citation II.

FEBRUARY 3, 1982: A new weight to height record for helicopters of 125,154lb (56,769kg) to 6,562ft (2,000m), is set by a giant Soviet Mil Mi-26.

FEBRUARY 6, 1982: Troubled Laker Airways collapses due to unfavourable economic conditions. However, the low-cost airline has paved the way for many successful budget airlines in the future.

T-35 Pilan **Feb 19, 1982:** Boeing 757 **Apr 3, 1982:** Airbus A310 **July 14, 1982:** Harbin Y-12 **July 27, 1982:** Kamov V-80 (Ka-50) **Aug 30. 1982:** Northrop F-20 **Sept 3, 1982:** Beech 1900 **Sept 10, 1982:** Mundry CAP X ▶

1980-89

1. 727 replacement

Boeing also developed the new model 757 alongside the 767, and the smaller aircraft makes its first flight on February 19, 1982. The 757 is a single-aisle aircraft with a capacity of between 137-186 passengers, designed to supersede the Boeing 727 on primarily domestic routes. (Boeing)

2. New Airbus

On April 3, 1982, Airbus successfully flies the new A310 - a smaller derivative of the original A300, designed to seat between 200-280 passengers. This example is one of three operated by Uzbekistan Airways. (Airbus)

3. Commuter Beech

Beech flies the first model 1900 on September 3, 1982. The aircraft is a twin-turboprop 19-seat commuter aircraft and is destined to see a number of variations in its design, making it a highly popular aircraft. (Beech)

4. Heavy lifter

The giant Antonov An-124 Condor makes its maiden flight on December 26, 1982. Eventually 115 are built to serve both military and civilian operators, among them, Polet - this aircraft is one of seven operated by the airline and is seen at Sharjah in November 1999. (KEY - Alan Warnes)

5. Quiet turboprop

De Havilland Canada designed the Dash-8 to meet the need for a quiet 30-40 seat airliner: the first example flies on June 20, 1983. The design proves highly successful and is subsequently developed into a variety of models for both commercial and military use. (de Havilland Canada)

6. Brasilia

Following the success of its EMB-110 Bandeirante, Brazilian manufacturer Embraer flies the first EMB-120 Brasilia on June 27, 1983. The aircraft is sold to both

SIGNIFICANT DATES

MARCH 1, 1982: Flight-testing of the first production Boeing Vertol CH-47D Chinook upgrade gets under way at the company's Philadelphia facility.

APRIL 2, 1982: Argentine forces invade the UK's Falkland Islands in the South Atlantic, setting in motion events that lead to the Falklands War.

MAY 1, 1982: In what is, at the time, the longest bombing raid in history, a single RAF Vulcan bomber attacks Port Stanley airfield on the Falklands so as to deny the use of the base to fast jets of the Argentine Air Force. The aircraft operates from Ascension Island in the Azores under the code name 'Black Buck'.

MAY 12, 1982: Braniff International ceases all operations - the North American carrier cites the current economic recession as the reason for its difficulties.

MAY 18, 1982: American Airlines celebrates a landmark when it carries its 500,000,000th passenger.

JUNE 14, 1982: Argentine forces surrender to the British at Port Stanley in the Falklands. Over 100 Argentine aircraft are shot down for the loss of just ten British aircraft in combat.

JUNE 29, 1982: Lockheed finishes modifying the fleet of 270 USAF C-141A Starlifters to the stretched C-141B specification. The lengthened transport aircraft now has an additional 2,171cu ft (61.48m³) of capacity.

JULY 3, 1982: The General Dynamics F-16XL, featuring a larger cranked delta wing constructed from composite materials, makes its first flight. Designed to carry twice the load of the existing F-16, the aircraft loses the battle for USAF orders to the McDonnell Douglas F-15E.

SEPTEMBER 20, 1982: The HAL Ajeet Trainer makes its first flight in India. It is a two-seat development of the Ajeet light fighter which was itself developed from the British Folland Gnat.

SEPTEMBER 30, 1982: The first circumnavigation by a helicopter is completed by a Bell 206L Long Ranger after beginning the flight on September 1. Over 26,000 miles (41,850km) are flown and 23 countries visited.

NOVEMBER 4, 1982: Pan Am commences Boeing 747SP services between Los Angeles and Sydney. The 7,487 mile (12,049km) journey is said to be the longest non-stop commercial service.

military and commercial operators, such as the Brazilian Air Force, illustrated here. (Embraer)

7. Futuristic Beech
The amazing Beech Starship combined the company's expertise in turboprop aircraft with Burt Rutan's design flair. The result is a quite amazing-looking aircraft which first flies on August 11, 1983. Highly efficient and able to carry up to ten passengers, it is primarily used as a business transport. (Beech)

8. Italian attacker
Italian helicopter manufacturer Agusta performs the first flight of its new A 129 Mangusta attack helicopter on September 15, 1983. The type has been the main Italian Army attack helicopter since 1989. (Agusta)

9. Airtech transport
A joint venture by Spain's CASA and IPTN of Indonesia produced the CN-235

transport, designed to meet both military and commercial requirements. It makes its first flight on November 11, 1983, and is sold to a wide variety of customers, including Turkey, (illustrated) which operates more than 50 of the type. (KEY collection)

10. Punchy Pilatus
Slovenia is one of many customers for the Pilatus PC-9 turboprop-powered advanced trainer/light attack aircraft. The prototype

flies for the first time on May 7, 1984. (KEY - Alan Warnes)

11. AMX
The joint Embraer-Aermacchi-Aeritalia AMX makes its maiden flight in Italy on May 15, 1984. The aircraft is used as an attack aircraft by the Brazilian and Italian air forces and has also been sold to Venezuela. (Embraer)

1980-89

DECEMBER 16, 1982: Boeing's AGM-86B air-launched cruise missile (ALCM) achieves initial operational capability aboard the USAF's Boeing B-52.

JANUARY 7, 1983: US Marine Corps squadron VMFA-314 based at MCAS El Toro in California, is the first operational unit equipped with the McDonnell Douglas F/A-18A Hornet.

JANUARY 25, 1983: The Saab 340 twin-turboprop airliner makes its maiden flight. It enjoys moderate sales success and is also used as the airframe for the Swedish Air Force's S.100B Argus AEW aircraft.

FEBRUARY 3, 1983: Dassault completes the first flight of the Mirage 2000N, a low-level nuclear capable strike version of the basic Mirage 2000.

APRIL 9, 1983: The Piper PA-48 Enforcer makes its maiden flight. The aircraft is a development of the wartime North American P-51 Mustang - power comes from a turboprop engine.

APRIL 25, 1983: Based on the wartime Dornier Do 24, the modern day Dornier company flies the Do 24TT technology demonstrator amphibian.

JULY 22, 1983: The first solo round-the-world helicopter flight is completed by Dick Smith, covering 35,258 miles (56,742km) in a Bell Jet Ranger III. He set off on August 5, 1982, and flew for some 320 hours.

AUGUST 1, 1983: America West commences operations from its base at Phoenix, Arizona.

SEPTEMBER 2, 1983: A Soviet Su-15 fighter shoots down an unarmed Korean Air Lines' Boeing 747 near the sensitive Sakhalin Island military base, well inside Soviet airspace. All 269 aboard the aircraft are killed and a major diplomatic incident occurs.

SEPTEMBER 15, 1983: The still classified Lockheed F-117A Nighthawk stealth fighter is declared operational with the 4450th TG at Tonopah, Nevada. It is a further six years before the aircraft is revealed to the public.

DECEMBER 9, 1983: The 1,000th Boeing 737 is rolled out at the company's Renton plant, Seattle, Washington.

FEBRUARY 24, 1984: The Boeing 737-300 makes its first flight. The aircraft is larger than the previous models, can seat up to 149 passengers and is powered by two CFM56 turbofans.

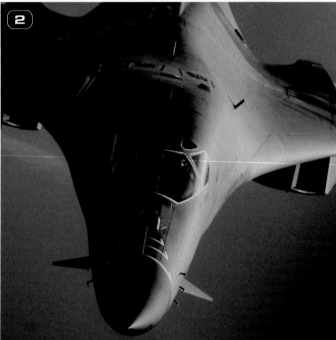

1. European transport

The ATR-42, jointly developed by Aérospatiale of France and Aeritalia of Italy, makes its first flight on August 16, 1984. The regional turboprop proves popular around the world, particularly in Europe . This example is one of 12 operated by Eurowings. (ATR)

2. Lancer flies

The reborn B-1 programme results in the first Rockwell B-1B taking to the air on October 18, 1984. The aircraft subsequently suffers many 'teething problems' but today, following numerous avionics and weapons upgrades, it is the USAF's fastest bomber. (USAF)

3. Japanese jet trainer

The Kawasaki T-4 intermediate trainer makes its first flight on July 29, 1985. The aircraft is the current mount of the Japanese aerobatic team, the Blue Impulse. (KEY - Steve Fletcher)

4. Gulf IV

Following the success of its earlier models, Gulfstream flies the first Gulfstream IV on September 19, 1985. The fast business jet can seat up to 19 passengers and has enjoyed buoyant sales, including many to military customers, such as the Koninklijke Luchtmacht (Royal Netherlands Air Force).

5. Fokker 50

The Fokker 50 is an advanced development of the original Fokker 27 Friendship and makes its first flight on December 28, 1985. New engines, six-blade composite propellers, avionics and equipment improvements and a capacity of up to 58 passengers mean that the aircraft is popular with airlines. (Fokker)

6. Attack Hawk

The British Aerospace Hawk 200 prototype

SIGNIFICANT DATES

MARCH 5, 1984: The first production Tornado F.2 ADV for the RAF makes its first flight.

MARCH 6, 1984: At Cardington, Bedfordshire, the British Airship Industries Skyship 600 makes a successful first flight.

MARCH 31, 1984: The final RAF Vulcan bombers with No 50 Squadron are retired from frontline service, leaving only a handful of Victor air refuelling tankers in service with the RAF to remind it of the heady days of the V Force.

JUNE 22, 1984: The Voyager Aircraft Inc Voyager, designed by Burt Rutan and flown by Dick Rutan, makes its maiden flight. The aircraft is designed to fly around the world non-stop and un-refuelled.

JULY 1, 1984: A rule change today opens up the transatlantic route to the new generation of large twin-engine jet airliners. Previously restrictions limited twin-jets to routes within one hour of a diversionary airport in case of engine failure. Today's highly reliable engines have extended this to two hours, opening up the north Atlantic airways to the likes of the Airbus A300 and A310 and the Boeing 767. By the year 2002 the rules have been further relaxed in view of the reliability of modern engines.

SEPTEMBER 21, 1984: The three-engine Dassault Falcon 900 makes its first flight. The executive jet is designed to carry up to 19 passengers over long distances.

NOVEMBER 8, 1984: The UK's Royal Navy reforms No 849 Squadron to operate the Sea King AEW.2 helicopter to provide the fleet's light carriers with an AEW capability. It is the world's first AEW helicopter unit.

DECEMBER 14, 1984: The Grumman X-29A, a forward swept wing research aircraft makes its first flight.

DECEMBER 17, 1984: A USAF C-5 Galaxy establishes a new all-up weight record when it lifts off at 920,836lb (417,691kg).

APRIL 22, 1985: United Air Lines buys all the Pacific routes plus all the Boeing 747s and a number of TriStars from Pan Am for $750 million. This is the start of the gradual disintegration of the once mighty Pan Am.

APRIL 30, 1985: British Aerospace flies the first of the RAF's Harrier GR.5 Harriers - the UK's version of the American AV-8B.

MAY 21, 1985: The world's first commercial aircraft to be made extensively from composite materials, the Dassault Falcon V

makes its first flight on May 19, 1986. The aircraft is designed as an attack version of the original Hawk trainer and can carry a wide variety of ordnance. With the ability to operate at night and to carry a variety of weapons, it proves to be an export success. This is a Malaysian Air Force example. (BAe)

7. Dassault's next generation

The new Dassault Rafale, planned to meet the needs of both the French Air Force and Navy, makes its maiden flight on July 4, 1986. The aircraft is highly versatile and can carry a wide variety of ordnance. It finally enters service with the French Navy in 2001. (Dassault)

8. Avanti!

Piaggio maintains its preference for pusher propulsion with the new P.180 Avanti which first flies on September 23, 1986. Able to seat up to nine passengers, the aircraft features a canard configuration while the rear-mounted engines ensure a very quiet cabin. (KEY - Malcolm English)

9. Strike Eagle

McDonnell Douglas develops a strike version of the highly successful F-15 Eagle and the new aircraft, the F-15E Strike Eagle, makes its first flight on December 11, 1986. It is destined to become the USAF's primary precision strike weapon of the 1990s and 2000s. (McDonnell Douglas)

10. Fly-by-wire Airbus

The Airbus A320 was designed as direct competition to the dominant Boeing 737. However, it features modern computer-controlled fly-by-wire avionics, a more spacious cabin, and the subsequent A318, A319 and A321 share a common cockpit. The aircraft first flies on February 22, 1987, and is to prove immensely popular with the airlines. (Airbus)

10F business jet, makes its first flight. Lightweight composit materials are to feature extensively in new aerospace designs.

MAY 24, 1985: Pan Am signs a $1 billion deal with Airbus for 16 A320s and 12 A310s plus options on a further 34 A320s and 132 A310s.

AUGUST 12, 1985: Five hundred and twenty people are killed in the worst ever single aircraft accident when a Japan Air Lines Boeing 747SR crashes into mountains north of Tokyo.

SEPTEMBER 13, 1985: The first (and only) destruction of an orbiting satellite by an aircraft is accomplished when a USAF F-15 launches an anti-satellite missile from an altitude of 40,000ft (12,190m)

SEPTEMBER 26, 1985: One of the largest defence orders ever placed (approximately $3.5billion) is agreed by Saudi Arabia with British Aerospace for 48 Tornado IDS, 24 Tornado ADVs, 30 Hawk trainers, two Jetstream 31s and 30 Pilatus PC-9s.

JANUARY 28, 1986: NASA and the world are stunned when the latest Space Shuttle mission, 51L using shuttle *Challenger*, ends in disaster 75 seconds after launch when the vehicle explodes, killing all seven astronauts.

JANUARY 31, 1986: de Havilland Canada is purchased by Boeing.

APRIL 14/15, 1986: Operation Eldorado Canyon takes place when a combined force of USAF and US Navy strike aircraft hit targets in Libya in response to alleged Libyan-sponsored terrorist attacks.

MAY 20, 1986: Work commences on London's latest airport - the London City Airport in the heart of the Docklands district of East London. The airport is to prove popular with the business community and its location dictates the use of small regional airlines of good short field performance.

MAY 25, 1986: Frenchwoman Nadin Vaujour uses an Alouette II helicopter to help her husband escape from Santé prison in Paris. A number of 'copycat' escape attempts follow elsewhere.

JULY 1, 1986: The West gets its first opportunity to view the Mikoyan MiG-29 *Fulcrum* when six aircraft make a goodwill visit to Rissala Air Base in Finland.

1980-89

1. Merlin magic
The EH Industries EH 101 makes its first flight on October 9, 1987. The aircraft is a true multi-role helicopter, at home on SAR duties, ASW duties, troop transport, cargo airlift or as a commercial helicopter. After a very long gestation period, the Merlin HM.1 is now in service with the Royal Navy: the HC.3 variant has joined the RAF. (Royal Navy)

2. New Jumbo
The latest variant of the Boeing 747 Jumbo Jet, the 747-400, makes its maiden flight at Everett, Washington, on April 29, 1988. The aircraft features many improvements over older models, notably with a two-man cockpit, improved aerodynamics such as winglets and greater range and payload capabilities. (Boeing)

3. Aerobatic Extra
The aerobatic Extra 300 makes its first flight on May 6, 1988, and proves to be a highly successful aircraft in its field. (KEY - Duncan Cubitt)

4. Swinging Swede
The Saab J 39 Gripen flies for the first time on December 9, 1988. Designed as a swing role fighter, it can switch from an air-to-air mission to a ground attack mission in seconds, providing operators with a truly flexible aircraft. (Saab/Katsuhiko Tokunaga)

5. Antonov's monster!
The largest and heaviest aircraft to fly, the six-engine Antonov An-225 makes its maiden flight on December 21, 1988. Only one is built and after a period of inaction it is once again available for outsize cargo transport. (Cliff Knox)

SIGNIFICANT DATES

AUGUST 6, 1986: The British Aerospace Advanced Turboprop (ATP - later called the Jetstream 61) makes its first flight.

AUGUST 8, 1986: British Aerospace's EAP technology demonstrator for the proposed Eurofighter programme makes a successful first flight.

AUGUST 11, 1986: Making use of advanced rotor blade technology, a Westland Lynx helicopter establishes a new world speed record of 249.09mph (400.87km/h).

AUGUST 20, 1986: A General Electric GE-36 unducted fan engine makes its first flight fitted to a modified Boeing 727. Despite much promise, the concept does not catch on.

NOVEMBER 30, 1986: Fokker completes a successful first flight of its new Fokker 100, an advanced development of the Fokker 28.

DECEMBER 4, 1986: McDonnell Douglas flies the MD-87 for the first time. The airliner is a short fuselage version of the MD-80, able to seat up to 130 passengers.

DECEMBER 14-23, 1986: The Rutan Voyager makes an historic non-stop and unrefuelled round-the world flight, flown by Dick Rutan and Jeana Yeager. Flight time is 9 days, 3 minutes and 44 seconds, and the distance flown is 24,986.664 miles (40,212.139km).

FEBRUARY 19, 1987: The Boeing E-6A communications relay aircraft makes its first flight. It is designed for use by the US Navy to provide command and control communications with the Navy's Trident missile-equipped submarines. By the end of the 1990s, the aircraft had also absorbed the duties of the USAF's EC-135 Looking Glass fleet of airborne command posts.

JUNE 26, 1987: McDonnell Douglas flies the first night attack variant of the AV-8B Harrier II. The aircraft is equipped with a FLIR system mounted in the nose and the system is eventually introduced on RAF aircraft, these becoming Harrier GR.7s.

JULY 16, 1987: British Airways announces that it is to purchase rival UK carrier British Caledonian.

MAY 29, 1987: German pilot Mathias Rust, just 19, defies the formidable Moscow defences when he lands a Cessna 172 in Red Square having flown from Helsinki, Finland.

APRIL 15, 1988: The world's first hydrogen-powered aircraft, the Tupolev Tu-155, makes its first flight.

1980-89

1. Tupolev twin
January 2, 1989, sees the maiden flight of the twin-engine Tupolev Tu-204 airliner. The medium-range airliner is also the first to be fitted with Western engines – the Rolls-Royce RB211-535E4. (Rolls-Royce)

2.Rotor revolution
The revolutionary Bell/Boeing V-22 Osprey makes its first flight on March 19, 1989. Designed to meet a US Marine Corps need for a fast troop insertion vehicle, the V-22 combines the vertical properties of a helicopter with the speed of a conventional aircraft by swivelling the rotors through 90 degrees. (US Navy)

3.Tai fighter
The AIDC Ching Kuo is Taiwan's first indigenous fighter and makes its maiden flight on May 28, 1989. The aircraft is designed to replace the Taiwanese Air Force F-104s and today serves alongside Taiwan's F-16s and Mirage 2000s. (AIDC)

4. Billion dollar bomber
Despite being the most expensive aircraft ever built, the Northrop B-2 Spirit stealth bomber is also one of the most capable, and flies for the first time at Palmdale, California, on July 17, 1989. The very distinctive flying wing can carry precision-guided munitions anywhere in the world from its home base in Missouri, as was illustrated in missions over Afghanistan in late 2001. (USAF)

SIGNIFICANT DATES

APRIL 16, 1988: The McDonnell Douglas/BAe T-45A Goshawk, a development of the BAe Hawk for the US Navy, makes its first flight.

JULY 1988: Chinese carrier Air China is formed by the Civil Aviation Administration of China (CAAC).

AUGUST 18, 1988: An electronic combat and reconnaissance version of the Panavia Tornado, the ECR, makes its first flight. The aircraft is to fulfil a West German Air Force requirement.

AUGUST 28, 1988: What is at the time the world's worst airshow accident occurs at Ramstein Air Base in West Germany, when three MB-339 aircraft of the Italian Frecce Tricolori display team collide. Over 40 people, including the three pilots, are killed and dozens more injured when wreckage of one aircraft crashes into the crowd. Afterwards West Germany bans all airshows while elsewhere regulations are considerably tightened up.

SEPTEMBER 19, 1988: The BAe Sea Harrier FRS.2, equipped with the Blue Fox radar, makes its first flight from the company's Dunsfold facility.

SEPTEMBER 28, 1988: The Soviet-built Ilyushin Il-96-300, a wide body airliner, makes its first flight.

OCTOBER 27, 1988: The first airliner to include considerable use of composite materials in its wings, the ATR-72, makes its first flight.

NOVEMBER 10, 1988: The USAF finally reveals the F-117A Nighthawk stealth fighter to the public, six years after it became operational.

JANUARY 5, 1989: Another incident between American and Libyan fighters occurs when two US Navy F-14 Tomcats shoot down a pair of Libyan MiG-23s.

JUNE 8, 1989: In what must rate as one of the luckiest escapes from a doomed aircraft, Russian test pilot Anatoli Kvochur ejects from his MiG-29 at the Paris airshow 2.1 seconds before impact. A bird strike in the starboard engine caused the crash, while the aircraft was performing a low-level manoeuvre.

JULY 4, 1989: A Soviet MiG-23 *Flogger* crashes close to Courtrai, Belgium, after its pilot had ejected over Poland. The unmanned aircraft was shadowed by USAF F-15 Eagles until it crashed. The F-15s had orders to shoot it down if it was at risk of hitting a populated area.

THE NEED FOR Speed

HAVING ACHIEVED POWERED FLIGHT, THE AVIATION WORLD HAS STRIVEN TO BUILD FASTER AND FASTER AIRCRAFT. MARK NICHOLLS CHARTS THE PROGRESS OF THIS QUEST FOR SPEED.

Man's ambition to further technological and engineering excellence has seen many marvels over the past 100 years but achieving greater speed has always grabbed the headlines. Be it ships, automobiles or trains, if the goal was to get between two points faster than before, it would be sure to capture the public's imagination. When the aeroplane was added to this list of man-made wonders, it presented an altogether more glamorous icon, albeit one that brought with it higher risks for those involved.

As with almost every technological advance, it is a combination of factors that has permitted the aeroplane to fly faster – more powerful engines, better aerodynamic design, better materials and improved manufacture. Although each of these individually can make an aircraft quicker, such as fitting a bigger engine to an existing design, when combined the effect is usually more pronounced.

Early developments

Before World War One early aircraft designers were just getting to grips with understanding the basics of aerodynamics and how to properly control an aircraft in flight. Materials used were mostly wood and fabric, although increasingly steel tubing was employed in the airframe. From an aerodynamic point of view, many early aircraft had the properties of a flying garden shed with parts of the airframe left uncovered and almost no attempt made to streamline the finished product. Drag was consequently high and when coupled to the low-power piston engines of the period, speeds were far from startling. Indeed, on August 29, 1909, the Curtiss Golden Flyer won the Gordon Bennett Trophy with a speed of 47mph (75km/h). The first officially recognised (by the FAI - Fédération Aéronautique Internationale) world speed record had been previously set on May 20, 1909, at 34.03mph (54.77km/h) by Paul Tissanddier flying a Wright biplane.

The first Schneider Trophy race was held in 1913 and was ultimately to play a significant part in the quest for speed (see page 162) but it was the outbreak of World War One that provided the greatest impetuous to develop the capabilities of the aeroplane. The dawning of air-to-air combat meant that whoever had the most manoeuvrable and fastest aircraft had the advantage. Achieving this aim resulted in many innovations from the likes of Anthony Fokker, Morane-Saulnier and Thomas Sopwith.

The arrival of the monoplane was highly significant, since an efficient single wing presents far fewer drag and weight penalties than a biplane arrangement, and when combined with a streamlined fuselage and more powerful engine, the result was a much faster aircraft. ▶

Despite earning a reputation as a killer, the Grenville Gee Bee established a new speed record on September 3, 1932. This replica gives some idea of just how small the aircraft was - dominated by the huge engine. (David Stephens Collection)

On July 28, 1976, an SR-71A established a record of 2,193.17mph (3,529.46km/h) for an air-breathing aircraft - and it still stands to this day. (Ted Carlson)

War by Other Means

THE DEBT THAT AVIATION OWES JACQUES SCHNEIDER CANNOT BE MEASURED. KEN ELLIS DISCUSSES THE LEGACY OF HIS FAMOUS COMPETITION.

A study of the history of powered flight will show that the over-riding spur to technological advance has been war or the threat of war. The pages of Century of Flight attest to this. With the 21st century barely started, the so-called 'War on Terrorism' has already provided a massive boost to the development of weapons, their delivery and command and control.

There are of course exceptions to this notion. For example, the pioneers of powered flight were driven largely by the fascination of the achievement, with hardly a thought given to any applications that their obsessions may generate. Also, as mass air transport grew in the 1950s and 1960s the airline industry became a driving force in its own right and has given rise to a incredible surge in technology spurred on by the two remaining giants, Airbus and Boeing.

There is one shining example of a 'private venture' that had a massive effect on the development of aviation, particularly in the 1920s when mediocrity seemed to be the rule of the day. This was the Schneider Trophy, a beautiful prize that became the Holy Grail for the nations of France, Italy, the UK and the USA. Its outright possession gave rise to the spending of vast sums of money to push the barriers forward for national honour.

The
SCHNEIDER TROPHY
Sept. 6th & 7th
CONTEST 1929

THE ROYAL AERO CLUB
Official
SOUVENIR PROGRAMME
Printed & Published by
GALE & POLDEN LTD, LONDON, ALDERSHOT & PORTSMOUTH
PRICE ONE SHILLING

These high-pressure races took on the semblance of the modern-day Formula One motor racing, and the technologies involved were no less impressive then as now. The monies poured in were also of similar proportions, although thankfully some items remained within the pockets of individuals even in the 1930s. The contests moved to a venue in the country of the winner, providing that same nomadic, globe-trotting image that is associated with F1. And the comparisons continue... Schneider was also huge crowd-puller and it needs be said that the nature of the 'race' was such that spectators probably saw very little of what was going on!

Psychologists would see no difference between such sports, calling them 'war by other means'. It is ironic that the main spin-off from the competitions was to benefit not

Above: **Not surprisingly, aircraft that competed in the Schneider contests were earmarked as national treasures, although a depressing number slipped the net. To the right is Italy's 1926 winner, the Macchi M.39, to the left the Macchi-Castoldi MC.72 of 1931. The latter took the absolute world speed record in 1933 and again in 1934, that time reaching 440mph (709km/h).** (Aermacchi)

civil aviation, but the military. Be that as it may, motivated by whatever means, the Schneider Trophy took on a stature like no other competition.

Born near Paris in 1879, Jacques Schneider was part of the influential and powerful family that owned the armament conglomerate centred on Le Cresuôt. He trained as a mining engineer but – like many others – was captivated by the sights and sounds generated by Wilbur Wright as he demonstrated his 'aerial carriage' in France in 1908. Jacques was also dazzled by high-speed boats and was nearly killed in one in 1910, leaving him permanently disabled. This misfortune did not deter Jacques - the following year he

became a qualified pilot of both powered aircraft and of balloons and in 1913 set a national altitude record in a balloon.

Speed and all things marine remained a passion for

● **The Schneider Trophy became a huge item of public interest and a major spectator sport. Tens of thousands thronged to the turning points around the Solent for the 1929 race.** (KEY collection)

● **The biplane format proved to be very tenacious but 1925 was the last time it took the honours. The impressive Curtiss R3C-2 was flown to victory by Lt James H Doolittle at 232.57mph (374.27km/h).** (KEY collection)

Schneider and he dreamed of scenarios in which 'hydravions' became the new passenger liners, taking people, freight and mail at great speed over long distances. He wanted to motivate the development of seaplanes of all kinds and as well as a beautiful trophy, he backed his vision of a new world with the award of 25,000 francs for three years running – a mind-boggling sum in those days.

Jacques hoped that such a glittering prize would transform the face of aviation. He was right, but he got the time-scale wrong and the competition was eventually rethought. The Great War intervened after only two contests had been staged, and the 1919 event was declared void with one crash, two non-starts, two retirements and

question that year is given with its maximum speed. (The HF.20 pre-dated fighters, but no matter.)

As can be seen the Deperdussin of 1913 and the Savoia of 1920 were both slower than contemporary 'equivalents'. But by 1925 the impetus of the Schneider Trophy becomes readily apparent. The shapely R3C-2 biplane floatplane was 72mph (115km/h) faster than the P-1A pursuit fighter – and both came from the same manufacturer.

The final 'race' – only the winner 'competed' – saw the Supermarine S.6B sizzle around the Solent at very nearly twice the speed of the Bristol Bulldog, the RAF's standard day fighter of the time. By then, 1931, the competitors were feeling the developmental pinch, and the costs were

escalating horrifically and the industry needed time to absorb the lessons it was learning.

Britain's final 'push' owed much to the financial intervention of Lady Houston, underlining the changing attitudes to the spin-off that such a contest could generate. But while there were to be no huge passenger-carrying flying-boats of the sort envisaged by Schneider, the competition fed much into the world of fighters and in engine development.

The legend that the S.6B quietly turned itself into the Spitfire five years later does not hold water under study of the reality. To use modern-day parlance, the S.6B was a 'technology demonstrator' for Supermarine, showing what could be done with aerodynamics, construction techniques and materials. For Rolls-Royce, the 2,350hp (1,753kW) Type 'R' V-12 was much more of a stepping-stone to the incredible Merlin. But this, as they say, is another story...

None of this considerable achievement was witnessed by the man of vision who had started and inspired it all. Jacques Schneider died, aged 49, on May 1, 1928, near Nice. By then his riches were much reduced, but his name had been carved indelibly into the history of aviation.

Below: **There can be no denying that another spin-off of the Schneider contest was the creation of some of the most beautiful looking aircraft. Supermarine S.6 N248 awaiting its turn at Calshot, 1929.** (Gordon Swanborough collection)

the Italian competitor flying the wrong lap pattern. At least he gained the right for Venice to be the venue the following year.

With each race the number of laps changed and so did the shape and form of the course, to take into account the peculiarities of the venue. The contest was not really a 'race' in the accepted sense, more a parade of aircraft built to very different specifications competing against the clock. From the 1920s the aircraft industry had seen the value of getting involved. The military was also brought in to a greater or lesser degree – national pride was at stake after all.

Three wins in a row was the new goal. Achieve this and the trophy would be held in perpetuity. The four competing nations threw themselves anew into a form of combat.

Statistics can prove anything that you want but the table accompanying this feature tells a little of the progress that Schneider kick-started. The winners of four the races are given with their speeds. To give an indication of the state-of-the-art at that time, a fighter operating in the country in

PUSHING THE BOUNDARIES

Race	Winner and Speed, mph (km/h)	Equivalent and Speed, mph (km/h)
1913	Deperdussin — 45.75 (73.62)	Henri Farman HF.20 — 102 (165)
1920	Savoia S.21 — 107.22 (172.54)	Ansaldo SVA.5 — 140 (226)
1925	Curtiss R3C-2 — 232.57 (374.27)	Curtiss P-1A — 160 (257)
1931	Supermarine S.6B — 340.08 (547.29)	Bristol Bulldog II — 174 (280)

SCHNEIDER TROPHY WINNERS

Date	Location	Pilot	Country	Type*	Speed, mph (km/h)
1913	Monaco	Maurice Prévost	France	Deperdussin	45.75 (73.62)
1914	Monaco	Howard Pixton	UK	Sopwith Tabloid	86.78 (139.65)
1919	Bournemouth	Guido Jannello	Italy	Savoia S.13*	race void
1920	Venice	Luigi Bologna	Italy	Savoia S.12*	107.22 (172.54)
1921	Venice	Giovannia de Briganti	Italy	Macchi M.7*	117.9 (189.73)
1922	Naples	Henri Biard	UK	Supermarine Sea Lion II	*145.7 (234.47)
1923	Cowes	David Rittenhouse	USA	Curtiss CR-3	177.38 (285.45)
1925	Baltimore	James H Doolittle	USA	Curtiss R3C-2	232.57 (374.27)
1926	Hampton Roads	Mario de Bernardi	Italy	Macchi M.39	246.5 (396.69)
1927	Venice	S N Webster	UK	Supermarine S.5	281.65 (453.25)
1929	Calshot	H R Waghorn	UK	Supermarine S.6	328.63 (528.86)
1931	Calshot	J N Boothman	UK	Supermarine S.6B	340.08 (547.29)

Notes: All of floatplane configuration other than those marked *, which were flying-boats. Source: The Schneider Trophy Races by Ralph Barker (Airlife, 1971) which remains by far the best study of the subject.

The ill-fated Blackburn Pellet gets airborne from the Solent on September 27, 1923. Its progress baulked by a small boat, it porpoised and crashed. Thankfully its pilot, R W Kenworthy, was rescued. (Gordon Swanborough collection)

Winner of the 1913 contest, the Sopwith Tabloid moored at Monaco. Piloted by Howard Pixton it achieved 86.78mph (139.65km/h). (Gordon Swanborough collection)

Between the wars

Immediately after World War One, the growth of commercial flying was pronounced, and particularly so during the 1920s and 1930s, when fledgling airlines faced a fiercely competitive market. Faster passenger aircraft were vital and so from the early types that could carry just a handful of people, to the arrival of the airliner proper, designers did all they could to build faster aircraft.

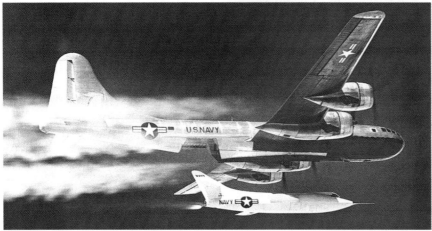

By now metal was being used more and more in aircraft construction. Offering strength at a light weight, it enabled great advances to be made in aircraft design, typified by the 1930s Boeing Monomail, the world's first all-metal monoplane. It was not long before aircraft such as the famous Douglas DC-3 Dakota were whisking passengers across the skies – but still at a relatively low speed.

The first aircraft to establish a speed record in excess of 400mph was the Supermarine S.6B floatplane racer which, on September 29, 1931, achieved 407.5mph (655.8km/h) at Ryde, Isle of Wight. Piston engine aircraft could not travel appreciably faster than this due to the limitations imposed on them by the propeller. However, air racing was becoming a popular sport and a number of aircraft, besides the Schneider Trophy seaplanes, were designed and built purely to compete. One of the most famous is the Grenville brothers' Gee Bee R-1 racer, which was basically a huge radial engine with wings. During the National Air Race on September 3, 1932, at Cleveland Ohio, Major J 'Jimmy' Doolittle set a new speed record for land-based aircraft of 296.287mph (476.828km/h).

Engine development was certainly playing its part by now, with Rolls-Royce in particular raising the horsepower stakes with its specialised racing R engine, forerunner of the famous Merlin. But it was the patent for a gas turbine engine, registered in 1930 by Frank Whittle, that had the biggest single impact on aircraft speed for the entire century – though it would not see much application until after World War Two.

The golden age

No one would refer to World War Two as 'a golden age' but the period it spanned certainly was as far as aircraft evolution was concerned. In the space of just six years, massive advances in engines and aircraft design were made in the name of national defence.

The 1930s had already seen major developments in

Left: **On October 14, 1947, Chuck Yeager became the world's fastest man when he took the Bell X-1 through the sound barrier and into the history books.** (NASA)

piston engines with powerful designs, both in air-cooled radial and liquid-cooled 'V' form. New streamlined fighters, such as the Supermarine Spitfire, Focke-Wulf Fw 190 and North American P-51 Mustang dominated air combat during the war, and speeds well over 400mph were commonplace. Even bombers were able to reach higher speeds than ever before, but it was the arrival of the jet engine in the early 1940s that was to change everything. Without the limitations of a propeller, the focus turned to improving aerodynamics and keeping weight in check to ensure aircraft could fly faster. The British Gloster Meteor and the German Messerschmitt Me 262 were the world's first operational jet fighters, although only the German aircraft saw any appreciable combat during World War Two. It incorporated many advanced features, most notably the swept wing, which was to play such a vital part in future aircraft design.

The invisible barrier

Piston engine fighters encountered what seemed like an insurmountable hurdle during World War Two. When diving at high speed pilots became aware of severe buffeting – sometimes control was lost, causing the aircraft to break up. What they were coming up against was the sound barrier, or more accurately a barrier caused by the aircraft going so fast that the air could not move out of the way and so became compressed. German designers had worked out that sweeping the wings back helped to improve airflow at these high speeds, and so applied them to the Me 262.

However, in the end, it was a straight wing aircraft, specially built for the task, that finally broke the sound barrier, the Bell X-1. Powered by a rocket engine, the X-1 became the world's first supersonic aircraft on October 14, 1947, when USAF test pilot Charles 'Chuck' Yeager exceeded Mach 1 for the first time over the Rogers Dry Lake in California.

From that moment onwards, the development of faster aircraft literally took off. With the added incentive provided by the Cold War, the USA, its allies and the Soviet Union raced ahead with new faster jet aircraft. This drive was equally felt by the engine manufacturers, and the power available from their jet engines multiplied at an astonishing rate (see pages 58-63). At the end of World War Two in 1945 jet engines were producing around 2,000lb of thrust, but less than 20 years later the two Pratt & Whitney J58s fitted to the SR-71A Blackbird were generating a massive 32,500lb each.

The jet age

From the late 1940s and throughout the 1950s there was an almost constant stream of new speed records, mostly set in the USA as new types of jet fighters and other high-speed research aircraft pushed the boundaries of aerodynamics and engine performance. Famous names, such as Scott Crossfield and Milburn Apt, were among the pioneers of faster-than-sound flight, though Chuck Yeager was also still setting records. Crossfield became

● **With the sound barrier broken, it was not long before aircraft pressed for even greater speeds. Scott Crossfield became the first man to exceed Mach 2 on November 20, 1953, in the Douglas D-558-2 Skyrocket.** (NASA)

● **Chuck Yeager poses beside the Bell X-1A after reaching Mach 2.44 on December 12, 1953. He momentarily lost control at this speed and plunged 50,000ft before recovering the aircraft.** (NASA)

● **The first aircraft to pass Mach 3 was the Bell X-2 flown by Milburn Apt. Sadly he lost control and was killed, despite managing to eject the escape capsule.** (NASA)

The fastest aircraft in the world is still the North American X-15A-2 which on October 3, 1967, reached an incredible Mach 6.72 or 4,534mph (7,296km/h). (NASA)

the first man to exceed Mach 2 on November 20, 1953, in the Douglas D-558-2 Skyrocket, followed by an amazing Mach 2.44 flight by Yeager in the Bell X-1A which almost cost him his life. On September 27, 1956, Milburn 'Mel' Apt became the world's fastest man when he took the Bell X-2 past Mach 3 but then lost control and was killed.

These records were all part of the research into overcoming the aerodynamic and heat generation problems of flying at such speeds. Similar work, though not as extensive, was also underway in the UK and France, as well as the Soviet Union, and each of these countries produced a number of experimental aircraft as well as high-speed fighters.

Numerous records have been established by military jets, but the outright speed record for an air breathing aircraft is held by the Lockheed SR-71A Blackbird at 2,193.17mph (3,529.56km/h) set on July 28, 1976.

The jet engine also revolutionised the airliner business

that grabbed the headlines, entering service in 1976. Today it is still the only Mach 2 airliner in service, flying regularly between London, Paris and New York.

Preparing for space

During the late 1950s as NASA began preparations for space flight, a number of very high-speed flights were made by the rocket-powered North American X-15. On October 3, 1967, after setting a number of amazing records, the X-15A-2 flown by Major William 'Pete' Knight pushed the record to 4,534mph – Mach 6.72 – the fastest speed ever achieved by an aircraft. This work, and much more undertaken by the likes of the X-24 and other lifting body craft, paved the way for the NASA Space Shuttle. Although effectively a spacecraft, it becomes an un-powered glider when it re-enters the Earth's atmosphere, at which point it is arguably the world's fastest aircraft, travelling at over 17,000mph (27,350km/h) just before re-entry.

SELECTED SPEED RECORDS

Date	Speed	Aircraft
May 20, 1909	34.04mph (54,795km/h)	Wright A
Aug 23, 1909	43.38mph (69,822km/h)	Curtis Reims Racer
Aug 28, 1909	47.81mph (76,956km/h)	Blériot XII
Apr 12, 1911	69.47mph (111,801km/h)	Blériot XI bis
June 12, 1911	77.67mph (125km/h)	Blériot XXIII
June 21, 1911	82.72mph (133,136km/h)	Nieuport IIG
Mar 2, 1912	104.33mph (167,910km/h)	Deperdussin
Sept 29, 1913	126.66mph (203,850km/h)	Deperdussin
Feb 7, 1920	171.41mph (275,862km/h)	Nieuport 29V
Oct 20, 1920	187.98mph (302,529km/h)	Nieuport 29V bis
Feb 15, 1923	233mph (375km/h)	Nieuport-Delage Sesquiplan
Nov 4, 1923	266.2mph (428,397km/h)	Curtiss R2C-1
Dec 11, 1924	278.48mph (448,171km/h)	Bernard V.2
Nov 4, 1927	297.825mph (479,290km/h)	Macchi M.52
Mar 30, 1928	318.632mph (512,776km/h)	Macchi M.52R
Sept 12, 1929	357.75mph (575,743km/h)	Supermarine S.6
Sept 29, 1931	407.5mph (655,798km/h)	Supermarine S.6B
Sept 3, 1932	296.287mph (476.828km/h)	Grenville Gee Bee R-1
Oct 23, 1934	440.683mph (709,209km/h)	Macchi-Castoldi MC.72
Mar 30, 1939	463.96mph (746,606km/h)	Heinkel He 100 V8
Apr 26, 1939	469.23mph (755,138km/h)	Messerschmitt Me 209 V1
Oct 2, 1941	623.85mph (1,003.96km/h)	Messerschmitt Me 163
Nov 7, 1945	606mph (975.464km/h)	Gloster Meteor F.III/IV
Sept 7, 1946	616mph (990.786km/h)	Gloster Meteor F.IV
June 19, 1947	623.738mph (1,003.594km/h)	Lockheed P-80R
Aug 20, 1947	644.663mph (1,030.820km/h)	Douglas D-558-1
Aug 25, 1947	650.8mph (1,047.130km/h)	Douglas D-558-1
Oct 14, 1947	670mph (1,078km/h)	Bell X-1
Nov 18, 1952	698.52mph (1,124.137km/h)	North American F-86D-20
July 16, 1953	715.76mph (1,151.883km/h)	North American F-86D-35
Sept 7, 1953	727.496mph (1,170.760km/h)	Hawker Hunter F.3
Sept 25, 1953	735.72mph (1,184km/h)	Supermarine Swift F.4
Oct 3, 1953	752.96mph (1,211.746km/h)	Douglas XF4D-1
Nov 20, 1953	1,291mph (2,077.6km/h)	Douglas D-558-2
Dec 12, 1953	1,650mph (2,655.34km/h)	Bell X-1A
Aug 20, 1955	822.29 mph (1,323.312km/h)	North American F-100C-1
Mar 10, 1956	1,131.76mph (1,822km/h)	Fairey FD.2
Sept 27, 1956	2,094mph (3,369.87km/h)	Bell X-2
Dec 12, 1957	1,202mph (1,943.5km/h)	McDonnell F-101A-5 Voodoo
May 16, 1958	1,403.19mph (2,259.538km/h)	Lockheed YF-104A
Oct 31, 1959	1,483.8mph (2,388km/h)	Mikoyan Ye-66
Dec 15, 1959	1,525.9mph (2,455.736km/h)	Convair F-106A
Nov 22, 1961	1,605.51mph (2,585,425km/h)	McDonnell XF4H-1
July 7, 1962	1,665.89mph (2,681km/h)	Mikoyan Ye-166
May 1, 1965	2,062mph (3,331.507km/h)	Lockheed YF-12A
Oct 3, 1967	4,534mph (7,296km/h)	North American X-15A-2
July 28, 1976	2,193.17mph (3,529.560km/h)	Lockheed SR-71A

Note: Figures include both measured course records and one-way speeds set by research aircraft.

and the ground-breaking de Havilland Comet was to set the standard when it entered service in 1952, shaving hours off commercial flights previously the forté of the piston-engine airliner. With the arrival of the Boeing 707 and Douglas DC-8 at the end of the 1950s, civil aviation was changed forever as these fast jet airliners effectively shrank the world. Two designs of supersonic airliner flew by the end of the 1960s, the Tupolev Tu-144 and the BAC/Aérospatiale Concorde. However, it was Concorde

Limitations

Considering the fact that powered flight is now celebrating its first centenary, it is perhaps a little surprising that many of the existing speed records were set over a quarter of a century ago. In reality, it is testimony to the ingenuity of the designers and engineers that they were able to build aircraft capable of pushing the aerodynamic limits so quickly. Within the atmosphere, especially at lower altitudes, it is air resistance and friction that pose the

greatest problems. However, the constant development of new heat-resistant composite materials may yet see even greater speeds reached. NASA is already testing its X-43 hypersonic test vehicles, which it hopes will eventually reach Mach 10.

On the commercial front, Boeing has proposed its Sonic Cruiser to fly in the transonic speed range, but at present there are no plans to build a replacement for Concorde. In this instance, it is not the technology but the sheer cost of such a project that is prohibitive.

Thirty years after the piston engine's heyday, a privately-owned P-51 Mustang used for air racing set a new record for a piston-engine aircraft of 499.047mph (803km/h). Steve Hinton's heavily modified aircraft was powered by a 3,800hp Rolls-Royce Griffon engine.

It is worth remembering just what amazing achievements man has made in relation to speed in the air. The very first record speed of 34.03mph (54.77km/h) was set in May 1909. Just 58 years later, this figure had risen to an incredible 4,534mph (7,296km/h) set by the X-15A-2. ◼

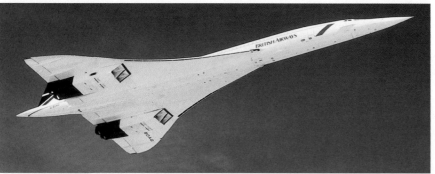

● **The highly modified P-51 Mustang Red Baron set a new world record for piston engine aircraft of 499mph (803km/h) on August 14, 1979.** (Dick Phillips)

● **Still the world's only supersonic airliner, Concorde flies daily at Mach 2 but could well be the only supersonic airliner to see regular service.** (British Airways)

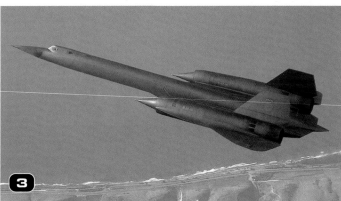

1990-99

1. Revamped trijet

On January 10, 1990, McDonnell Douglas carries out the maiden flight of its MD-11 trijet, derived from the earlier DC-10, at its Long Beach, California facility. The new aircraft features updated avionics and the addition of winglets, as well as a number of other improvements over the original DC-10. (McDonnell Douglas)

2. South African teeth

The South African Atlas Aircraft Corporation XH-2 Rooivalk attack helicopter makes its first flight on February 11, 1990, having been rolled out on January 15. (Atlas)

3. Bowing out with a bang

On March 6, 1990, while being retired to

SIGNIFICANT DATES

JANUARY 5, 1990: First flight of a Boeing E-3D (Sentry AEW.1) at Boeing Field, one of seven on order for the RAF. When the final aircraft is rolled out in May 1991, it becomes the last 707 airframe to be built.

JANUARY 11, 1990: The US Department of Defense awards a $123 million development contract for the V-22 tilt-rotor aircraft to Bell Helicopter Textron and Boeing Vertol.

JANUARY 26, 1990: Boeing flies the first of two presidential VC-25As, a heavily modified 747-200, from its Wichita, Kansas, facility prior to delivery to the US Air Force for use as 'Air Force One'.

FEBRUARY 19, 1990: The Boeing 737 surpasses the Boeing 727 as the world's most prolific airliner when the 1,833rd example emerges from the production line at Renton, Washington.

FEBRUARY 25, 1990: Smoking is banned from all US airline flights in North America.

MARCH 10, 1990: The 10,000th Boeing jetliner, a 767 for Britannia Airways, is delivered.

JUNE 1, 1990: The first special operations version of the CH-47 Chinook, the MH-47E, completes its maiden flight.

JUNE 16, 1990: The latest version of the BAe 125 business jet, the 125-1000, made its maiden flight at Chester. The aircraft, powered by two Pratt & Whitney Canada PW305 engines, is designed to fly almost 4,200 miles (6,759km) with six passengers.

JUNE 29, 1990: Bombardier buys up the Learjet company, adding a range of business jets to its extensive aviation product line.

JUNE 29, 1990: The last of 329 Saab Viggens, a JA 37, is delivered to the Swedish Air Force's F16 wing at Uppsala.

JULY 18, 1990: Maiden flight of the Embraer CBA-123 takes place at the company's São José dos Campos facility in Brazil. The aircraft is the product of a co-operative venture with Argentinean firm FAMA but it is destined not to be a success.

AUGUST 2, 1990: Iraqi forces, supported by the Iraqi Air Force, invade the kingdom of Kuwait in an unprovoked attack. The UN responds with a massive build up of forces in the Gulf.

OCTOBER 11, 1990: Maiden flight of the joint USA/Germany developed Rockwell/MBB X-31A fighter manoeuvrability demonstrator.

OCTOBER 23, 1990: United Air Lines buys up Pan American World Airways' routes from the US to London and from Dallas to Paris, thus ending Pan Am's transatlantic operations.

OCTOBER 31, 1990: Australian airlines are deregulated, permitting the carriers to set their own fares and decide their own routes. This opens up the country's commercial aviation sector to more competition.

JANUARY 13, 1991: The first Boeing 727 (N7001U) is retired by United Air Lines after achieving 64,492 flying hours, 48,057 cycles and carrying over 3 million passengers. The aircraft is donated to the Seattle Museum of Flight and repainted in its original livery.

JANUARY 18, 1991: US carrier Eastern Airlines collapses with debts of $3.2 billion.

1990-99

the Smithsonian Museum in Washington DC SR-71A Blackbird 64-17972 establishes a new point-to-point record for crossing the continental USA. It makes the 2,404-mile (3,868km) flight from the Pacific to Atlantic coasts in 1 hour 8 minutes and 7 seconds - an average speed of 2,112mph (3,398km/h). (USAF)

4. ATF contenders fly
The maiden flight of the Northrop/McDonnell Douglas YF-23A takes place on August 27, 1990, the aircraft is a contender for the USAF's Advanced Tactical Fighter (ATF) programme. (Northrop)

5.
The second contender for the ATF programme, the Lockheed/General Dynamics/Boeing YF-22A, makes its first flight on September 29, 1990. (Lockheed)

6. New Asian trainer
On November 21, 1990, the jointly developed Nanching Aircraft Manufacturing Company/

Pakistan Aeronautical Complex (NAMC PAC) K-8 trainer and light attack aircraft makes its first flight. (KEY - Alan Warnes)

7. Airbus A340 flies
On October 25, 1991, the first Airbus A340 four-engine long-range airliner takes to the sky for its maiden flight at Toulouse, France, with test pilot Pierre Baud at the controls. This is the only aircraft in the world capable of challenging the 20-year reign of the Boeing 747 in the high

capacity, long distance market. (Airbus)

8. Advanced transport
September 15, 1991, witnesses the first flight of the McDonnell Douglas C-17 Globemaster III, a new strategic airlifter able to perform tactical airlift missions from rough strips. The aircraft can carry heavy payloads and large items of cargo but needs only three crew members, thanks to its technologically advanced cockpit and avionics. (McDonnell Douglas)

FEBRUARY 2, 1991: The latest version of the popular Cessna Citation, the Citation VII, completes a successful first flight from Wichita, Kansas.

FEBRUARY 19, 1991: First flight of the Dassault Mirage 2000D, strike variant of the successful Mirage 2000. The final 2000D was not delivered to the French air Force until 2001.

MARCH 22, 1991: First flight of the Pond Racer, a twin-engined aircraft designed by Scaled Composites that is designed to break the speed record for piston-engined aircraft, currently standing at around 530mph.

MARCH 27, 1991: First flight of the Socata TB 200 Tobago XL.

APRIL 5, 1991: The US Army selects a joint Boeing/Sikorsky design to fulfil its requirement for a new light helicopter. The aircraft will be low observable and fly-by-wire, and will be called the RAH-66 Comanche. Anticipated procurement stands at almost 1,300 aircraft.

APRIL 10, 1991: First flight of the Aviones de Colombia AC-05 Pijao agricultural aircraft.

APRIL 23, 1991: The Lockheed/General Dynamics/Boeing YF-22A is declared the winner of the USAF's Advanced Tactical Fighter programme.

APRIL 29, 1991: Maiden flight of the Cessna 525 CitationJet, a new business jet designed to fly four passengers a distance of 1,730 miles (2,784km).

MAY 2, 1991: Trans World Airlines sells the rights to three of its transatlantic routes to London to American Airlines, marking the beginning of the end of TWA's international operations.

MAY 24, 1991: A specially modified El Al 747-200 combi makes it into the record books by carrying the largest ever number of people in one aircraft, when it airlifts 1,200 Ethiopian Jews from Addis Ababa to Israel.

MAY 31, 1991: Swiss manufacturer Pilatus commences flight-testing of its new PC-12 single-engined utility transport. The sleek aircraft features large winglets and is designed to compete in the lucrative large capacity utility transport market. A military variant for intelligence and surveillance duties is also available.

JUNE 13, 1991: The new Learjet 60, designed to carry up to nine passengers, makes its first flight. It is the first Learjet to be powered by Pratt & Whitney engines.

JUNE 17, 1991: Alaska Airlines commences scheduled services from Alaska to the former Soviet Union, the first flight being a Boeing 727 from Anchorage to Magadan and Khabarovsk.

JUNE 18, 1991: First flight of the BAe RJ70 regional airliner, a development of the BAe 146.

JULY 1, 1991: The last RAF Shackleton AEW.2 is retired from service by No.8 Squadron marking the end of over 40 years of RAF Shackleton operations. The venerable aircraft has been replaced by the new Boeing Sentry AEW.1.

1990-99

1. Gulf War

Operation Desert Storm commences on January 16, 1991, as Coalition forces begin operations to evict invading Iraqi forces from Kuwait. The conflict makes considerable use of new technology, introducing stealth and precision weapons to a battlefield that is dominated by air power. Just three years after it was revealed to the public, the Lockheed Martin F-117A Nighthawk stealth fighter plays a pivotal role during the conflict. (Lockheed Martin)

2. Regional winner

On May 10, 1991, the Canadair Regional Jet makes its first flight and goes on to lay the foundations for a highly successful line of regional airliners. Over the next ten years further models are added to the product line to compete primarily with regional airliners offered by Embraer of Brazil. (Bombardier)

3. Small but sleek

The Swearingen SJ-30, arguably the world's smallest business jet, makes its first flight on February 13, 1991, from San Antonio, Texas. Up to eight passengers can be carried at speeds in excess of 500mph (804km/h) for distances up to 2,500 miles (4,023km). (Swearingen)

4. K-Max lifts off

December 23, 1991, sees the fist flight of the new Kaman K-Max high-lift crane helicopter. The unusual helicopter features a small body with intermeshing rotors but offers excellent heavy lift capabilities, particularly at altitude, it is also a study in practicality over looks. (Kaman)

5. Tiger flies

On April 27, 1991, the prototype of the Eurocopter Tiger attack helicopter makes its first flight at Marignane, France. The new helicopter is also designed to fill the scout and escort roles, putting it in competition with the likes of the Bell AH-1 Cobra, the McDonnell Douglas AH-64 Apache, the Westland Lynx and the Agusta A129 Mangusta. (Eurocopter)

SIGNIFICANT DATES

JULY 1, 1991: Piper Aircraft files for Chapter 11 bankruptcy protection after running up debts of £28 million.

JULY 26, 1991: Air Russia is formed by British Airways and Aeroflot to open up air traffic between Russia and the West. The new airline is based in Moscow and will operate Boeing 767 aircraft.

AUGUST 12, 1991: Delta Airlines takes over a large number of Pan Am routes and services following a $1.4 billion deal. In April Pan Am surrendered a number of transatlantic routes to London to United Air Lines.

SEPTEMBER 18, 1991: Polish company PLZ flies the PZL-130TB Turbo-Orlik for the first time, adding yet another turboprop-powered aircraft to the highly-competitive turboprop trainer field.

NOVEMBER 1, 1991: Connoisseur class is launched by United Air Lines to cater for the international business traveller. The service features gourmet food, fine wines and larger, more roomy seats and sets the scene for an ongoing battle to see who can pamper their customers the most.

NOVEMBER 23, 1991: First flight of the Chinese XAC Y7-200B turboprop-powered transport aircraft.

DECEMBER 4, 1991: The last Pan Am Clipper flight, Clipper 436 from Bridgetown, Barbados, to Miami International Airport, touched down at 5.23pm bringing to an end operations by the historic Pan American World Airways.

DECEMBER 19, 1991: Following the collapse of the Soviet Bloc, Russian carrier Aeroflot reveals that 40% of its fleet is grounded due to the nation's economic crisis and a chronic shortage of fuel.

JANUARY 24, 1992: Textron Inc agrees a deal to buy Cessna Aircraft from General Dynamics for $600 million.

MARCH 23, 1992: Beechcraft, now a part of the Raytheon company, delivers its 50,000th aircraft, a King Air 90B.

AUGUST 14, 1992: Tupolev flies the Tu-204 airliner to be powered by Roll-Royce RB211-535E4 engines.

AUGUST 20, 1992: Indian manufacturer Hindustan Aeronautics Limited flies the ALH (Advanced Light Helicopter) for the first time.

SEPTEMBER 12, 1992: First flight of the UK-built Europa Aviation Europa two-seat light aircraft.

SEPTEMBER 17, 1992: First flight of the uprated SIAI-Marchetti S.211A jet trainer, one of the contenders for the American JPATS programme.

NOVEMBER 8, 1992: British Airways agrees a deal to buy Dan Air for £1, though it will also take on the struggling carrier's £58 million debt.

NOVEMBER 27, 1992: Avro International Aerospace performs the first flight of the RJ85 - this version has been developed from the BAe 146 and is designed to carry between 85-112 passengers.

DECEMBER 10, 1992: First flight of the Fokker 50 Maritime Enforcer.

DECEMBER 18, 1992: First flight of the Let L-610G, a derivative of the Czech design equipped with American avionics and powered by two

6. Revamped Hawk

February 29, 1992, sees BAe fly the first Hawk 100, the latest development of the successful advanced jet trainer that is equally at home in the light attack role. (BAe)

7. Lethal Apache

McDonnell Douglas flies the first prototype of the upgraded AH-64D Apache Longbow attack helicopter at its Mesa, Arizona, facility on April 15, 1992. The upgraded helicopter features a new mast-mounted millimetre wavelength fire control radar as well as many other avionics and airframe improvements. (Boeing)

8. New Saab turboprop

March 26, 1992, witnesses the maiden flight of the twin turboprop Saab 2000 regional airliner, a larger stable mate to the company's Saab 340. Saloes were less than fantastic and it is now out of production. (Saab)

9. Biggest Airbus twin

On November 2, 1992, Airbus successfully flies the latest addition to its range of airliners, the twin-engine Airbus A330. The new airliner is basically the same airframe as the A340 but utilises a pair of powerful turbofan engines rather than four. (Airbus)

10. New Falcon

French manufacturer Dassault adds another business jet to its extensive line-up when it flies the Falcon 2000 for the first time on March 4, 1993. (Dassault)

11. Largest single-aisle Airbus

March 11, 1993, sees the first flight of the Airbus A321, the largest of the single-aisle A320 family designed to carry up to 200 passengers, though more typically it will be configured for 185. Airbus is pursueing the goal of being able to offer airlines a complete package of aircraft to meet all their needs. (Airbus)

1990-99

General Electric turboprop engines.

DECEMBER 18, 1992: Maiden flight of the McDonnell Douglas Explorer eight-seat commercial helicopter.

JANUARY 15, 1993: First flight of the Rockwell/DASA Ranger 2000 jet-powered trainer.

JANUARY 31, 1993: Sikorsky flies the first UH-60Q Medevac version of the UH-60 Black Hawk.

FEBRUARY 22, 1993: Maiden flight of the McDonnell Douglas MD-90, a medium haul twin-jet designed to typically carry 153 passengers 2,600 miles (4,184km).

MARCH 4, 1993: Saab flies the first production JAS 39 Gripen, destined for the Swedish Air Force.

MARCH 12, 1993: Lockheed Martin completes a $1.5 billion deal to buy up the General Dynamics Military aircraft division and with it the very successful F-16 Fighting Falcon.

MARCH 31, 1993: Qantas and Australian Airlines, both government-controlled carriers, are merged under the Qantas banner.

MAY 8, 1993: The two-seat Aerotek Hummingbird observation and utility aircraft makes its first flight in South Africa.

MAY 10, 1993: Maiden flight of the Aero Vodochody L-139 Albatros, powered by a Garrett TFE731-4 engine and equipped with Bendix/King avionics.

MAY 15, 1993: Embraer successfully flies the EMB-312H Super Tucano, an uprated and improved version of its military turboprop-powered trainer.

JUNE 1, 1993: BAe reveals it has sold its Corporate Jets division to US-based Raytheon for £250 million.

SEPTEMBER 10, 1993: The 1,000th Boeing 747 is rolled out at the company's Everett facility near Seattle, Washington.

SEPTEMBER 30, 1993: The RAF retires the last of its Buccaneer strike aircraft, the type having originally been built for the Royal Navy.

OCTOBER 15, 1993: The V-bomber era comes to a close as the RAF retires the final three operational Victor K.2 refuelling tankers serving with No.55 Squadron at RAF Marham.

DECEMBER 2, 1993: First flight of the Airbus A300-600F freighter.

DECEMBER 17, 1993: The first operational B-2A Spirit stealth bomber is delivered to the USAF's 509th BW at Whiteman AFB, Missouri, by Northrop.

DECEMBER 18, 1993: First flight of the Sukhoi Su-34 two-seat, long-range bomber version of the Su-27 Flanker.

DECEMBER 21, 1993: Cessna flies the first 750 Citation X long-range, high-speed business jet, designed to operate at Mach 0.9 and carry up to 12 passengers.

JANUARY 17, 1994: Saab flies the first AEW&C variant of its 340 regional airliner. The Saab 340 AEW&C is equipped with the Ericsson Erieye radar.

1

2

3

4

5

6

1. New Jumbo freighter
Boeing flies the first 747-400F freighter on May 7, 1993. Unlike the passenger version of the -400, the freighter does not have the distinctive winglets. (Boeing)

2. Tornado mid-life upgrade
On May 29, 1993, BAe flies the first fully-fitted midlife update trials Tornado GR.4 aircraft. A number of avionics upgrades and the addition of a forward-looking infrared (FLIR) sensor form the core of the upgrade. (BAe)

3. Canadian Amphibian
The maiden flight of the Canadair CL-415 amphibian - a turboprop powered development of the CL-215 - takes place on December 6, 1993. Improved performance is one of the key attractions of the new aircraft, a type that is primarily aimed at the fire-fighting market. (Canadair)

4. Eurocopter first flight
The first flight of the Eurocopter EC-135 helicopter, designed to carry up to seven passengers, occurs on February 15, 1994. The sleek helicopter is the first brand new product to emerge from the recently-formed Eurocopter consortium. (Eurocopter)

5. Eurofighter takes off
After much political interference and amid continued financial uncertainty, the first Eurofighter 2000 prototype makes its maiden flight at Manching, Germany, on March 27, 1994. In total seven development aircraft are built by the participating nations - Germany, Italy, Spain and the UK. (DASA)

6. Giant Boeing twin
After a highly comprehensive and thorough design, manufacture and testing phase, the Boeing 777, the world's largest twin-engine airliner, makes its maiden flight from Everett, Washington, on June 12, 1994. (Boeing)

7. Look no pilot!
July 3, 1994, witnesses the first flight of the General Atomics Predator unmanned aerial vehicle (UAV), designed to perform tactical medium-altitude reconnaissance with an array of on-board sensors. (KEY - Alan Warnes)

SIGNIFICANT DATES

APRIL 10, 1994: GKN acquires Yeovil-based Westland Helicopters, the new company being named GKN Westland Helicopters.

APRIL 21, 1994: Maiden flight of the Bell 407 concept demonstrator helicopter.

APRIL 26, 1994: First flight of the PZL-Mielec I-22 Iryda M-93V powered by Rolls-Royce viper engines.

MAY 10, 1994: The BAe Jetstream 61, developed from the Jetstream ATP (Advanced Turboprop), makes its first flight at Prestwick.

MAY 18, 1994: The Northrop Grumman Corporation is formed following a successful $2.17 billion takeover bid of the Grumman Corporation by the Northrop Corporation.

JUNE 22, 1994: Airbus reveals its plans for the A3XX 'super jumbo', a double-deck airliner designed to carry between 530 and 965 passengers.

JUNE 23, 1994: Maiden flight of the Antonov An-38 transport aircraft takes place at Novosibirsk in Ukraine.

JULY 7, 1994: First flight of the Mundry CAP 232 aerobatic aircraft.

AUGUST 18, 1994: Maiden flight of the Israel Aircraft Industries Astra SPX business jet.

AUGUST 29, 1994: Kansai International Airport opens in Japan after eight years of construction work. The $15 billion project required the airport to be built in Osaka Bay on a 1,260-acre man-made island. Being well away from any population centres, the airport can operate on a 24-hour basis.

AUGUST 30, 1994: In another consolidation of the US aviation industry, the Lockheed Corporation and the Martin Marietta Corporation agree a $10 billion deal to form the Lockheed Martin Corporation, America's largest military contractor.

NOVEMBER 21, 1994: Engine maker Rolls-Royce completes a $525 million deal to buy the Allison Engine Company, thus giving it a much greater presence in the USA.

DECEMBER 7, 1994: Brazilian aerospace company Embraer is privatised when the government sells its 55.4% controlling stake.

MARCH 31, 1995: Maiden flight of the experimental Grob G-850 Strato 2C research aircraft. Designed to perform high-altitude environmental scientific research, the aircraft has a two-man crew and can carry two scientists/researchers.

MAY 31, 1995: The Schweizer RU-38A Twin Condor surveillance aircraft makes its first flight at Elmira, New York.

JUNE 1, 1995: Maiden flight of the Dassault Falcon 900EX, a long-range development of the Falcon 900 business jet.

JUNE 20, 1995: Maiden flight of the Boeing 767-300F freighter.

JUNE 22, 1995: The Beech/BAe licence-built development of the Pilatus PC-9 is selected by the US DoD as the winner of the JPATS

7

11

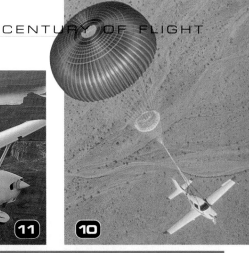

10

8

12

13

9

8. Flying whale
The massive and aptly-named Airbus A300-600ST Beluga, designed to carry large aircraft components and other outsized cargo, makes its first flight at Toulouse on September 13, 1994.
(Airbus)

9. New Antonov
The latest in a long line of transport aircraft from Antonov, the four turboprop powered An-70 makes a successful maiden flight at Kiev in the Ukraine on December

16, 1994. As well as a clean and streamlined appearance, the aircraft's turboprop engines and propellers produce a distinctive sound.
(KEY - Duncan Cubitt)

10. Parachute please
On March 31, 1995, the Cirrus SR-20 light aircraft makes its first flight and is unique in having its own parachute. In a severe emergency, such as an engine failure, the pilot can deploy the parachute enabling the aircraft to drift slowly to earth. (Cirrus)

11. Cessna reborn
The first flight of a new-build Cessna 172 takes place on April 19, 1995. The type was reintroduced after the California Product Liability Law, which had practically stopped single-engine general aviation aircraft production in the USA, was dropped following the introduction of the General Aviation Revitalization Act by President Bill Clinton. Shortly afterwards Cessna also began new production of a number of older designs such as the Ce 182. (Cessna)

12. Embraer shapes up
Brazilian manufacturer Embraer takes the regional airliner market by storm when it flies its sleek EMB-145 50-seat regional jet prototype at its São José dos Campos facility on August 11, 1995. (Embraer)

13. Bigger better Hornet
November 29, 1995, sees the McDonnell Douglas F/A-18E Super Hornet, a completely re-engineered, larger and more capable version of the original Hornet, make its first flight at St Louis, Missouri. (Boeing)

1990-99

---

competition. The new aircraft will equip both the USAF and the US Navy, replacing the T-37 and T-34 respectively.

AUGUST 4, 1995: The Grob G 850 Strato 2C establishes a new world altitude record for a piston-engined aircraft by reaching 60,866ft (18,552m).

AUGUST 10, 1995: First flight of the Indonesian IPTN N-250 turboprop regional airliner.

AUGUST 15, 1995: The Beriev Be-32K twin-turboprop airliner makes its first flight at Irkutsk, Siberia.

AUGUST 16, 1995: A chartered Air France Concorde establishes a new round-the-world record for an airliner, beginning and ending at New York's JF Kennedy Airport, after a flight

lasting 31 hours and 27 minutes.

AUGUST 16, 1995: The first production Northrop Grumman E-8C J-STARS battlefield surveillance aircraft completes its maiden flight.

SEPTEMBER 1, 1995: The German Luftwaffe undertakes its first combat mission since World War Two when JbG 32 Tornado ECRs take part in a Deny Flight sortie over the former Yugoslavia.

OCTOBER 7, 1995: The prototype of a new Japanese fighter, the Mitsubishi XF-2A, takes to the air for the first time at Nagoya. The aircraft is very similar to the Lockheed Martin F-16 from which it was developed.

OCTOBER 7, 1995: First flight of the latest version of the Bombardier Learjet, the

Learjet 45, takes place at Wichita, Kansas.

NOVEMBER 28, 1995: Gulfstream Aerospace successfully flies its new Gulfstream V business jet at Savannah, Georgia.

JANUARY 1, 1996: Aero International (Regional) is formed by combining ATR and BAe subsidiaries Avro RJ and Jetstream.

MARCH 16, 1996: Famous Dutch aircraft manufacturer Fokker is declared bankrupt and the company ceases trading. A new company, Fokker Aviation BV is established to provide product support and services to existing Fokker operators.

MARCH 19, 1996: McDonnell Douglas unveils the X-36 tailless unmanned research aircraft at St Louis, Missouri. The aircraft is intended

to investigate flight controlled purely by ailerons and thrust vectoring.

APRIL 2, 1996: First flight of the Extra EA 200 aerobatic and training aircraft.

APRIL 19,1996: The Chinese Shenyang Aircraft Corporation (SAC) flies the F-8 IIM, an upgraded version of the F-8 II - the export version of the J-8 Finback.

APRIL 24, 1996: First flight of the Aermacchi MB-339CD equipped with new digital cockpit and avionics, designed for the Italian Air Force as an advanced lead-in trainer.

APRIL 25, 1996: First flight of the Yakovlev Yak-130 military jet trainer, just over a month after the competing MiG-AT.

1990-99

1. New Euro helicopter
The latest European helicopter, the NH Industries NH 90 multi-role helicopter, makes its maiden flight on December 18, 1995, at Marignane, France. (NH Industries)

2. Stealth helicopter
On January 4, 1996, the Boeing/Sikorsky YRAH-66 Comanche reconnaissance attack helicopter prototype makes its maiden flight at West Palm Beach, Florida. The helicopter is designed to be a low-observable replacement for the OH-58D Kiowa and to supplement the AH-64 Apace attack helicopter with the US Army. (Boeing/Sikorsky)

3. New Russian trainer
The MiG-AT military jet trainer makes its first flight on March 16, 1996, entering a highly competitive jet trainer market. (KEY collection)

4. Super-agile Flanker
Sukhoi flies its highly manoeuvrable Sukhoi Su-37 thrust-vectoring fighter on April 2, 1996. The aircraft stuns airshow crowds with some quite extraordinary manoeuvres. (KEY - Duncan Cubitt)

5. Extra sleek
On April 4, 1996, the Extra EA 400, a touring/business aircraft designed to carry five passengers, makes its first flight. The aircraft features a high wing and a particularly clean and streamlined airframe. (Extra)

6. Modernised Hercules
The maiden flight of the latest version of the Lockheed Martin C-130 Hercules, the C-130J, takes place at Marietta on April 5, 1996. The aircraft features new avionics and uprated engines, giving it a considerable performance advantage over older model C-130s. (Lockheed Martin)

SIGNIFICANT DATES

JUNE 5, 1996: US company Fairchild acquires an 80% stake in German manufacturer Dornier Luftfahrt.

JUNE 17, 1996: The extraordinary Scaled Composites Boomerang makes its first flight. The Burt Rutan designed aircraft is another example of his radical thinking - although it is twin-engined it has an asymmetrical appearance.

JUNE 24, 1996: Raytheon delivers the 5,000th example of the Beech King Air twin-engined business aircraft, in this case a turboprop-powered -300 variant.

JULY 3, 1996: Cessna opens its new aircraft factory at Independence, Kansas, having recommenced production of its range of single-engined products.

JULY 25, 1996: The UK MoD announces it has selected a modernised version of the existing Nimrod MR.2 to fulfil the RAF's maritime reconnaissance requirements. The aircraft, to be called the MRA.4 will be almost completely rebuilt with new wings and Rolls-Royce/BMW BR710 turbofan engines, new avionics, new cockpit and a revised and updated mission suite.

AUGUST 6, 1996: Maiden flight of the Kawasaki XOH-1 two-seat military reconnaissance helicopter designed to replace the Hughes OH-6D with the Japanese military.

AUGUST 9, 1996: Maiden flight of the first Boeing 767 AWACS aircraft, this one forming part of a four-aircraft order for the Japanese Air Self Defence Force.

AUGUST 15, 1996: Boeing reveals that it has purchased Rockwell International's Space & Defence sector for $3.2 billion, thus adding the B-1B Lancer and the Space Shuttle to its books.

SEPTEMBER 2, 1996: Boeing launches the 757-300 featuring a stretched fuselage and offering a seating capacity increase of 20% over the -200 series.

NOVEMBER 16, 1996: Boeing and Lockheed Martin are both awarded contracts for the concept demonstration phase of the Joint Strike Fighter (JSF) programme.

NOVEMBER 16, 1996: Maiden flight of the prototype VisionAire VA-10 Vantage, a single turbofan-powered six-seat business jet.

NOVEMBER 27, 1996: The Australian government announces that it has selected the BAe Hawk 100 as the new lead-in fighter trainer for the Royal Australian Air Force. An order for 33 aircraft is signed on June 24, 1997.

NOVEMBER 29, 1996: The Tupolev Tu-144LL supersonic airliner flies again at Zhukovsky in Russia as part of a $15 million high-speed research programme in conjunction with NASA.

DECEMBER 26, 1996: China flies its first indigenous helicopter, the Jingdezhen Z-11 general purpose helicopter designed to seat up to seven passengers.

APRIL 23, 1997: The BAe Hawk Mk 115 is selected to equip the new NATO Flying Training in Canada (NFTC) programme. An order for 18 aircraft is agreed on November 17.

Aug 25, 1995: Airbus A319 Nov 28, 1995: Gulfstream V Nov 29, 1995: McDD F/A-18E Dec 18, 1995: NH Industries NH-90 Jan 4, 1996: Boeing Sikorsky RAH-66 Mar 16, 1996: MiG-AT Apr 4, 1996: Extra EA 400 Apr 5, 1996: Lockheed Martin C-130J

7

8

9

10

11

12

13

7. Canada's global jet

The Bombardier Global Express corporate jet, the latest to emerge from the Canadian company's workshops, makes its maiden flight at Downsview, Canada, on October 13, 1996. (Bombardier)

8. Revamped 737

February 9, 1997, sees the maiden flight of the first Next Generation Boeing 737-700 which introduces new technology, avionics, engines and airframe components to the original and highly successful Boeing 737 design. (Boeing)

9. Tailless flight

McDonnell Douglas puts its X-36 unmanned research aircraft through its first flight at Edwards AFB, California, on May 17, 1997. The unusual aircraft features a main wing and a small canard-like forward wing but no tail surfaces. (NASA)

10. Air dominance

The first pre-production Lockheed Martin/Boeing F-22A Raptor air superiority/dominance fighter takes to the air at Marietta, Georgia, on September 7, 1997. The stealthy, high-technology winner of the USAF's ATF competition is designed to dominate any future aerial battlefield. (Lockheed Martin)

11. New CASA transport

Spain's CASA performs the first flight of its C-295 transport aircraft, a stretched derivative of the successful CN-235, on November 28, 1997. (CASA)

12. Potent Fulcrum

The Russian MiG-29 *Fulcrum* gets a welcome new lease of life with the first flight of the upgraded MiG-29SMT on November 29, 1997. The modernised fighter features considerable avionics and airframe improvements as well as increased fuel capacity and an air-to-air refuelling capability. (KEY collection)

13. Fairchild Dornier goes jet

Fairchild Dornier carries out the first flight of its Do 328JET on January 20, 1998. The new regional airliner is a turbofan-powered variant of the popular Do 328 turboprop regional airliner. (Fairchild Dornier)

1990-99

APRIL 28, 1997: The first of five initial production V-22 tiltrotor aircraft is delivered to the US Marine Corps.

MAY 22, 1997: Maiden flight of the Romanian Avioane IAR-99 Soim jet trainer and light attack aircraft fitted with advanced Lancer-type avionics.

AUGUST 1, 1997: Boeing completes a huge deal, in excess of $13 billion, to merge with its former commercial airliner rival McDonnell Douglas. Only the Boeing name lives on but the deal makes it the world's largest aerospace company.

AUGUST 2, 1997: First flight of the Aero Vodochody L-159 light combat aircraft/advanced trainer, the latest development of the original L-39 Albatros.

AUGUST 15, 1997: The first circumnavigation of the world by a piston-engined helicopter is achieved by Jennifer Murray and Quentin Smith. They arrive back at Denham after a 97-day flight in a Robinson R44 helicopter.

AUGUST 22, 1997: Maiden flight of the AASI Jetcruzer 500, a six-seat business aircraft featuring a canard and rear main wing configuration propelled by a single pusher turboprop.

SEPTEMBER 10, 1997: Cessna delivers its 2,500th Citation, a Citation X.

SEPTEMBER 17, 1997: First flight of the Antonov An-140 twin turboprop short-range transport/airliner.

SEPTEMBER 25, 1997: The Sukhoi S-37 Berkut fighter demonstrator, featuring an unconventional forward swept wing, makes its first flight.

OCTOBER 7, 1997: The new Oslo Airport is opened by King Harold of Norway and has the capacity to handle up to 17 million passengers a year.

OCTOBER 21, 1997: The Boeing/BAe T-45C Goshawk, equipped with Cockpit 21 digital avionics, makes its first flight.

NOVEMBER 3, 1997: European manufacturer Airbus secures a 124-aircraft order from US Airways for a mix of A319 and A320 airliners, one of a number of significant North American orders received by Airbus.

NOVEMBER 3, 1997: British Airways takes delivery of its 50th Boeing 747-400 - the airline operates more 747-400s than any other carrier.

NOVEMBER 5, 1997: Maiden flight of the four-seat Diamond DA 40 Katana, derived from the earlier two-seat version.

DECEMBER 22, 1997: The Eurofighter 2000 is finally cleared for production following agreement by the four participating countries; Germany, Italy, Spain and the UK. However, it will be another five years before the first aircraft flies.

JANUARY 23, 1998: First flight by the Explorer Aircraft Corporation Explorer single-engined, multi-role utility transport takes place in Australia.

JANUARY 31, 1998: Maiden flight of the Bombardier (de Havilland Canada) Dash 8Q 400 stretched version of the Dash 8, designed to seat up to 78 passengers.

1990-99

1. Globally unmanned
On February 28, 1998, Teledyne Ryan's RQ-4A Global Hawk reconnaissance UAV makes its maiden flight at Edwards AFB, California. The craft is designed to operate autonomously at high altitudes with a long loiter capability, employing various sensors, including synthetic aperture radar, in the strategic reconnaissance role. (USAF)

2. Space lifeboat
The first flight of the X-38 Crew Return Vehicle development aircraft takes place on March 12, 1998, after it is dropped from the NASA NB-52 mother ship. The X-38 is a vital element in the development of an emergency crew return vehicle for astronauts who will man the international space station. (NASA)

3. New Texan
One of the most famous names associated with aviation training, the Texan, is resurrected on July 15, 1998, with the maiden flight of the first production Raytheon T-6A Texan II (Pilatus PC-9 Mk II). (Raytheon)

4. Strange Proteus
Arguably one of the strangest-looking aircraft ever to fly takes to the air for the first time on July 26, 1998. The Scaled Composites Proteus High Altitude Long Operation (HALO) communications relay and surveillance/reconnaissance aircraft is certainly quite an unusual design but then Scaled Composites and designer Burt Rutan have a reputation for producing aircraft of an unconventional appearance. (KEY - Alan Warnes)

5. New Russian amphibian
The maiden flight of the Beriev Be-200 amphibious transport/fire-fighting aircraft takes place on September 24, 1998. (Yefim Gordon)

6. Sleek Raytheon
On December 22, 1998, Raytheon undertakes the maiden flight of its Raytheon Premier 1 twin turbofan light business jet, one of the most attractive small business jets ever built. (Raytheon)

SIGNIFICANT DATES

MARCH 19, 1998: Eighty-two-year-old Wing Commander Ken Wallis sets a new E.3 (Autogyro) climb-to-height record by reaching 9,842ft (3,000m) in 7 minutes 20 seconds.

MARCH 24, 1998: Reported date for the first flight of the Chinese CAC J-10 single-engined advanced fighter.

APRIL 1, 1998: The RAF loses its nuclear capability with the retirement of the WE.177 free-fall tactical nuclear bombs.

APRIL 30, 1998: BAe announces its intention to take a 30% stake in Swedish company Saab.

JUNE 18, 1998: The UK MoD announces that the Grob G-115E Tutor has been selected to replace the Scottish Aviation Bulldog T.1 with the University Air Squadrons and Air Experience Flights.

JULY 4, 1998: The Embraer ERJ-135 37-seat regional airliner makes its first flight at São José dos Campos in Brazil.

AUGUST 2, 1998: First flight of the stretched Boeing 757-300.

AUGUST 21, 1998: First flight of the Piper PA-46-400TP Malibu Meridian, a six-seat turboprop-powered business/private light transport aircraft.

SEPTEMBER 2, 1998: The 100-seat Boeing 717-200, derived from the McDonnell Douglas MD-95, makes its first flight at Long Beach, California.

SEPTEMBER 4, 1998: The first flight of the Boeing BBJ (Boeing Business Jet), based on the 737-700 Next Generation airframe.

SEPTEMBER 25, 1998: The USAF retires the last examples of the EC-135C Looking Glass airborne command and control posts after nearly 40 years of service. The role is now handled by the US Navy's E-6A/B Mercury aircraft.

OCTOBER 1, 1998: Korean Aerospace Industries is officially formed marking the consolidation of South Korean aerospace firms Daewoo Heavy Aircraft Industries, Hyundai Space & Aircraft and Samsung Aerospace.

NOVEMBER 12, 1998: Airbus flies the first A319CJ Airbus Corporate Jet, based on the A319 airliner.

NOVEMBER 17, 1998: German company Daimler Benz AG and the Chrysler Corporation merge to form DaimlerChrysler Aerospace.

NOVEMBER 18, 1998: South Africa announces it has selected the BAe/Saab JAS 39 Gripen, the BAe Hawk and the Agusta A109 for the South African Air Force as part of a huge defence upgrade package.

10

7

8

11

9

7. Helibus takes flight

The Sikorsky S-92 Helibus twin-turboshaft, medium-lift helicopter makes its first flight on December 23, 1998. The helicopter is designed to compete in the lucrative but competitive medium-lift category with potential for both military and commercial use. (Sikorsky)

8. New Russian airliner

After years of delays caused by funding shortages, the 102-seat Tupolev Tu-334 twin turbofan, medium-range airliner finally makes its first flight on February 8, 1999. (Yefim Gordon)

9. NATO attacks Serbia

On March 24, 1999, and for the first time in its 50-year history, NATO launches an attack on a sovereign nation when it commences Operation Allied Force, beginning with air strikes against Serbian forces in Kosovo and Serbia. This follows intense diplomatic efforts to protect the ethnic Albanian population in Kosovo from Serbian forces seemingly intent on committing genocide. The conflict lasts for 78 days and then a stabilization force enters Kosovo. (KEY - Steve Fletcher)

10. Brazilian AEW&C

The first flight of the Embraer EMB-145SA (R-99A) AEW&C variant, equipped with the Ericsson PS-890 Erieye dorsal-mounted radar, occurs on May 22, 1999, at São José dos Campos. (Embraer)

11. Spartan flies

The joint US-Italian Lockheed Martin Alenia C-27J Spartan, a development of the 1970s G222 tactical transport aircraft, completes its first flight on September 25, 1999. The aircraft is being developed and marketed alongside the new Lockheed Martin C-130J, with the C-27J featuring much of the new technology used on the C-130J. So far all C-27Js have been produced by remanufacturing existing G222 airframes. (KEY - Duncan Cubitt)

DECEMBER 9, 1998: The US and the UK launch Operation Desert Strike, a four-day offensive against targets in Iraq following the country's failure to comply with UN arms inspections.

FEBRUARY 1, 1999: The surveillance/rescue and maritime patrol version of the ATR-42, the ATR-42MP Surveyor, makes its first flight.

FEBRUARY 1, 1999: Five major airlines – American Airlines, British Airways, Canadian Airlines, Cathay Pacific Airways and Qantas Airways – announced the formation of the oneworld global alliance.

MARCH 12, 1999: The Czech Republic, Hungary and Poland are accepted into NATO, opening up opportunities for western aerospace companies to bid for modernisation contracts for their air forces. However, financial difficulties delay new aquisitions.

MAY 14, 1999: The first production Bell-Boeing MV-22B Osprey for the US Marine Corps is rolled out and handed over at Arlington, Texas. The aircraft had already flown on April 30.

MAY 18, 1999: Airbus delivers its 2,000th airliner, an A340-300 for Lufthansa.

MAY 27, 1999: Bombardier flies the first CRJ700 regional airliner, a larger version of the original Canadair Regional Jet.

JUNE 14, 1999: Brazilian manufacturer Embraer officially launches the new ERJ-170 and ERJ-190 regional airliners at the Paris Airshow with a launch order for 30 of each from Swiss carrier Crossair.

JUNE 15, 1999: Raytheon is declared as the winner of the RAF's Airborne STand-Off Radar (ASTOR) competition. The aircraft chosen is the Bombardier Global Express with five aircraft to be delivered, fitted out with a complex suite of sensors including an advanced synthetic aperture radar and moving target indicator.

AUGUST 17, 1999: Maiden flight of the Kazan Ansat twin-turbine light helicopter.

OCTOBER 9, 1999: First flight of the Boeing 767-400ER stretched variant able to seat 304 passengers in a two-class layout and with a maximum range of 6,444 miles (10,371km).

OCTOBER 14, 1999: The European aerospace sector takes another step towards almost complete consolidation with the formation of the European Aeronautic, Defence and Space Company (EADS). The new entity is the result of the merger of Aérospatiale Matra SA and DaimlerChrysler Aerospace AG (DASA).

NOVEMBER 30, 1999: BAE and Marconi electronic systems merge to form BAE Systems - the final consolidation of the UK aerospace industry?

Be-200 **Nov 12, 1998:** Airbus A319CJ **Dec 10, 1998:** Kamov Ka-60 **Dec 22, 1998:** Raytheon Premier 1 **Dec 23, 1998:** Sikorsky S-92 **Feb 8, 1999:** Tupolev Tu-334 **May 27, 1999:** Bombardier CRJ700 **Sept 25, 1999:** Lockheed Martin Alenia C-27J

SO YOU WANT TO BE A
pilot?

SO YOU WANT TO LEARN TO FLY, AND YOU WANT A CAREER IN THE AIR – BUT WITH SO MANY AVENUES TO PURSUE, STEPHEN BRIDGEWATER ASKS WHICH ONE SHOULD YOU FOLLOW?

Whether you are bored with the nine-to-five routine of your current job or are a school-leaver looking for gainful employment, opting for a career in aviation is a tempting prospect for anybody interested in aircraft and flight. However with such a diverse range of occupations and employers available there are many choices to make, the first of which is between military or civil aviation. While the entry qualifications detailed in this article refer to careers in the UK, there is very little difference between the requirements of the armed forces and airlines around the globe. In fact many of the world's airlines recruit pilots from overseas offering a chance to relocate to new areas and experience different cultures.

There are a whole variety of career paths in aviation that do not even require your feet to leave the ground, from maintenance to air traffic control and check-in staff to aircraft design but in this short overview of the industry we will focus on piloting careers.

So you want to be a military pilot?

One route open to a budding pilot is to join the military, but which armed service should you choose? The obvious choice seems to be the RAF – after all, they're the people with the aeroplanes, right? WRONG!

Both the Royal Navy and the Army have flying sections and both have their own fleet of aircraft and helicopters.

All three services actively seek out potential pilots, primarily from schools, colleges and universities, but also from other walks of life.

Taking up a career in the British armed forces gives a potential pilot superb training in all aspects of flying and aircraft operations. Whether you find yourself flying at low level through Welsh valleys in an RAF fast jet, lurking behind trees in an Army helicopter or searching for submarines with the Fleet Air Arm, you'll be guaranteed a flying career surpassing all others in terms of excitement.

Above: **Life in the fast lane – prospective fast jet pilots begin flying on the BAE Hawk T.1, pictured in the foreground. Those pilots 'making the grade' may graduate from the course to fly one of the RAF's current fast jet aircraft, such as the Tornado F.3 as shown here.** (Rick Brewell/RAFPR)

However, it's not all about excitement - a career in the armed forces is an important and responsible position, vital not only to the defence of the nation and its allies, but also to the well-being of citizens around the world. Deployments of British armed forces are often involved in the humanitarian role, aiding people in distress because of natural or personal disaster. In recent years we have seen our troops flying as far afield as Sierra Leone and Kosovo to fulfil this role. They also provide emergency support in the UK, as demonstrated last winter when military helicopters helped secure flood defences to protect residents in areas surrounding rising rivers.

Entry qualifications and criteria differ among the three services, as does the type of work involved. In this short piece we will try to give a brief overview of the job and give you some indication of the qualifications required and the training involved.

During our research, we found that the entry criteria changed on a fairly regular basis and, although the facts were correct at the time of going to press, we would strongly recommend anyone interested in joining the armed forces to contact their local armed forces careers office before making any definite career or education choices.

Royal Air Force
THE JOB
The RAF's equipment is undergoing a major change, as new aircraft - such as the Eurofighter Typhoon and C-130J Hercules - enter service, but one thing never changes, the high standards expected of RAF aircrew.

The RAF employs both officers and aircrew, male and female, in flying roles including pilot, navigator and air engineer.

THE TRAINING
The selection process for all aircrew takes place at RAF College Cranwell, Lincs, although you will have had initial

interviews at your local careers office before getting through to the three-day assessment. For the successful candidates, aptitude and intelligence tests will be followed by interviews and leadership exercises.

If you are offered a commission as an RAF officer, your training will begin with a 24-week Initial Officer Training Course at Cranwell. From here you will begin your flying training on the T67 Firefly at the Joint Elementary Flying Training School (JEFTS) at RAF Barkston Heath. Advanced flying training takes three different forms, depending on the type of aircraft you have been selected to fly in squadron service. 'Fast jet' pilots will progress through the Tucano and Hawk, whilst helicopter pilots will be trained on the Squirrel and Griffin helicopters. Pilots selected to fly multi-engine aircraft will train on the Jetstream before going on to operational types such as the Nimrod.

Navigators will remain at Cranwell for most of their training, although those selected for fast-jet types move

to RAF Valley in Wales for Hawk flying. Having completed initial training, aircrew will also carry out much of their training at Cranwell.

On completion of flying training and, where appropriate operational conversion training, newly-qualified aircrew join their first squadron - welcome to the sharp end of the RAF!

The Army Air Corps
THE JOB
The job of the AAC is vital to the operational success of the army, both in peacetime and during war, and as an AAC pilot you may find yourself flying alongside crews from other nations in support of NATO or UN missions across the globe.

In addition to armed action (actually destroying enemy tanks), an AAC helicopter pilot must be able to perform many other tasks essential to the smooth running of any operation, from reconnaissance missions, to finding enemy strongholds, to delivering much-needed supplies to the front line. This means that an AAC pilot's job is a very varied one.

THE TRAINING
As a potential AAC officer, your first contact with the army will probably be at one of the careers offices. This will be followed by a visit to RAF Cranwell to undertake the initial selection tests. You will then have an overnight visit to the AAC headquarters at Middle Wallop, Hampshire, where you will sample army life and meet serving pilots. If the AAC decides to sponsor you through training, you will begin with one year of initial training at Sandhurst, which will include courses on leadership, battle skills and army organisation. This training is common to all army officers and soldiers, but for an AAC pilot it is followed by an intensive 16-month flight-training course. After mastering a fixed wing aircraft, you will progress onto helicopters before gaining your wings. Once you are a qualified helicopter pilot, you will be trained to fly one of the operational helicopters of the AAC before being posted to your first regiment.

Above: **Flying with the Royal Navy is one of the most demanding and exhilarating jobs a pilot could ask for. This AEW Sea King flies past its operational base, HMS Invincible.** (Joe Mercer/HMS Invincible)

Above: **In the hot seat - at the end of pilot training with the air force you could find yourself flying an aircraft such as the SEPECAT Jaguar.** (Jack Pritchard/RAFPR)

The Fleet Air Arm

THE JOB

If you like a challenge, they don't come any better than this. Try to imagine yourself landing a multi-million pound jet fighter on an aircraft carrier, maybe at night, perhaps even in bad weather. If that sounds like the sort of challenge that appeals to you, a job with the Fleet Air Arm could be just what you're looking for.

The Fleet Air Arm (FAA) operates the Sea Harrier F/A.2 as its main combat aircraft. However, it's not all about fast jets, and helicopters carry out a number of FAA roles.

THE TRAINING

Your training will begin with 39 weeks at Britannia Royal Naval College, Dartmouth, where you will learn about the Navy way of life. Pilot candidates then move to RAF Cranwell for 26 weeks for ground school and flying training, initially on the JEFTS Fireflies. After learning to fly, pilots are selected for either Sea Harrier or rotary wing training. To train as a Sea Harrier pilot, a pupil must show excellent flying skills and must also be judged as having the right character to get though the intensive

and demanding training course.

Pilots who go on to fly rotary wing aircraft will move to RAF Shawbury for 21 weeks for the same basic course as their RAF counterparts. Once again, the training is intense, but those who succeed will be taught to fly the Lynx or Sea King before being awarded their wings.

So you want to be an Airline Pilot?

Many Private Pilot Licence (PPL) holders or even budding GA pilots dream of flying for a living and turning their hobby into a career.

Perhaps it is the money that attracts people to the job, maybe it's a status thing, or maybe it's just a love of flying and the opportunity to travel the world.

These days we are becoming ever more reliant on air travel – whether for holidays or business – and it now plays a huge part in the British economy, employing hundreds of thousands of people in diverse areas of work. There are an increasing number of openings for commercial pilots and here we intend to provide a broad overview of how you can embark upon this career path.

Of course, if you mention airlines to anyone, the first job that springs to mind is that of the pilot's, and every passenger flight in the UK must have two pilots on board – a captain and a co-pilot – regardless of whether it's a long-haul trip or just a short 'hop'.

A PILOT'S DAY

The pilot's day begins several hours before take-off, as he or she will be responsible for arranging a flight plan for that day's route, supervising the refuelling and loading of the aircraft, as well as briefing the cabin crew before flight.

Just before take-off, the pre-flight checks are completed by the captain and co-pilot, who then communicate with Air Traffic Control (ATC) to confirm take-off arrangements.

After take-off, the autopilot will be switched on but, as with all flying, the crew must remain vigilant at all times, monitoring the weather and the aircraft's performance and location.

After landing at the destination, the final task is to write a report on the flight noting any incidents and updating the aircraft's log books with information about the flight.

"WHAT SORT OF PERSON DO I NEED TO BE?"

It may be surprisingly to learn that it is not necessary to have a PPL to begin training as an airline pilot, although some flying experience would undoubtedly look good on a CV. Airlines are more concerned with the type of person you are, than your flying experience, as the job requires very specific personal qualities.

An airline pilot must be reliable, calm and level-headed, with above average co-ordination and technical skills. An effective pilot will also be a team leader, who is able to take charge of his colleagues should circumstances demand it.

In addition, you need to be a confident communicator, able to speak clearly and calmly on the radio to ATC, and in a polite and friendly manner to fellow cabin staff and passengers.

Lastly you must be in excellent general health and be physically fit, as commercial pilots must pass regular medical check-ups throughout their career. You should

---

FOR MORE INFORMATION

Contact your local armed forces careers office, or contact the military direct at the following addresses:

Army Air Corps
Recruitment Liaison Officer, Regimental Headquarters AAC, Middle Wallop, Stockbridge, Hants, SO20 8DY.
Telephone Army Careers on 08457 300111 or check out its website at www.army.mod.uk

Fleet Air Arm
Royal Navy & Royal Marines Careers Service, Freepost GL672, Cirencester, Gloucestershire, GL17 1BR.
Telephone Royal Navy Careers on 08456 075555 or check out its website at www.royal-navy.mod.uk

Royal Air Force
The RAF does not have a main address to write to for information, preferring instead that you contact your local careers office.
Telephone Royal Air Force Careers on 0345 300100 or check out its website at www.rafcareers.com

Above: **The Army Air Corps' new Westland Apache attack helicopter is among the best of its breed in the world. Could a career flying a potent fighting machine such as this be just around the corner for you?** (McDD)

Above: **With their checks nearly completed, this Boeing 747 crew prepare for departure – if this is the type of flying career that appeals there are a number of options available to you.** (KEY Collection)

have good hearing and normal colour vision, but whilst good eyesight is essential, spectacles may be allowed.

"DO I NEED ANY QUALIFICATIONS?"

Flying training in the UK is carried out by private organisations, and as such, entry qualifications for commercial licences can vary. As a rough guide, the Civil Aviation Authority advises applicants to have a minimum of five GCSE Grades A to C (or equivalent) including Mathematics, English and a Science, and many training schools will ask for these as a minimum. Some training schools, however, may require higher grades as they consider that these indicate that pupils will respond better to training.

In order to fly passengers, you will need to gain a CAA Commercial Pilots Licence (CPL) which is granted upon completion of the relevant exams but will be 'frozen' until you have flown a minimum number of hours.

"WHAT ARE THE AGE REQUIREMENTS?"

The minimum age at which a pilot can begin studying for a commercial licence is 17 or 18 years depending upon the school involved. Training will take around 26 weeks and will include all aspects of your flight training.

Many fledgling CPLs begin their careers on turboprop aircraft such as this ATR-42. (KEY - Duncan Cubitt)

There is no upper age limit set by the training schools but it is unlikely that anybody over 35 will find a job with the airlines, unless they are already qualified and moving from one airline to another.

"WHAT DO I HAVE TO LEARN?"

Many people gain their PPL before deciding they would like to become a commercial pilot, but it is also possible to enrol on courses that will teach people with no previous flying experience.

As part of the CPL course you will need to sit a number of ground exams in both navigation and technical subjects. These are shown in the accompanying table.

The CPL course is a structured package that starts on a small single-engined aircraft and progresses, with appropriate ground school and simulator raining, onto twin-engined aircraft. As with all pilot training, the CPL course is a mixture of learning theory in the classroom then putting this theory into practice in the air.

"OK, HOW MUCH?"

It had to come didn't it? That dreaded question - "How much?" Well, to enrol at one of the private residential training courses and study for a CPL will cost you somewhere in the region of £30,000! However, a number of schools, both in the UK and abroad, offer a variety of prices

and packages tailored to suit the needs of most pilots.

"IS THERE NO OTHER WAY?"

Yes, fortunately there are other options. Many of the large airlines in Britain will fully or partly sponsor you through the expensive training course. Airlines will generally require the same five GCSE A to C grades, plus at least two A' Level passes, preferably in Maths and Physics.

Applicants are usually aged between 18 and 28 years of age and will agree to work for the airline for a minimum amount of time after being awarded their ATPL. These schemes vary, but most airlines require you to repay the training costs out of your wages over the first few years following graduation.

CAA CPL(A) GROUND EXAMINATION REQUIREMENTS	
Navigation	**Technical**
1) Aviation Law, Flight Rules & Procedures	1) Principles of Flight (Aeroplanes)
2) Signals	2) Engines
3) Human performance & Limitations	3) Electrics & Automatic Flight
4) Radio Aids	4) Airframe Systems (Aeroplanes)
5) Flight Planning	5) Loading
6) Instruments	6) Performance (A, C, D, E or U)*
7) Meteorology (Theory)	*Appropriate to the type/class of
8) Meteorology (Practice)	aeroplane used on the CPL(A) Skill
9) Navigation	Test.

Above: **Even if you are not destined for the flight deck, there are many other careers in aviation - including cabin crew.** (KEY - Tony Dixon)

Above: **Climbing away from McCarran Airport in Las Vegas this United Airlines' Boeing 747 is just one of the types that a commercial pilot might fly at the pinnacle of their career. America is the largest market for commercial pilots by virtue of its vast internal flight network.** (KEY - Mark Nicholls)

The modern-day RAF Jaguar pilot is typical of many fighter 'jocks' around the world. His practical but lightweight flying suit and equipment has gone through an extensive evolution to reach this stage. (KEY - Duncan Cubitt)

A CENTURY OF FLYING
Clothing

FLYING CLOTHING IS 100 YEARS OLD – PETER WHITE EXAMINES HOW AIRCREW CLOTHING HAS ADAPTED TO DEVELOPMENTS WITHIN POWERED FLIGHT.

Above: **The early pioneer pilots had very little to protect themselves against the weather, and headgear was basic to say the least.** (KEY collection)
Right: **Sopwith 1½ Strutters form the backdrop of this 1916 image, which clearly illustrates the flying apparel of the period.** (KEY collection)

The human element of any flying machine was initially concerned with staying warm, and the clothing chosen was often similar to that used in another then relatively new pursuit – motoring. The motorcar was an 'open-cockpit' affair in the early days, so the hats and coats worn by early motorists were simply adapted for the pioneers of flight.

Pioneering years

Companies like Roold in France and Burberry in Britain developed flying suits - a variation of the working overall known as the 'boiler suit'. As aircraft developed and became likely to stay aloft for longer scarves and tweed hats were supplemented with more substantial headgear. Besides the leather 'flying cap', which was borrowed and then adapted, from the motor world, safety helmets were devised. Because of the high-risk factor in open cockpit flying machines, which were usually devoid of any form of harness or straps, a Mr Warren of Hendon, with others like Roold, Brown and Dunhill and Gamages, produced a padded flying helmet. The helmets were made of cork and fabric and usually leather covered, and although each manufacturer had its own styling, the principle was the same. The safety helmet and its later models were used during the First World War and beyond.

Goggles were another essential item 'borrowed' from the early motorists. These came in many shapes and sizes with rubber, leather or fabric masks to hold the glass lenses.

The world was becoming aware of the aeroplane and its uses as an observation platform as well as a means of transport. Yet heavier-than-air craft were treated with suspicion by the British Government and it saw little future in their use in any fighting scenario! When the First World War started, the small fleet of basic machines operated by the Royal Flying Corps and Royal Naval Air Service were still as flimsy as their early predecessors. In times of war, technology advances ten fold due to necessity - aircraft became faster and heavier and were able to fly higher and for a longer duration. Now the only thing to do was to improve the kit worn by the flyers so they were able to cope with new demands placed upon them by the advancement of flight.

Influence of war

The War Office issued blanket-lined leather coats and jackets, plus fur-lined flying helmets to help combat the colder conditions now being experienced at higher altitudes. This basic issue was supplemented by 'private purchase' items from well-known suppliers of the time (eg Pride and Clark, Burberry, Gamages, etc) for those that could afford the extra luxury. The average squadron could be seen in an assortment of styles of leather or fur coats, with leather full-cowl helmets and open-front helmets with protective leather facemasks. As well as the issued leather riding boots, or shorter brown examples, 'Fug boots' were also worn. These were long sheepskin wader-like boots that covered the leg to the top of the thigh.

Flying gauntlets also comprised many different types because of privately purchased and issued examples being utilised and usually worn with an under glove of wool or silk for extra warmth.

Later in the war, the famous 'Sidcot Suit' was developed and the story goes... a young pilot, Sidney Cotton, went flying after working on his aircraft but he and his overalls were still covered in grease and oil and this he found worked as a windbreak and kept the body warmer than usual. Using this knowledge, he produced a wind-proofed flying suit with a double maternity front, fur-lined knee pockets, chest map pocket and a fur collar to protect the neck from prop wash. The highly successful 'Sidcot Suit' was born and was used in different guises the world over, forming the pattern for some years as the ultimate flying overall.

Between the wars

Between the two world wars aviation development and exploration entered an exciting era, yet the types of aircraft initially available were surplus war machines which were subsequently improved and developed until by the 1930s new and radical, for the time, designs took to the air, like the Supermarine Spitfire.

Flying clothing took the same course and looking at early photographs of pioneers like Charles Kingsford Smith, you notice the World War One Sidcot Suit and leather helmet were still considered adequate for the job in hand. The post-war barnstorming boom was very big in the US and many of the aviators were ex service so they used their military flying kit, while others were able to buy from the plentiful stocks of government surplus. Fashion became involved and large stores like Harrods and Pride and Clark offered tailored and customised flying attire in different colour leathers and fabrics. War surplus Mk.1 and Mk.2 goggles were available, some having been updated and remarketed by firms like William Stephens and Sons Ltd; and others, such as Luxor, Rocket, Resistal, Wilson, Seesall, Visionaire and Triplex, offered a wide variety of styles.

The military side of flying was generally a lot quieter after World War One and with Britain's commitment to the Empire it stretched the much-reduced air force and its budget. Therefore the clothing worn by service personnel reflected

Above: **Between the two world wars aircrew clothing improved dramatically, both in terms of headgear and the quality and warmth of flying jackets.** (KEY collection)

this and the earlier leather coats, jackets and Sidcot Suits continued as the main form of protection into the 1920s and early 30s. The Sidcot Suit was improved and the 1930 pattern was available in a rubberised linen fabric in light grey or green and had the luxury of zips and a detachable fur collar. To complete the picture, layers of under garments and gloves were worn topped by a fur-lined leather Mk.1 or 1930 Pattern helmet with 'Gosport tubes' for crew communication and or earphones if required.

Goggles used were mainly the Triplex Mk.1 and Mk.2 until 1933 when they were superseded by the Mk.3/3A models, these had curved Perspex lenses mounted on a leather and chamois mask, which gave a better view than earlier models.

Oxygen was now needed as aircraft flew higher and the first masks available, leather and fur-trimmed Mk.1 and Mk.2 of the early 1920s were replaced by the leather A, B and C models in the 1930s which had provision for microphones and could be strapped to the 1930 pattern flying helmet. The D-type cloth mask with chamois lining was introduced in 1936 in conjunction with the B-type helmet and this combination became very well known as the headgear of early World War Two and the Battle of Britain period.

In warmer climes, the flying clothing worn would have been shorts, boots and a lightweight jacket, and the helmet needed to be of cotton or other lightweight materials, sometimes with a neck flap. From the 1930s the British aviators wore an A-type helmet, which was basically a cloth-covered cork toupee with earflaps and a strap under the chin, the brim shielding the wearer from the sun.

Flying boots also became more user friendly for instance the British 1930 pattern boot was sheepskin lined with brown suede outer and a rubber-covered welt and foot section. The upper calf area of the boot was wide enough to take a bulky flying suit leg and had a leather strap for security and fit.

Later in the decade both the Americans and British were using 'thermally insulated' suits and these consisted of a sheepskin-lined jacket with a full length front zip with separate sheepskin-lined high-rise trousers held up by braces. The US Shearling Suit was made up of type A3 trousers and type B3 jacket, and the British equivalent was known as the Irvin Suit. Due to the bulkiness of the trousers, the jacket was often worn on its own and saw service for a number of years as the Irvin flying jacket.

The rumblings of a possible conflict were on the horizon and some far-sighted people had begun to plan ahead but most of the world was still flying fairly old and sometimes obsolete designs, and often the flying clothing being worn, matched the craft.

More war - more clothing

September 1939, and once again Britain was at war and as mentioned earlier, this state of affairs usually hastens product development of most kinds, especially flying machines and their necessary accessories. The next six years saw a tremendous leap from bi-plane fighters to rockets and jet-powered aircraft. Although the main players of World War Two were Britain, Germany, Russia, Japan and the USA, the whole world benefited from the progress gained.

An 83 Squadron crew after returning from another sortie over enemy territory. By now oxygen provision was essential to cope with high-altitude operations. (KEY collection)

Flying clothing became more specialised and some items were developed for specific purposes; for example the GQ and Irvin parasuits. It was made to fit the torso and upper legs, with an integral life preserver and parachute harness for either a front-mounted chest pack or a seat-type 'chute. Ideal for the confines of the Boulton Paul Defiant rear turret position or similar stations on our early World War Two bombers. Later in the conflict, and used more by the US forces, flak suits were made of many layers of silk fabric to protect gunners in their vulnerable positions aboard B-17, B-25, B-24 and other such craft. Another protection for the bomber crews was an adaptation of the 'tin helmet' suitably modified and used in battle situations by the British, Germans and Americans.

The Irvin Suit was used extensively by bomber crew, as was the 1940 Pattern flying suit (from the Sidcot lineage), a heavy gabardine twill material, usually worn over a kapok lining or a 'teddy bear' suit. The pale yellow Taylor Suit was a favourite with the gunners, being very snug with its kapok lining and buoyancy pads, which gave some reassurance in the event of ditching in the sea. The Taylor and Irvin Suits could also be put on over an electrically-heated lining, which in turn could be attached to EH socks, and glove liners worn under leather gloves or mitts. The 1941 Pattern Sidcot Suit had an integral wiring loom with press-stud connectors for the EH gloves and EH socks.

Fighter pilots did not require such heavy and extreme kit, as their missions were of a shorter duration and not normally at the high altitudes of the bomber boys - so

they often flew in their uniforms and when available, battledress tops and trousers. Roll collar pullovers were allowed under the uniform instead of a shirt and tie, and often a silk scarf was worn for warmth and to 'lubricate' the neck. All aircrew wore a life preserver to keep them afloat if they were unlucky enough to land in water.

The waistcoat, life-saving, inflatable 1932 Pattern was still in service as a life preserver in the early part of WW2 and was usually worn half inflated to save time in the event of a ditching. By 1941 a new model was being used, known affectionately as a Mae West after the buxom actress, whose assets the fully-inflated life preserver was supposed to resemble. The yellow Mae West was inflated by a CO_2 bottle and contained a first-aid kit, shark repellent, orange dye for identification, a torch, plus escape items and attachment straps.

The B-type helmet was superseded in 1941 by the C-type, also of leather but with rubber cups to hold the earphones. A number of variants were available with different goggle strap details, and fittings for the Mk.4 goggles could be attached. Later models also had provision for an internal wiring loom. This versatile helmet was still in military use by the late 1950s, and was even worn by some jet pilots despite the advent of the 'bone dome' protective helmet. The Royal Navy used the C-type but retained the earlier B-type 'doughnut' ear pieces so that both earphones and 'Gosport tubes' could be fitted together for non-detectable crew communication whilst in flight, as well as using the radio.

Above: **The Mae West arrived in the early 1940s and has remained a vital element of aircrew kit ever since.** (KEY collection)

Above: **US Eighth Air Force P-51 Mustang pilots take a break between missions. The need for warm clothing in the cold unheated fighter cockpits was essential - but pilots still felt the effects of the sub-zero temperatures.**

For the hotter regions, the D-type canvas helmet was used, similar to the C in shape but with a protective neck flap. Later, this was available with an internal wiring loom and the Fleet Air Arm also had a version tailored to its needs. A mesh helmet, the E-type, for low-level long-distance operators, like Coastal Command, was ideal to prevent the head overheating. Other forces within the Allies, the American and the Axis, all had similar types of headgear and other flying clothing items, but space does not allow for a more in-depth survey.

World War Two flying boots were a progressive development of the earlier mentioned 1930 Pattern, some in suede and others in leather or fabric, but one example is particularly worth highlighting. The British 1943 Pattern or 'escape boot' was interesting because of its

carrier developed through the rubber E and F models, to the very successful G-type and this was superseded in 1945 by the H-type mask, which in its different forms was still being used in the 1970s.

The more exacting flying has become, the more specialised the equipment has had to be, and oxygen masks since the 1980s may have differed little in appearance but the materials used and the fittings have advanced greatly. Flying suits and coveralls have become more user friendly and specific to aircraft type or operation, with pockets for maps, manuals, flying gloves, escape items, calculators and pockets with plastic windows for making notes with a Chinagraph pencil. Since World War Two, the colours of flying suits have been in various shades of blue or grey, depending on the mark

worn under the flying suit or over it, depending on the model - those worn outside have the necessary pockets attached. Modern flying boots are worn under trousers and are normally made from soft but firm black or brown leather to just above the ankle.

Although the needs of the military have accelerated the development of flying clothing, man's 'race to space' has been responsible for the most recent introduction of new materials and styling. With the dawning of the era of helmet-mounted sights, fly-by-wire and other modern technology, the military pilot is still vulnerable, and needs to be protected because however advanced the machine, it still needs the aircrew, apart from UAVs of course.

Today military flying clothing has undergone a revolution. Many spin-offs from the NASA space

Above: **Lighter weight equipment was already arriving in the early 1950s, as illustrated by this shot of 85 Squadron following a training sortie in Meteor NF.14s.** (KEY collection)
Right: **Royal Canadian Air Force CF-104 pilots pose with their aircraft. By now it was a case of get in and plug in - the arrival of the ejector seat also had a bearing on flying suit design.** (KEY collection)

dual purpose, the foot section looked like a standard black lace-up Oxford shoe with the calf area in black leather or suede and a central zip. The sheepskin leg lining featured a small pocket containing a knife, which could used to cut the stitching so that the top section could be removed - thus leaving a passable shoe for escape purposes if the unlucky wearer found himself behind enemy lines. Other escape items were secreted in clothing, such as a compass in a button, saw blade in a jacket collar and tissue or silk escape maps which could assist the downed airman with his escape.

Jet- and rocket-powered aircraft had appeared towards the end of World War Two heralding a new era of aviation, and due to the advance of speed, flying clothing had to develop pretty quickly so as not to hinder progress.

Flying helmets saw the first dramatic changes - when the Mk.1 bone dome arrived it was worn as a protective covering over a cloth F-type helmet and later the G-type, which contained the earphones and electrical harness, as well as retaining clips for the oxygen masks. The Mk.1 became the Mk.1A when an adjustable visor and mount were fitted, and became the standard helmet for years, though it was relegated to helicopter duties and non-ejector seat types when later models arrived. From the Mk.2 'bone dome' to the present day Mk.10, Alpha and beyond, the electrical harness and earphones have been an integral part of the helmet and, depending on the aircraft type and or task, either single or double visors are fitted.

During World War Two, the oxygen mask/microphone

number, but in the 1970s a wish to conform to NATO standards resulted in flying suits adopting the olive drab/khaki scheme, along with other items of equipment.

The jet era

The jet age created another development, the anti-g suit, a necessity to prevent the rapid movement of blood around the body and its inherent bad effects, due to high acceleration and high-speed manoeuvres. These can be

programme have brought forward advanced lightweight materials that permit strong garments to be produced that are considerably lighter than their predecessors. Flying helmets now include heads-up display information projected onto the visor and when coupled with the helmet-mounted sight, allow the pilot to have constant access to flight and target data regardless of where he is looking. In 100 years flying clothing has indeed come a long, long way. ◼▭

Above: **The modern day flying helmet is a world apart from the leather varieties worn by pilots during World War One. Integral displays provide pilots with flight and target information right before their eyes.** (Pilkington Optronics)
Left: **Crews of the SR-71A Blackbird flew in pressurised space suits due to the extreme high altitude at which the aircraft operated. In later years the suits were the same as worn by Space Shuttle astronauts.** (NASA)

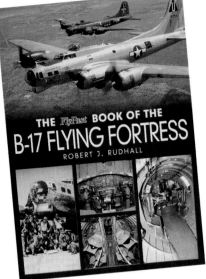
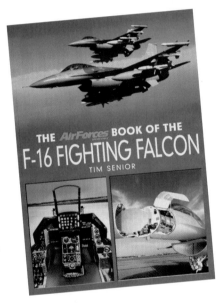
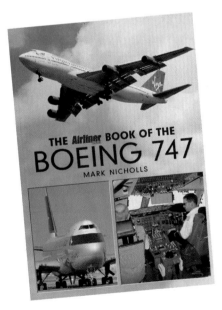

2003 A Year of Celebration

A host of aviation events is being planned for 2003 to celebrate the centenary of powered flight. Not surprisingly, the United States is leading the way as it was there, on December 17, 1903, that it all began. However, in the UK, Europe and around the world, many airshows, museums and other aviation events have special plans to mark the occasion.

Modern technology is allowing access to information about the vast majority of these events through the Internet. Check out Key Publishing's website (www.keypublishing.com) for links to many of these.

On the other hand, you might wish to visit the site of the first controlled flight – Kitty Hawk in North Carolina. The Wright Brothers National Memorial is likely to receive a record number of visitors in 2003, but equally the many aviation museum collections across the USA and elsewhere can expect higher than normal interest. Many UK aviation museums are also planning special events or attractions. The RAF Museum at Hendon is opening a new 'Milestones of Flight' extension – appropriately enough on December 17, 2003. The Yorkshire Air Museum at Elvington will have a replica of the Wright Flyer on show and is holding a special 'Centuries of Flight' display on July 6, 2003. If you want to see the actual Wright Flyer, visit the Smithsonian Museum in Washington DC.

In the USA, a special First Flight Centennial Celebration is to take place between December 13-17, 2003, at Kill Devil Hills, Kitty Hawk, and will include a recreation of the Wright Brothers' first flight with the EAA's replica Wright Flyer.

It was originally planned to mark the 100 years of powered flight with a huge Aviation World's Fair at Newport News, Virginia, in April 2003, but the State of Virginia recently withdrew funding, and as we close for press the event has been cancelled. The organisers are trying to find an alternative venue and should this be forthcoming, details will appear in most of Key Publishing's magazines and on the website.

Elsewhere in 2003 dozens of major aerospace events, such as the Avalon Airshow in Australia (February), the Paris Airshow in France (June), Aero India (February), MAKS Airshow in Moscow, Russia (August) and the Seoul Airshow, South Korea (October) are all planning centenary events. Besides these, many other airshows will be majoring on the 'Century of Flight' theme, with one of the biggest expected to be the International show at Dayton, Ohio, on July 17-20, 2003. However, it can almost be guaranteed that nearly every airshow in North America will mark the centenary of flight.

UK airshow organisers will follow a similar path with the Royal International Air Tattoo at RAF Fairford expected to hold a large-scale event, provided that international support is better than in 2002. However, smaller organisations, such as the Shuttleworth collection at Old Warden, Bedfordshire, can expect much interest next year as their collection of vintage aircraft represent the formative years of the century of flight. The major RAF airshow at Waddington will mark the event and the Imperial War Museum (IWM) at Duxford is planning a Century of flight airshow on September 7 and 8. The IWM is also staging a special photographic exhibition and a series of special events and lectures, for details visit their website (www.iwm.org.uk/duxford).

The Royal Aeronautical Society (RAS) is co-ordinating a number of events in the UK in 2003, with the aid of sponsors such as BAE SYSTEMS, British Airways, Rolls-Royce, Lockheed Martin and Smiths. The RAS is also setting up a Scholarship Fund to inspire a new generation to take up careers in aerospace – for more details visit the website (www.100yearsofflight.org.uk).

For further details of 2003 events, keep up-to-date by visiting the Key Publishing website or by reading *FlyPast* each month and *Airshow 2003*, on sale in April.

Above: **The largest aerospace trade show in 2003 will be the Paris Air Salon at Le Bourget. It will makr the centenary of flight as well as showing off all the latest aviation hardware.** (KEY - Duncan Cubitt)

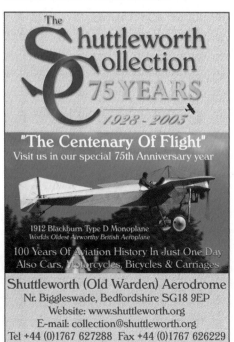

2000-2002

2000-2002

1 Boeing JSF
The Boeing JSF demonstrator makes its first flight on September 18, 2000. The aircraft features a direct engine lift system and a host of advanced features. (Boeing)

2 Lockheed JSF
Lockheed's demonstrator for the JSF programme, the X-35A, makes its maiden flight on October 24, 2000. Lockheed's JSF features both engine lift and a lift fan for use in the STOVL variant. (Lockheed)

3 Super Cobra
The first upgraded Bell AH-1Z Super Cobra makes its first flight at Bell Helicopter Textron's Arlington Flight Research Center in Texas on December 7, 2000. A total of 180 US Marine Corps AH-1W Super Cobras are scheduled for upgrade to the new standard. (Bell)

4 Indian LCA
On January 4, 2001, India's indigenous Light Combat Aircraft (LCA), designed by the Aeronautical Development Agency and built by Hindustan Aeronautics Ltd, made its first flight from Bangalore. (KEY - Alan Warnes)

SIGNIFICANT DATES

JANUARY 4, 2000: The latest arrival on the European low-cost scene, Buzz, commences operations from its base at London-Stansted.

MAY 17, 2000: A new Cyprus-based charter airline - Helios - commences operations.

JULY 6, 2000: BAE Systems formally hands over the first Hawk Mk 115 at CFB Moose Jaw, Canada, for the NATO Flying Training in Canada (NFTC) programme. The aircraft is the first of 21 due to join NFTC.

JULY 18, 2000: The first WAH-64 Apache to be assembled in the UK by GKN Westland Helicopters makes its first flight from the company airfield at Yeovil, Somerset. The helicopter is one of 67 on order for the UK Army Air Corps.

JULY 21, 2000: China announces plans to merge existing carriers into three major airline groups in a massive restructuring of the country's airline industry, which will see three new groups based around Air China, China Eastern Airlines and China Southern Airlines.

JULY 24, 2000: Ibis Aerospace's Ae270P Ibis single-turboprop ten-seat business and light utility aircraft makes its first flight from the Aero Vodochody factory airfield at Kbely, near Prague, in the Czech Republic.

JULY 25, 2000: In a freak accident, Air France Concorde F-BTSC crashes in the Paris suburbs after a metal strip from a Continental Airlines DC-10 on the runway at Charles de Gaulle causes a tyre blow-out and punctures the aircraft's fuel tanks. The accident, the first in the type's history, subsequently leads to the fleet being

grounded while modifications are undertaken to prevent a recurrence. The aircraft are eventually returned to service on November 7, 2001.

JULY 26, 2000: Agusta and GKN Westland announce that their helicopter businesses are to be merged under a new company, AgustaWestland.

JULY 28, 2000: The prototype of a new twin-piston, multi-role utility aircraft, the Wolfsberg-Evektor Raven 257, makes its first flight from Kunovice in the Czech Republic.

AUGUST 3, 2000: The ultra-stretched Boeing 737-900 makes its first flight from Renton Municipal Airport, Washington. The aircraft is the largest variant of the 1960s design, albeit of the updated Next Generation 737 family.

SEPTEMBER 4, 2000: The UK Ministry of Defence confirms that a contract has been signed for the RAF to lease four Boeing C-17A Globemaster III transports to fulfil the Short-Term Strategic Airlifter requirement. This is the first international deal for the C-17.

NOVEMBER 30, 2000: Sino Swearingen SJ30-2 business jet conforming prototype makes its first flight at San Antonio International Airport, Texas.

DECEMBER 12, 2000: The V-22 Osprey tilt-rotor programme is grounded after two fatal accidents involving US Marine Corps aircraft. Following an extensive review and modifications to the aircraft, flights are resumed on May 29, 2002.

DECEMBER 19, 2000: An Airbus Supervisory Board meeting formally gives the go-ahead

Feb 29, 2000: Mikoyan MiG 1.44 July 24, 2000: Ibis Aerospace Ae270P Nov 30, 2000: Sino Swearingen SJ30-2 Dec 7, 2000: Bell AH-1Z Super Cobra Jan 4, 2001: HAL LCA Feb 2, 2001: Bell/Agusta AB 139 Feb 21,

5 AB 139

On February 2, 2001, the Bell Agusta Aerospace AB 139 utility helicopter prototype makes its first flight from Agusta's Cascina Costa facility in Italy. The helicopter is pitched in the highly competitive medium size category. (Bell/Agusta)

6 Stretched Bombardier

Bombardier's 86-seat CRJ900 prototype, a stretch of the CRJ700, makes its first flight from Montreal Mirabel International Airport, Canada, on February 21, 2001. The aircraft has already generated considerable orders. (Bombardier)

7 Executive Embraer

March 31, 2001, sees the first flight of Embraer's new ECJ-135 Legacy business jet at São José dos Campos, Brazil. (Embrear)

8 Ultra-long Airbus

The prototype Airbus A340-600 makes its first flight from Toulouse. The aircraft represents the ultimate stretch of the A340 and can carry more passengers further than any other Airbus. (Airbus)

9 Baby Airbus

The Airbus A318 prototype makes its first flight on January 15, 2002. The 107-seat aircraft, the smallest member of the Airbus family, is set to compete with a number of regional airliner types already on the market. (Airbus)

for launch of the 555-seat A3XX as the A380, with the baseline model now designated the A380-800. Launch commitments stood at 50 firm orders and 42 options, the minimum of firm orders that the company had said it wanted to reach before committing to the project.

DECEMBER 20, 2000: Australia signs the $1 billion contract for Project Wedgetail, under which it will acquire four Boeing 737-700 airborne early warning and control aircraft, with options on a further three.

JANUARY 10, 2001: American Airlines announces a complex and far-reaching deal to acquire the assets of Trans World Airlines (TWA). This will mean the end of the TWA name, one of the oldest in the US airline industry. The deal is sealed on April 9.

JANUARY 26, 2001: SkyStar Aircraft, manufacturers of the popular Kitfox range of homebuilt aircraft, flies its latest design, the new Kitfox Lite2 two-seater, which can be flown in the USA without FAA certification.

MARCH 29, 2001: Boeing unveils the Sonic Cruiser, a radically different airliner design which will fly just below the speed of sound. It is designed to fly faster, higher and more quietly over long ranges.

APRIL 28, 2001: The prototype Avro RJX-85 makes its first flight from BAE Systems' airfield at Woodford, Cheshire. The RJX programme, a development of the BAe 146, is subsequently abandoned in November.

MAY 1, 2001: General Dynamics reveals that it is to acquire Galaxy Aerospace, adding the

Astra and Galaxy to its portfolio of business jets, which already includes the Gulfstream range, acquired in 1999.

JUNE 25, 2001: Boeing flies the first upgraded CH-47F Chinook, which features the more powerful Honeywell T55-GA-A4A-714 engines, plus avionics and mission equipment upgrades.

JULY 21, 2001: Dick Rutan flies a rocket-powered version of the Scaled Composites Long EZ, dubbed the EZ-Rocket, for the first time at Mojave Airport, California. The aircraft is fitted with two 400lb thrust rocket motors and will be used as a test-bed for engines developed by XCOR Aerospace.

AUGUST 21, 2002: No.31 Squadron, the last RAF squadron to be equipped with the Tornado GR.4, leaves Germany, ending almost 50 years of RAF presence.

AUGUST 31, 2001: First Gulfstream V-SP test article makes its first flight from Savannah, Georgia. The aircraft features an advanced cockpit, improved performance and more advanced safety features.

SEPTEMBER 11, 2001: A day which changes the face of air travel forever. In the most unprecedented and horrific hijackings to date, four commercial airliners are commandeered by terrorists. Two are subsequently flown into the twin towers of the World Trade Center in New York, a third is deliberately crashed into the Pentagon, and the fourth crashes in open countryside southeast of Pittsburgh, Pennsylvania. The huge death toll of these suicide attacks stuns the world and will have far-reaching effects on the aviation industry worldwide.

1

2

3

4

5

1 Embraer's gamble

On February 19, 2002, the prototype Embraer 170 makes its first flight from São José dos Campos, Brazil. Hopes are that the aircraft will mean a secure future for the Brazilian manufacturer – thus far orders for the new aircraft are backing this up. (Embraer)

2 Unmanned combat

May 22, 2002, and the Boeing's X-45A Unmanned Combat Air Vehicle prototype makes its first flight from Edwards AFB, California. The Americans see the UCAV as the way ahead for the more dangerous combat strike missions – by taking the pilot out of the cockpit and letting computers (with a little human assistance) run the show. (Boeing)

3 L-159B

On June 1, 2002, Czech company Aero Vodochody test-flies its new L 159B advanced jet training aircraft prior its debut at the SBAC Farnborough airshow. The aircraft is an advanced two-seat trainer which is also able to undertake light combat missions. Flights with an air-to-air refuelling probe have already been accomplished. (Aero Vodochody)

4 Pilatus PC-21

The new Pilatus PC-21 advanced turboprop trainer makes its first flight from Stans on July 1, 2002. This is the latest and most advanced in a long and successful line of military trainer aircraft from the Swiss company. (Pilatus)

5 T-50 flies

Korea Aerospace Industries (KAI) completes a successful first flight of its new T-50 Golden Eagle advanced supersonic jet trainer at its Sachon facility on August 20, 2002. The aircraft has been developed jointly with Lockheed Martin and so far orders for 50 T-50s and 44 A-50 light combat versions have been placed by the Republic of Korea Air Force. (Lockheed Martin)

SIGNIFICANT DATES

SEPTEMBER 24, 2001: Swissair announces it is to seek creditor protection, cut down its fleet and amalgamate operations with Crossair under a new name, Swiss Air Lines.

OCTOBER 7, 2001: Start of combat operations by American and British aircraft against Taliban and al-Qaeda targets in Afghanistan as part of the 'war against terror' which follows the September 11 attacks in the USA. Missions include the longest-ever bombing raids, carried out by USAF B-2 stealth bombers flying from their home base at Whiteman, Missouri.

OCTOBER 26, 2001: Lockheed Martin is announced as the clear winner of the Joint Strike Fighter (JSF) competition, and on the same day is awarded an $18.98 billion contract for the System Development and Demonstration phase of the JSF programme.

NOVEMBER 7, 2001: Belgian national carrier Sabena becomes another post-September 11 victim, filing for bankruptcy after all rescue attempts have failed.

NOVEMBER 28, 2001: Diamond Aircraft Industries Diamond Star DA40 TDI prototype, the first production GA type powered by a diesel engine, made its first flight.

DECEMBER 20, 2001: Bell Helicopter Textron's prototype UH-1Y, an upgraded UH-1N, makes its first flight at the Arlington Flight Research Center, Texas. The US Marine Corps plans to have 100 of its UH-1Ns upgraded to UH-1Ys.

FEBRUARY 11, 2002: Prototype Airbus A340-500 makes its first flight from Toulouse/Blagnac International Airport, France. The aircraft has the longest range of any Airbus aircraft.

FEBRUARY 26, 2002: Boeing announces that it has now formally offered the 747-X Quiet Longer Range derivatives of its 747-400 to customers. The aircraft will be quieter, have a higher take-off weight, longer range and higher reliability.

MAY 3, 2002: London-Luton-based low-cost carrier easyJet announces that it is in exclusive negotiations to purchase rival Go.

SEPTEMBER 6, 2002: The first example of the latest Saab Gripen, JAS 39C is handed over to the Swedish Air Force.

SEPTEMBER 17, 2002: The US Air Force Chief of Staff, General John P Jumper, announces that the Lockheed Martin/Boeing F-22 has been redesignated as the F/A-22, reflecting its additional attack mission capability.

SEPTEMBER 30, 2002: The UK Ministry of Defence confirms that the RAF and Royal Navy are to acquire 150 Lockheed Martin F-35B STOVL JSFs to replace the existing Harrier and Sea Harrier fleets.

OCTOBER 2, 2002: In a move directing opposing the current trend for low-cost travel, Air Canada's chief executive officer, Robert Milton, announces that the airline will launch yet another offshoot, Elite, which will provide business class travel in Airbus A319s configured with only 40 seats.

OCTOBER 14, 2002: Luton-based low-cost carrier easyJet becomes the first such carrier to operate both Boeing and Airbus aircraft when it reveals that it is to acquire 120 Airbus A319s, with options on a further 120. The deal is said to offer considerable cost savings to Europe's largest low-cost carrier.

REACHING FOR
SPACE

OF ALL MAN'S ACHIEVEMENTS IN THE FIELD OF AERONAUTICS, LEAVING THE EARTH'S ATMOSPHERE AND REACHING FOR THE STARS MUST BE THE MOST IMPRESSIVE. DAVID BAKER TAKES A BRIEF LOOK AT THE VERY RAPID DEVELOPMENTS IN THE FIELD OF SPACE FLIGHT.

The Space Shuttle *Endeavour* makes a spectacular blast-off from Cape Kennedy on another mission. The reusable vehicle is one of man's greatest achievements in space flight. (NASA)

Right: **On February 20, 1962, John Glenn was the first American astronaut to successfully obit the earth aboard the Mercury 6 'Friendship 7' spacecraft.** (NASA)

Below: **Yuri Gagarin was the first man in space and at the time the Soviet Union was ahead in the space race – a position that did not last for very long.** (KEY collection)

In an astonishing burst of technical development and human endeavour during the last 50 years, space-faring nations have sent people into orbit, walked on the moon, built the first permanently habitable space stations and sent spacecraft beyond the solar system. Few could have foreseen the enormous strides in research and exploration made possible by technologies unknown when man first ventured into the air with powered flying machines a century ago.

Paving the way

Not until March 16, 1926, did US physics professor Robert Goddard successfully launch the world's first liquid propellant rocket - into a cabbage patch at Auburn, Massachusetts - on a flight that lasted less than three seconds. Liquid-fuelled motors offered greater flexibility than solid propellant rockets and promised the opportunity to put objects in orbit, people in space and humans on the planets. Moreover, they used lighter propellants than solid rocket motors and could be designed to operate with much greater efficiency - cutting weight and improving performance over their solid contemporaries.

Goddard invented the world's first liquid propellant rocket motor because he wanted to send instruments to the top of the atmosphere and measure conditions at the edge of space. In designing the motor he was following exactly the same principle adopted by those a decade later who would produce the world's first jet engines for aircraft. The only real difference between the two types of engine is that the rocket motor burns fuel using oxidiser carried along in a special tank, whereas the jet engine ingests air as it travels through the atmosphere. Both are reaction motors and both require combustion chambers to combine fuel with oxidiser in a burning cycle. It all comes down to Isaac Newton's three laws of motion - the most important of which says that for every action there must be a reaction. In both jet and rocket, the product (exhaust) generates thrust (the action) producing motion (the reaction).

Attributed to the Chinese, the development of black powder rockets preceded Robert Goddard by at least 1,500 years but in that time they made little progress, culminating in the Congreve and Hale rockets used in battle by the British and the Americans in the 19th century. Powder rockets were useful in naval warfare because they imparted no recoil but visionaries saw a greater potential for plying the oceans of space.

A propulsive device that carried within its structure everything it needed to create combustion and produce a motivating force seemed the only way to leave the atmosphere and travel to other worlds. Science fiction took on new vigour and writers such as H G Wells and Jules Verne gave vent to imagination.

Around the turn of the century, Konstantin Tsiolkovsky, a mathematics teacher living outside Moscow, published prophetic works explaining how space stations could be assembled using rockets powered by liquid hydrogen and liquid oxygen - the most efficient liquid propellants, albeit the most difficult to handle. With more than twice the efficiency of powder rockets, he described cryogenic propellants for liquid-propelled motors a century ahead of their time and inspired Lenin's revolutionary zealots with thoughts of liberating the masses from autocratic oppression, setting up orbiting communes populated by individuals free to control their own destiny. Seized upon as a hero of Soviet ideals, Tsiolkovsky was hailed as the father of space travel while a decade later Goddard would be acclaimed as the father of modern rocketry.

War changes everything

In Germany and Russia, progress during the 1930s was swift but whereas the German Army ensured money and resources were available for ballistic missiles powered by liquid motors, politics and the Stalin purges stripped Russia of its scientific elite. While Germany built the V-2 ballistic missile, the Russians focused on battlefield rockets such as the famous Katyusha. When British and American troops seized V-2 components and test fired them in the North Sea and in the USA it changed the future and created prospects for space travel.

Within a decade of the end of World War Two, Russia and America were developing intercontinental missiles propelled at first by liquid propellant motors inspired by

Above: **The German V-2 rocket of World War Two was the world's first ballistic missile. Its technology paved the way for manned space exploration.** (NASA)

Above: **Astronauts Charles Conrad and Gordon Cooper prepare for launch aboard the Gemini 5 spacecraft at Cape Canaveral. The Gemini series laid the foundations for the successful Apollo missions to the Moon.** (NASA)

the powerful V-2 and then by solid propellant motors capable of long-term storage. These liquid propellant motors powered the first satellite launchers for Russia's Sputnik 1 on October 4, 1957 and Explorer 1 on January 31, 1958. Whereas Robert Goddard had given the world the liquid propellant rocket, it was Germany's Wernher von Braun that led America's effort toward space. In Russia, Tsiolkovsky's vision was made real through the efforts of Sergei Korolev, who convinced Soviet Premier Nikita Kruschev to fund the world's first manned space flight which put Yuri Gagarin into orbit on April 12, 1961.

Space race

In direct response to Sputnik 1, on October 1, 1958, America's National Advisory Committee for Aeronautics (NACA) had been renamed the National Aeronautics and Space Administration (NASA). Formed in 1917, NACA underpinned commercial and military aeronautical science and engineering through its research centres at Langley Field, Virginia, and the Ames Aeronautical Laboratory, California. These and other research laboratories were absorbed into NASA.

The US Army rocket development centre at Huntsville, Alabama, became the NASA Marshall Space Flight Centre where Saturn moon rockets were designed under the leadership of von Braun. Launch facilities at Cape Canaveral, Florida, and at the Vandenberg Air Force Base, California, were expanded to meet the demands of the space race.

The surge into space was energised by fears that Russian successes would tip the uncommitted world toward Soviet-style Communism discouraging belief in American capitalism as a way forward to the future. When Gagarin went into space, beating NASA's Mercury astronaut Alan Shepard to that historic slot by less than one month, it galvanised the US Congress into support for John F Kennedy's bold challenge to race the Russians to the Moon.

In an address before a joint session of Congress on May 25, 1961, Mercury's proposed successor, Project Apollo,

A Soviet Soyuz is launched from the Baikonur Cosmosdrome – the Soviets were always very close to the Americans with regard to rocket development, it was lack of finance that finally lost them the space race. (KEY collection)

was redirected from an earth-orbiting observation platform into a spacecraft for lunar landings. That goal would be achieved in little more than eight years despite a 21-month delay when astronauts Grissom, White and Chaffee were killed in their spacecraft during a launch pad rehearsal on January 27, 1967.

Between Mercury and Apollo, NASA flew a total of ten two-man Gemini missions in 1965 and 1966 during which rendezvous and docking in orbit, space walking and flights of up to 14 days in duration paved the way for moon missions, a period in which the Russians were noticeably silent. Following eight flights between 1961 and early 1965, the Soviets launched two flights in tandem, put the first woman (Valentina Tereshkova) into orbit, conducted the first three-man flight and performed the world's first space walk.

Only in 1964, three years after Kennedy threw down the gauntlet, did the Russians pick up the challenge and

frantically scramble for their own Moon plan. Whereas the Russians had been in the vanguard of exploring the Moon and the nearest planets with unmanned spacecraft, they were late in believing the Americans were serious about manned lunar landings. By the mid-1960s, the Americans had equalled Russia's early lead in powerful carrier rockets and with von Braun's Saturn V capable of throwing 40 tonnes at the Moon NASA won the weight-lifting contest.

Bedevilled by in-fighting and mischievous politics, Russia's equivalent, the colossal N-1 rocket, designed to send cosmonauts to the Moon was late and unreliable, not one of its four flight attempts successfully got into space. Yet, even as the space race fuelled by Kennedy's Apollo challenge was reaching its climacteric with the landing of Armstrong and Aldrin on the lunar surface on July 20, 1969, the high dollar price for access to space forced engineers to search for cheaper ways to get into orbit.

Above: **Buzz Aldrin steps out on to the lunar surface on July 20, 1969. The historic Apollo 11 mission achieved President John F Kennedy's pledge to put a man on the Moon before the end of the 1960s.** (NASA)

Above: **The sheer noise of a Saturn V launch will live forever in the memories of whoever witnessed it. Here Apollo 16 lifts off – the Apollo missions were frightfully expensive but at a time of continued rivalry with the USSR, they were a very public way of emphasising America's supremacy.** (NASA)

Aerospace spin-offs

While the Russians abandoned their plans to put cosmonauts on the Moon and, in 1971, started assembling the first in a long succession of space stations, NASA turned to reusable winged space vehicles, and the Shuttle emerged as a potential low-cost successor to expendable rockets. In parallel, as the space programme was moving toward more commercial activities, with satellites for communications, broadcasting, navigation, weather and remote sensing, the technologies that underpinned the great achievements of the 1960s were finding application elsewhere.

Grumman took a major weight-saving technique it developed for the Apollo Lunar Module and applied it to the F-14 Tomcat. First in a new generation of twin-fin blended wing-body combat aircraft, the F-14 was equipped with titanium tubing fitted together by a cold-weld technique whereby the separate pipes are first chilled in a liquid nitrogen bath and then brazed. The Grumman F-14 embodied the synergy between low-weight and high-reliability and soon several aeronautical projects advanced the state of aeronautical engineering built upon the extraordinary demands and the unique requirements of satellites, spacecraft and launch vehicles. It was a natural application.

Before early ballistic missiles had been converted to put the Mercury and Gemini astronauts into space, the adventurous brigade of 1950s American test pilots riding rocket powered X-series research aircraft to high speed and high altitude, believed they would be the first ones to pin astronaut wings on their flight jackets. It was not to be. The panic spread by Sputnik 1 allowed little time to develop new winged space planes and the first astronauts rode into space on ballistic capsules carried by adapted military rockets. Nevertheless, when studies during the 1960s heralded a new age of winged re-entry vehicles for cheaper access to space lifting bodies provided pilots with the opportunity to pave the way for the Shuttle.

The amazing M2-F2 lifting body played a vital part in 'lifting body' research that was to ultimately lead to the Space Shuttle. (NASA)

Reusable dream

In a series of tests from Edwards Air Force Base, California, Lifting Bodies designed and built by NASA and the US Air Force assembled vast quantities of data 'feeling' the atmosphere under various conditions and in various configurations. This research converged with new developments in reusable, throttleable, rocket motors combining with large solid rocket boosters to provide lift for a reusable spaceship – the winged Shuttle – formally approved by President Nixon in January 1972, just eleven months before the last of six Apollo moon landings.

Launched on April 12, 1981, exactly 20 years to the day since the flight of the first man into space, veteran astronaut John Young accompanied rookie Bob Crippen on the first Shuttle flight, returning to Earth two days later. For almost five years, four Shuttles carried satellites, laboratory modules and spacecraft into orbit

and back until, on January 28, 1986, *Challenger* was destroyed when a solid rocket booster failed shortly after lift-off killing all seven crew, including a teacher expecting to enthral children with lessons from orbit. Grounded for 32 months, the Shuttle returned to operations in late September 1988. Less than two years later, Russia launched its own Shuttle called Buran. By this time the Russian economy was almost bankrupt and within two years, the Communist system imploded and Buran was grounded.

The only way is up

The Cold War was over, removing the fuel from the space race, that now transformed itself into an era of international co-operation and joint endeavour, where Russians and Americans worked together to build an international space station. Assembly began in 1998 and will continue for several years yet, with Shuttle flights now expected to continue until at least 2020. Over the 45 years of reaching into space, the most exciting endeavour attempted by humans had transformed a propaganda race into an industry that today employs 1.1 million people worldwide, with revenues in excess of US$100 billion and growth at 9% per year.

Today, where once space budgets came from governments and taxpayers, 85% of all money spent on satellites, launch vehicles and spacecraft comes from private companies and giant corporations. In a commercial sense it has been a great success. In technical terms it has forged new industries, provided new capabilities and invented new materials, manufacturing processes and management techniques, much of which has fed across into aviation. Yet to be realised is the legacy in hypersonic flight with air breathing scramjets promising hemispheric journeys in less than one hour and trips to Australia for a weekend vacation making the orient as accessible to the occident as Paris is to London. Then, aviation and space will have truly converged and rightfully come of age. ■

Above: **The Space Shuttle *Endeavour* lands at Cape Kennedy** – all the lifting body research work made it possible to land this vehicle from earth orbit completely without engine power. (NASA)

Above: **The HL-10 lifting body about to touch down at Edwards AFB, California, in 1966.** (NASA)

Recce Test!

WIN £100 OF AVIATION BOOKS

KEY PUBLISHING IS OFFERING TWO LUCKY READERS THE CHANCE TO WIN £100-WORTH OF AVIATION BOOKS. TO ENTER, ALL YOU HAVE TO DO IS IDENTIFY THE 12 AIRCRAFT ILLUSTRATED, WRITING YOUR ANSWERS IN THE SPACES BELOW.

RECCE TEST!

Name: ....

Address: ....

....

....

Postcode: .... Country: ....

Tel: .... Fax: ....

E-mail: ....

Closing date: February 28, 2003

Send your answers to:
Century of Flight Competition, Key Publishing Ltd, PO Box 100, Stamford, Lincs PE9 1XQ, UK.

1 ....

2 ....

3 ....

4 ....

5 ....

6 ....

7 ....

8 ....

9 ....

10 ....

11 ....

12 ....